COL

DICTIONARY OF

INFORMATION TECHNOLOGY

To Richard, with love

COLLINS

DICTIONARY OF

INFORMATION TECHNOLOGY

Eric Deeson

HarperCollins*Publishers*

HarperCollins Publishers 1991
P.O. Box, Glasgow G4 0NB

First published 1991

© Eric Deeson 1991

The Author asserts the moral right to be identified as the Author of this work.

Reprint 10 9 8 7 6 5 4 3 2 1 0

ISBN 0 00 434371 9 (paperback)
ISBN 0 00 434375 1 (cased)

British Library Cataloguing in Publication Data
Deeson, Eric
  Collins Dictionary of information technology. –
  (Collins subject dictionaries).
  1. Information systems
  I. Title
  302.2

All rights reserved. No part of this publication may be reproduced, stored in a retrieval system or transmitted, in any form or by any means, electronic, mechanical, photocopying, recording or otherwise, without the prior permission of the publisher.

This book is sold subject to the conditions that it shall not, by way of trade or otherwise, be lent, re-sold, hired out or otherwise circulated without the publisher's prior consent in any form of binding or cover other than that in which it is published and without a similar condition including this condition being imposed on the subsequent purchaser.

Typeset in Bembo 10pt. solid by Morton Word Processing Ltd., Scarborough.

Printed in Great Britain by HarperCollins Manufacturing Glasgow

PREFACE

This book has been written to meet the needs of students taking courses in information technology, computing and business studies, and professionals looking for guidance in the field of information technology generally. The publishers and author would be interested to hear from readers about changes which they feel would make the book more useful to them.

The abbreviation IT is used throughout the book for 'information technology'. Words in **bold** are used to show both the initial word in entries, and related terms within specific entries. Words in SMALL CAPITALS are cross-references to other entries within the book.

THE AUTHOR

ERIC DEESON was until recently Director of Resources and Information Technology at Joseph Chamberlain College, Birmingham. He is the author of Collins Gem *Basic Facts: Physics* (3rd. edition 1991), *Computing and Information Technology* (Blackwell 1988) and *Managing with Information Technology* (Kogan Page 1987).

A

abbreviated calling, *n.* calling out on a phone or fax machine with just one or two key presses. The most often used numbers are programmed into a store.

abend, *n.* an abnormal, or aborted, end, when a program stops other than in the normal way as a result of a bug, user input error, or escape key press.

abort, *vb.* to stop an activity or a program run before its normal end. An **abort timer** (time out) is a software device (a loop) that aborts the current task if something does not happen within a certain time, for example if the system cannot get through the phone network to a remote database.

absolute, *adj.* fixed in value rather than relative. An **absolute address** is the most basic form of ADDRESSING; the instruction's address field (operand) contains the address of the storage cell it is to use. **Absolute code** is an alternative term for MACHINE CODE. An **absolute loader** is a LOADER that always puts the loaded program in the same part of the store. The **absolute value** of a number is its magnitude (size), taking no account of sign. Thus −7 has a greater absolute value than +5. In many program languages, the function **ABS** returns the absolute value of its argument.

absorption, *n.* an alternative term for ATTENUATION.

AC, *abbrev. for* AIR CONDITIONING and ALTERNATING CURRENT.

ACC *symb. for* the ACCUMULATOR register of a processor's ARITHMETIC and logic unit. See also MACHINE (Figure).

accelerating voltage, *n.* **1.** the high voltage inside a CATHODE RAY TUBE that accelerates the electron beam towards the screen. **2.** the voltage between cathode and anode in the electron gun.

acceptance testing, *n.* the testing of a new system before the user accepts (and pays for) it. This is one of the later stages of SYSTEMS ANALYSIS and design.

acceptor, *n.* a type of substance which, when added as an impurity to an intrinsic semiconductor, removes electrons and so makes the semiconductor p-type. An acceptor is usually an element of valency 3 (e.g. boron).

access, *n.* the means of obtaining data from whatever stores it, e.g. a chip, tape or disk (see also DIRECT ACCESS). **Access time**

ACCORDION FOLD

is the length of time a system takes to find (or store) a given data item. In the case of access from disk, it is the sum of SEEK TIME (the time taken by the head to move to the right track), SEARCH TIME (or LATENCY, the time for the disk to rotate to the right spot), and READ/WRITE TIME (the actual data transfer time, usually far less then either of the others).

An **access arm** (**access mechanism**) is the part of a disk DRIVE that moves the head(s) in and out over the disk surface(s). An **access point** is another name for a key as used in searching a file.

Not all systems are on **open access** (available for anyone to use); you may have to subscribe to the system, work through a complex logging-on process, or give one or more passwords. **Access control** is about making such security methods effective. In the field of communications, **access barring** lets data transfer one way only. An **access line** is a permanently open private (possibly leased) line between a user's system and an exchange (switching centre).

accordion fold, *n*. an alternative term for FAN FOLD (printer) paper.

accounts, *n*. financial records. These form a major area of IT in the office, with software (specially written, or general purpose such as database managers and spreadsheets) used to help keep accurate up-to-date financial records. Previously, people kept accounts manually in large books called ledgers: the general (nominal) ledger, and ledgers for sales and purchases. A good accounts software package uses a similar structure, but also has relational database features to duplicate entries in various places.

accumulator, *n*. the central register (a parallel ADDER) in a processor's arithmetic and logic unit, the place where in effect all processing takes place; and thus the major bottleneck in a system that does not use parallel processing.

accuracy, *n*. the measure of how close a result is to its correct value depending on freedom from, for instance, ROUNDING ERRORS.

ACE, *n*. the Automatic Computer Engine, a first generation computer built in 1951 at Britain's National Physical Laboratory.

ACK, *symb. for* acknowledge, a code sent from a communications unit to say either:
  (a) the unit is ready to receive data, or
  (b) it has just received a data block without error (and so is ready for the next one).

ADDER

acoustic, *adj.* of or related to sound. An **acoustic coupler** is a type of MODEM into which a phone handset is pressed; sound waves then carry the data for part of the path. An **acoustic delay line** is a delay line which depends for its action on the slow speed of sound signals compared with electric signals.

action frame, *n.* a viewdata RESPONSE FRAME.

action message, *n.* a message from a system's operating software asking for action from the operating staff (e.g. to change a disk or put new paper into a printer).

active, *adj.* in use. An **active file** is one with a non-zero level of activity, even if it is an open file; an **active peripheral** is on-line and working; an **active device** is an electronic unit such as a transistor or electron tube that can amplify signals (thus needing a power supply).

activity, activity ratio, activity level or **hit rate,** *n.* the fraction of records in a file accessed or amended in, say, a working day. **Activity loading** is a way to ensure a file's most active records are easiest to access.

An **activity report** is a printout of actions taken by a system during a period of time. See also LOG.

ACU, *abbrev. for* automatic call unit. See AUTO-DIALLER.

A/D, *abbrev. for* analog to digital.

Ada, *n.* a high-level program language (published 1980), with Pascal roots and main strength in the structured coding of real-time systems, best known for its use in nuclear power station control and US weapons systems, but of fast growing value to commerce.

adaptive channel location, *n.* an 'intelligent' style of MULTIPLEXING in which the usage of given channels depends on demand. **Adaptive routing** is an approach to PACKET SWITCHING in which the system sends each packet along the route which is most convenient at a given moment.

ADC, *abbrev. for* ANALOG TO DIGITAL CONVERTER.

adder, *n.* a logic circuit for adding input bits to give an output. The truth table below shows the rules for adding two bits (inputs I1 and I2):

	I1	I2	C	S
0 + 0 = 00 or	0	0	0	0
0 + 1 = 01	0	1	0	1
1 + 0 = 01	1	0	0	1
1 + 1 = 10	1	1	1	0

ADDER

The carry column (C) is the output of an AND GATE, while the sum (S) is that of an exclusive-or. The logic circuit with this truth table (a **half adder**) is therefore as in Fig. 1. This half adder is sufficient for adding single bits.

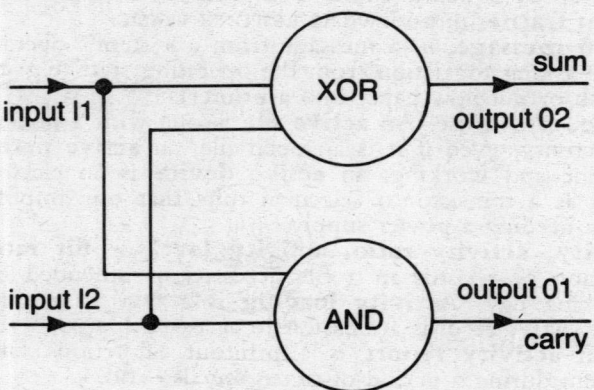

adder. Fig 1. Half adder circuit.

To add two binary numbers, however, an adder with a third input is needed, for the carry from the previous addition. This is a **full adder**, built from two half adders (Fig. 2).

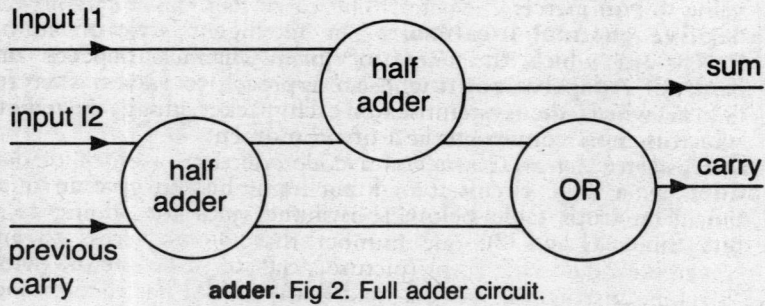

adder. Fig 2. Full adder circuit.

A single full adder can add two binary numbers of any length by taking a pair of bits at a time. This is the **serial adder** in Fig. 3. **Serial adding** is slow, so the **parallel adder** is more common. This has a full adder for each pair of bits, and so is as long as the system's word length. Parallel addition, as shown overleaf, is not quite parallel because of the carries at each stage; techniques exist to speed it up further (at an increased cost in money).

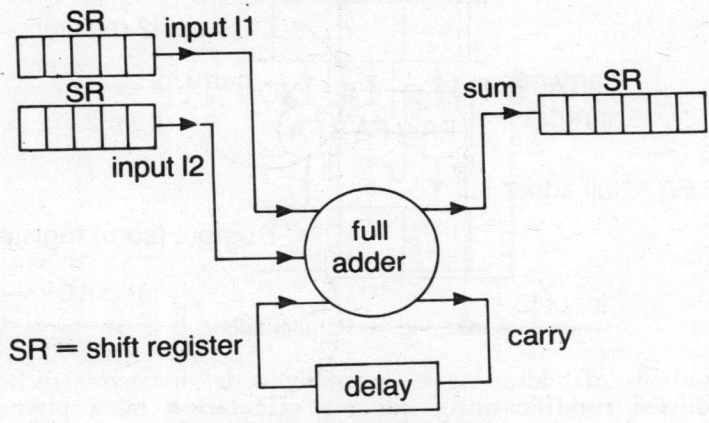

adder. Fig. 3. Serial adder.

All the above applies to **two-input adders**; three-input adders are much the same in principle. When the parallel adder acts as an ACCUMULATOR, the carry out line in Figure 4 can pass a carry bit to the flag register. The carry flag will then show if addition has led to overflow.

The add/subtract unit next to a processor's accumulator consists of a parallel adder whose carry in line passes a bit for addition but not for subtraction. This procedure is related to the complementation method of subtraction.

address, *n.* **1.** (*communications*) a code added to a block of data in transfer (e.g. a packet in a packet switching system or an email message) to show where it should go.

2. (*computing*) the unique number that allows access to any given storage or screen (picture) cell or disk sector. Most machine instructions have a field (part) for the instruction code and an **address field** so the system knows where in store to find or put the data concerned. (Pulses along the **address bus** will then open the right gates). During the processor's MACHINE CYCLE, the address field contents appear in the **address (selection) register** (**ASR**). As there are various

ADDRESSABILITY

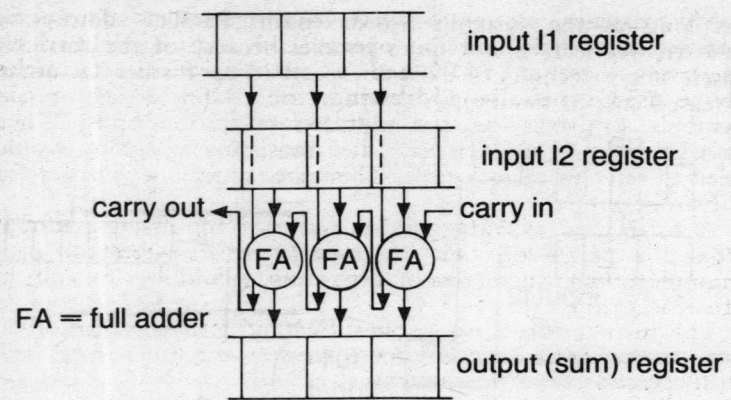

adder. Fig. 4. Parallel adder.

methods of addressing in assembly code, however (such as **address modification**), **address calculation** takes place to obtain the correct value. A similar process ensures the effective saving to, and loading from disk, of data blocks.

addressability, *n.* the number of addressable points or cells in a given space (e.g. a screen). An **addressable cursor** (like most cursors now in use) is one you can program to move to any part of the screen.

addressing, *n.* methods of using the ADDRESS FIELDS of instructions to allow efficient and speedy access to the storage cells. We can describe processors (and, therefore, the instructions they accept) on the basis of the number of addresses each instruction can have. **Zero-address instructions** have no attached addresses, and so must work with a stack. **One-address instructions** are most common, but some systems allow two, or even three, adddress instructions. For example:

0 ADD	add the top two numbers in the stack and leave the result there;
1 ADD a	add the value of 'a' to the accumulator, leaving the result;
2 ADD a b	add the value of 'a' to the accumulator, storing the result in 'b';
3 ADD a b c	add the values of 'a' and 'b', and store the result in 'c'.

Most machine instructions have two main parts, the operation (opcode) field and the operand, or address, field(s); respectively these are ADD and 'a' etc. above. The examples above used **symbolic addressing**: the address fields contain symbols, or labels, for the addresses of the operands. When translating such instructions, the translating program would need to refer to a label table. This takes time, but is easier for the programmer.

A balance of advantage exists for each addressing method, from the points of view of the system architect, the programmer, and the users of programs who look for quick, efficient action.

The main **addressing modes** (methods) in use (not all in any one system) are as follows (names are given first, and then the address field contents):

immediate: the actual data to be used;
direct: the address of the storage cell involved;
extended: no address field, the address being the next word after the opcode;
indirect: the address of the storage cell that contains the address needed;
indexed: the number to be added to a base value held in an index register;
modified: address field contents change (e.g. increment) each time used;
relative: the number to be added to the current address value;
symbolic: see above.

adjacency, *n.* in optical character reading, an indication of whether characters are too close for accurate reading.

ADP *abbrev. (outdated) for* automatic data processing, or (business) computing.

aerial, *n.* or **antenna,** a device for accepting (as a receiver) radio waves to give an electric signal, or (as a transmitter) for converting an electric signal to radio waves. A **dish aerial** is parabolic in shape. In receive mode, this lets it focus (and thus strengthen) a weak input parallel beam, e.g. one from a satellite. A transmitting dish produces a parallel beam. See also BEAM WIDTH.

a.f., *abbrev. for* audio frequency, i.e. with a frequency in the range of audible sound waves, 25–20000 hertz. See RADIO.

AFC, *abbrev. for* AUTO FREQUENCY CONTROL.

afterglow, *n.* an alternative term for PERSISTENCE.

AGC, *abbrev. for* AUTO GAIN CONTROL.

AI

AI, *abbrev. for* artificial intelligence. See also MACHINE INTELLIGENCE where both terms are discussed.

air conditioning (AC), *n.* a system for controlling temperature and humidity useful in IT areas. It may be controlled by a processor. See ENERGY MANAGEMENT and ENVIRONMENT CONTROL.

airline booking, *n.* an important example of real-time processing, where the travel agent needs near-instant access to stored data plus the power to add and amend records.

alarm, *n.* a signal, e.g. through a speaker and/or on screen, to warn of some special event or to remind the user to do something. Many personal computers now have alarm utilities, sometimes simple 'alarm clocks' or else more complex systems linked with their desktop diary and calendar routines.

Alarm handling, to some, means interrupt or error handling. An **alarm signal** is a code sent in advance of a distress message to switch on automatic alarm receivers.

Algol, *n. acronym for* 'Algorithmic oriented language', the first structured high level language (devised in 1962), forerunner of Pascal. The name relates to the way Algol programmers can start by developing an algorithm before extending it to code. This originally made the language very popular in science and technology, but it has not made much progress since, except in education.

algorithm, *n.* a set of precise steps that can solve a given problem, or a proof that the problem has no solution. In IT people express algorithms in various ways:

(a) in clear English sentences;

(b) in PSEUDO-CODE, somewhat like program code (and, indeed, a program is an algorithm itself);

(c) as a STRUCTURE CHART;

(d) as a FLOW CHART.

The solutions of all but the most simple problems involve branching; making a decision and then taking one of two or more paths. The decisions are of two types, conditionals and loops, there being five most common structures in all. These are illustrated on the accompanying pages using flow chart symbols, where a diamond stands for a decision and an oblong for a set of actions.

(a) IF (condition(s)) THEN (action(s)1) ELSE (action(s)2). See Figure 1. Known as the *binary conditional*.

Some program languages have no ELSE (in which case the system assumes it); in others IF, THEN and ELSE form

ALGORITHM

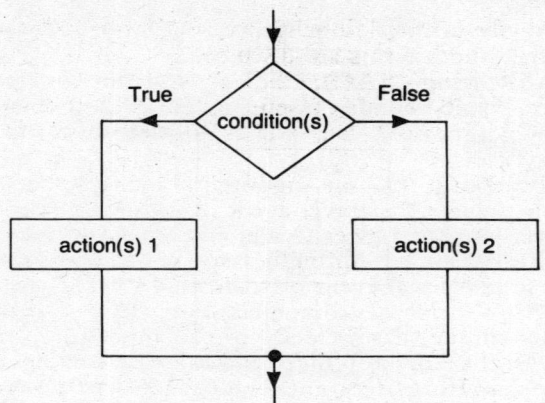

algorithm. Fig.1. The IF structure.

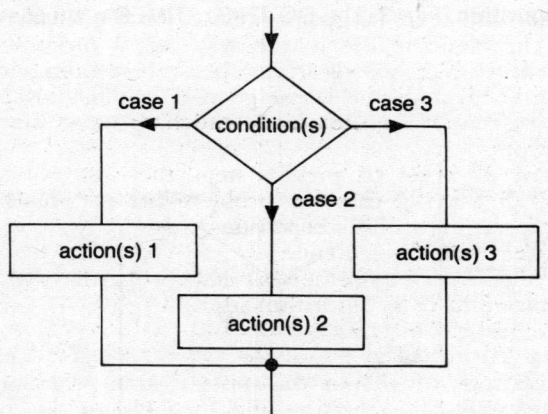

algorithm. Fig. 2. The CASE structure.

separate statements, so we also need an ENDIF to mark the end of the structure.

(b) CASE (label) / (condition(s)1) (action(s)1) / (condition(s)2) (action(s)2) / (condition(s)3) (action(s)3) /.../ END-CASE. See Figure 2.

Known as the *multiple conditional*.

ALGORITHM

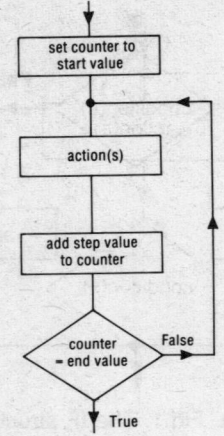

algorithm. Fig. 3. The DO THIS... TIMES n structure.

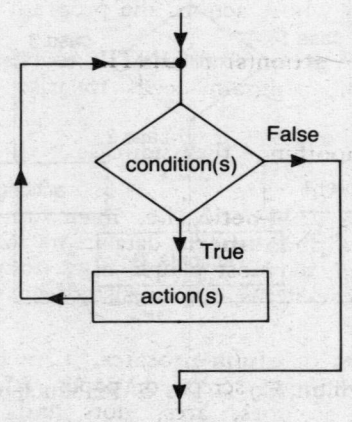

algorithm. Fig. 4. The WHILE structure.

(c) DOTHIS / (action(s) / TIMES *n* or FOR (label) = (start value) TO (end value) STEP (step value). See Figure 3.

This is used for *fixed loops*, when the programmer knows how many times the program needs to carry out the actions.

ALPHA-GEOMETRICS

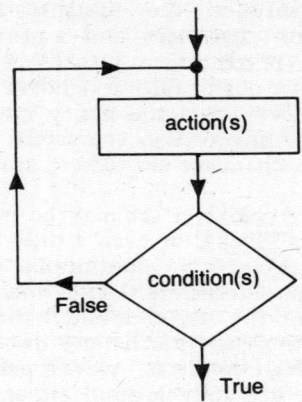

algorithm. Fig. 5. The REPEAT structure.

(d) WHILE (condition(s)) / action(s) / ENDWHILE. Used for *non-fixed loops* whose actions the program may not need at all. See Figure 4.

(e) REPEAT / action(s) / UNTIL (condition(s)). Used for *non-fixed loops* the program needs to pass through at least once. See Fig. 5.

aliasing, *n.* 'smoothing the staircase' edges of computer graphics.

alpha, *abbrev. for* **alphabetic**, i.e. made up of letters alone. **Alphameric** or **alphanumeric** data items may contain letters and digits; indeed, to most people now, these terms describe STRING data, whose items can consist of any set of keyboard characters.

alpha-geometrics or **alpha-mosaics,** *n.* methods of building up a graphic design on screen or paper. An alpha-geometric design consists of lines, arcs, dots and other geometric structures. With the appropriate software, you can zoom in on such a design without any loss of smoothness.

An alpha-mosaic is often much simpler to construct (and can be output from a printer rather than needing a plotter), since it is just a pattern of dots. However, when you zoom in, the dots become larger.

ALTERNATE CHARACTER SET

alternate character set, *n.* the modern **ASCII** system provides 128 codes for characters and control signals. To transfer each character needs seven bits ($2^7 = 128$), fitting, with a parity (check) bit, neatly into a standard eight-bit byte. If, on the other hand, we avoid the parity bit (e.g. within a micro), a byte can code any of 256 characters. The extra 128 can form an alternative character set. There are other ways to achieve this effect.

A system's alternative character set may be italic versions of the normal set, graphics blocks, or even a different font.

alternating current (AC), *n.* a continuous electric current that reverses direction alternately. The main(s) electricity supply in most parts of the world is alternating: the applied voltage, and therefore the current, changes direction regularly, at the rate of 50 or 60 Hz (hertz, waves per second). The 'average' voltage V_θ is generally around either 110 V or 240 V.

It is not hard to use the mains supply as a carrier for voice or data signals. Many intercom units carry speech round a building this way; electric power firms often use the high voltage trunk lines for messages too. This technique of power line data transfer is now quite common for networking data and environment control signals in a building.

alternative mode, *n.* a means of allowing two users (e.g. on a network) to access and amend a given file in turn without clashes.

ALU, *abbrev. for* ARITHMETIC AND LOGIC UNIT.

AM, *abbrev. for* AMPLITUDE MODULATION.

amateur radio, *n.* the use of powerful radio transmitters and receivers by qualified but amateur hobbyists for world-wide voice and data signal transfer.

ambiguity, *n.* a lack of clear meaning. It is common in human languages, but not allowed when using a program language (because an IT system cannot 'know what you mean').

amplification, *n.* increasing the AMPLITUDE of a signal, thus making it stronger, by using an **amplifier**, a powered electronic system as in a phone signal REPEATER.

amplitude, *n.* the amount a wave's value varies round its central (or average) value. The larger the amplitude, the larger the wave's energy content. What amplitude means in practice depends on the wave type; thus it relates to brightness in the case of light waves and to loudness with sound waves.

ANALOG(UE)

Amplitude Modulation (AM) is a common way to let a high frequency wave (the 'carrier') carry a lower frequency signal; AM radio signals are the best known example. See also MODULATION.

analog(ue), *adj.* describing quantities that are wavy. An analog signal (e.g. the output from a light sensor) is wavy in that it can have a value anywhere in the range allowed. Digital signals, on the other hand, can have only a small number of values (levels) within the range.

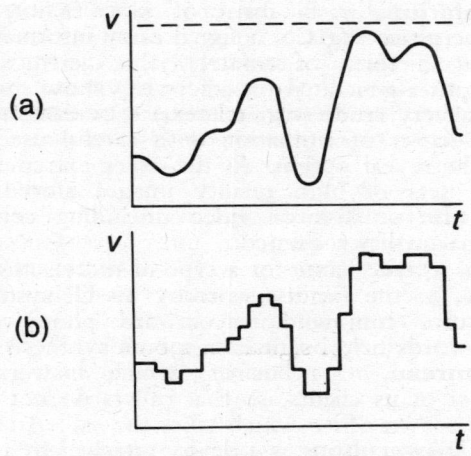

analog. Analog (a) and digital (b) signals.

An **analog computer** has analog inputs and analog outputs, and analog (rather than digital) central processing circuits to maximise its efficiency. However, analog processing cannot be general purpose because analog electronics cannot effectively deal with continuous signals, so people design analog computers only for specific tasks. Flight simulators are a major example.

A hybrid computer has analog inputs and outputs but uses digital processing. This gives it a general purpose nature, but means it needs **analog to digital converters** (**ADCs**) at the inputs and DIGITAL TO ANALOG CONVERTERS (DACS) at the outputs.

Most IT systems are digital. When digital data is transferred through an analog phone system, it needs ADCs and DACs;

ANALYSIS

these are provided in modems. To avoid that need, the first fax machines were analog; **analog fax** ('Group 1') is now rare, however.

analysis, *n.* the breaking of something into its separate parts, at least in thought. SYSTEMS ANALYSIS therefore means finding the parts of a system. In practice, though, systems **analysts** design and develop as well as analyse.

AND, *n.* a GATE (circuit or element) with an output only if all inputs are 1.

angle modulation, *n.* a form of MODULATION in which changes in the phase angle of a signal carry information.

animation, *n.* a form of PRESENTATION GRAPHICS in which images (computer-generated or otherwise) show movement or change. Even very crude (e.g. teletext) BLOCK GRAPHICS screens can show a degree of animation with careful use of flashing sections or the reveal option. At the other extreme, the rapid screening of sets of high quality images stored in an IT system, on film or disk or video (including compact) disc gives a cinema-quality sequence.

ansaphone, *n.* a trade name for a type of ANSWERING MACHINE.

answer back, *n.* the facility whereby an IT system can respond to voice commands or inward phone calls using messages or words held on disk or speech synthesis.

answering bureau, *n.* a business which answers telephone calls on behalf of its clients, so that callers do not notice it is not the client's own office which takes the call. An **answering machine** or **answerphone** is a device attached to a phone line to pass on messages to callers and record on tape what they say. Some machines allow the user to phone in and hear what is on the tape.

answerphone, see ANSWERING MACHINE.

antenna, *n.* an alternative term for AERIAL.

anticipatory staging, *n.* a technique for moving blocks of data from backing store to main store, or from main store to cache, in anticipation of their being needed shortly, rather than moving them on demand.

aperture card, *n.* a type of microform with a single image mounted in a window in the centre of a card (for ease of and flexibility in filing).

APL, *n.* 'A program language', a powerful programming language which can handle great power arrays of several dimensions.

apogee, *n.* the point in a satellite's orbit when it is furthest from the Earth, and when signals from it to Earth are weakest.

application, *n.* the use to which someone puts an IT system. An **application package** and **application software** are programs for a particular use, while an **application programmer** writes to meet users' specific needs. An **(application) program generator** is a program that guides users through their needs in detail and then produces working (though not always efficient) programs for the application.

approval, *n.* a sign or statement that a country's telecommunications authority accepts a given hardware design for use with the telephone network.

architecture, *n.* the specification of structure of, for instance, a network or computer, that states exactly the hardware and how software controls it, and the data transfer techniques employed.

archive, 1. *n.* a backing store.

2. *vb.* to save data in backing store. An **archive file** is a file in backing store.

Strictly, archives are stores of data or information held for future reference rather than amendment: microform or video (including compact) disc are the best media in this case. If a user expects a significant level of future change, then it is best to use computer backing storage such as magnetic tape or disk.

argument(s), *n.* the value(s) on which a function operates, such as 'angle' in SIN(angle) and 'name' and '5' in LEFT$(name,5).

arithmetic, *n.* numerical calculations such as addition and subtraction. In digital IT systems, this takes place in and around the accumulator of the processor's **arithmetic and logic unit (ALU)** (or **arithmetic unit**), and includes all processing actions other than logical ones (comparisons). The accumulator is in essence an **adder**; all arithmetic operations take place in binary and reduce to adding as follows:

Add: The rules are as in DENARY, where

$$0 + 0 = 0 \text{ carry } 0$$
$$0 + 1 = 1 \text{ carry } 0$$
$$1 + 0 = 1 \text{ carry } 0$$
$$1 + 1 = 0 \text{ carry } 1$$

Thus for 1010 + 0111:

ARITHMETIC

$$\begin{array}{r} 1010 \\ 0111\ + \\ \hline = 0001 \end{array} \text{ carry } 1\ (\times 2^4)$$

Subtract: To subtract number B from number A, the system adds the complement of number B to number A; it ignores any carry. For example, 1010 − 0111 becomes

$$\begin{array}{r} 1010 \\ 1001\ + \\ \hline = 0011 \end{array} \text{ (carry 1 ignored)}$$

Multiply: The rules are as in denary, where we use the 1 times table:

$$0 \times 1 = 0$$
$$1 \times 1 = 1$$

Thus
$$\begin{array}{r} 1010 \\ 0111\ \times \\ \hline 1010 \\ 10100 \\ 101000\ + \\ \hline = 1000110 \end{array}$$

This is, however, the same as shifting number A left each time there is a 1 in number B, and adding those results. The shift involved is an **arithmetic shift**, the same as a logical shift, but keeping any sign bit untouched.

Divide: In much the same way, division becomes a process of right shifting and subtraction; i.e. right shifting, complementing, and adding. In this case, though, unless the system is working in **integer arithmetic** (when it ignores any remainders), the process will continue past the position of the binary point. Indeed, all the above applies as much to binary fractions as to integers.

More important, it also applies to operations on data that does not represent numbers. For instance to change 'Collins' to 'collins', the program would involve a function which would add 32 to the ASCII value of the initial letter.

The **arithmetic feature** of a word processor concerns how you may use it to work out sums, either with a pull-down calculator or at the cursor. Thus you can add a percentage profit or carry out a sum, with little break in the typing.

Arithmetic operators are symbols used in a program language for arithmetic operations. In most cases, these are +, -, * (for times), / (divide), and ^ (raise to the power of). The

ARRAY

arithmetic register, or A register, of a processor is for storing intermediate results for later in an arithmetic operation.

ARQ, *symb. for* automatic request for correction (or repetition). It is a signal from data receiver to sender that received data contains errors (compare ACK).

array, *n.* **1.** (*telecommunications*) a set of identical aerials that work together on a given task.

2. (*computing*) a data structure, available in most program languages, for storing a fixed length list (one-dimensional array) or table (two- or multi-dimensional array) of items.

Unless the array is very small, the programmer must set in advance (declare) the size of the structure, i.e. the **array bounds** or **array dimensions**. Few program languages let you then change the setting. The number of dimensions allowed in a given case depends on the operating software, the program language, the type of data item in question, and the storage space on offer.

The three Figures below show how we may think of arrays (i.e. their logical structure), in one, two, and three dimensions. They also give declaration statements in Basic and Pascal.

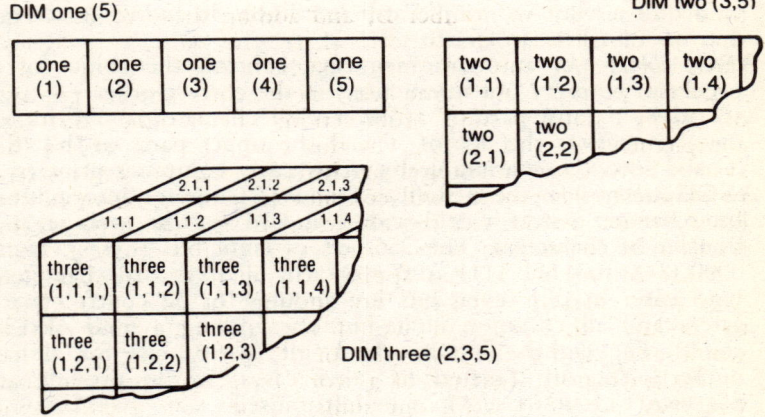

array. 1D, 2D and 3D arrays.

As with other data structures, an array has a single label (name); thus instructions can work on the whole or on

17

ART SOFTWARE

selected parts (the **array elements**, each having one or more 'subscripts' (= co-ordinates) to describe it). See also DATA STRUCTURE.

An **array processor** is a type of parallel processor (a set of processors working in parallel, with another in control); its design lets it handle at speed the tasks of processing array elements. Such tasks include those of matrix mathematics as well as, for instance, searching and sorting.

art software, *n.* a type of application program (GRAPHICS SOFTWARE) for producing on screen, editing, storing and printing pictures. Features may include some of those of COMPUTER AIDED DRAWING, but such programs mainly offer various approaches to freehand drawing and painting, a range of text fonts and sizes, access to stored video screens, animation, and special effects. Block features may include block move (cut and paste), block copy, and transformations such as shearing, turning, reflecting, and inverting foreground and background. Picture processing is an excellent introduction to IT for young people.

artificial cognition, *n.* an outdated term for OPTICAL CHARACTER READING.

artificial intelligence (AI), *n.* the ability of artificial systems to act in a way we would call intelligent in living creatures. See MACHINE INTELLIGENCE.

ASC, *abbrev. for* automatic sequence control, the ability of a processor to carry out instructions in the correct order.

ascender, *n.* any part of a lower case character above its X-HEIGHT, such as the dot of 'i' and the upper parts of 'b', 'd', 'f' and so on, not printable by many early computer printers.

ASCII, *abbrev. for* the American Standard Code for Information Interchange, a near world-wide standard for the storage and transfer of characters. The 256 sets of eight bits (bytes), from 0000 0000 to 1111 1111, can represent all keyboard characters with ease. In fact seven bits are enough for 32 control characters and all common alpha-numerics giving a total of 128 codes. The eighth bit is a check bit (parity bit) for alpha-numeric data in transfer; in other cases, it can provide an ALTERNATE CHARACTER SET or be left unused.

An **ASCII keyboard** provides keys (including combinations) for at least the 128 ASCII codes and characters. Until recently, not all keyboards did so.

aspect, attribute, characteristic or **view,** *n.* a feature of an object. A display's **aspect ratio**, is the ratio of the horizontal and vertical sides, typical values being 4:3 for television screens and standard computer displays and 3:2 for photograph and cinema screens.

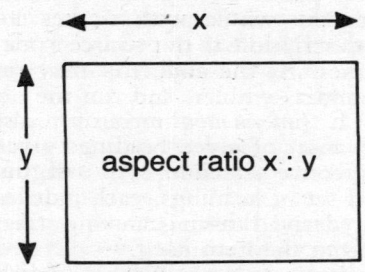

aspect. Aspect ratio.

An **aspect card** in an information retrieval system lists, for a given topic, the serial numbers and/or locations of relevant documents or items.

ASPIC, *abbrev. for* the Author's Symbolic Pre-press Interfacing Code; a set of codes which can be added to word processed text to allow the disk to be read by an automatic typesetting system.

ASR, *abbrev. for* **1.** (*communications*) automatic send/receive, describing a telex, fax, or email system that can send signals at set times (e.g. at night) and receive signals without anyone being present.
2. (*computing*) ADDRESS SELECTION REGISTER.

assemble, *vb.* to convert **assembly code** (a source program written in **assembly language**) into machine code, an **assembler** being the translation program that carries out the conversion. The instructions of an assembly language have a one-to-one relation with those in machine code (which is not the case with higher level program languages). Each instruction may have four parts (fields):
    (a) a label to allow jumps;
    (b) the operation code (opcode);
    (c) the storage cell address concerned (operand);
    (d) a comment (remark) by the programmer.
Of these only the opcode is essential in all cases, though most opcodes also require an operand.
The process of translation (i.e. **assembly**) involves converting

each opcode into the corresponding bit pattern, and each operand and address label into an absolute or relative value (see **addressing**); comments are ignored. Normally this whole process needs two passes through the source code. **Assembly time** is how long this whole process takes: longer than it may seem from the description if the source code contains macros and/or sub-routines. At the end, you may remove from store the source code and assembler, and run the object program.

assignment, *n.* **1.** (*information processing*, also called **assignment indexing**) a set of index headings given to each item in store to allow effective searching. An **assigned term index** is one using a fixed set of headings, each indexed item taking the right subset. In derived term indexing (as in a book), the headings come from the item itself.
2. (*computing*) giving a value to a label (variable). The **assignment instructions** that do this have various forms. A simple example is LET vat_rate = 15 (though many program languages do not use the LET keyword, and ':=', for instance, may replace '='). In an interactive program, the input instruction also includes assignment; non-interactive software may READ from DATA statements instead to give the same effect.

associative storage or **content addressed storage,** *n.* a form of storage where the contents of the cells identify them, rather than their addresses or the labels used for the contents. A standard processor cannot handle a content addressed store; an **associative processor** (one specially designed for the task) is, however, very fast. See also PARALLEL SEARCH.

asynchronous transfer, *n.* in which the bytes, blocks, or packets transfer when ready, and therefore at irregular intervals, rather than as a result of timing pulses from some type of clock. An **asynchronous computer** also carries out each operation when the previous one is done, rather than when a timing pulse appears.

Atanasoff, John Vincent a US engineer who developed the concept of the programmable electronic (vacuum tube) calculator in the late 1930s and early 1940s. His ABC machine was a forerunner of ENIAC, and first to use binary.

Atlas, *n.* the first commercial computer with such now standard features as:
  (a) transistors rather than valves (making it second GENERATION);
  (b) virtual storage, with the main (core) store backed by a

magnetic drum;
(c) operating system in software rather than being hard wired.

Design started at Manchester University (UK) in 1956 and, after support from Ferranti, production of what was then the world's most powerful computer started in 1963.

ATM *abbrev. for* AUTOMATIC TELLER (MACHINE).

attached processor, *n.* a secondary (slave) processor linked to the main one (master), in most cases sharing the latter's store, and able to carry out tasks assigned by the master.

attenuation, absorption or **loss,** *n.* a signal's fall in strength (i.e. energy or AMPLITUDE) with distance from its source. To restore the amplitude, an analog signal needs REPEATERS, but these amplify noise as well as signal. The REGENERATORS of digital systems perform this function more successfully.

attribute, *n.* the aspect of a data ENTITY (the content of a record of a file) held in a field.

audio, *adj.* relating to sound or hearing. (Of a system) handling signals of **audio frequency (a.f.)**, i.e. in the range 25–20000 hertz. See SPECTRUM. A magnetic **audio cassette/tape** stores such signals. An **audio response unit** is a type of MODEM that links inward voice phone calls to a computer able to reply with synthesized speech.

audit trail, *n.* **1.** a feature that lets a computer user check back on the steps that produce a given output.
2. (also called **audit log**) a security record of every transaction in an IT system, including logging on and off and what users do while on line.

authentication, *n.* the verification of user identity by means of passwords and personal identity numbers, including checking that these have not been changed without proper reason.

author(ing) language, *n.* a cross between a high level program language and a program generator, mainly used to produce computer-aided learning software. The tutor/author designs lessons either by coding within the program language or, if this presents problems, by working with the much simpler and more natural **author interface**.

authority file, *n.* a file whose records set up standards for the records, fields, cross-references, and so on, of an information retrieval system. A THESAURUS is a type of authority file.

authorization code, *n.* an IT system user's set of personal identity numbers or codes, passwords, etc.

auto-, automated or **automatic,** *prefix* or *adj.* working with-

AUTO

out human presence or control. An **auto answer** system handles inward phone calls; an example is an **auto line switch** that passes faxes to a fax system, email messages to a computer, and voice calls to a phone handset or answering machine. An **auto caller (ACU)** or **auto dialler**, on the other hand, makes outward calls on its own, perhaps to broadcast a recorded or synthesized message or a set of faxes, or for polling other units, or just for testing lines. **Auto call distribution** is a feature of key phone and some fax networks. Inward calls go to different extensions at different times of day.

Some visual displays offer **auto contrast control**. This attempts to keep the contrast within a set range. **Auto resolution control** is a similar feature of some fax machines: they adjust the fineness of scanning to suit the detail on the sheets they scan. **Auto frequency control (AFC)** is the way most receivers and transmitters stay finely tuned to a given frequency (wavelength). Many audio systems have **auto volume control (AVC)** to prevent the output sound from becoming too loud or soft; this may be the result of **auto gain control (AGC)** in the control circuit or amplifier (gain = amplification).

An **auto feeder** is a SHEET FEEDER: a printer attachment to pass single sheets through as needed. In fax, **auto group select** lets the sending system react to the other's acknowledgement (which includes a code for the group or type) and then send at the correct rate. Some fax systems are not compatible in this way with those of other groups, however. However, all modern machines and cards have an **auto identify** routine, as do most other electronic systems that link to the phone or telex network; the routine may include a RECEIVE ID message as well as codes to tell the sender how and when to transfer data. **Auto reduction** is the way a machine scales down an inward fax to fit the printer paper.

Word processors and desktop publishing software (DTP) may offer a number of features with special 'auto' names. Thus **auto kerning** allows automatic space compensation for characters which should overlap each other's space. See KERNING.

Automated bibliography, **automated dictionary**, **automated glossary**, **automated lexicon** and **automated thesaurus** are automatic files which a word processor or DTP user can call on, and perhaps extend and/or extract from, at

AUTO

any time. They also appear in many COMPUTER AIDED TRANSLATION systems. Respectively these files offer:

(a) detailed records of books and other resources you may wish to access;
(b) word lists for spelling checking;
(c) the same, but with notes;
(d) the same, with or without notes;
(e) the same, with the lists set up by meaning to allow the user to find synonyms.

Also in the fields word processing and DTP, **auto(matic) abstracting** allows a user to extract the main points from a document to produce a very short summary. **Auto(matic) indexing** software generates an index from a paged document, working with a standard set of key words and phrases, or one compiled by the author. **Automatic letter writing** is an outdated term for MAIL MERGE. **Automatic widow/orphan adjust** is how some word processors and DTP programs avoid a short single line of text at the top of a page or column (a widow) or a heading or single line of text at the foot (orphan). **Automatic decimal alignment/tab** allows numbers to be lined up in columns with their decimal points under each other. **Automatic footnote tie-in** ensures that if you move a block of text to a new page, the footnotes that relate to it move too.

Automated stock control software helps users handle ordering and deliveries and sales, keep accounts, and predict demand. This is an important area of IT application. **Automatic data processing (ADP)** is an outdated term for computing which was used mainly in a business context.

In communications, **automatic log-on** describes how an intelligent terminal or computer program will send all necessary control codes, passwords and call signs when the user wants to access a given remote data base. **Automatic message routing** is how a packet switching centre or other data transfer exchange passes inward signals to the correct outward channel.

Many modern phones and fax systems have an **automatic re-try** feature: if a call or fax does not succeed (e.g. because of a busy line), the software will try again after (say) a couple of minutes. In some cases, it will do this an indefinite number of times.

Automatic speech processing includes a number of IT techniques, for instance, the digital transfer and storage of

AUTOCODING

voice messages, and speech recognition.

An **auto(matic)teller (machine) (ATM)** is a bank's cash dispenser. Modern ATMs, linked to the correct central computer on demand, can show the balances of your accounts and let you move funds between them. An ATM can also issue statements, and allow the user to order printed ones which will be sent by mail. Cheque books can also be ordered using an ATM.

autocoding, *n.* a system for translating symbolic code to machine code, i.e. a form of assembly.

automation, *n.* control by automatic systems based on processors. An **automaton** (an outdated term for a robot) is any device that processes an input and converts it either to an instruction it can carry out or to an output. A TURING MACHINE is one major type.

autonomy, *n.* the ability to act without outside control. **Autonomous** peripherals are ones which are not DUMB.

auxiliary, *adj.* in support. **Auxiliary hardware** is part of a system not on-line to the central processor (e.g. a fax machine that can work on its own as well as when part of a network), and **auxiliary store** is backing store.

availability, *n.* the fraction of time a user can work with a processor, i.e. when it is not working with other users or on lengthy tasks.

AVC, *abbrev. for* AUTO VOLUME CONTROL.

B

b, *symbol for* BIT.
B, *symbol for* BYTE.
Babbage, Charles (1792–1871) an English professor of mathematics (despite being self-taught), who carried out important work on logarithms (until the 1950s a crucial calculating aid). To help with the vast numbers of calculations needed to build logarithm tables, he designed (with considerable state support) various high power general purpose calculating machines (called difference and analytical engines). Making the parts accurately enough was, however, not possible at the time so the projects failed.

All the same, most people think of Babbage as the 'parent of modern computing'. Ada Lovelace was an important colleague, who developed with him concepts of programming and stored program control.

Babbage played a major role in many aspects of nineteenth century British life: engineering, politics, code breaking, social reform, physics, and operations research.

babble *n.* interference between data transfer channels.
background, 1. *adj.* describing a low priority task (for example a **background job** such as printing) carried out by a multi-tasking system, in slack times between giving attention to higher priority jobs (e.g. handling users). This is known as **background processing**.
2. *n.* on a graphics screen, the equivalent of the sheet of paper. **Background ink** is a high reflection ink used for printing background text (i.e. text to be ignored) on sheets that will undergo optical character reading. The ink reflects nearly as much as the paper, so the OCR system does not detect it.
backing store or **extension store,** *n.* a slow, large capacity storage system that supports the fast, small costly main store of a general purpose IT system. A single purpose system needs no backing store - the main store can carry all the software and other data it requires. In the case of general purpose systems, on the other hand, there tends to be a frequent transfer of data between main store and backing store (saving

BACKPLANE

for later use), and the other way (loading for current needs).
Like main storage, a backing store can involve both read only
and read and write units. For read and write, MAGNETIC MEDIA
are by far the most common; however, certain OPTICAL MEDIA
are fast growing in importance for this, as well as being the
main form of read only media.

As their price goes on falling, chips are also being used
more widely for backing storage, particularly in very small
computers (as they take up little space and need little power).
See EPROM.

backplane, *n.* an alternative term for MOTHERBOARD.

back up, 1. *vb.* to provide support for occasions when
problems arise.
2. *adj.* describing anything created for the purposes of support
in IT processing. Thus a **backup file** is an extra copy saved in
case the main copy is lost, and **backup hardware** is equipment kept in reserve for when the usual hardware fails or
cannot cope with its load.

Backus-Naur form (BNF), *n.* a system (metalanguage) used
to describe the syntax (grammar) of a program language.
Developed by **John Backus** of IBM (founder of Fortran) from
Backus normal form (an incorrect name) and first used to
define Algol, BNF depends mainly on three symbols, used in
this simple example:

$$<vowel> ::= a|e|i|o|u$$

We read this as 'the meta-variable called 'vowel' is defined as
one of the set of terminal symbols 'a', 'e', 'i', 'o' or 'u'.' Thus
the three main symbols are:

<...> a metavariable, e.g. a data type or program instruction;
::= meaning 'is defined as';
| meaning 'or'

BNF defines a decimal number thus:

```
          <point> ::= .|,
          <digit> ::= 0|1|2|3|4|5|6|7|8|9
         <number> ::= <digit>|<digit><number>
 <decimal number> ::= <number><point><number>|
                     <point><number>
```

There are various ways to parse sample variables to check that
they are correct in terms of BNF definitions.

backward chain, *n.* a way of using a knowledge-based expert system to prove a hypothesis, by working back from the hypothesis into the knowledge base, rather than the reverse (compare FORWARD CHAIN).

backward channel, *n.* the channel between receiver and sender in a data transfer, used for control signals.

backward recovery, *n.* a means of getting back out of an error by a series of 'undo' actions in reverse order to the ones that led to the problem.

Bain, Alexander (1810–1877) a Scottish electrical engineer who was the first person to succeed (in 1842) in scanning an image and sending the result through a telegraph, thus making the first fax system. The design of his scanner (a set of linked electric pendulums) was too complex for success; however, within thirty years it led to popular working facsimile telegraphs.

Baird, John Logie (1888–1946) a Scottish engineer who started research into television in 1922, with the first demonstrations in 1926 (the same year as his patents for using television waves in a radar system). The British Broadcasting Corporation started to use his 30-line mechanically scanned system in 1929, moving to 240 lines in 1936, and an electronically scanned 405-line system the next year. Baird produced the first 3D and colour television systems in 1944.

band *n.* **1.** a recording area on a magnetic tape (or drum).
2. a range of frequencies, as in, for instance, audio band, long wave (radio) band, and BROAD BAND networks. A **band pass filter** is a circuit that lets a given band through but not signals with frequencies outside that range. **Bandwidth** is the range of frequencies a filter, channel or other system can pass or handle.

banking, *n.* the business engaged in by a bank, a major application area for all aspects of IT, where there are many uses for computing, telecommunications, electronics and video. Banking becomes more efficient in the use of electronic funds transfer (rather than the use of cash, cheques and other forms of paper) and of on-line data bases of various kinds. The world-wide banking electronic network is therefore very large and complex.

See also AUTO TELLER and HOME/office banking, both systems that give clients the power to carry out transactions without having to enter a bank.

bar code, *n.* also called PIECE IDENTITY NUMBER (PIN), this is a form of MACHINE READABLE INPUT very widely used in trade

BARREL PRINTER

and stock control. The bar code itself is a set of black lines and spaces of varying thickness, used to carry information about the nature and source of the product concerned. A **bar code reader/scanner** measures the reflected light level from the bars and spaces and outputs to a processor a corresponding signal. Software may then do such tasks as:

(a) noting the passage of the item through a warehouse or checkout;

(b) changing the stock level value in a stock file;

(c) showing the price on a display (after referring to a prices file).

A **bar code printer** is a printer that prints bar codes onto labels (for instance) after software has translated the data into the right form.

barrel printer, *n.* an alternative term for DRUM PRINTER.

barring, *n.* the prevention of access to some or all of a system's facilities.

base, *n.* the storage cell, with its **base address**, to which relative ADDRESSING relates at any point in an assembly program. During the assembly of a program which includes relative addresses, **base offset assembly** is the process of changing them to absolute addresses. The assembler adds the base value to each relative value.

A **base band** is a frequency band (range) used to transmit certain television and telephone signals. A **base plate** is an interface for an electric or electronic typewriter that allows its use as a true word processor. A **base station** is a transmitter/receiver at the centre of a cell in a CELL PHONE network, linked to the 'mobile switching centre' (exchange) for the local group of cells.

Basic, *n. acronym for* Beginners' All-purpose Symbolic Instruction Code, the most widely available program language for use with micros. Being so widespread, this general purpose language exists in a vast number of dialects (varieties), with almost every new micro extending its features to provide extra facilities. The standard, if there is one, does not differ much from that set up originally in 1964, though John Kemeny and Thomas Kurtz (Dartmouth College, US) designed it for non-interactive use on main frames.

The design was, as the name implies, to help train programmers. Basic was, and remains, a friendly system, easy to pick up and extend. Much of that ease derives, however, from its use of line numbers, so being interpreted rather than compiled, and its flexibility. These factors, all still shown by most modern versions, do not endear Basic to professional programmers; it is now, however, often very well structured, extremely powerful and effective.

batch, *n.* a set of programs or program tasks passed to a computer for **batch processing**, that is, for action without people being involved. Most computing jobs are designed for batching, in order to trouble users as little as possible. Batch processing is the main mode of operation of main frame systems; the operating software includes a JOB CONTROL LANGUAGE (JCL) for the purpose.

Some people wrongly use 'batch processing' to mean BACKGROUND working.

battery, *n.* a set of one or more cells used as an electric power source (supply). The supply is now one of the main limiting factors in pocket and laptop micros, whose users may need to work away from mains power for many hours at a time. The best alternative on cost grounds is to use rechargeable cells – but these last for an even shorter time than standard ones. Various lines of research hold out hope of batteries that by the mid-1990s could:

(a) weigh 20% of current types;
(b) take up less space;
(c) work at full stretch for several days before needing a recharge;
(d) survive many hundred recharges. Systems based on solid conducting polymer sheets are particularly exciting and are likely to be cheap and hazard-free.

baud, *n.* the main unit of data transfer speed ('**baud rate**'), one baud often being the same as one bit per second. Strictly, a baud is one signal event (state change) per second; it is a bit per second only in the case of a binary channel. In other cases it may be a digit, symbol or byte per second.

The name comes from that of Emil **Baudot**, who devised the first standard telegraph code in 1877. The **Baudot code** concept was a great advance, but being still the standard for telex, is a major factor in the decline of that technology. The problem is that the code uses five bits (Baudot's operators had five-key keypads), giving a total of only 62 control codes and characters. (2^5 is 32, but making one code a shift lock gives access to a second set of 32, also including a shift lock.)

BCD *abbrev. for* BINARY CODED DECIMAL.

bead, *n.* an alternative term for a module in a program

BEAM STORE

developed by MODULAR PROGRAMMING, the programmer grouping BEADS together in threads.

beam store, *n.* an obsolete term for a BACKING STORE in a cathode ray tube in which electron beams write and read data.

beam width, *n.* the angle (strictly, solid angle) within which an aerial can send or receive useful signals.

bearer, *n. a* BROAD BAND channel with high band width.

beginning marker, *n.* a type of control code to mark the start of something, e.g. a **beginning of file (BOF)** marker in a computer file. A beginning marker can also mark the start of a signal. A **beginning of information marker (BIM)** is a transparent or reflective leader at the start of a magnetic tape. A sensor in the drive can then detect when the tape is ready for use.

bell character, *n.* a control code (ASCII 7) which sounds a bell or beeper to alert the user.

Bell code, *n.* a code system for passing commands to a computer-aided phototypesetter.

belt printer, *n.* a device similar to a **chain printer**, with the characters on the surface of an endless belt.

benchmark, *n.* a standard test used to compare the accuracy, efficiency or speed of an IT unit or program.

bibliography, *n.* a description of documents, books and/or other information sources. **Bibliographic coupling** is a measure of how close two such sources are in content, based on the number of other sources they cite in common. **Bibliographic data bases** are computer based bibliographies. Many include much more than just details of title and origin: they may store the whole of each document (or at least an abstract) in electronic form.

bi-conditional, *adj.* an alternative term for equivalence (see EQUIVALENCE GATE).

bi-directional printer, *n.* a printer which prints consecutive lines in opposite directions, thus saving a lot of time. See BOUSTROPHEDON PRINTING.

BIM, *abbrev. for* BEGINNING OF INFORMATION MARKER.

binary, *adj.* describing any system with only two states, e.g. a simple on/off power switch. The **binary system** uses **binary numbers** for base two counting and arithmetic. Here, **binary notation** involves only two **binary digits** (bits), 0 and 1, with a **binary point** (.) used in the same way as the decimal point in denary to make **binary fractions**.

A binary number is therefore of the form 0010 1011.0110 (it

BINARY

is normal in writing to group the bits in fours rather than threes:- four bits equal one hexadecimal digit in value). The usual rules of place value apply, with 1 (2^0), 2 (2^1), 4 (2^2), 8 (2^3) ... passing left from the point, and 0.5 ($1/2^1$), 0.25 ($1/2^2$), 0.125 ($1/2^3$) ... to the right. The usual rules of ARITHMETIC apply as well.

In an IT system, there is a number of ways to handle denary (base ten) numbers. If the programmer wishes to treat them as digit strings, ASCII codes 48 (for 0) to 57 (for 9) apply. To carry out arithmetic tasks, the system must handle numbers as numbers. In that case only a small range of values, or a low level of precision, results from putting one value in one word. Working with integers only is one way to reduce this problem; others are to use SIGN AND MAGNITUDE and/or FLOATING POINT forms. See also COMPLEMENT.

Part way between numbers as strings and numbers as numbers is some form of **binary coded decimal (BCD)** system. Here the software codes and handles each denary digit as a binary number. Thus 1993 could appear as 0001 1001 1001 0011. As this simple BCD needs four bits per denary digit but does not use the values from 1010 to 1111, various extended BCD systems have evolved. The most important is EBCDIC, which, like ASCII, is an eight-bit data handling system with many other characters than digits.

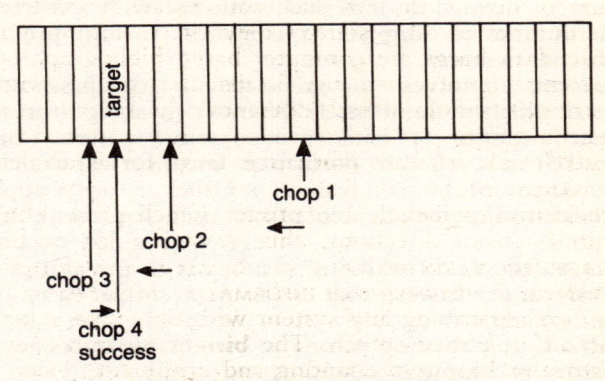

binary. The binary chop (search).

A **binary chop** or **binary search** is a very efficient way to search a list (for instance) for a particular value, as long as the

BINDING

list's search field contents are in order. It involves looping through this process until the search succeeds or until it is clear the target is not in the list (See Figure). The sequence is: move to the item at or next below the centre of the list; if the target is less than that item, discard the second half of the list; otherwise, discard the first half.

A **binary tree** is a TREE with no more than two branches from each node.

binding, *n*. an alternative term for linking (see LINK).

bioelectronics, *n*. microelectronics using a proportion of organic materials and with possible biological links in mind. The main area of current interest is medicine. Here microelectronic implants have proved of immense value for monitoring (using a biosensor), for prosthesis (e.g. heart pacers), and for delivering drugs.

A **biosensor** is a microelectronic implant with a radio transmitter to send readings outside the body of the patient or research subject. Such sensors, able to work full time for a year or more, interfere little (if at all) with biological systems. Typical biosensors can be used, for example, to monitor temperature, pressure, strain, organ size, and the electric activity of major nerves.

Bioelectronics includes the development of **biochips** from biosensors. These chips range from biosensors with a biologically active coating, to ones that work not with semiconductors but with proteins (digital) or enzymes (analog) produced by genetic engineering.

Bioaccess involves the replacement of passwords and personal identity numbers (PINs) by checking (for instance) the user's finger or hand prints, retina pattern, or voice. (These schemes relate to **computer biometrics**, the electronic measurement of human features.) Other security applications of bioelectronics include biosensors used for bomb and drug detection.

bionics, *n*. the study of living systems with the aim of making hardware and software that work in a similar way (see also NEURAL COMPUTER).

bistable, 1. *adj*. existing in one of two stable states, depending on history and input.
2. *n*. a name for the FLIP FLOP, a two-state circuit of great importance in, for example, chip data storage.

bisynchronous, *adj*. capable of sending frequent synchronisation signals both ways during a data transfer.

bit (b), *n.* a binary digit, 0 or 1. The **bit density** of a storage medium is the number of bits it can store (strictly, but rarely, in a standard length (as in **bits per inch (BPI)** of tape, area or volume). For **bit map**, see MAP. The **bit rate** of a data transfer is the number of **bits per second (BPS)** passed. A **bit stream** is a set of related bits in transfer, while a **bit string** is any other set of related bits; in both cases, people refer to the value in a particular **bit position**. **Bit location**, on the other hand, is a field in a record able to store just one bit (e.g. a logical field).

Bit slice systems have large powerful processors, of any desired word length, made of a set of identical processors each able to handle, say, four bits. Custom microprogramming then sets each system up as required, with each of the unit processors left to work on a specific task. A bit slice system is thus a type of parallel processor. **Bit stuffing** is adding extra 'make weight' bits into a sequence before transfer, the receiver taking them away to restore the original signal.

bite, *n.* an alternative term for BYTE.

black box, *n.* a jargon term for a system of which only the function, not the design, matters.

black signal, *n.* the signal produced by scanning the darkest parts of a fax original or a television scene. See also BRIGHTNESS.

bleeding, *n.* the spreading of ink outside the edge of a printed character, causing problems for OPTICAL character readers.

bleeper, *n.* a type of PAGER.

blind, *vb.* to program a system so it will ignore unwanted inward data.

blind keyboard, *n.* one which gives the user no visual copy.

blinking, *n.* flashing on a screen, a feature of many cursors and priority messages.

blip, *n.* 1. a small, perhaps unwanted, signal on a display screen.

2. a mark on a document, or a pulse on a tape, that causes some specific action when a reader detects it.

block, 1. *n.* part of a text in a word processor, a spreadsheet table, or other file that the system can handle as a whole. A given word processor's **block handling** features may include saving, printing, deleting, moving, searching and spell checking the current marked block. In the same way, in a graphics (art) program, you may be able to move, copy, save, print a block and/or transform it in such ways as twisting and turning.

BLOCK

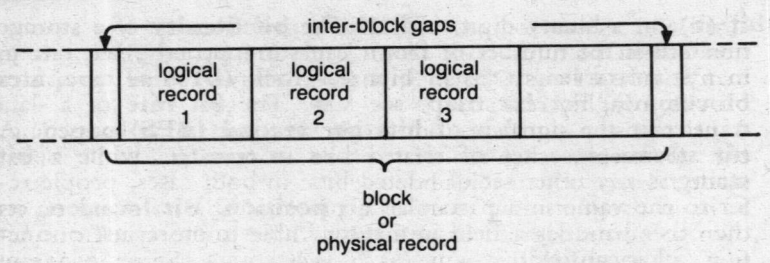

block. Fig. 1. Magnetic tape blocking.

2. *n.* the fixed-length part of a computer file the system handles as a whole. In backing storage, one block is the largest amount of data the processor can read or write at a time, this being **block transfer**. The block is therefore the size of a disk sector (the disk's smallest addressable area) and the size of the backing storage buffer register. A tape file is as shown in Figure 1.

A block does not have to equate to a single record in a file, though in many systems the block size is the upper limit of record size. **Blocking** is the creation of a block from two or more logical records (the block then being the physical record); the system's **blocking factor** is the number of logical records in a block.

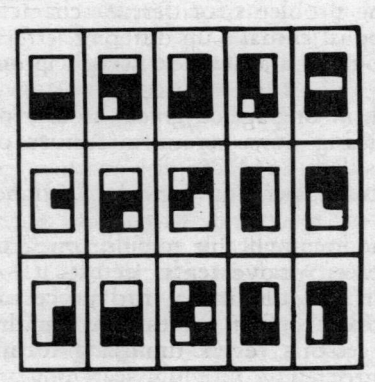

block. Fig. 2. Some graphics blocks.

3. *n.* a rectangle, with a **block diagram** being the structure chart of a system or process. **Block graphics** are low resolution screen pictures built from large groups of pixels, as in many VIDEOTEX systems. Figure 2 shows some **graphics blocks**, roughly real size.

4. *vb*. to use a signal or code to prevent something happening, e.g. to keep a channel clear or to stop outside calls being made from an extension phone.

5. *n*. in programming, part of a program able to stand on its own to some degree, or defined to have some specific function. It is much the same as a PROCEDURE. Some program languages demand a block structure. In Cobol the blocks are termed divisions, for example.

blocking, 1. *n.* (*word processing*) justification (see also FLUSH).
2. *vb*. to start a paragraph without an indent on the first line.

blow back, *vb*. to make a full sized image on screen or paper of a microform page.

blowing, *n*. using a special interface between store and PROM chip to program the chip.

BNF, *abbrev. for* BACKUS-NAUR form, a way to describe the syntax (grammar) and structures of a program language.

board, *n*. a printed circuit board. See also MOTHERBOARD.

body, *n*. the main text of a word-processed document (i.e. other than headings, footnotes, boxes, captions, etc.), **body size** being the size (in points) of the **body type**.

BOF, *abbrev. for* BEGINNING OF FILE MARKER.

boilerplating, *n*. the use of different sets of word processed standard paragraphs to make up different letters.

bomb, *n*. a fatal error made when using a program that causes the loss of the program (see also LOGIC BOMB).

book, *n*. a large set of pages in main store. A **book message** is a signal broadcast to two or more receivers.

Boole, George (1815–1864) English mathematician. He started work as a school teacher in Lincoln at the age of 14, and taught himself first several languages, then science, then mathematics, and was still able to find time for active work in various social reform movements. In 1844, Boole received the Royal Society's first gold medal for mathematics, and a few years later became the first professor of mathematics at University College, Cork, even though he had no secondary education or degree.

Described by Bertrand Russell a century later as the founder of pure mathematics, Boole's major work at Cork was to devise the form of mathematics called symbolic logic. His

BOOLEAN

aim, as a highly religious person, was to try to express human thought in mathematical terms, and Boolean algebra is the basis for modern computer theory.

Boole also developed binary arithmetic, set theory, differential equations and statistics.

Boolean, *adj.* the logical data type (**Boolean element**), one with only two values (**Boolean values**: true or false, 1 or 0).

Boolean algebra (or **Boolean calculus** or **Boolean logic**) deals with logical statements, i.e. binary ones that can be only true or false. These statements, or propositions, involve **Boolean operators** such as 'and' (symbol ∧), 'not' (complement, ') and 'or' (∨), and, being binary, relate directly to the action of a processor's arithmetic and logic unit. The **Boolean operations** handled by the operators are often expressed in **Boolean tables**. See TRUTH TABLE, GATE.

The rules of Boolean algebra follow, x, y and z being any Boolean elements.

(a) Null rules:
$x \vee 1 \equiv 1$
$x \wedge 0 \equiv 0$

(b) Identity rules:
$x \vee 0 \equiv x$
$x \wedge 1 \equiv x$

(c) Complement rules:
$x \vee x' \equiv 1$
$x \wedge x' \equiv 0$

(d) Idempotent rules:
$x \vee x \equiv x$
$x \wedge x \equiv x$

(e) Commutative rules:
$x \vee y \equiv y \vee x$
$x \wedge y \equiv y \wedge x$

(f) Associative rules:
$x \vee (y \vee z) \equiv (x \vee y) \vee z$
$x \wedge (y \wedge z) \equiv (x \wedge y) \wedge z$

(g) Distributive rules:
$x \wedge (y \vee z) \equiv (x \wedge y) \vee (x \wedge z)$
$x \vee (y \wedge z) \equiv (x \vee y) \wedge (x \vee z)$

(h) Absorption rules:
$x \vee (x \wedge y) \equiv x$
$x \wedge (x \vee y) \equiv x$

boom, *n.* a frame for holding the elements of an aerial array, or a microphone.

booting or **cold boot** or **cold start,** *n.* a computer's automatic preparation for a user's instructions when the machine is switched on. This process needs the **bootstrap** instructions hard wired in the system; those instructions may include a **bootstrap loader** to copy operating software or other programs from backing store to main store. The word comes from the phrase 'to pull yourself up by your bootstraps [shoe laces]'.

boustrophedon printing, *n.* a form of printing in which the head prints one line in one direction and the next line in the other, i.e. bidirectional printing. The word comes from the Greek, meaning 'as the ox ploughs'.

box, *n.* a frame on screen or in a document for a section of important text, or an urgent message to the user, or the text or message itself.

BPI, *abbrev. for* BITS PER INCH.

BPS, *abbrev. for* BITS PER SECOND. See also BAUD.

brain, *n.* the co-ordinating centre of the nervous system in vertebrates, the model at which many IT system designers aim. The human brain has 14 thousand million neurons, so the target is a distant one. Interestingly enough, a supercomputer model of a 10000 cell brain (hippocampus) built in 1990 produced signals very much like human brainwaves. The origin of these waves is no more clear in the case of the model than it is in that of the brain itself. See also NEURAL.

branch, *n.* 1. a point in a program where the system will choose between two or more actions.
2. the link which exists between a node and a child (or descendant) in a tree.

breadboard, *n.* 1. a circuit set up for development and testing rather than for production.
2. a general purpose printed circuit board used for building such circuits.

break, *vb.* to interrupt a program run, perhaps by using a break or escape key press, or by a special input at a **break point** in the program (a DEBUGGING aid).

bridge, *n.* 1. a full-wave RECTIFIER circuit, with AC input and DC output.
2. a circuit that automatically smooths the effects of temperature change.
3. a circuit linking two networks, or two computers (strictly termed GATEWAY).
4. a blob of solder linking two tracks on a circuit board by mistake.

brightness, *n.* the intensity of all or part of a screen display or scanned sheet. **Brightness ratio** is a measure of the contrast between the lightest and darkest parts.

broad band, *adj.* describing a channel of much wider band width than normal (BASE band), and able to carry data at very

BROADCAST

high rates, or a number of separate signals at once (by MULTI-PLEXING). A **broad band network** is one whose coaxial cable (band width up to 300 MHz) carries a mix of signal types, e.g. high speed digital data, voice and video. Links to individual hardware units are by radio frequency transceivers (modems). Data transfers through these networks are either one way only, or two way using a head end control unit to handle the routing.

broadcast, *vb.* to send a given signal to a number of receivers or network stations at the same time or, in the case of fax, consecutively. In a **broadcast network**, all signals are in packets, each headed with an address code for the target station(s). Various methods exist (e.g. token passing) to prevent clashes between packets.

A **broadcast satellite** is one used for radio and television broadcasting rather than one-to-one communications. **Broadcast videotex** is an alternative name for TELETEXT.

brushes, *n.* a set of electric contacts used to read punched cards and tape.

bubble, *n.* a small isolated magnetic domain. **Bubble storage** holds BITS as bubbles in a pipeline. A bubble domain is a very small region with opposite polarity to its surroundings (normally the surface layer of a garnet crystal). The bubble store holds data as a set of domains (1s) and gaps (0s), each set, or train (thousands of words long) being held in a loop-shaped track (called a pipeline). To erase, rewrite or read a train, the system transfers the train to the main loop through a transfer site. See Figure.

Bubble storage is therefore not fully direct access; it is, all the same, fast acting, highly robust and non-volatile. While costs have not yet fallen as much as expected, the technique is used in main or backing store in a number of systems (e.g. military). See also CHARGE-COUPLED DEVICE (CCD).

A **bubble sort** is a widely used method of SORTING data items; in it the lowest value items 'bubble' up toward the top of the list.

bucket, *n.* a block or sector of storage, or its contents.

buffer, *n.* a store for data in transfer where the two units work at different speeds, **buffering** being the use of buffer storage so that the processor and program need not wait for a slow peripheral. The **storage buffer register** of a central processing unit lies at the junction between main and backing store.

bug, *n.* an error in a program that means the program does

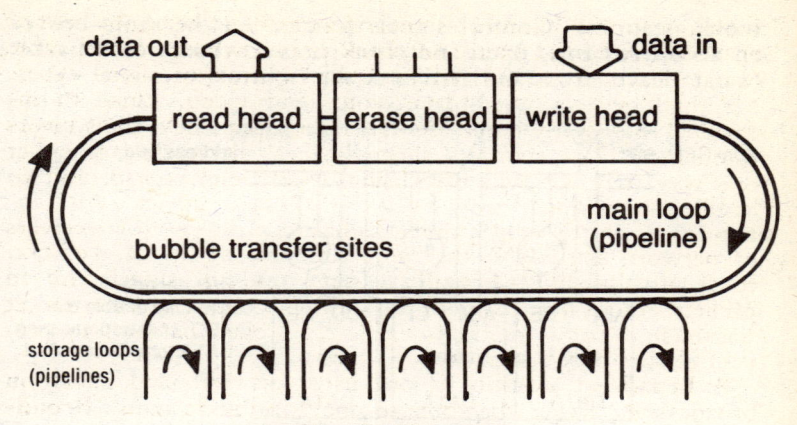

bubble. Bubble storage.

data out — read head — erase head — write head — *data in*

bubble transfer sites — main loop (pipeline)

storage loops (pipelines)

not work as it should. **Debugging** is the process of finding and removing bugs.

buggy, *n.* a floor robot with its own processor, or driven by a linked computer.

bulk storage, *n.* an alternative term for BACKING STORE.

bulk update terminal, *n.* a terminal used for editing **videotex** pages.

bulletin board, *n.* a computer messaging, conferring and mailing system, mainly for remote micro users, and often short-lived.

bundling, *n.* the practice of including software (e.g. word processor or games) when selling a micro.

bureau, *n.* a firm that provides IT services for others, e.g. COMPUTER BUREAU, FAX BUREAU.

burn, *vb.* to program a ROM chip by setting the circuits permanently.

burst, 1. *n.* a short, high frequency signal or data transfer. **Burst traffic** is a number of such signals in a channel and a **burst modem** is a modem able to handle them.

2. *vb.* to separate pages of continuous printout by hand or with a **burster**.

bus, *n.* a major path for parallel data or signals. A **bus driver** is an amplifier for the signals (see LINE DRIVER), and a **bus terminus** is a balancing circuit at the end. The bus may serve a very large number of circuits (or, in the case of a **bus net-**

BUSINESS SYSTEMS

work, stations). Control signals (carried on the same bus or on a **control bus**) open and close gates to ensure each packet of data leaves from and arrives at the right places.

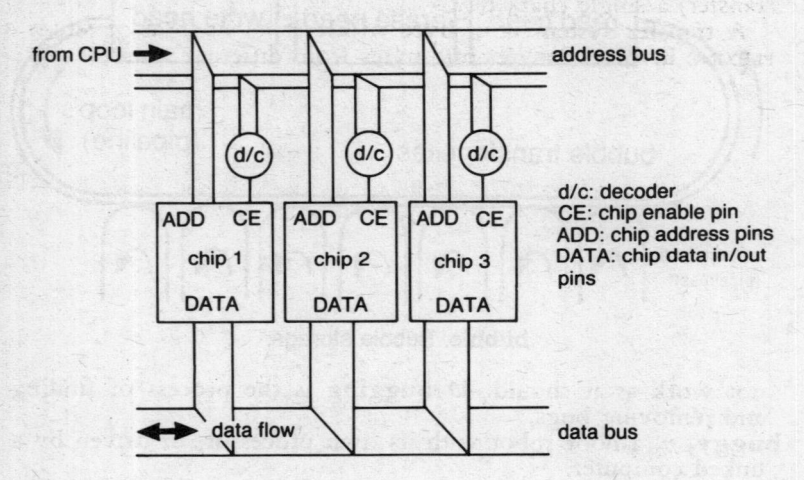

```
from CPU →                                          address bus

         (d/c)         (d/c)         (d/c)
                                                    d/c: decoder
      ADD   CE      ADD   CE      ADD   CE          CE: chip enable pin
                                                    ADD: chip address pins
      chip 1        chip 2        chip 3            DATA: chip data in/out
                                                    pins
      DATA          DATA          DATA


      ↔ data flow                                   data bus
```

bus. Address and data buses linking read/write storage chips.

Systems may have separate buses for data words (**data bus**), control signals and addresses (**address bus**) (See Figure). On the other hand, one bus may carry all these types of traffic, with a large enough set of lines for each. Such a multi-purpose bus will need lines for each of the bits in the system's word, for each of the bits in the control signal word, and for each bit in the largest address. The S100 bus has a hundred lines. This is very costly, but it is also very fast and effective.

business systems, *n.* hardware and software used for business information handling. The main areas of **business software** are word processing, spreadsheet work, database management, communications control, and graphics. Many packages now integrate these, while other programs, e.g. accounts, stock control, and project management, are important too.

A **business graphics** program, as opposed to art software, converts sets of figures to graph form, e.g. line graph, bar chart, and pie diagram. See also GRAPHICS and PRESENTATION GRAPHICS.

BYTE

byte (B) or **bite,** *n.* a set of bits of standard length handled as a unit. It is normal now to work only with eight-bit bytes (as in this book); one such byte can handle (store, process, transfer) a single character.

A transfer system is in **byte mode** if its method of MULTI-PLEXING involves interleaving bytes from different sources.

C

C, *n.* a high level program language, fairly recent and therefore well designed in the light of experience. C is a general purpose language that offers both a high level of structure and many low level features to aid translation to efficient machine code. Like PASCAL, it is block structured rather than having procedures; indeed it is not as elegant as Pascal, but is fast growing in popularity, especially for writing systems software.

C band, *n.* the range of RADIO frequencies from 3.9 to 6.2 gigahertz (GHz).

cable, *n.* one or more conductors in an insulating sheath (e.g. CO-AX), used to carry power or signals. **Cable TV (cablecasting)** is a system for distributing broadcast and/or local radio and/or television signals through a cable network linking all, or most, places in an area; broad band techniques mean that the cable can carry signals in both directions (e.g. for interactive TV), and that telephone, video phone, data, viewdata and other transfer services may be on offer too. See also FIBRE OPTICS.

cache, *n.* a high speed store situated logically, if not physically, between a processor and its main store. The operating software has the task of trying to predict which blocks of data in main store will next be wanted by the processor, and transfers these to the cache in advance of demand. Success rates of 80% or better are typical.

CAD, *abbrev. for* COMPUTER AIDED DESIGN or COMPUTER AIDED DRAWING.

CAD(/C)AM, *abbrev. for* COMPUTER AIDED DESIGN AND MANUFACTURE.

CAE, *abbrev. for* COMPUTER AIDED EDUCATION.

CAI, *abbrev. for* COMPUTER AIDED INSTRUCTION.

CAL, *abbrev. for* COMPUTER AIDED LEARNING.

calculator, *n.* a device, normally hand-held or desktop, that carries special purpose mathematical software. As well as helping the user with simple arithmetic, statistical and trigonometric calculations, many calculators now are programmable; some have backing store; some have graphic output; some have printers.

call, *n.* **1.** a one-way or two-way telephone, fax or radio transaction. **Call barring** involves programming a telephone handset, fax system or radio transmitter so that it cannot call everywhere. **Call confirmation** is a message to the sender that a fax or telex has got through. A **call directing code** is a code used to direct a message or signal between two stations, while **call forwarding** and **call transfer**, available in some telephone exchanges and local networks, is the automatic transfer of an unanswered call to a second handset. **Call pick-up** is a manual version of these last two systems.

A **call logger** stores details of all calls made (and, in the case of fax, received). It then gives the user or owner of the system a printout for, for instance, billing purposes.
2. access to a separate program or routine from or by the one in current use.
calligraphic plotter, *n.* a graphics monitor.
CAM, *abbrev. for* COMPUTER AIDED MANUFACTURE.
camera-ready copy (CRC), *n.* sheets of printout (text and/or graphics) ready for platemaking in a print shop.
camping, *n.* a technique whereby a busy telephone or fax machine can take an inward call as soon as it is free.
candidate key, *n.* a type of primary key in relational database searching.
canned text, *n.* files of word-processed text used for BOILERPLATING.
capacitance electronic disc (CED) or **capacitative disc,** *n.* a type of contact VIDEO DISC which stores the signal in the form of electric charge at each point on the surface.
carbonless paper, *n.* a multipart printer paper for making copies of printout without the use of carbon paper. This allows the user to make more copies, as printers can handle only a limited thickness of paper, and the use of carbon paper therefore limits numbers of copies.
card, *n.* **1.** a type of PUNCHED MEDIA, now rarely used except in such contexts as the KIMBALL TAG. The card stores data as patterns of holes punched in **card columns**. A **card punch** is an offline device for punching these hole patterns, a **card reader** being able to sense the patterns; both machines have a **card feed** to carry cards through quickly and efficiently.
2. an alternative term for printed circuit board (PCB); as in, for instance, **fax card** (a PCB that gives a computer fax facilities) and **hard card** (a PCB that carries a hard disk unit and control circuits).

CAROUSEL

3. a small plastic rectangle imprinted with a form of machine readable store used, for instance, as a credit or debit card or for identifying the bearer. A **stripe card** is one whose store is a strip of magnetic material, though optical stripe versions now exist (one type being the **Drexon card**). Compare SMART CARD.

carousel, *n.* a display system that loops through a sequence of screens again and again, for information or demonstration.

car phone, *n.* a mobile telephone for use (permanently or mainly) in a vehicle. Cellphones are now common in this context (see CELLULAR RADIO). See also SMART CAR.

carriage return, *n.* **1.** the typewriter key or lever that returns the carriage at the end of a line ready for typing the next.
2. the code (ASCII 13) that causes the same effect on a telex set, type setter, or computer printer.
3. the key (RETURN or ENTER) on a computer keyboard that gives that code.

carrier signal or **carrier wave,** *n.* a signal or wave that transfers coded information, either by adding higher frequency components, or by MODULATION. At the receiver, suitable circuits remove the carrier to leave the sent information.

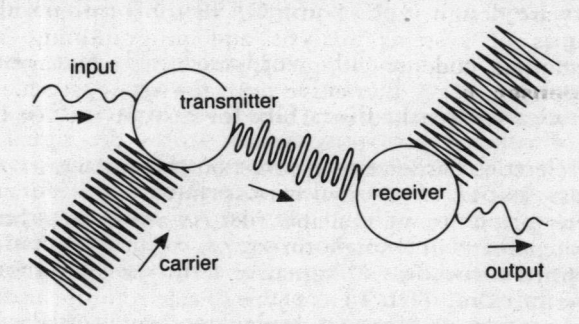

carrier signal. Transfer of a modulated carrier wave.

carry, *vb.* to transfer (when adding or multiplying) a number from one column to the neighbour with higher place value (the next one on the left). In computer arithmetic, a **carry bit** is a carry from the most significant column; the bit may set a **carry flag** in a flag register, showing that the sum has led to overflow.

cartridge, *n.* a compact hardware, firmware or backing storage pack, e.g. a tape loop or a backing storage chip in a box which is easy to insert and remove.

CAS, *n.* a recent standard for data transfers between computers. The program sits in the background, and can be called up at any time with a simple key press. It will then send the current file to the modem for onward transfer to a second computer or fax machine.

case, *n.* see LOWER CASE, UPPER CASE.

CASE, 1. *n.* one of the five main ALGORITHM structures, handling a multiple decision (branch).

2. *acronym for* computer aided SOFTWARE ENGINEERING. Programs giving help in this area are now a major industry. They tend to let the user work with a graphics screen, and, since they need a great deal of storage, are best used on a network rather than a stand-alone system. The interpretation of CASE depends on the context of the programmer; needs differ greatly. When such systems first appeared in the early 1970s, the needs of those who used them were fairly clear. Even now, one may expect a data dictionary (a store for all the data items available to the system under development). Also, one finds help in the areas of software specification, architecture design, and software design itself. Some CASE tools (programs) assist other areas of systems analysis and programming such as documentation, code development, and project management.

cash dispenser, *n.* an alternative term for AUTO TELLER.

cassette, *n.* a tape packed in a box for ease of use, or the box itself.

CAT, *abbrev. for* COMPUTER AIDED TEACHING, COMPUTER AIDED TRANSLATION, COMPUTER AIDED TYPE-SETTING.

catalog(ue), *n.* a list of available files on a disk or other backing store, perhaps in a single directory.

catastrophic error, *n.* an alternative term for FATAL ERROR.

cathode-ray tube, (CRT) *n.* a type of electron tube used as the basis of many kinds of visual display. A focussed beam of electrons (charged particles) from the electron gun converts to a spot of light when it strikes the coated screen. A deflection assembly uses signals to move the spot to any part of the screen, either by electrostatic means (as in oscilloscopes and monitors) or by electromagnetism (as in television and radar sets). See also ACCELERATING VOLTAGE.

CATV, *abbrev. for* COMMUNITY AERIAL (ANTENNA) TV.

Cauzin strip, *n.* a form of parallel MACHINE READABLE INPUT, sometimes used to transfer programs printed in books and

CB

magazines to small computers and robots fitted with a **Cauzin reader**.

CB, *abbrev. for* CITIZENS' BAND.
CBT, *abbrev. for* COMPUTER BASED TRAINING.
CCD, *abbrev. for* CHARGE-COUPLED DEVICE.
CCTV, *abbrev. for* CLOSED CIRCUIT TV.
CCU, *abbrev. for* COMMUNICATIONS CONTROL UNIT.
CD *abbrev. for* COMPACT DISC.
CDI, see COMPACT DISC.
CD-ROM, see COMPACT DISC.
CD-ROM XA, see COMPACT DISC.
CDU, see COMPACT DISC.
CED, *abbrev. for* CAPACITANCE ELECTRONIC DISC.
cell, *n.* one of the small identical units which make up a whole. See PIXEL, STORAGE CELL.
cellular radio, *n.* a growing type of network for mobile (e.g. car) telephones, or **cellphones**. The call from a **cell telephone** passes to the base station of the cell it is in at the time; the base station transfers it by cable to the MOBILE SWITCHING CENTRE that handles a group of cells; this passes it in turn to the nearby telephone exchange (see Figure). The reverse

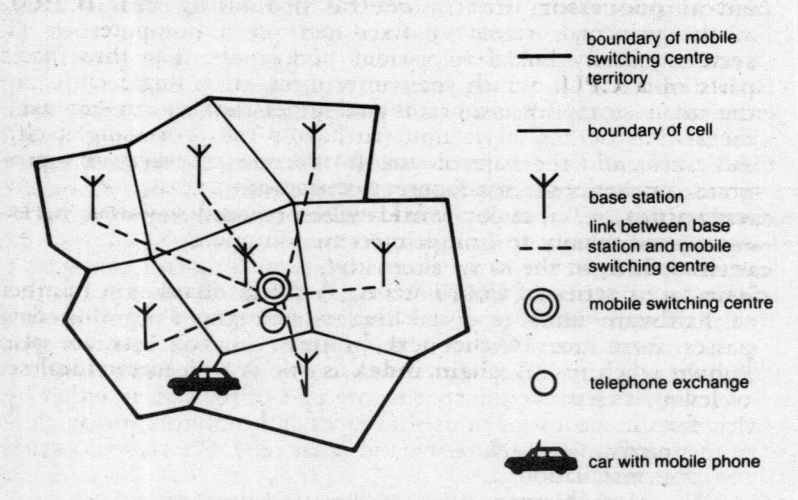

cellular radio. Part of a cellphone network.

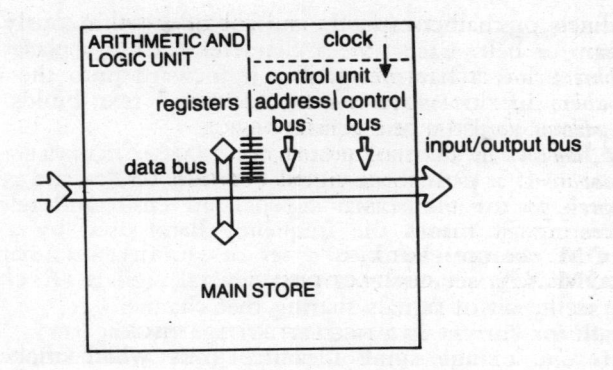

central processor. The main parts of a central processing unit.

happens to contact the receiving telephone. As the calling and receiving telephones move between cells, computers transfer the signals between the base stations without loss of channel.

central office, *n.* an alternative term for TELEPHONE EXCHANGE.

central processor unit or **central processing unit (CPU),** *n.* the principal, relatively fixed part of a computer or IT system, usually linked to various peripherals. The three basic parts of a CPU, which may now exist on a single chip, are the main store (for programs and other data in current use), the arithmetic and logic unit (to handle the processing itself), the clock, and the control unit (to decode and carry out program instructions). See Figure. See MACHINE CYCLE.

Centronics, *n.* a major world-wide standard PARALLEL INTERFACE, used mainly to link printers to computers.

certification, *n.* the same as APPROVAL.

chain, *n.* a series of linked items. A **daisy chain** is a number of hardware units (e.g. backing stores) joined so that data passes from one to the next in turn. Linked lists are also known as chains. A **chain index** is one with a hierarchical set of levels, as in:

fax ...
   card ...
      installation ...
         problems ...

In a **chain search**, each record found contains some means of pointing to the next. A **chain printer** (or belt printer) carries

CHANGE FILE

several sets of characters in the surface of a continuously moving chain or belt. Each time a character reaches a place where it should print, a hammer strikes it forward onto the ribbon and paper. In this way, a line of printed text builds up (a chain printer is also a line printer).

change file, *n.* an alternative term for TRANSACTION FILE.

channel, *n.* **1.** a path for a signal between sender and receiver (and perhaps for the return signals). In radio and television broadcasting, it means the frequency band used by a given station. A **channel bank** is a set of MULTIPLEXING hardware used to share a channel between several signals. A **channel group** is the set of signals sharing that channel.
2. a path for current in a FIELD EFFECT TRANSISTOR (FET).

character, *n.* a single symbol, control code, punctuation mark, digit or letter with a specific meaning, in essence the result of any keyboard key press. A **character string** is a set of none, one or more characters. A **character block** is the rectangle of dots on screen or printout that can form a character. A **character generator** is the hardware and/or software in control, while **character codes** are how a system stores, processes and transfers its complete **character set**.

Character density measures the number of characters (or bytes) a store holds per unit length, area, or volume.

Character fill is a process of hiding GARBAGE in a store for security reasons by putting a character such as 0 or X in place of each byte of garbage. For optical **character reading/recognition (OCR)** see OPTICAL CHARACTER READING. In OCR, **character skew** describes when a character is twisted from the vertical, making reading much harder. Also in OCR, **character strokes** are the strokes, marks and dots that make up a given character, while **character style** describes its actual structure. See also FOUNT.

In a display or printout, a **character space** is the area a character takes up; as characters vary in size, proportional spacing can help to make a text more legible. A **character spacing display** is a visual display that can show a text with proportional spacing. For CHARACTERS PER SECOND (CPS) see CPS.

charge-coupled device (CCD), *n.* a type of volatile storage cell built on a semiconductor chip and also used in image sensing. A CCD store works very much like a BUBBLE STORE; here, though, tiny groups of electric charge make up the data words in the pipelines just below the chip surface.

In a CCD camera, a lens focuses light from the viewed

scene onto a grid of CCDs, one per pixel; charge builds up in each cell to an extent that depends on brightness. Electronics then reads the grid's charge pattern to produce an electronic version of the scene.

chat mode, *n.* the use of EMAIL, computer conferring or fax machines to pass messages to and fro in a type of electronic conversation.

check, *adj.* concerned with testing for corruption (spoilage) of transferred data. A **check bit** (PARITY bit) at the end of each transferred computer word allows for such testing, as does a **check character** or **check digit** in the case of longer data strings. With whole blocks or whole messages, a final **check sum** has the same function.

In each case, the sending system works out the check values and transmits them with the signal. The system at the other end repeats the calculations and reports if the calculated values differ from those received.

checkpoint, *n.* a point in a program at which the system saves a specified set of values (e.g. the status of all current files, and the contents of all registers). Then if something goes wrong, the operator can resume at the last checkpoint rather than at the beginning of the job (this is **checkpoint re-start**).

chief operator, *n.* the person in charge of all operating STAFF on a large computer site.

child, *n.* **1.** a descendent node in a TREE.
2. the product of a merge between parent and transaction files, the child being the parent in the next GENERATION.

childboard, SEE MOTHERBOARD.

chip or **microchip** *n.* an integrated circuit or a similar kind of circuit in a protective covering, or package. The actual chip is a prepared square of semiconductor (in most cases silicon, hence **silicon chip**). See WAFER for details of manufacture. The chip is centred in the package, with fine gold wires leading to the links to the pins, the whole then being coated for protection (see Figure).

Chip architecture is the term used to describe the design of the chip itself (in terms of diodes, transistors, and so on), the linking between chip edge connectors, pins and outside circuits; and/or the linking of a number of chips on a printed circuit board to make a final product. A **chip card** is the same as a SMART CARD; one with its own chip and therefore a degree of 'intelligence'.

chrominance signal, *n.* the part of a colour video signal that

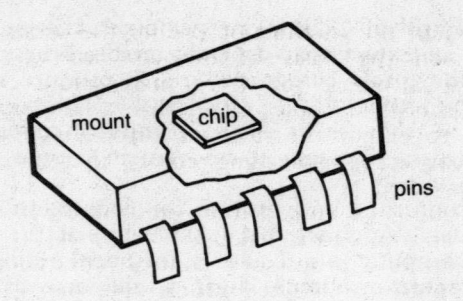

chip. A chip in its mount.

carries the image's colour details, with luminance handling brightness.

CIM, *abbrev. for* COMPUTER INPUT ON MICROFORM, COMPUTER INTEGRATED MANUFACTURE.

CIR, *abbrev. for* CURRENT INSTRUCTION REGISTER.

circuit, *n.* a complete working set of power supply, **circuit elements** (components, such as resistors, chips, fuses) and conducting links. **Circuit analysis** is finding out what a circuit does and how it does it, while **circuit design** is the planning and testing of circuits.

In telecommunications, a circuit is a complete to-and-fro channel between two sets (e.g. telephones, fax and telex machines).

Circuit switching is the provision of exchanges (switching centres) in a telephone or telegraph network so that any set can link with any other. The **circuit switched public data network (CSPDN)** is the system of exchanges and lines that handles data communications.

circular file, *n.* a file set up so that as each new record comes in, the oldest record goes out.

citizens' band (CB), *n.* a public local radiotelephony system which allows users to communicate by voice between vehicles and sites over a distance of, perhaps, 30 km. Such a system may offer only a few tens of frequency bands, so if there are many users, there is interference and lack of privacy.

clash, *n.* the system breakdown which occurs when a system tries to carry out two incompatible actions at the same moment, e.g. to send two data packets down a channel simultaneously.

classification, *n.* the method of coding the items in a library or database on the basis of the contents of each. **Close classification** is where there are many close codes (e.g. a thousand to handle IT topics rather than a hundred).

clear, 1. *vb.* to empty the store of current user data, the instruction **clear screen** meaning empty that part holding an image of the screen.
2. *adj.* describing an uncoded or unscrambled signal. **Clear language** is an uncoded signal.

clock, *n.* a part of a processor's control unit, with the task of sending out pulses at a fixed **clock rate** (e.g. 10 MHz, ten million pulses a second). Clock rates above about 30 MHz cause difficulties as a result of circuit limitations and access to storage cells. Some people believe that an upper limit is likely to be 50 MHz (unless there are very significant changes in technology); others look to 150 MHz by the end of the century.

The clock's pulses are the means by which the control unit synchronizes all the system's actions. The **clock track** of a backing store medium is the track which holds synchronizing pulses.

close classification, *n.* a finely-tuned type of CLASSIFICATION system.

closed, *adj.* the reverse of OPEN. Thus **closed circuit TV (CCTV)** broadcasts its signals only to a small number of receivers linked to the centre by cable. A **closed coordinated index** is an index using a fixed and unchanging number of key terms: **closed indexing** means setting up such an index.

A **closed file** is one in main or backing store, but not in current use, while a **closed loop** describes a system with automatic FEEDBACK. In a program, a **closed sub-routine** is a sub-routine kept separate from the main (calling) program, and supplied with a heading name and a closing return (or similar) instruction. Lastly, a **closed user group (CUG)** is a group within an electronic mail or fax network whose members alone can communicate with each other.

cluster, *n.* an alternative term for a STAR in the case of a network. A **cluster system** is such a network set up mainly for the sharing of resources (software and hardware).

CMC, *abbrev. for* any code for MAGNETIC INK CHARACTERS, also for COMPUTER MEDIATED COMMUNICATION.

CML, *abbrev. for* COMPUTER MANAGED LEARNING.

CMOS, *abbrev. for* COMPLEMENTARY METAL OXIDE SEMI-

CONDUCTOR. See MOS and field effect TRANSISTOR.

CNC, *abbrev. for* COMPUTER NUMERIC CONTROL.

co-ax cable or **coaxial cable,** *n.* a cable with a single central conductor (core), very well insulated from the earthed, protective conductor (sheath).

Cobol, *n.* Common Business-Oriented Language, an old but still widespread high level program language designed for office software. Produced by the US Department of Defense in 1959, Cobol is very well able to handle extremely large data files. It is the most readable program language because all instructions are written like simple English sentences. This, however, makes a Cobol program slow, and costly as far as storage space is concerned. Microbased Cobol versions are therefore rare.

code, *n.* **1.** a symbol for a CHARACTER handled by an IT system. See, for example, ASCII, BAR CODING, and BINARY CODED DECIMAL. As more than a few 'standard' code sets exist, **code conversion** must take place when units based on different sets communicate. **Code extension** involves adding codes for your own special needs to a set. **Coding**, or ENCODING, is producing a standard code from a non-standard one.

Pressing a **code key** (e.g. ESCAPE) on a keyboard warns the system you are going to send an instruction rather than make a normal input.

2. a computer program, usually in a machine or assembly language. **Coding** is the same as programming.

codec, *n.* jargon for an encoder/decoder unit, a type of CODE converter.

coding, *n.* **1.** the production of a computer program from a specification with a **coding sheet**. This is a specially printed table to help in drafting, based on the special needs of the program language in use.

2. the devising of standard short forms for data item values, e.g. M or F in the gender field of a file. Not only does this save storage space, it cuts down typing errors and the danger of missing relevant records in a search (as when someone might enter 'male' or 'man' in the gender field).

3. (also ENCODING) producing a standard code output from a non-standard input. See also ENCRYPTION.

coherence, *n.* **1.** a measure of how well the parts of an IT system work together.

2. the property of laser light whereby the waves produced keep in step. It is this quality that makes lasers so worthwhile in many contexts, including communications.

cold boot or **cold start,** *n.* an alternative term for BOOTING.

collision, *n.* see CLASH. **Collision detection** is a feature of network control which, for example, prevents data packets from colliding (using the cable at the same time).

Colossus, *n.* the first general purpose programmable electronic calculator series. A number of these were running in Britain during the Second World War on code-breaking work.

colour, *n.* an aspect of the often most communicative displays and printouts, with **colour displays** and printers designed to give good colour images. **Colour microform** is microform able to show colour, although this is rare; most microform systems work with text, illustrated, if at all, in black and white. **Colour bars** are a video image sent to a colour display in order to test it.

There are various types of **colour printer**. These include standard types with ribbons with up to seven bands of coloured ink, and ink jet machines with reservoirs for each colour. Colour laser printers are beginning to appear in the early 1990s, though the technology (just like that used in colour copiers) is straightforward. At the top of the range are machines using ribbons of dye the width of the image and very large thermal print heads with thousands of elements. These can offer millions of colours and shades, but are extremely bulky and costly.

COM, *abbrev. for* COMPUTER OUTPUT ON MICROFORM.

Comal, *n. acronym for* the Common Algorithmic Language, a computer program language extended from what was then standard unstructured Basic to give it more structure (explicitly for those learning how to program).

combiner, *n.* a simple multiplexer able to send two signals down one channel.

command, *n.* a direct instruction to an IT system, i.e. one carried out at once rather than being in a program. In order to allow this, the system must be **command driven** or in **command mode**, and the user must work with a standard **command language**. A **command file** is a series of commands stored together and run in order, and so is, in fact, a kind of program. Working with commands is faster but less friendly than working with MENUS.

comment, *n.* a note (sometimes called REMARK) put in a program as a type of documentation. Its aim is later to inform the programmer (or others) what is going on at each stage.

COMMON

common, *adj.* shared by two or more users. A **common carrier** is a name for a country's tele-communications provider, while **common software** describes programs that look and work the same on different incompatible machines.

communicating word processor, *n.* (now a rare term) a special purpose word processor that can link to a network in order to send text signals out quickly.

communications, *n.* the IT-based transfer of data between people and/or hardware. A **communications control unit (CCU)** supervises this from moment to moment in a network, and **communications software** are programs designed to help. Most people wish to transfer data or information in various ways that depend on context. A company's **communications mix** is its combination of communications systems.

A **communications satellite** performs tasks relating to person-to-person and/or broadcast communications. **Communications theory** involves making mathematical models of communications systems; its two main fields are information theory (sources and channels) and coding theory. See also SHANNON, TELECOMMUNICATIONS.

community aerial (antenna) TV (CATV), *n.* the oldest type of cable radio or television system. A large central aerial collects the broadcast signals (such as those beamed by a **community aerial television relay**, a transmitter sending by microwave). The central system then amplifies and distributes them.

compact disc (CD), *n.* a small optical disc, normally 120 mm across (though 90 mm discs are becoming common). The disc is very widely used to store audio, but is being used increasingly as a computer backing store. Then it is called **compact disc ROM (CD-ROM)**. ROM means *read-only memory*. Capacity can be up to 600 MB (although one technique provides 2400 MB). Access times are fairly long (up to a second), though again rapid progress is being made, and the 23 ms target (the access time of a hard disk) was reached in 1989.

A more recent development is **compact disc video (CDV)** for storing video stills and sequences; here five minutes on a disc is the normal capacity, though research attempts to increase this to an hour had been successful by the beginning of 1991. **Compact disc interactive (CDI)** involves storing a mix of software, data, audio and compressed video for flexible

COMPACTION

interactive use under processor control; this has more potential power than interactive video. See also INTERATIVE VIDEO and MULTI-MEDIA.

The disc stores its contents in digital form along a spiral of pits. The read head consists of a low power laser plus a photo-cell to detect the reflected light. Light reflects poorly from the pits themselves, but reflects well from the lands between the pits (see Figure).

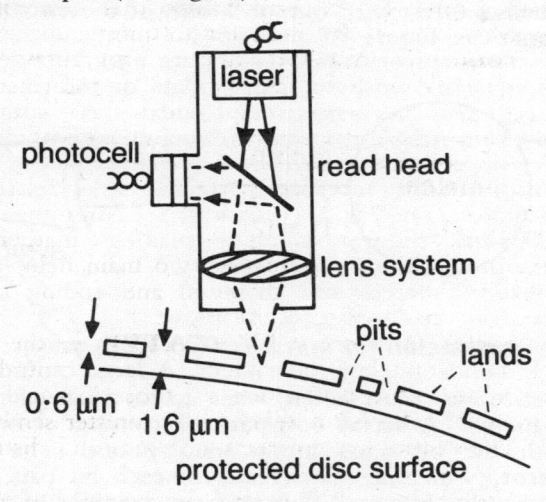

compact disc. Reading a compact disc.

The spiral, perhaps several kilometres long, is a serial access arrangement, although users may think of CD storage as direct access because it is so rapid. It can be possible to find a given data item within a second or two in a 600MB CD-ROM.

The designers of standard compact computer disks did not foresee their use for non-text data storage: CD-ROMs work with audio and moving video only with great difficulty. **CD-ROM XA** (XA for extended architecture) is a collective term for attempts to overcome this problem, but at the end of the 1980s, no agreed standard had yet appeared.

compaction, *n.* **1.** an alternative term for COMPRESSION.
2. a method of GARBAGE COLLECTION on a read/write disk. All

COMPANDING

wanted data comes together at the start of the disk, leaving all garbage at the end.

companding, *n.* an alternative term for COMPRESSION.

comparator, *n.* a logic circuit that compares two input bit trains and outputs a bit that depends on whether or not the inputs are the same. The output of some comparators is three-state; these can also mark which input is the greater.

The simplest comparator is a match (equivalence) GATE (non-exclusive OR), with output 1 only if the two input bits are the same (see Figure 1).

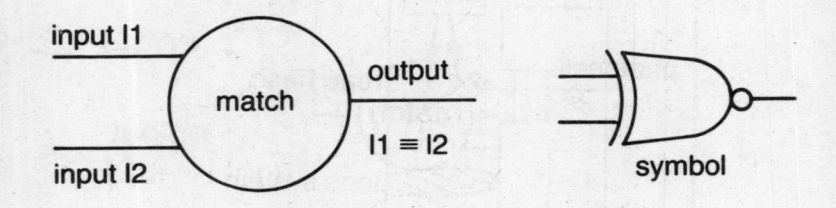

comparator. Fig. 1. A match (not XOR) gate.

In practice we most often want to compare data words rather than bits. A **serial comparator** consists of one match gate, with the bit pairs input one by one. The **parallel comparator**, with one match gate for each bit pair, is faster but more costly. Figure 2 illustrates an example of a four-bit parallel system.

compatibility, *n.* a measure of how well two different systems can work together in sharing programs, files and other data. Most manufacturers now ensure their new systems are compatible with those they have previously sold. This is termed **upward compatibility** from the latter's point of view and DOWNWARD COMPATIBILITY from that of the former. See also CONNECTIVITY.

competing carriers, *n.* any COMMON CARRIERS that can supply similar services to the same clients (as when, for instance, two telephone networks serve the same area).

compiler, *n.* the software which translates a high-level language program into machine code to allow the system to run it.

Compilation is the process of translating, with **compila-**

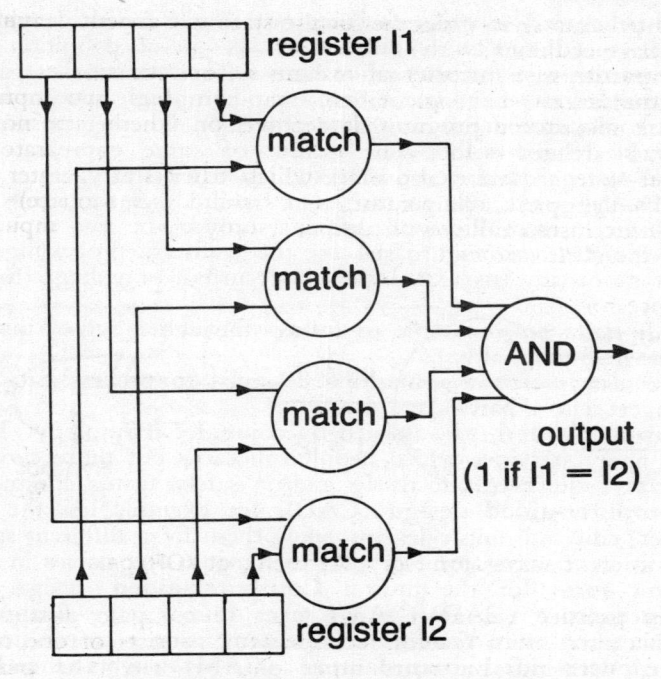

comparator. Fig. 2. A four-bit comparator.

tion errors being those that then come to light, and **compilation time** the time the translating takes.

complement, *n.* a method of storing negative numbers to make processing simpler. See ARITHMETIC, ONES COMPLEMENT and TWOS COMPLEMENT. **Complementation** is the conversion process.

complementary metal oxide semiconductor (CMOS), *n.* or *adj.*. See MOS and field effect TRANSISTOR.

compression, compaction or **companding,** *n.* the cutting down of the amount of data needed for a given amount of information. A **compression** or **compaction algorithm** is the means whereby the system achieves this. There are many such systems. MODIFIED HUFFMAN and MODIFIED READ are world standards in the case of fax.

computer, *n.* a system that links hardware and software (con-

COMPUTER-AIDED

trol programs) in order to carry out simple repetitive tasks at great speed and with little error. A useful definition that covers the vast majority of machines from the smallest micro to the largest main frame, is: a modern, high speed, digital electronic, stored program data processor. These terms can in turn be defined as follows:

(a) *modern*: developed during the last half century;

(b) *high speed*: able to carry out hundreds of thousands, or, in some cases, millions of actions a second;

(c) *digital electronic*: based on the transfer, processing and storage of tiny (two-state) pulses of current or voltage (for instance);

(d) *stored program*: able to follow through a set of instructions held internally;

(e) *data processor*: a machine designed to process data (i.e. convert it to a particular form).

computer-aided, *adj.* assisted by computer technology. There are many activities which people can carry out more cheaply, reliably, quickly, effectively and/or safely using computers. **Computer-aided design (CAD)**, for example lets the user enter, edit and polish designs, view them from different angles in different ways, print or plot them, and save copies in electronic form for the future. **Computer-aided design and manufacture (CAD(/C)AM)** takes this a stage further by driving robots to manufacture an item using a stored design. **Computer-aided manufacture (CAM)** covers the latter applications only, but see also COMPUTER-INTEGRATED MANUFACTURE.

Computer-aided drawing (or drafting, CAD) is less complex than computer-aided design: pictures in this case are in two dimensions only, and there may be no library of standard shapes to call on. At the same time, the user will have many aids to improve freehand drawing (e.g. shapes such as lines, circles, blocks), and the two CADs overlap considerably. See also GRAPHICS SOFTWARE.

Computer-aided education (CAE), instruction (CAI), learning (CAL), and **teaching (CAT)** are some of the many names for the use of computers to aid learning, by use of topic-specific programs. Learners also often use business software (word processors, graphics programs, and so on), but generally speaking, the term CAE does not include these. For **computer-aided software engineering**, see CASE.

Computer-aided translation (CAT) is the use of

programmable machines (including electronic pocket dictionaries and phrase books) to help people translate between human languages. **Computer-aided typesetting** (also abbreviated as CAT) is the use of computers to prepare typeset text, perhaps as CAMERA-READY COPY, or to automatically feed suitably coded (e.g. ASPIC) word processed text into a typesetting system.

computer-assisted, *adj.* an alternative term for **computer-aided**.

computer based training (CBT), *n.* the provision of training programmes in which computers (and, often, other IT systems such as interactive video) play a major role.

computer bureau, *n.* a firm that offers computer based services to other firms, e.g. the running of their monthly payroll programs.

computer conferring or **conferencing,** *n.* a type of EMAIL in which two or more people contribute when they can to a computer-based conference or discussion. The people involved log on, read, and add their comments and ideas at the time they choose.

computer generations, *n.* a method of classifying computers historically on the basis of the electronics used: first, electron tubes (valves); second, transistors; third, chips; fourth (current), highly integrated chips. See GENERATIONS sense 2.

computer graphics, *n.* the use of a computer to generate on screen (and to print out) pictures and designs. Such programs, on a range from art (paint) software to computer-aided design (CAD), have much the same features in essence as a word processor. The pictures produced vary from low RESOLUTION (where the individual blocks making up the picture are most obvious) to very high resolution (similar to that of a photo or video screen). See also GRAPHICS.

computer input from microform (CIM), *n.* a technique whereby a computer can screen an image held on MICROFORM for the user to edit and/or add to a document. See also FOSDIC.

computer integrated manufacture (CIM), *n.* fully automated factory work, where all actions and activities are programmed into robots and electronically controlled machine tools. This is more advanced than COMPUTER AIDED MANUFACTURE in that people have no direct role to play other than in design.

computer language, *n.* a set of instruction types, data types and rules for writing computer programs. See PROGRAM LANGUAGE.

COMPUTER LITERACY

computer literacy, *n.* a basic knowledge of what computers are and how to use them.

computer managed learning (CML), *n.* a style of computer aided learning in which the computer keeps track of each learner's progress and gives advice as to what next to do at each stage.

computer mediated communication (CMC), *n.* the use of computers to aid and improve human communication, e.g. EMAIL and computer conferring.

computer numeric control (CNC), *n.* a system in which one or more automated machines and systems work in a network with instructions from a central processor with no human operator in charge. (DIRECT NUMERIC CONTROL is the same but with a person in charge.)

computer operator, *n.* a person concerned with the running of a large computer system (see STAFF), with such tasks to do as changing disks and printer paper.

computer output on microform (COM), *n.* the production of hard copy on film in miniature form rather than on paper. This is of great value where a system involves a large amount of hard copy; microform is much cheaper to produce and store than paper printout, and COM machines work up to a hundred times faster than printers.

computer program, *n.* a set of instructions which instruct a computer to carry out a given task. See ALGORITHM and PROGRAM.

computer system, *n.* a fully working set of hardware items and driving software.

computerization, *n.* the transfer of tasks in particular contexts from manual methods to computer-based ones (still sometimes part of the work of a SYSTEMS ANALYST).

COMSAT, *abbrev. for* COMMUNICATIONS SATELLITE, strictly a trade name.

concentrator, *n.* a type of MULTIPLEXING system, for sharing a channel between several signals.

concertina fold, see FAN FOLD.

concurrency, *n.* a method in which a system carries out a number of jobs during the same period, sharing time and resources between them as required. True concurrency is, however, parallel processing. See also MULTI-PROCESSING.

conditional jump, *n.* a branch to a new set of program instructions that the system follows only if some condition is true. All the major ALGORITHM structures involve conditional

CONSUMER IT

jumps.

conditioning, *n.* the use of procedures and/or protocols to ensure that a data transfer does not suffer too many errors.

configuration, *n.* the set of settings of a computer system that makes it work as it should in a given context. A **configuration program** is a utility that helps the user choose the best settings and then stores them until changed again.

confirmation, *n.* an acknowledgement of successful action. A **call confirmation** is a message from the system that a telex or fax has been received safely.

conflation, *n.* (*database and file searching*) the use of a **conflation algorithm** to improve efficiency. The algorithm reduces all search key words to roots. Thus, for instance, the system can pick up all references to words that start with 'compu' (like computation and computing) when the searcher enters 'computer'.

connectionism, *n.* the study of the behaviour of NEURAL NETWORKS.

connectivity, *n.* the power to link incompatible systems (e.g. in a network) so that they can exchange data. This is a major current aim in IT.

connector, *n.* the line and symbols linking two sheets in a flow chart or structure chart. A **logical connector** is a Boolean operator (e.g AND, OR, NOT) used to define targets for a database or file search.

console, *n.* the terminal used by a large computer's operating staff to send job instructions and to receive messages (such as 'Put tape 1453 on drive 16').

constant, *n.* a data item that is fixed in value (e.g. the firm's name, or PI, 3.14159...) throughout a program. **Constant length (size, width)**, as applied to fields for instance, is the same as FIXED LENGTH.

consultant, *n.* a person who gives advice on IT problems to different clients for a fee.

consumables, *n.* the parts of a system that need frequent replacement (e.g. disks and printer heads) as opposed to capital items.

consumer IT, *n.* the application of IT to consumer goods. Already, microprocessors appear as dedicated systems in control of a range of consumer goods such as tools and kitchen, leisure and home office goods (such as sewing machines, video and audio units and telephones). Home computers are of value for game playing and children's learning, and also for word

CONTACT VIDEO DISC

processing, accounts, communications (including access to bank accounts) and other aspects of working at home.

The use of IT to control the consumer home environment has started, with microprocessors being used in the central heating 'programmer'. In some high-tech homes, computers deal too with lighting and energy balance and may allow the family members to input commands by simple voice control or key pads, even from a remote telephone.

contact video disc, *n*. a VIDEO DISC whose surface the read head actually touches all the time (rather than floating above). The main type of contact video disc now in use is the CAPACITATIVE system.

content addressed storage, *n*. an alternative term for ASSOCIATIVE STORAGE.

contention, *n*. the situation which arises when two or more network stations try to access shared hardware or programs at the same time. It is the task of the operating software to handle such problems without damage.

contiguous graphics, *n*. a method of producing graphics in which the graphic BLOCKS have no space left between them. Also known as continuous graphics (see CONTINUOUS). Compare SEPARATED GRAPHICS.

continuation page, *n*. a videotex page you can access only from the main page, i.e. one with no address of its own.

continuous, *adj*. 'going on without a break'. **Continuous graphics** are pictures made up from graphics blocks without gaps left between them. Compare SEPARATED GRAPHICS.

Continuous processing is non-stop processing, often to be found in environment control systems and large batch processing computers. **Continuous stationery** is printer paper other than in separate sheets (i.e. fan fold or roll). A **continuous tone** picture is one with a large GREY SCALE rather than only one or two grey tones.

contrast, *n*. a measure of the brightness difference between the darkest and lightest parts of a screen image or of material on paper ready for scanning.

control, *n*. **1.** the power to direct actions. A **control area** or **control block** is the part of an IT system's store that holds overall control information. A **control character/code/ variable** is a code which, when sent with a signal, has an effect on hardware (e.g. to ring a bell or to roll up the printer paper to the next new page).

A **control program** is an outdated term for operating soft-

CONTROL

ware; **control program for micros (CP/M)** was the main world standard until MS-DOS appeared in the early 1980s. See also MP/M.

A **control total** is a type of CHECK sum, produced by adding the value in a given field of each record; a HASH TOTAL is a meaningless control total. Thus in an exam mark file, we could use the sum of the IT exam marks as a control total, but the sum of the learners' ages would be a hash total (accurate for checking ages, but having no meaning in the context of the examinee's marks). A tape's **control track** carries pulses used for synchronization and/or searching.

The **control unit** of a processor has the function of decoding instructions and opening gates to carry them out. See MACHINE CYCLE.

2. the whole field of automating and managing processes and the action of machines; it includes the use of ROBOTS. The system accepts inputs from manual controls and automatic sensors, processes these on the basis of a stored program, and outputs actions. In a good control system, there is a clear FEEDBACK loop between output and input; in other words, the sensors measure the output actions, and so keep these within limits. The Figure shows a simple control system intended to keep the thickness of rolled sheet metal within a desired range. The detector monitors the thickness of the sheet

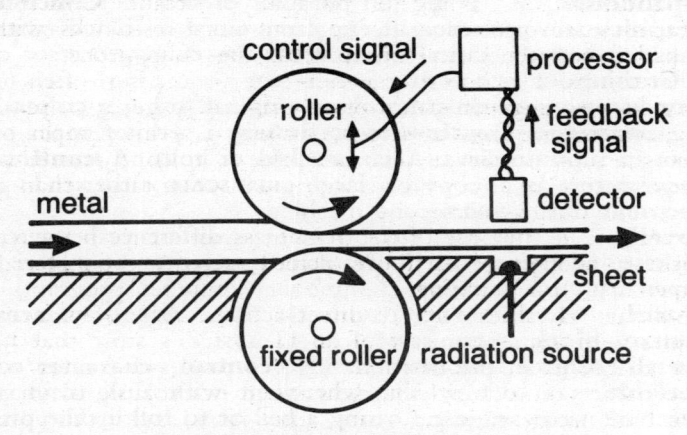

control. Feedback in process control.

CONTROLLED VOCABULARY

and feeds information back to the rollers via the processor.

controlled vocabulary, *n.* the restricted set of keywords you may use when searching a file or database.

convergence, *n.* the coming together of previously unrelated technologies, common in IT. For example, interactive video brings together computer and video concepts, while the electronic office has brought information technology and information science closer to one another.

conversational mode, *n.* a two-way interaction between a computer and a user, with each message or command from one leading to a response or action from the other.

converter, *n.* a device able to transfer data from one physical form to another (e.g. from chip to video disc). **Convert speed** is the rate at which this takes place.

copier, *n.* a system used to produce hard copies of an original sheet or flat object. The machine scans the original to produce an image, often using XEROGRAPHY, on a drum. That image attracts the toner powder, which in turn passes to the blank sheet where it is made permanent by the use of heat which bakes the image on the paper. Modern copiers use chips to extend their features significantly. For instance, some machines now allow users to move a block of the image of the original to a new place and to colour it and/or add a frame before making copies.

co-processor, *n.* a special purpose processor slaved to a system's main processor. It can carry out a restricted range of tasks (e.g. mathematical ones) while the main processor does other things.

copy, *n.* an image on paper of an original (using a COPIER), or of a microform reader screen, or of an area of main store (using a dump utility). A fax machine is in **copy mode** if set to produce a local copy of the original rather than sending an electronic image to a second machine.

copyright, *n.* the right to produce copies of your own 'intellectual property' (i.e. the result of your own thought, e.g. a dictionary, broadcast programme or computer program) and to obtain royalties (fee payments) from others who make copies with your permission.

core store, *n.* an out-dated term for a processor's main store. The name comes from the days when nonvolatile main store was built from magnetic 'cores' (tiny rings), with the polarity of each ring giving one bit value.

corporate communication, *n.* information circulated from a firm's management to the staff, in the form of a newsletter or video, for instance.

corruption, *n.* the introduction of errors into a block of data as a result of some problem in hardware, software (e.g. a bug) or transfer (e.g. noise).

cover sheet, *n.* a sheet sent in advance of the main fax, on which the sender writes covering notes and states who the signal is addressed to, and how many sheets are being sent in total.

CPA, *abbrev. for* CRITICAL PATH ANALYSIS.

CP/M, *abbrev. for* CONTROL PROGRAM FOR MICROS.

CPS, *abbrev. for* **1.** characters per second (a data transfer or printing rate).
2. frequency in cycles per second. This use is now outdated and has been replaced by hertz (Hz).

CPU, *abbrev. for* CENTRAL PROCESSING UNIT.

crash, *vb.* to stop working as a result of a hardware problem or fatal software error (bug).

CRC, *abbrev. for* CAMERA-READY COPY.

credit card, *n.* a plastic card with identifying data stored in a magnetic or optical stripe or in a chip, with which you can obtain cash from an auto teller and purchase goods and services on credit. A **credit card reader** has a slot through which the card is passed; the system can then check the typed personal identity number (PIN) and send transaction details to a central computer.

critical path analysis (CPA), *n.* a way of breaking a project or scheme into its individual steps. The steps appear as lines on a chart with a note in each case of the least time required to finish each step; the chart structure shows which steps depend on which. It is then easy to see what must be done when, and how to recover from delays with the minimum loss of time. Computers make critical path analysis very straightforward, so this type of software (also called a PROJECT SCHEDULER) is very important in many fields.

cross fire, *n.* interference between signals in two channels of the same or different types (e.g. between telephone and telegraph lines).

cross talk, *n.* the transfer of energy between two channels or tracks, leading to INTERFERENCE and/or corruption.

CRT, *abbrev. for* CATHODE-RAY TUBE.

cryptography, see ENCRYPTION.

CSPDN, *abbrev. for* CIRCUIT SWITCHED PUBLIC DATA NETWORK.

CUE TRACK

cue track, *n.* the track on a video tape used for voice instructions to, and codes for, the editor.

CUG, *abbrev. for* CLOSED USER GROUP.

cursor, *n.* a line or blob (often flashing) on screen to show where the next input will appear. In many programs you can use a mouse or the **cursor keys** on a keyboard to move the cursor.

cut and paste, *n.* a process which allows the movement of a block (chunk of text or part of a picture) from one part of a document to another. Most word processors allow this to be done by deleting the block, moving the cursor, and inserting it back from store. In graphics programs, on the other hand, a mouse can often be used to carry out the action clearly on screen.

cybernetics, *n.* the study of communication and control systems, with particular interest in how living and machine systems compare, in order to improve the efficiency of the latter.

cycle, *n.* one of a set of similar repeated actions; e.g. a MACHINE CYCLE is the action in a processor which leads to the carrying out of one instruction. **Cycle time** is the time a system takes to pass through one machine cycle, or the time to read a word from store and write it back again. **Cycle stealing** is a name for DIRECT MEMORY ACCESS.

Cyclic code is the same as unit code (e.g. GRAY CODE), a code for counting in binary where each value differs from the next in only one bit. A **cyclic shift** is a shift in which each bit that drops off one end goes back at the other:
single right cyclic shift:

$$1001\ 0101 \rightarrow 1100\ 1010$$

double left cyclic shift:

$$1001\ 0101 \rightarrow 0010\ 1011 \rightarrow 0101\ 0110$$

cylinder, *n.* a drum shaped object. **Cylinder scanner** is an alternative term for a drum scanner, and **cylinder printer** is an alternative term for a drum printer.

D

DAA, *abbrev. for* DIRECT ACCESS ARRANGEMENT.
DAC, *abbrev. for* DIGITAL TO ANALOG CONVERTER.
DAI, *abbrev. for* DISTRIBUTED ARTIFICIAL INTELLIGENCE.
daisywheel printer, *n.* a high quality but slow printer with the letters set at the ends of the 'petals' of a wheel. To print, the wheel spins to the correct position, and then a hammer pushes the letter against the ribbon. Now that cheap printers can produce flexible, fast, high quality output, the daisywheel machine is in decline. For **daisy chain**, see CHAIN.
dark trace monitor, *n.* a cathode ray tube display whose image is dark on white rather than the reverse. The aim is to reproduce the effect of an image on a sheet of paper.
DAT, *abbrev. for* DIGITAL AUDIO TAPE.
data, *n.* a set of one or more items of information inside an IT system, i.e. being stored, processed or transferred. The word has changed from plural to singular in recent years; instead of **datum**, we now use **data item** to mean the singular (a unit of data).

A **data bank** and a **data base** are both large collections of data; many people use the phrases to mean the same thing. Strictly, though, a data base is a collection that is essential to a person or firm, while a data bank is a wider collection, more like a library. A **data base management system (DBMS)** is a software package designed to help the user work efficiently and easily with a data base (amending, sorting and searching the data held), while **data base control** is the task of one or more members of a computing department's STAFF. A **data base umbrella** is a firm that handles the data base management needs of others.

We can view a data base hierarchically, i.e. as a tree, as shown in the Figure.

In a true hierarchical data base, however, the records themselves are at different levels. See HIERARCHICAL DATA BASE, compare RELATIONAL DATA BASE.

A **data bus** is a BUS that carries data in large volumes between the parts of a central processor; the system designers

DATA

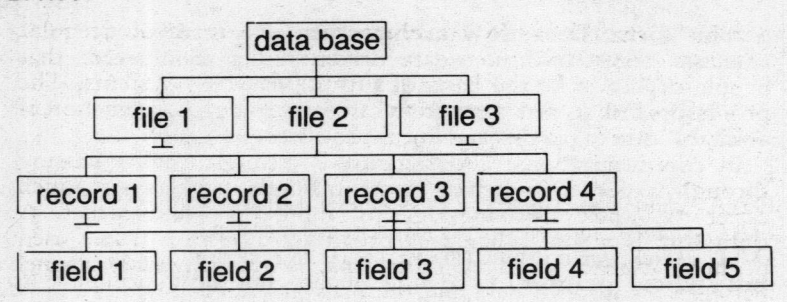

data base. A data base viewed as a tree.

may link it with the address and control buses, or keep them separate.

Data capture involves collecting data in a form an IT system can process. It includes two automatic methods. The first method, in the case of environmental data, uses sensors linked to an input interface. The second involves MACHINE READABLE INPUT, as, for example, with bar codes and stripe cards (the media holding these are called **data carriers**). In other contexts, people write the data onto carefully designed **data capture forms**; others can then key it in at speed (this is known as **data entry**. See DATA PREPARATION, below). Often we can use **data collection** for data capture, but a **data collection platform** is an automatic communications satellite.

After collection (capture), it is often important to reduce the bulk of the data so that it needs less storage space and transfer time. There are various methods of **data compaction** or **data compression** (see COMPRESSION). For much the same reason, it is useful to let several data transfer signals share one channel. A **data concentrator** is one way of achieving this. See CONCENTRATOR and MULTIPLEXING.

Data control may mean the same as database control (see above); it also has the more specific meaning of checking that the data that enters and leaves an IT system is in the correct form. In either case, the people concerned may use a **data dictionary** to show all the necessary details or a **data directory** (a summary). See DICTIONARY.

Data flow is part of the responsibility of data control staff; it concerns data transfers inside the IT system and between it and the outside world; a **data flow chart** shows these transfers in

DATA

graphic form. **Data flow architecture** is a form of irregular PARALLEL COMPUTING, i.e. data driven rather than fixed, that people expect to be the basis of fifth GENERATION systems. The processors link so that the system can carry out each instruction as a suitable mix of parallel and linear processes.

In communications, a **datagram** is a single packet passing through a packet switching system; single packets are much easier to handle than messages of more than one packet. A **data line** is a screen line in a broadcast television frame used to hold teletext data. A **data link** is the physical channel between a source of data and the place it has to reach.

Data logging is the process of collecting data from the environment automatically: i.e. using sensors, analog-to-digital converters, and suitable software to time, bank and later analyse the results. A **data network** is a network which shares data (but not hardware) between its stations.

Data preparation was (originally) the use of card and tape punches to store input information in machine readable form. Few systems now use PUNCHED MEDIA apart from, for example, Kimball tags for data entry. Instead, **direct data entry** is the norm. Here the data preparation (data entry) STAFF use some kind of KEY TO STORE terminal to type the data straight in to the system.

Data processing (DP) (a now little used term for business computing) is the same as computing in cases where there are large amounts of data to handle. It covers all the stages from data collection to output: data collection (capture), preparation (entry), storage, processing, and the storage and output of the results. Those stages make up the **data processing cycle**. A **data processing system** is the hardware and software involved, as well, perhaps, as the people (the LIVEWARE) including the *data processing manager (DPM)*.

Data protection is any legal safeguard against the abuse of personal information held in IT systems. National laws differ in the details of how they try to protect people's PRIVACY in this context. A **data subject** is a person about whom there is a record in a file; the **data user** is the owner of the file and its contents.

The British Data Protection Act 1984 gives data subjects the rights to know what is on file about them, and to appeal against it if they wish. It also gives data users the duties to register their files and their uses for data held, and to keep the data secure, and up-to-date.

DATA

Data radio covers all situations where data is broadcast over a region using radio waves. Teletext (broadcast videotex) data comes on spare lines in a television picture signal, but there are various other methods of 'data-casting', including the broadcast of weather and road condition data for decoding and display by special car radio sets.

Data reduction includes CODING and COMPRESSION and other methods of cutting down the size of a large set of data. **Data retrieval** is the process of searching a data base or file for specific information; this is a major reason for having the data base or file in the first place. **Data security** concerns preventing unauthorized people from gaining access to stored data. See SECURITY.

A **data set**, as well as being a set of data, is an old (now rarely used) term for modem, a **data set adapter** being the interface between modem and computer that handles serial/parallel and parallel/serial conversion. See also LINE TERMINATION UNIT. A **data sink** is the destination of data in transfer; in a terminal, a circuit with this name may exist to handle error checking. On the other hand, a **data source** is where the transferred data comes from.

Data structures are different logical ways of viewing sets of data; each has advantages for processing in different contexts. A single **data item** is the simplest data structure; it may be an integer, a real number, a character string, or a Boolean element (an item with only two possible values); these are different **data types**. We can picture a data item as a zero-dimensional data structure (like a mathematical point).

We view a logically one-dimensional (1D) data structure as a set of data items in a row, all of the same type. The three special 1D data structures differ in how you (i.e. your software) can access the elements (individual data items). A STACK has only one open end: to add an element, you push it onto the top of the stack; to remove a data item, you must pop the one at the top of the stack. This is the simplest 1D structure in that the system needs only one pointer; the address of the open end.

A QUEUE has two open ends, one for adding items (the tail), and one for removing them (the head); it needs two pointers, one for each end. A LINKED LIST allows access at any point; you can add new elements or remove old ones where you like. The system now has a pointer to the head of the list, and each item in the list carries a pointer to the next one. A RING is a linked list whose tail element points to the head.

To programmers, the most common 1D data structure is a 1D ARRAY, or list. Indeed, it is common practice to use a 1D array to provide the other 1D structures. Once set up (declared), an array is fixed in size; it is easy to access any element by giving its subscript (the number that refers to its place in the list). The strength of an array compared to the other 1D structures is that you can, if you wish, process all elements the same way at the same time.

Arrays do not, however, need to be 1D; you can have an array of any number of dimensions as long as it can fit into the store. We can view a 2D array as a set of rows and columns, and access any element by quoting its two subscripts.

A TREE is a 2D structure with a branching, rather than rectangular, shape. Each element, or node, can have any number of branches to elements at the next level down. A picture of a tree is very much like that of a data base (above): data bases and files are data structures too. Indeed the hierarchical file is a very important structure: we can view it as an array in which the fields (columns or lists) do not need to be of the same data type.

A **data tablet** is a GRAPHICS TABLET, an input unit on which you can draw or write. **Data tags** are codes that identify types of data in a document in a bibliographic data base; they provide an aid to searching. **Data transfer** concerns passing data from one place to another, while **data transfer rate** is the number of bits (or, sometimes, bytes) passed in a second. There are many methods of data transfer, and a wide range of **data transfer standards** exist to reduce problems.

The **data type** of a data item describes its characteristics in the context of storage and processing. Numbers (numeric types) may be integer (whole), real (i.e. with a decimal point), or complex (with a $\sqrt{-1}$ component). Other data types are Booleans (able to have only two values, e.g. true and false), and characters or strings of characters. Some program languages offer data structures as types (as with linked lists in Lisp and arrays in most Basics); others, e.g. PASCAL, let you define, as part of the declaration process, the special types you wish to use in a program.

Data vetting is the checking of input data for correctness; VALIDATION, VERIFICATION and the use of CHECK BITS, etc., are common methods.

DB, *abbrev. for* DATA BASE.

dB, abbrev. for DECIBEL.
DBMS, abbrev. for DATA BASE MANAGEMENT SYSTEM.
DBS, abbrev. for DIRECT BROADCAST (BY) SATELLITE.
DC, abbrev. for DIRECT CURRENT.
DCTL, abbrev. for DIRECT COUPLED TRANSISTOR LOGIC. See LOGIC (ELECTRONIC LOGIC).
DDC, abbrev. for DIRECT DIGITAL CONTROL.
DDD, abbrev. for DIRECT DISTANCE DIALLING.
DDE, abbrev. for DIRECT DATA ENTRY.
DDS, abbrev. for DOCUMENT DELIVERY SYSTEM.
deadlock or **deadly embrace,** *n.* a situation where two programs demand use of a certain file or peripheral at the same time, no priority having been set.
debit card, *n.* a personal plastic card, with data stored on a magnetic or optical stripe or in a chip, for use with EFTPOS systems. At the point of sale, the cashier passes ('swipes') the card through a reader, and enters the amount of money to be paid. The card's owner types his/her personal identity number (PIN). If the central computers approve the purchase, they automatically transfer the amount from the card owner's bank account to that of the trader.
debugging, *n.* the process of removing (squashing) BUGS in a program or hardware unit. The hardest part of debugging is finding the problems in the first place; tests need careful design so they cover as many situations as possible.
decade, *n.* a group of ten items, e.g. of storage cells.
decibel (dB) *n.* the unit of power or sound level. The measure is strictly a ratio, comparing the level in question with some standard. Thus, we use decibels to measure the gain of an amplifier, by treating the input and output power levels, P_i and P_o, like this:

$$\text{gain in decibels} = 10 \log(P_o / P_i)$$

It follows that a 3dB rise/fall occurs when the power is doubled/halved. This rather strange system of measurement follows a classical law of physiology: if one sound appears twice as loud as another, it is 3dB greater. This applies to all senses.
decision table, *n.* in program documentation, a table listing all labels (variables) in the program with their meanings, and with notes on what should happen if they hold certain values.
deck, *n.* **1.** a tape DRIVE.
2. a set of punched cards that holds a program or data file.
declaration, *n.* a statement at the start of a program (e.g. in

DEDICATED

Pascal and some assemblers) that defines a label with its data type, or some other data structure with its size and type. That is a **global declaration**; a **local declaration** does the same at the start of a procedure, and applies only within that procedure. A **declarative program language** is one used to build up an expert system, in which the knowledge engineer declares all relevant facts and principles before defining problems the system should deal with.

decoder, *n.* a circuit with a large number of output lines, only one of which carries a pulse, that one depending on the pattern of inputs (see Figure). A printer contains a decoder; each character or control code output follows a particular input ASCII pattern on the eight input lines.

To some people, the decoders driving output units are the only true kind; they convert input data to information for users. However, the same principles apply in many other parts of an IT system. In particular, an **instruction decoder** links the control unit in the operation register with the circuits that provide the various operations. Also, an **address decoder** locates a given storage cell on the basis of the contents of the address selection register (see MACHINE CYCLE).

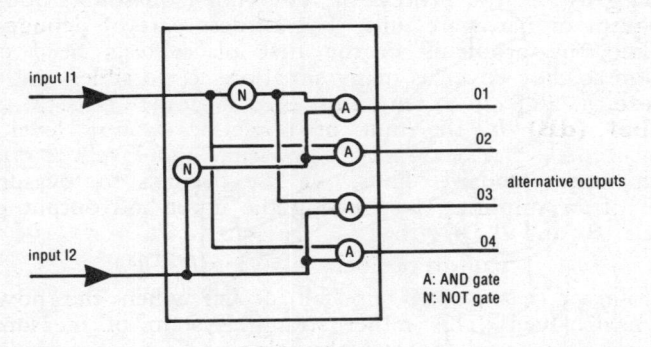

decoder. An *n*-input decoder can have up to 2^n unique output lines.

de-collate, *vb.* to separate (burst) the sheets of multi-part printer paper after printing. A **de-collater** (burster) is a machine designed for this purpose.

dedicated, *adj.* set aside for a single special use, e.g. a printer used for address labels only. A **dedicated port** is an interface

DEFAULT

with a communications channel that handles only one type of data transfer.

default, *adj.* applying in the absence of other instructions. For instance, a computer's default printer is the one it uses unless told to send to another; the default value of a numeric label (variable) is often 0.

definition, *n.* the measure of the amount of detail a screen or printout picture can produce. See RESOLUTION.

deformable mirror device (DMD), *n.* a silicon chip with, on the surface, perhaps 256 000 tiny two-state square mirrors. The control system can switch each mirror from one position to the other at the same time, and to do so (in theory) thousands of times a second. A DMD chip in a light beam can therefore project a very large video image onto a wall-sized screen. A rotating three-colour filter over the chip would produce colour pictures.

degradation, *n.* the loss of quality of a signal because of, for instance, noise or interference.

degrees of freedom, *n.* the different types of movement a robot has. The robot arm in the Figure has seven degrees of freedom. Each arrow shows a direction of movement.

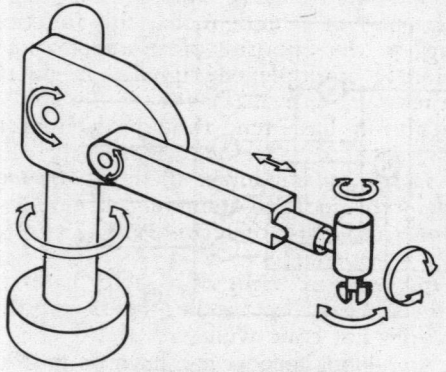

degree of freedom.

delay line, *n.* a line down which data passes and returns to delay its transfer, for instance for data storage or to put it in step with other data. An **acoustic delay line** converts the signal to sound (which travels much more slowly than electric effects). An **electromagnetic delay line** passes the signal, still in electric form, through a set of capacitors and inductors to slow it down. A **magnetic delay line** uses magnetic waves for the same purpose.

delayed send, *n.* a feature of some fax and telex units that enables the send time to be set some distance in the future (e.g. at night when charges are lower).

delimiter, *n.* a special code (character) that marks the start or end of, for instance, a string or file. See also END MARKER and BEGINNING MARKER.

delivery, *n.* the full process of transfer of a signal.

Delivery time refers to the time lapse between the start of sending the signal and its completion.

delta modulation, *n.* a form of pulse code modulation.

demand, *n.* a request, with 'on demand' meaning 'as required'. Thus a **demand multiplexer** is one which allocates time slots between users as needed rather than giving them all the same slot. **Demand processing** is the processing of data on input, rather than first storing it. **Demand staging** involves moving blocks of data from backing store when called for, rather than in advance (ANTICIPATORY STAGING).

demodulation, *n.* the opposite of MODULATION, i.e. the removal of the carrier to leave the original signal. A **demodulator,** e.g. part of a modem, has this function.

demultiplexing, *n.* the opposite of MULTIPLEXING, i.e. separating the previously multiplexed signals. A **de-multiplexor** has this function.

denary, *adj.* denoting base ten, though decimal is the more common word.

derived term index, *n.* an index made up of terms (words, phrases) found in the indexed item (e.g. a book), rather than of extracts from a fixed list of terms (this is an ASSIGNED TERM INDEX).

descender, *n.* the part (or 'tail') of a lower case character that passes below the normal bottom line (as in g, j, p ...). Some early printers could not cope well with these.

descripter, SEE KEY WORD.

desktop, *adj.* relating to the surface of a desk. A **desktop environment** is a user interface that is supposed to look and work like a desktop. A **desktop computer** is one small enough to fit entirely on a table with room to spare (i.e. a personal computer).

Desktop publishing (DTP) is the use of a versatile word processor (one with, for instance, many text styles and sizes,

DESTRUCTIVE READING

columns and the power to include graphics) with a high quality printer. The output of a DTP system is camera-ready copy. These are sheets which can be photocopied or sent to a print shop for plate making.

Desktop video combines broadcast quality video with computer power in a micro. Inputs may be from camera or video tape or disc, and the system takes (or 'grabs') single frames or a sequence and puts them in store. Then the user can edit them for printout or for display in a screen window. Such systems also offer the power to display video from broadcast or local sources in a small screen window while work continues on normal tasks. In the other direction, desktop video systems can be the basis of video publishing, with screen graphics going to a video display or to tape. The hardware needs of such systems are not bulky or costly. A television tuner, 'frame grabber' and massive store all go on a card in the computer. Some systems also accept images from compact and video discs.

destructive reading, *n.* the copying of data from store without leaving the original in place (in fact now a rare form of reading other than when working with a stack).

device, *n.* a hardware unit, either part of a larger system or able to work independently. In the former case, a **device driver** is a program in the system's operating software that ensures the device works as it should in relation to the rest of the system.

DFS, *abbrev. for* disk filing system, i.e. DISK OPERATING SYSTEM.

diacritic, *n.* a mark ('accent') placed above or below a letter to show stress or a special pronunciation. Few word processors and printers can handle many diacritics.

diagnostic, *adj.* denoting anything suitable for understanding the cause of (i.e. diagnosing) errors. **Diagnostic aids** for programmers include breakpoints, tracing, input testing systems and **diagnostic messages** (error reports), all provided perhaps by a **diagnostic program** in the program language software.

dialect, *n.* a non-standard version of a program language. Basic suffers more than most from dialects (there are hundreds in this case). The problem is that a program written in one dialect for one machine will not transfer easily to a different computer. On the other hand, allowing dialects allows fast development; so Basic has now become much more powerful than most other program languages.

dial-up, *adj.* describing a computer which can be accessed by

DIGITAL

dialling the relevant telephone number from a linked terminal.

diary, *n.* **1.** a pop-up utility in many DESKTOP environments that gives you all the features on screen of a paper diary, and others (such as speedy searching and alarms)

2. (or JOURNAL) a log of all activity on a large computer, listing, among other things, the date and time of each access from a terminal, with the terminal's code, the user's code, and details of the programs run and files viewed. This is of value for SECURITY.

dibit, *n.* a pair of bits treated together, e.g. in four-phase modulation. A dibit can have one of four values: 00, 01, 10, 11.

dictionary, *n.* **1.** the file of words with which a spelling checker works. In most cases, the user can extend this file to cover his/her special vocabulary.

2. (or DATA DICTIONARY) a full statement of a system's use of data; for each data item and label, it gives the meaning, relationship with others, form, type and usage. The purpose is to ensure system efficiency and to help with changes. A *data directory* is a summary of a data dictionary.

diffuser, *n.* a ground glass screen that spreads light evenly. Most microform readers, and some computer monitors, use diffusers.

digital, *adj.* **1.** displaying information as numbers.

2. able to take only a restricted number of values between the bottom and top of the permitted range (whereas an ANALOG measure can have any value in the range). Most IT systems (including **digital computers**) are BINARY digital, with only two values allowed, called 0 and 1. See also ARITHMETIC.

Digital audio tape (DAT) is high density magnetic tape used to store data or sound in digital form. Unlike COMPACT DISCS, which are also able to store data or sound at high density, data on DAT is re-recordable; given the right hardware, you can write to it as well as reading from it. A major use in computing is to provide fast, high capacity backup for a hard disk pack; digital audio tapes can now handle up to 1.4 GB. Used as backing store, such a tape still gives a mean access time of around 20 seconds. A **digital camera** is a video camera with a digital output; this makes it well suited to feeding scenes to a computer. (You need to feed the output of an analog camera through a digitizer first.) **Digital optical disc (DOD)** and **digital optical recording (DOR)** are terms relevant to the recording of digital data on an optical medium

DIGITIZER

(compact or video disc, or optical tape).

Digital paper is a fairly new data storage system; its great potential is shown by the fact that a digital paper disk offers the capacity of a hard disk at the price of a floppy. The inputs to a **digital plotter** are the true coordinates of the points to be plotted; compare INCREMENTAL PLOTTER.

Digital speech is synthesized SPEECH, each phoneme (speech sound unit) going to the speaker as a digital pattern, with a **digital to analog converter (DAC)** as part of the interface between the digital system and the speaker, an analog output unit. **Digital transfer** is the transfer of data in digital form, as between stations on a local area network and in digital broadcasting.

digitizer, *n.* the name given to various units that convert analog input to digital output on a large scale: e.g. graphics tablet or the interface between an analog camera and a digital computer.

DIL, *abbrev.* for DUAL-IN-LINE PACKAGE.

diode, *n.* a basic element of (micro-)electronic circuits, an element which passes current one way only, i.e. a RECTIFIER. A SEMICONDUCTOR diode, very common in integrated circuits, is a p-n junction; i.e. a scrap of silicon (in most cases) that is p-type on one side and n-type on the other. The Figure shows (a) a typical structure, (b) the relevant circuit symbol, and (c) rectification effect.

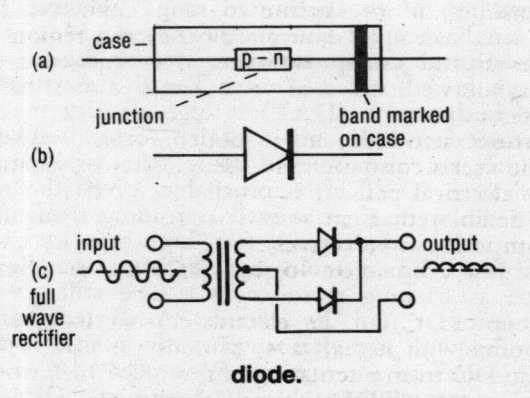

diode.

A LIGHT-EMITTING DIODE (LED) is a common light source for modern mains-powered systems. It is a semiconductor diode

DIRECT DATA ENTRY (DDE)

set to conduct: electron interactions produce light of brightness that depends on current and of a precise frequency. The last feature is why the LED is the basis of the semiconductor LASER.

diode transistor logic (DTL), see LOGIC (ELECTRONIC LOGIC).

DIP, *abbrev. for* DUAL-IN-LINE PACKAGE. **DIP switches** are small switches in a set (of up to eight or so) mounted on a chip-like base, and so are able to fit a standard chip socket.

diplex, *adj.* (of a channel) able to carry two signals at the same time in the same direction, i.e. the simplest form of MULTI-PLEXING.

direct access, *n.* (sometimes wrongly called RANDOM ACCESS) contact with any point (e.g. any cell in store or any sector on disk) by using the address, rather than starting at the beginning and working through (SERIAL ACCESS). Direct access is far faster than serial access in most cases, though in fact serial access to a data item on a compact disc is so fast that it appears to be direct access.

A **direct access arrangement (DAA)** is a protective device used on telephone lines, to prevent damage from a fault in a connected unit.

direct addressing, *n.* a form of ADDRESSING in which the address part of an instruction contains the actual address in store to be used.

direct broadcast (by) satellite (DBS), *n.* using a geostationary communications satellite to send radio and television broadcasts to a region 24 hours a day. In the region is a mix of large dishes (see AERIAL) which feed an amplified signal to sites throughout a local area, and small dishes feeding individual sites.

direct connect modem, *n.* a modem which transfers data between the user's computer and the telephone system through an entirely electrical path. It is much more reliable (but somewhat less flexible) than an ACOUSTIC COUPLER (part of whose transfer path is by sound waves).

direct coupled transistor logic (DCTL), see (ELECTRONIC LOGIC).

direct current (DC), *n.* an electric current in one direction only, and often, but not always, of constant value. A rectifier can produce DC from alternating current (AC). See DIODE.

direct data entry (DDE), *n.* the typing of new input data directly into an IT system, rather than typing it off line onto cards (for instance) for later reading into the system. See also

DIRECT DIAL IN

KEY TO STORE.

direct dial in, *n.* a feature of some private branch exchanges which let outside callers dial straight through to a particular handset or fax machine.

direct digital control (DDC), *n.* a common approach to hybrid computing; a digital processing unit carries out the work of the central simulator of a pure analog computer.

direct distance dialling (DDD), *n.* the ability to telephone places outside the exchange area without calling on an operator.

direct line, *n.* a telephone or fax link that does not pass through an exchange (switching centre), making it more secure.

direct memory access (DMA), *n.* allowing an input or output unit to have access to a system's main store for the transfer of a small amount of data. This takes one MACHINE CYCLE, during which time the processor suspends its current work (hence the name 'cycle stealing').

direct numeric control (DNC), *n.* the operating system of a network of programmable machines, with a central computer and operator supervising all activity.

directives, *n.* the statements in an assembly code program that define symbols and storage areas. During assembly, the assembler translates and acts on these statements; it does not, however, produce machine code instructions from them.

directory, *n.* **1.** a table of names and details (including addresses) of stored data items, e.g. of files on a disk; or a summary version of a data DICTIONARY.
2. a logical sub-section of backing store, e.g. you may use one directory for letters and a second for reports. Some systems allow meaningful names for these directories; others offer only one character. Again some allow a hierarchy of directories, while others offer only one level.

direct output, *n.* the same as ON LINE output (the reverse of feeding output to a storage medium and then reading that off line).

direct outward dialling, *n.* a feature of most modern private branch exchanges, allowing users to obtain an outside line without troubling the switchboard staff.

direct read after write (DRAW), *n.* a method of checking data newly stored on an optical disc. If the stored data does not match the source, a new copy goes to the disc. As most optical discs do not allow data to be erased, the new copy goes to a new place, and the address in the directory entry is changed.

direct transmission satellite, *n.* a communications satellite used to beam signals to individual receivers (for example, personal messages) rather than to be broadcast.

direct voice input, *n.* the use of speech recognition techniques to allow a user to speak directly to an IT system. Many applications require this (e.g. where users need to keep their hands free), and more and more offer it (albeit as yet with only fairly restricted vocabularies of, perhaps, no more than a couple of hundred words).

disable, *vb.* to bar use of a feature (such as an escape key). This involves masking the corresponding INTERRUPT signals so they do not get through to the interrupt register.

IT can help **disabled people** in a number of ways: e.g., by setting up special input and output units and systems where standard ones are not accessible. Thus telephones for the deaf may have displays to show messages typed at the other end, while mouth- or eye-operated 'keyboards' allow quadriplegics to type.

disassembler, *n.* a program that translates machine code to assembly language. The usual aim is to find out how someone else dealt with a problem so you can improve the technique.

disc see DISK.

discretionary hyphen or **soft hyphen,** *n.* a hyphen entered by the user of a word processor to break a word at the end of a line. Should the word later move away from the end of the line, the system removes the hyphen automatically. See HYPHENATION.

dish, *n.* a parabolic AERIAL used to concentrate weak signals (in reception) or to focus output signals to a narrow beam.

disk or **disc,** *n.* a circular backing storage medium placed in a DRIVE for reading (and writing, if allowed). The nature of the disk surface and drive are of two main types; magnetic (erasable, re-writable, and writable) and optical (in most cases only readable). Magnetic disks, or **diskettes**, are small in size (not defined, but often 5.25 inches, 13 cm). For details of optical discs, see COMPACT DISC and VIDEO DISC.

Magnetic disks come in two main types; hard and flexible (floppy). Most **hard disks** (whether single or in packs) stay fixed in their drives, though more and more removable systems are now on offer (giving greater flexibility and security: and greater risk). Hard disk capacities range from 10

DISK

MB. The usual data storage density is up to about 100000 bits per square millimetre (though the 1980s record was 15 Mbit/mm^2, fairly close to current optical disc densities).

Floppy disks are always removable. This is necessary as their data capacity is only a few hundred kilobytes (although much higher density disks are being developed). They differ in diameter (in inches/centimetres: 8/20, 5.25/13, 3.5/8.9 and 3/7.6 are the most common; though 2/5.0 disks able to store a megabyte appeared at the end of the 1980s), and in the degree of protection their cases provide. Disks of different sizes sometimes have special names; e.g. diskette, minifloppy, but these are not standard. Most drives read both sides of a disk; **flippy disks** (which can be turned over) are available for use in single-sided drives.

Whatever the magnetic disk type, the physical organization of data on the surface is as shown in the Figure. There are concentric tracks and radial sectors. Each sector carries a block of data, which is clearly more concentrated the closer it is to the centre of the disk.

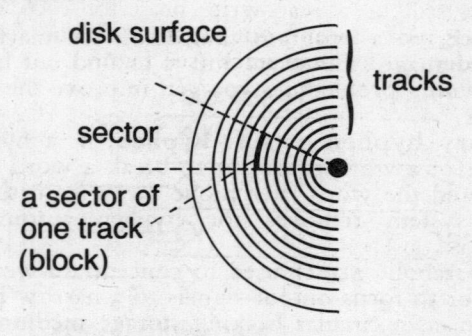

disk. Fig. 1. Disk surface organization.

In use, the disk spins continuously in the **disk drive** (or **disk unit**), at tens of revolutions a second in the case of hard disks, on demand (and more slowly) with floppies. A motor moves the access arm that carries the read/write head in or out to the correct radius, and when the disk has spun to bring the right sector to the head, reading/writing starts. The head floats on a cushion of air a tiny distance away from the surface. See DRIVE.

A **disk crash** occurs when the drive head touches the disk

DISPLAY

surface. This almost always leads to loss of data; if the data lost includes **disk management** details, the disk may no longer be usable. This possibility is one reason for frequent BACK UP.

Most important among the management details stored on a disk is the directory (index). Keeping this up to date is a task of the **disk filing system (DFS)**, or **disk operating system**. This is part of the operating software, but is such an important part that many operating software packages include 'disk' in their names (MS-DOS is a major example).

Disk formatting, preparing a new disk for use in a drive (or making an old one ready for re-use), is another important operating software task. It involves checking all the sectors for damage and laying down magnetic markers to separate and identify the tracks and sectors.

A **disk pack** is a set of two or more hard disks mounted on a common central spindle. Although the two outer surfaces will not be used (they are the ones most likely to suffer damage), this arrangement increases capacity at fairly low cost. There must still be a read/write head for each surface used. All the heads move in and out together on the access arm to a given cylinder, rather than track (see Figure).

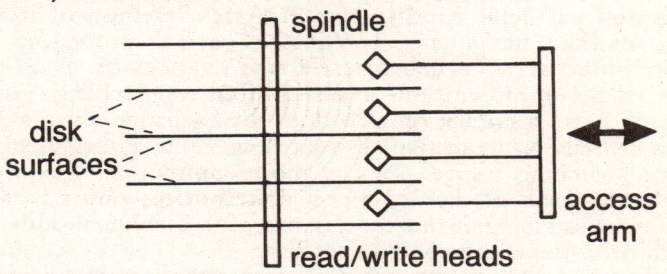

disk. Fig. 2. Disk pack organization.

display, *n.* **1.** a 'soft' visual output (i.e. one on some kind of screen) of an IT system.
2. the screen itself. The traditional bulky mains powered systems have CATHODE RAY TUBES at the centre, but flat screen displays are increasingly common. Most flat screens are LIQUID CRYSTAL DISPLAYS, but GAS PLASMA DISPLAYS are less rare than they were. All these display techniques depend on a rectangular array of addressable cells (PIXELS); the more cells there

DISTANCE LEARNING

are, the higher the definition (RESOLUTION) of the display.

3. the name (also **display type**) of the largest sizes of type, as used in headlines for instance.

distance learning, *n.* an approach to higher education (and in some countries, secondary education) and training, in which the learners mostly stay at a distance from the central campus. The learning programmes are a mix of printed, audio-visual, broadcast, and computer based material, with the telephone and/or computer conference often having a major role in discussion. Distance learning is cheap to deliver, yet very effective for people in thinly populated areas and those who, for personal or employment reasons, cannot enter a full-time programme.

distortion, *n.* a change in the shape of a signal, often as a result of interference, somewhere along the channel.

distributed, *adj.* denoting spread out, rather than having just one centre. In computing, all **distributed systems** involve some form of **distributed logic**, or **distributed processing**, with a number of processors in a network able to carry out different but related tasks. Special cases are the **distributed data base** (where files are held in different places for many people to access; see also INTEGRATED DATA BASE) and **distributed artificial intelligence (DAI)**, a method of increasing machine intelligence by linking several processors. For **distributed array processor**, see ARRAY PROCESSOR.

In telecommunications, **distributed switching** is an approach to spreading the load of an exchange over a wide area by having many small switching units rather than one large switching centre. This is most common in the case of cable television networks; here a **distribution point** is where the main cable branches to a number of individual addresses, with or without distributed switching.

division, *n.* sharing, as in sharing a channel between a number of signals by MULTIPLEXING

DMA, *abbrev. for* DIRECT MEMORY ACCESS.

DMD, *abbrev. for* DEFORMABLE MIRROR DEVICE.

DNC, *abbrev. for* DIRECT NUMERIC CONTROL.

docfax, *n.* an outdated jargon term for FAX.

document, *n.* a set of information able to stand alone, traditionally in printed form, but now often found as microform or a file in computer store. In word processing and DTP, **document assembly** concerns the linking of separate files to make a whole document (e.g. files for the chapters of a book).

A document delivery system (DDS) is a method of giving people easy access to documents, however stored. **Document retrieval** is crucial here: the use of data base management techniques or similar to find details (including addresses) of all relevant documents as defined in a search. You may then need a **document fulfilment agency** to supply copies of the material that interests you. However, increasingly a **document retrieval system (DRS)**, as well as finding details, can now hold material in full in backing store, so searchers can view what interests them on screen or obtain printouts.

documentation, *n.* the set of user instructions, background information, and notes on possible further development that (should) come with a hardware system or software package. As storage costs fall, it is more and more common to find most of the documentation on disk rather than in print. Most system designers and programmers do not write well, and/or do not think documentation important. As a result this material, though crucial, is often skimped or written by someone without full knowledge of the product.

documents per minute (DPM), *n.* a measure of the rate of processing (e.g. in searching) stored DOCUMENTS.

docuterm, *n.* a word or phrase that sums up the contents of a DOCUMENT or file, which is of value when searching.

DOD, *abbrev. for* digital optical disc. See COMPACT DISC.

Dolby system, *n. Trademark* a method of cutting down the effects of noise in an analog or digital audio record. The manufactures claim that analog cassettes can now produce signals as good as those of digital tape. All the systems use special circuits to separate signal from noise, boosting the former and filtering out the latter.

domain, *n.* **1.** a small region of one type of magnetic polarity (north-seeking or south-seeking) surrounded by regions of the other polarity. A magnetic BUBBLE is a particularly small yet permanent domain, and so is the basis of bubble storage.
2. any area of human knowledge as, for instance, stored in a knowledge based expert system.

donor, *n.* a type of substance which, when added as an impurity to an intrinsic semiconductor, adds extra conduction electrons. Thus the semiconductor becomes n-type. A donor is an element of valency 5, such as phosphorus.

DOR, *abbrev. for* DIGITAL OPTICAL RECORDING.

DOS, *abbrev. for* DISK OPERATING SYSTEM.

DOT

dot, *n.* the smallest addressable unit of a display or sheet of paper. See CELL. The smaller (and therefore more numerous) the dots in a given area, the higher the resolution. We measure resolution in the case of displays by (number of dots across) × (number of dots down), e.g. 1000 × 700. The number of *dots per inch* (*DPI*) (or centimetre or millimetre) is the corresponding measure for images on paper (e.g. a scanner may be able to resolve 40 dots per mm, or a page printer to print 120 dots per cm).

A **dot matrix** is a rectangular grid of dots able to form a human-readable character on screen or in printout. A **dot matrix printer** prints characters this way and can also produce graphic output (see Figure). The most common type of matrix printer has a print head with a vertical row of pins (typically in the range 9–24); the system drives the right pattern of pins forward against the ribbon to make a vertical row of dots. An INK JET PRINTER does the same, but with tiny drops of ink rather than pins. See also ELECTROSENSITIVE PRINTER.

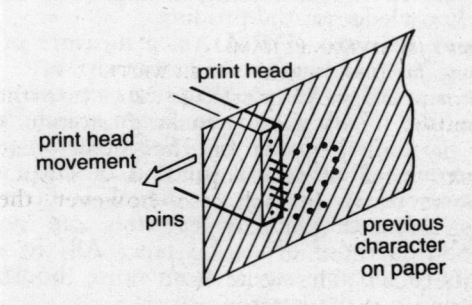

dot. A dot matrix printer.

double, *adj.* two-fold. See also DUAL. **Double buffering** is a process of data transfer which uses two buffers alternately, one buffer's contents are transferred or processed while the other fills. This raises working rate significantly. A major example is when a processor is carrying out a search of a file in backing store: it transfers a block of data into one buffer, and, while searching that, transfers the next block into the other buffer, and so on.

A **double (length) word** is a bit string of twice the system's normal word length, e.g. of 64 bits in a 32-bit

DRIVE

computer. A **double length register** is two one-word registers the system can treat together or separately as required. Together they might hold the full value obtained by multiplying two word-length numbers (giving **double precision** arithmetic); separately they may hold the integer answer and the remainder of a division (SEE NUMBER).

down, *prep.* or *adj* **1.** indicating a fall to a lower (less powerful) state; a computer **goes down** when it crashes. **Down time** is the period a crashed system is not working.

2. indicating a fall to a lower (less powerful) system; a computer is **downwardly compatible** if it can work in a network with, or run programs from, an older computer. To **download** is to transfer useful programs and files from a computer to a less powerful one (e.g. via videotex). A system is **downstream** of a second if it is further from the centre of the network.

DP, *abbrev. for* DATA PROCESSING.

DPI, *abbrev. for* DOTS per inch.

DPM, *abbrev. for* **1.** data processing manager (SEE STAFF).

2. DOCUMENTS PER MINUTE.

DRAM, *abbrev. for* DYNAMIC RAM.

DRAW, *abbrev. for* DIRECT READ AFTER WRITE.

drive, *n.* a form of backing storage hardware that supports, writes to and/or reads from, backing storage media. The structure of a drive depends on the media concerned (e.g. magnetic disk, stripe or tape, optical disc, stripe or tape, or punched tape or card). In each case, however, there needs to be some type of head (the part that does the writing and/or reading) and some method (the drive itself) of moving the media past the head. The write head must be able to output the set of actions that corresponds to each electric code received from the system. The read head converts each pattern detected into an electric code to pass back into the system.

(a) PUNCHED MEDIA: the write head is a set of blunt pins able to make patterns of holes in a column of the paper tape or card. The read head is either a set of brushes (electric contacts) on one side and a metal plate on the other, or a set of lamps on one side and a set of photocells on the other. The drive itself is a set of rollers in the case of cards and a sprocket unit for paper tape.

(b) MAGNETIC MEDIA: here it is normal for the read and write heads to be the same: an electromagnet to produce a magnetic field pattern that depends on the electric input, or, working in

DRIVER

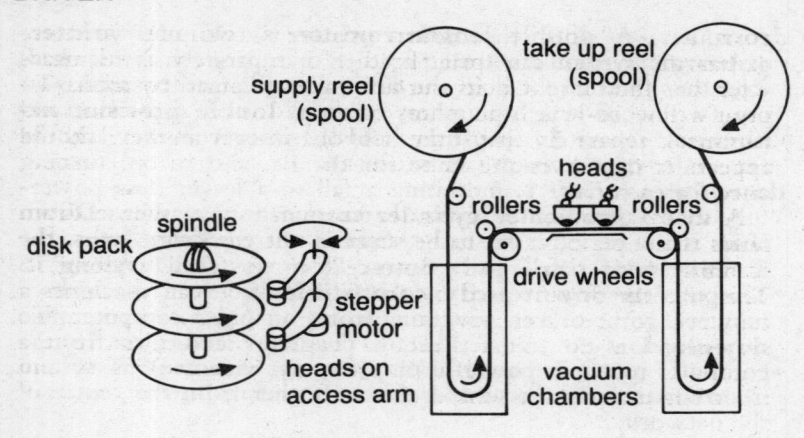

drive. Magnetic disks and tape drives.

reverse, to induce an output electric current that depends on the magnetic field pattern on the disk or tape surface. In the case of a disk system, the drive itself spins the disk, while an access arm moves the head(s) in or out to the correct radius. The Figure shows the structure of a drive for a pack of three hard disks, and also gives the general layout of a magnetic tape drive. See also DRUM STORE.

(c) See OPTICAL MEDIA.

driver, *n.* a program, part of operating software or a separate utility, that controls the working of, and data transfers to/from, a peripheral. Thus word processing software generally comes with a large range of **printer drivers**, one for each of the world's main printer models. See also BUS DRIVER and DEVICE DRIVER.

drop, *vb.* **1.** to fall out of action. A **dropped line** is a line (telephone line, for instance) that loses contact during a conversation or data transfer. **Drop out** is a brief loss of signal strength, e.g. in a data transfer or in a magnetically recorded file.

2. to make a downstream link. A **drop line** (or **drop wire**) is the link between an individual system (e.g. extension telephone or cable television set) and the distribution cable. See also MULTI-DROP.

DRS, *abbrev. for* DOCUMENT RETRIEVAL SYSTEM.

drum, *n.* a cylinder. In a **drum printer** or **cylinder printer**, or **barrel printer**, the 'print head' is a drum with a full character set embossed on its surface in each print position. To print a line of type, the drum turns to the 'A' position, and hammers press As onto the ribbon wherever they should appear. It then does the same for the Bs, and so on, turning once for each line.

A **drum scanner** or **cylinder scanner** is one whose drum holds the sheet of paper to be scanned. As the drum spins, the scanning head (lamp and photo-cell) moves slowly along it. This was the system used by the first effective fax machines a century ago, but it is now found only in certain reprographic systems. On the other hand, a **drum plotter** (as in the Figure) is much the same, with the write head moving to and fro while the paper on the drum moves up and down.

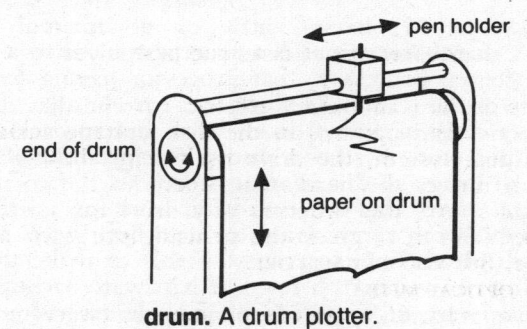

drum. A drum plotter.

The **drum store** was the first effective type of direct access magnetic backing storage system, designed in the late 1950s but probably never used now. The large cylinder spins all the time, at up to 100 revolutions a second; magnetic read/write heads (see DRIVE) all along the side transfer data to and from its magnetic surface.

dry run, *n.* working through a program 'by hand' but as a computer would, in order to seek errors: an important part of program development and testing.

DTL, *abbrev. for* DIODE TRANSISTOR LOGIC. See LOGIC (ELECTRONIC LOGIC).

DTP, *abbrev. for* DESKTOP PUBLISHING.

dual, *adj.* twofold. See also DOUBLE. A **dual density** disk is one whose magnetic surface is able to carry data at twice the normal density, so the disk can hold twice as much data as the norm. It may do this by being able to have twice as many tracks as usual, but, whatever the method, the heads must be able to cope; it is the head size that restricts density rather than the magnetic coating.

A **dual-in-line (package) (DIL)** or **(DIP)** is the standard design for a chip mounting: two rows of pins that both provide strong support and link the chip electrically to the socket that holds it. The number of pins in each row depends on the chip's function: more complex chips (e.g. microprocessors) have more pins than, say, storage chips. See also DIP SWITCH.

A **dual processor** is a type of parallel processor with two central processing units running in parallel, specializing in different types of task, or providing back-up in the case of failure

dumb, *adj.* in IT, having little or no internal processing power. A **dumb terminal** is a true peripheral to a multi-user system's central processor, that processor having to look after all aspects of the terminal's work.

dump, *n.* a copy of part of main store sent to backing store or to an output unit. A **screen dump** is a printout of the screen (there is an image of this in main store).

duplex, *adj.* two fold or two-way, such as a data transfer channel which can carry signals or data both ways at the same time. A **duplexer** is a MULTIPLEXER able to make this happen. **Duplexing**, however, is a form of hardware backup, doubling up the hardware of a system to provide reserve units in the case of failure.

Dvorak keyboard, *n.* a keyboard designed for fast typing, with the most commonly used keys in easy reach of the typist's fingers. See also MALTRON.

dyadic, *adj.* with a dual relationship, twofold. Thus a **dyadic function** has two arguments, while a **dyadic operator** has two operands.

Dynabook, *n.* a concept of the late 1960s of a highly flexible portable personal computer (developed in the US by Alan Kay). A laptop micro with a CD-ROM drive appeared with this name in 1989, but did not offer all the features of the original concept.

dynamic, *adj.* ever-moving, as opposed to STATIC. The contents of **dynamic RAM (DRAM)** chips need a pulse of power (refreshing current) every millisecond or so. This is

DYNAMIC

because the system involves storing each bit as an electric charge in a tiny capacitor, and the capacitors leak. STATIC RAM, on the other hand, loses its contents only when you switch off the system. DRAM chips offer much higher data storage densities, however, so are in very wide use. This is so, despite serious shortages in the late 1980s, at a time when the storage capacity was rising to the 500 kB level. 8 MB DRAMs should be common by the mid-1990s.

The **dynamic range** of a system is the ratio (in decibels) of the highest amplitude (signal) it can accept without damage to the system, to the lowest amplitude it can accept without loss of signal.

E

EAPROM, *acronym for* electrically alterable programmable read-only memory; a type of EPROM.

EAROM, *acronym for* electrically alterable read-only memory, an alternative term for EEROM.

earth, *n.* a low resistance electric link to the ground or to some other large conducting object (e.g. the frame of a plane or the hull of a ship).

The **earth segment** is the ground-based part of a satellite communications system. An **earth station** is a ground-based terminal able to communicate with a satellite and process received signals.

EBCDIC, *abbrev. for* EXTENDED BINARY CODED DECIMAL/DENARY INTERCHANGE CODE. See BINARY.

EBR, *abbrev. for* ELECTRON BEAM RECORDING.

echo, *n.* **1.** the reflection of a signal from an obstacle sufficient to cause interference (ghosting in the case of video) with the direct signal. **Echo location**, as used in **echo sounders** (ASDIC or sonar systems), involves studying sound waves reflected back to the sender in order to learn about the environment.
2. the feeding back to a keyboard operator of what has been typed or generated by the system to allow checking for errors. **Echo checking** is the same process on a larger scale: the sending of a copy of a signal back to the sender so the sender can point out errors or re-transmit.

ECL *abbrev. for* EMITTER COUPLED LOGIC. See LOGIC (ELECTRONIC LOGIC).

ECMA symbols, *n.* the standard set of FLOW CHART symbols. ECMA is the European Computer Makers' Association.

E-cycle, *abbrev. for* EXECUTE CYCLE.

edge board or **edge card,** *n.* a printed circuit board with contacts along one edge. An **edge connector** is the socket on another board (mother board) into which it is plugged.

editing, *n.* the making of changes to a program or data file. The standard changes are:

(a) amending statements/records (changing their internal structure);

(b) adding statements/records;
(c) removing statements/records.

In **text editing** (i.e. word processing) a document (text) can be edited in the same kind of way. An **editor** is a system that aids the editing of a program; it puts it on screen so you can work with it as with a word processor.

A **linkage editor** is a program that automatically edits machine code programs during linkage to make a seamless whole.

editorial process centre, *n.* a network used by writers, journalists, editors and typesetters in a publishing house. These people all have access to texts (stored electronically), and so can work on them with less effort and wasted time than when the material is on paper.

EDP, *acronym for* ELECTRONIC DATA PROCESSING. Related abbreviations (also out dated) are **EDPE** (electronic data processing equipment), **EDPM** (electronic data processing machine), and **EDPS** (electronic data processing system).

EDS, *acronym for* **1.** electronic data storage (the replacement in the electronic office of filing cabinets with backing store).
2. electronic document storage. See DOCUMENT, which also gives notes on **EDDS,** electronic DOCUMENT DELIVERY SYSTEMS.

EDSAC, *acronym for* the Electronic Delay Storage Automatic Calculator, the second computer using von Neumann's stored program concept to begin work (in 1949, design having begun in 1946 in Cambridge, UK). The delay storage system in fact used an ACOUSTIC DELAY LINE. Being based on electron tubes (valves), this was a first GENERATION machine.

education, *n.* the organization and delivery of learning. IT, in the form of, for example, COMPUTER AIDED LEARNING, COMPUTER BASED TRAINING, and COMPUTER MANAGED LEARNING plays an ever more significant role. **Educational technology** includes educational IT, as well as such fields as audiovisual learning systems (including DISTANCE LEARNING) and reprographics.

EDVAC *acronym for* the Electronic Discrete Variable Automatic Calculator, the first stored program computer to be designed, in 1944 by John von Neumann in Pennsylvania US; although it did not start working until 1952 (*cf.* MANCHESTER I 1948 and EDSAC 1949). Based on electron tubes (valves), this was a first GENERATION machine.

EEPROM, *acronym for* electrically erasable programmable read-only memory, a type of PROM chip.

EEROM

EEROM *acronym for* electrically erasable read-only memory, and much the same in practice as EAROM. READ ONLY MEMORY (ROM) storage chips are non-volatile: as the name implies, you can read data from them, but not write to them. All the same, in the case of EAROMS and EEROMS, you can wipe the contents with an electric current, and then reuse the chip. See also EPROM.

efficiency, *n.* some measure of the success of a program that does what it should. Efficiency takes into account speed of action and use of storage space: an efficient program is fast and compact.

EFT, *abbrev. for* ELECTRONIC FUNDS TRANSFER.

EFTPOS, *acronym for* ELECTRONIC FUNDS TRANSFER AT THE POINT OF SALE.

EHF, *abbrev. for* extra high frequency. See RADIO.

elastic buffer *or* **elastic store,** *n.* a buffer (or store) that is not of fixed length, but changes in size to meet demand. Elastic buffers are of special value in communications.

electroacoustic tablet, *n.* a type of GRAPHICS TABLET. From moment to moment the system checks where a finger or stylus ('pen') is on the tablet by sending out high frequency sound (acoustic) waves and sensing the return of their reflections.

electromagnetic, *adj.* concerned with electromagnetism (cases where electric current produces magnetic effects and vice versa) and/or with electromagnetic waves (which include light and radio waves; see SPECTRUM). An **electromagnetic delay line** is a type of DELAY LINE that produces its effect by passing the data down a series of inductors and capacitors.

electron beam recording (EBR), *n.* the process behind COMPUTER OUTPUT ON MICROFORM. The output signals from the computer go to control the electron beam in a type of cathode ray tube. Instead of a screen is a microform plate, which when exposed and developed gives the microform image used for data storage.

electron tube, *n.* a modern term for electronic valve, any electronic device whose action depends on a current of electrons in a VACUUM (see VACUUM DEVICE). The first tubes were truly valves; they passed current in one direction only; they had two electrodes, and so gained the name diode. Now vacuum diodes are very rarely used, but semiconductor diodes are numerous in every chip.

Electron tubes led to the technology of electronics: the study and use of small ('light') currents, i.e. those much less than an ampere. Semiconductor systems work with far smaller currents still (milliamps or less), so led to the technology of microelectronics, now firmly based on chips (integrated circuits).

Microelectronic units such as the semiconductor diode have very significant advantages over electron tubes; for example, they:

(a) use far less current, therefore cost less to run and require less cooling;
(b) are far smaller;
(c) are far more robust.

This applies just as much to systems built from them, i.e. audio, video, computer, and control.

However, one type of electron tube is still found everywhere: the CATHODE-RAY TUBE. By the time this has fully disappeared in favour of flat screens, it is likely that people will have developed miniaturized types of vacuum tube for new uses. Research and development in the early 1990s are moving towards chip-scale assemblies of vacuum diodes and triodes (triodes are equivalent to transistors). These have all the advantages of semiconductor units listed above, and great potential in television, microwave, and X-ray applications. They are many thousand times smaller than the traditional vacuum devices.

electronic, *adj.* concerned with small ('light') electric currents (much less than an ampere). People often use electronic loosely to denote technological information.

An **electronic blackboard** was originally the trade name for a system which sensed the movement of chalk on a special chalkboard, passing the results to displays. It now tends to cover any somewhat uninspired use of IT with learners, e.g. programs which do little processing but simply present screen after screen of text. See COMPUTER-AIDED LEARNING and EDUCATION.

Electronic composition is any process in which IT aids the preparation of material for printing; it therefore includes DESKTOP PUBLISHING and professional systems of that kind.

Electronic data processing (EDP) is an outdated term for business computing; EDP and EDS are related acronyms.

The term **electronic cottage** was first used by Alvin Toffler; it concerns the shift of work place from large central units (e.g. labour-intensive factories and office blocks) to small

ELECTRONIC

ones at street level and in the home. IT, mainly computing, telecommunications and robotics, is making this shift possible, and there are good reasons (human, social and economic) for society to encourage it. See also GLOBAL VILLAGE and TELECOMMUTER.

Electronic funds transfer (EFT) is one of the most far reaching applications of IT. It covers a number of ways in which IT stores, processes and transfers money with as little use of real cash and paper as possible. Electronic funds transfer includes the use of credit cards, debit cards, smart cards, auto teller machines, magnetic ink characters on cheques, and home/office banking. Banks and other finance houses use these systems on a huge scale.

Electronic funds transfer at the point of sale (EFTPOS) is the use of EFT systems where money would in the past have changed hands, e.g. at a checkout or sales desk. The buyer offers a debit card (stripe card or smart card) and types in the personal identity number. The cashier enters the details of the goods at the pos terminal; then, if the central computers accept the transaction, they transfer the money concerned electronically between the buyer's and the trader's bank accounts.

Electronic glass is a transparent conducting substance used for touch screens, for instance. As it is a conductor, a system based on it can detect where the user's pointing finger is at any moment, and take the right action. For ELECTRONIC LOGIC, see LOGIC.

There are various special forms of electronic communication between people. **Electronic mail** (see EMAIL) is the storing of personal messages in a central computer (host) in a wide area network, or in the central store of a local area network. Each time users log on to such a system, they can access their stored messages, acknowledge, reply to or forward them, or take other action. Email is one type of **electronic messaging**, others are COMPUTER CONFERRING and VIEWDATA; all in essence two-way systems. **Electronic publishing**, on the other hand, is a one way system; it includes publishing material for general access (by subscribers or the public) on compact or magnetic disc or by VIDEOTEX. An **electronic periodical/journal** is an electronic publication in any of those forms that comes out as a new issue every so often; but a major advantage of electronic publishing is that the information providers can continually update the material, rather than (for example) making readers wait for a new issue or edition.

The **electronic office** is jargon for today's (or tomorrow's) paperless office, a business information centre in which all information handling (input, processing, storage, access, and output) is electronic rather than paper-based. The Figure shows the flow of goods, information and money in such an office. See under electronic funds transfer (above), for the advantages of electronic rather than paper-based information. The present use of EFTPOS is a demonstration of the fact that money is information too, and the electronic office handles cash flow in just the same way as information flow. The Figure is a diagrammatic representation of the information handling needs of a typical office. Almost every aspect of office communication is now open to information technology. However, the Figure does not show a completely automated office; there are, and will remain for some time, many crucial tasks for people to perform.

Electronic speech systems include SPEECH SYNTHESIS (automated speech production) and SPEECH RECOGNITION (the use of software to accept, decode and act on speech inputs). An **electronic stylus** is a name for a LIGHT PEN or other sort of pen (e.g. that of a GRAPHICS TABLET) used for data input.

Electronic switching is a system used in a digital telephone exchange which offers many special services as well as fast, reliable call connection. An **electronic tutor** is a rare name for a COMPUTER AIDED LEARNING (CAL) system.

electronics, *n.* the science and technology of small currents (less than about an ampere) and of circuits working with them. In particular the subject covers conduction through gases, vacuum, and semiconductors. The last is the special field of solid-state MICRO-ELECTRONICS.

electro-sensitive printer, *n.* a very compact dot matrix printer, in which current from the print head changes the surface of the paper to produce the image. The print head produces a spark which burns off the top layer of the special paper, to reveal the darker layer below.

electrostatic, *adj.* describing stationary electric charge rather than moving charge (current). **Electrostatic deflection** is a method of moving a cathode ray tube beam to any part of the screen, as used with most computer monitors. An **electrostatic printer** is a page printer that works by XEROGRAPHY (the basis of most modern copiers). The image of the page first builds up as a pattern of electric charge on a drum; the

ELECTROSTATIC

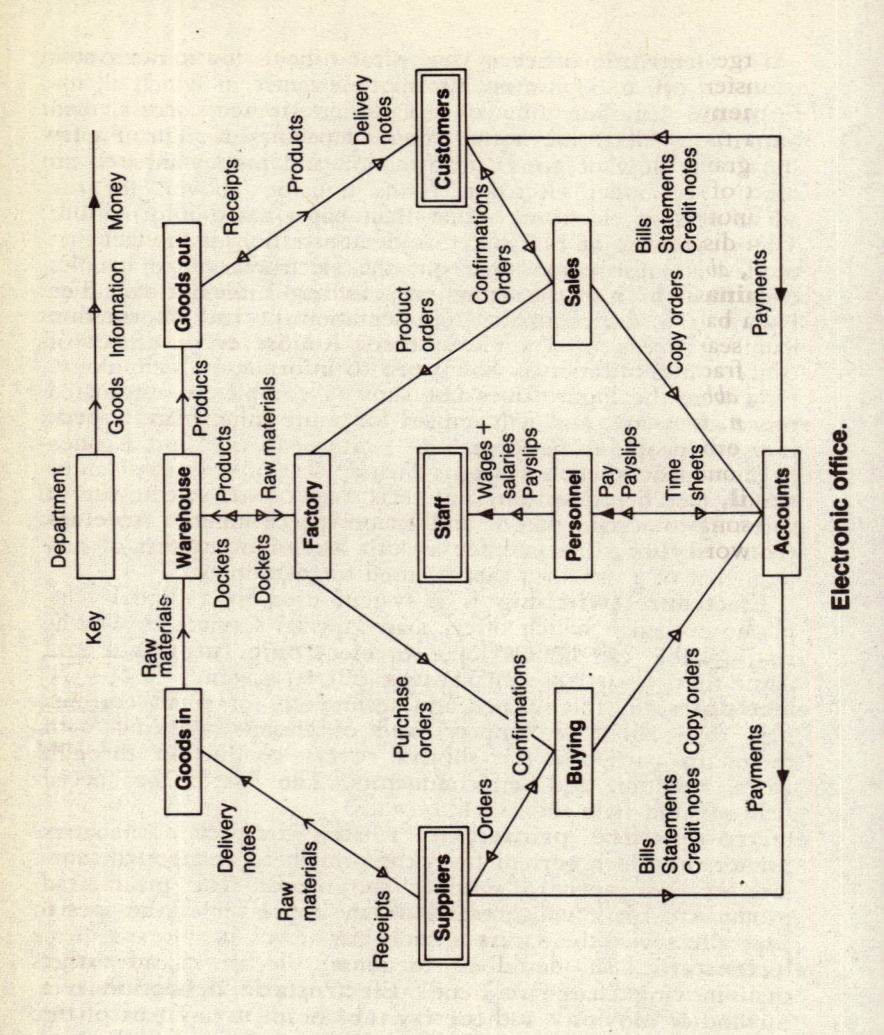

Key

Department

Goods → Information → Money

Diagram: Electronic office.

- Customers ← Delivery notes ← Goods out ← Products ← Warehouse
- Customers → Receipts → Goods out
- Warehouse ↔ Products/Dockets ↔ Factory
- Factory ← Raw materials ← Warehouse (Dockets)
- Goods in → Raw materials → Warehouse
- Suppliers → Delivery notes → Goods in
- Suppliers → Raw materials → Goods in
- Goods in → Receipts → Suppliers
- Factory → Product orders → Sales
- Sales → Confirmations / Orders → Customers
- Customers → Orders → Sales
- Factory ← Purchase orders ← Buying
- Buying → Orders → Suppliers
- Suppliers → Confirmations → Buying
- Personnel ← Time sheets ← Accounts
- Personnel → Pay / Payslips → Staff
- Staff → Wages + salaries / Payslips
- Accounts → Bills / Statements / Credit notes → Customers
- Customers → Payments → Accounts
- Sales → Copy orders → Accounts
- Buying → Copy orders → Accounts
- Accounts → Payments → Suppliers
- Suppliers → Bills / Statements / Credit notes → Accounts

98

charge attracts toner (very fine plastic dust) which the system transfers to, and bakes on, the sheet of paper.

element, *n.* **1.** a member of a set of similar items. An element of a DATA STRUCTURE is one of its data items, though in a few program languages an element is a single data item that is not part of a structure.
2. another term for GATE or logic circuit
3. a discrete part of an electr(on)ic circuit, i.e. component.

ELF, *abbrev. for* extra low frequency. See RADIO.

elimination *n.* the ignoring, in searching a file (or document data base), of those records (or documents) which do not meet the search description. The **elimination factor** of a search is the fraction of records (documents) eliminated.

EM, *abbrev. for* ELECTROMAGNETIC.

em, *n.* the space taken up by the letter 'm' in any size of type. An **em dash** is a long dash (—) rather than a short hyphen-like one, the en dash (–).

email, *n.* a common name for ELECTRONIC MAIL, the storing of personal messages in a central computer (host) in a wide area network (or in the central store of a local area network).

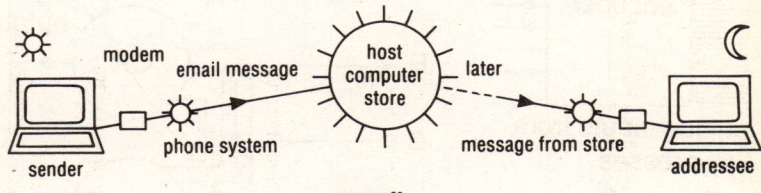

email.

Each time users log on to an email system, they can access their stored messages, acknowledge, reply to or forward them, or take other action. There are many nation-wide and international email systems (**email bureau**) but as yet few moves to link them effectively. As a result far fewer people and firms use email than should be the case, despite its advantages (compared to 'snail mail', the post) of speedy message transfer, low cost, flexibility and (in theory) ease of use. To encourage new members, most email systems dilute their effort by adding on-line data bases.

EMMS, *abbrev. for* ELECTRONIC mail and message system(s).
EMS, *abbrev. for* any ELECTRONIC MESSAGING system.

EMULATION

emulation, *n.* the use of software (and maybe hardware) in one IT system to make it act like another. Thus many non-standard computers have **emulators** that allow them to act like standard computers; some word processors include telex emulation.

en, *n.* the space taken up by the letter 'n' in any size of type. An en dash is a short hyphen-like dash (–) rather than a long one, the em dash (—).

encoding, *n.* the changing, by means of a suitable **encoder** (circuit or program), of input data into a coded form that the system can cope with. Most encoders are chips, with a large number of input lines, a signal on each line coming out as a unique pattern (e.g. in ASCII) on the smaller set of output lines. In the keyboard encoder shown in the Figure, there is one input line for each key (plus a system for handling cases where the user presses two or more keys at once, on purpose

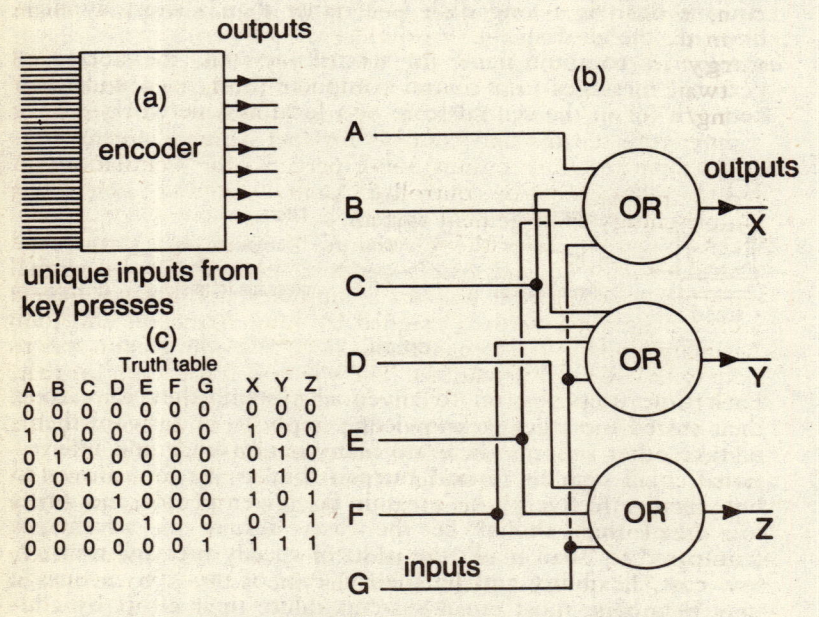

A	B	C	D	E	F	G	X	Y	Z
0	0	0	0	0	0	0	0	0	0
1	0	0	0	0	0	0	1	0	0
0	1	0	0	0	0	0	0	1	0
0	0	1	0	0	0	0	1	1	0
0	0	0	1	0	0	0	1	0	1
0	0	0	0	1	0	0	0	1	1
0	0	0	0	0	1	1	1	1	1

encoder. (a) Keyboard (seven-bit) and (b) and (c) three-bit encoder and truth table.

or in error). ASCII output needs seven lines, though the encoder may have a subcircuit to add a parity bit on an eighth line if so desired.

encryption, *n*. the changing of data, in store or in transit, to a secret (e.g. scrambled) form, or code, for reasons of SECURITY. *Cryptography* is the science or study of this type of coding.

end marker, *n*. a special character or other code that marks the end of a signal or chunk of data. Important examples are for end of block (*EOB*), end of file (*EOF*), end of job (*EOJ*), end of message (*EOM*), end of record (*EOR*), end of string (*EOS*), end of text (*EOT*), end of transferred block (*ETB*), and end of transferred text (*ETX*).

end page, *n*. in VIDEOTEX, a screen of actual information rather than a menu or routing screen, perhaps a leaf in the videotex tree.

end user, *n*. the final user of an IT product or set of information, rather than any other person or firm along the chain from the original maker or provider.

energy management, *n*. the use of real time processor and software to control the usage of fuel in an industrial process or living/working area. Such a system involves an array of temperature sensors and controls for fuel delivery mechanisms (e.g. switches and pumps) and perhaps for ventilation. A home microprocessor-controlled central heating unit is a simple energy management system.

ENIAC, *acronym for* the Electronic Numeric Integrator And Calculator, the second (after COLOSSUS) general purpose digital electronic calculator. It was not a computer as it did not have a stored program system. Designed by John Atanasoff and John Mauchly, and built in Pennsylvania (US) 1943–46, its aim was to help with ballistic calculations. The war ended too soon for that, so it became an important scientific calculator. One often quoted feat was to find the fifth power of a five figure number in half a second: but in doing so its 18000 valves used 200 kW of power.

entity, *n*. the person or thing whose details take up a record in a computer file. In the context of DATA PROTECTION, an entity is a data subject.

envelope, *n*. **1.** a set of bits added to a PACKET of data ready for transfer to give such details as the address to which it should be sent.
2. the carrier wave part of a modulated signal (see MODULATION).
3. aspects of the shape of a complete sound, such as its change

of loudness (and maybe pitch) during growth and decay, and its overall length (duration).

environment, *n.* **1.** surroundings in general. **Environmental control** is the use of processors, software and various items of hardware to sense aspects of the environment and take appropriate action. It includes ENERGY MANAGEMENT, air-conditioning control, and surveillance.

2. the set of hardware and software needed by a program. In this sense, **environmental control** is the work of operating software, in particular network operating software (network control).

EOB, *abbrev. for* end of block. See END MARKER.
EOF, *abbrev. for* end of file. See END MARKER.
EOJ, *abbrev. for* end of job. See END MARKER.
EOM, *abbrev. for* end of message. See END MARKER.
EOR, *abbrev. for* end of record. See END MARKER.
EOR, *n.* the exclusive OR GATE (circuit, element), with an output only if just one input is 1.
EOS, *abbrev. for* end of string. See END MARKER.
EOT, *abbrev. for* end of transmission (transfer). See END MARKER.
EPC, *abbrev. for* EDITORIAL PROCESS CENTRE, an integrated approach to the use of IT to aid publishing.
EPROM, *abbrev. for* erasable programmable read-only memory, a type of read-only storage chip also called electrically alterable programmable read-only memory (EAPROM). The chip has a window over the actual integrated circuit; shining ultraviolet light through this for a few minutes breaks the bonds formed in programming and thus erases the contents. You can then re-program the chip from scratch. See also READ-ONLY MEMORY.
equalization, *n.* the removing of any distortion in a signal after transfer.
equivalence gate, *n.* also called MATCH, a GATE (circuit, element) with an output only if all inputs are the same.
erasability, *n.* a feature of some storage systems (e.g. magnetic) that allows the contents to be deleted and new data to be stored. All read-and-write stores are erasable; most read-only ones are not.
ergonomics, *n.* the study of how people relate to a particular environment. In IT, ergonomics includes the biology and engineering aspects of work with computers, etc., and thus the design of hardware, related furniture, lighting, heating/air

conditioning, and so on. Ergonomics overlaps health and safety in its attempts to minimize such hazards as stress, backache, eye strain, and fatigue, as well as damage (e.g. eye disease, repetitive strain injury, and miscarriage).

Ergonomic keyboards are aimed at fast, strain-free typing. The most common are the MALTRON, DVORAK, and MICROWRITER, but all are rare compared to the standard QWERTY and AZERTY systems. See also HUMAN-COMPUTER INTERFACE.

ERIC, *acronym for* Educational Resources Information Center, a major international educational data base and publisher.

Erlang factor, *n.* a measure of the density of traffic in a channel or network. One way to find it is to multiply the number of calls carried in an hour by their average length in hours. A second way is to express that result as a fraction of the maximum possible.

error, *n.* a fault in a system, either long term (i.e. a BUG in hardware or software) or casual (e.g. an incorrect input). Most, if not all, IT systems have some degree of **error control**; communications networks or hardware may offer **error detection** and even **error correction** (see HAMMING CODE and PARITY), while a program's DIAGNOSTIC routines give it the ability to screen or print out **error messages** (**error reports**). The error in a correctly computed value is how far it differs from the correct value as a result of, for instance, inadequate precision (ROUNDING ERROR).

There are various classes of **program error**. A **syntax error** occurs where an instruction does not follow the program language's rules (syntax); it may be a programmer's slip of memory (e.g. forgetting to close a bracket) or of typing (e.g. putting 'ON ERORR' rather than 'ON ERROR'). **Semantic errors** include such things as using the same label for two different purposes, or referring to a label that does not exist. The translating program will pick up and report both these types of error; unless translation is by interpretation, they are assembly or **compilation errors**. Some modern program languages attempt to correct translation errors automatically; there is much debate as to whether this is a good thing or not.

Much more serious are errors that survive translation; these are true software bugs if even fairly heavy testing does not detect them. **Run-time (execution) errors** are errors picked up when the program runs (they cause an **error interrupt**): as when an input leads to overflow (e.g. an attempt to divide by zero) or underflow. Neither translation nor running will pick up **logical errors**, however, e.g. using < rather than > in a condition. Errors like these occur where the program does not carry out the design task; the only way to find them is by dry-running and/or by using test data and checking the output values.

ESC, *symbol for* the **escape** key on a keyboard, or its effect (**escape character** or **escape code**, 27 in ASCII). The usual function of the key is to interrupt a system's current activity, temporarily or permanently (though there may be a break key for the latter purpose). The usual function of the escape code is to inform the operating software that a control code follows it, the whole string (escape code plus control code) is an **escape sequence**. Many programs use escape sequences to let the user interrupt normal activity and pass a command for a special effect. Often indeed the escape key press makes a command menu or command line appear.

ESI, *abbrev. for* EXTERNALLY SPECIFIED INDEX.

ESS, *abbrev. for* ELECTRONIC SWITCHING system, a digital telephone exchange.

ETB, *abbrev. for* end of transmission (transfer) of block of data. See END MARKER.

ETX, *abbrev. for* end of text transfer. See END MARKER.

even parity, *n.* a PARITY system which sets the parity bit to 0 or 1 in order that there be an even number of 1s in each byte. On this basis, the parity bit for 1010 111 would be 1, making the byte 1010 1111.

event, *n.* anything that happens. A *significant* event to a processor is the end of an action or the receipt of a new command (either of these being marked by an interrupt).

exchangeable disk pack, *n.* a set of hard DISKS which can be taken out of a computer, stored, carried around and replaced. Such packs are costly, but they offer advantages of security, data transfer and storage extension over the more usual fixed disks.

exchange centre, switching centre or **node,** *n.* a unit within a network with the function of controlling links between stations in the area, and between any of them and other exchange areas or networks. The line from each station (telephone handset or device, or telex machine, for instance) ends in the exchange. There it can link with any other such local line, or with a trunk line to a second exchange in the case of a non-local call (see Figure). In a manual exchange, as on a

EXIT

manual switchboard, the links are made by hand; traditional automatic exchanges have electro-mechanical links; modern digital exchanges use electronic switching. The CELL phone system also links into the telephone exchange network.

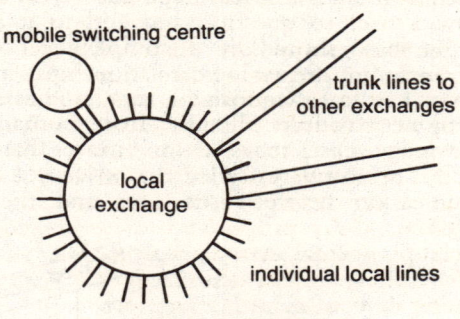

exchange centre.

exclusive OR, *n.* a GATE (circuit, element), called EOR or XOR, with an output only if just one input is 1.
execute cycle or **E-cycle,** *n.* a processor's fetch-execute-reset cycle. See MACHINE CYCLE. The **execute phase** is the part of that cycle in which the system carries out the current instruction.
execution, *n.* the carrying out (running) of a command or program (set of instructions). An **execution error** is the same as a run-time ERROR, an error in coding a program that shows only when the system runs the program. An **executable program** has been translated into machine code and linked (see LINK), so is ready to run.
executive, *n.* a control program. The term may be used for:
  (a) operating software;
  (b) that part of operating software handling the peripherals (i.e. input and output);
  (c) any program that oversees the work of subordinate programs;
  (d) an alternative term for MONITOR or SUPERVISOR.
exhaustivity, *n.* a measure of how thoroughly a file is indexed for retrieval, e.g. how many key words (index terms) attach on average to each record.
exit, *vb.* to transfer control from a sub-routine or procedure back to whatever called it, or from a main program back to

EXPANDER

the operating software.

expander, *n.* a circuit able to expand the amplitude range (volume range) of a signal, a sort of amplifier.

expert system, *n.* a major application of MACHINE INTELLIGENCE research which combines a knowledge base with suitable software to allow a user to question and add to it (see Figure). The knowledge base should be a complete set of facts and relationships (including fuzzy logic relationships) in the subject of interest (e.g. medical diagnosis or rock studies). A qualified knowledge engineer collects all these from human experts, so a good knowledge base may 'know' more than any single human expert. The software, called the INFERENCE ENGINE, controls communication between the user and the knowledge base.

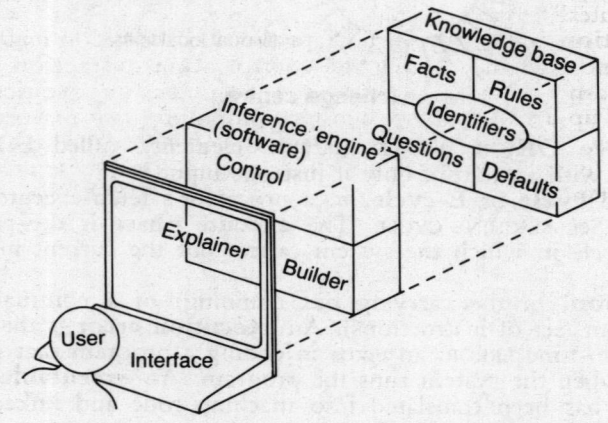

expert system. The parts of a knowledge-based expert system.

Expert system research and development have continued now for several decades, with some excellent results in areas like law and aspects of science and technology. An aim is to provide a complete expert system on a chip. See KNOWLEDGE BASED (EXPERT) SYSTEM.

exponent, *n.* the part of a floating-point number that gives the power of 10 (denary) or of 2 (binary) by which you multiply the other part, the mantissa. Thus, in denary standard (scientific) form, the number of particles in a mole is $6.025 \times$

10^{23}; here 6.025 is the mantissa and 23 is the exponent. See also NUMBER.

extended binary coded decimal/denary interchange code (EBCDIC), *n.* a system for coding all characters in the same kind of way as does ASCII. See BINARY CODED DECIMAL.

extension store, *n.* see BACKING STORE.

external label, *n.* a label, not usually machine readable, fixed to a backing store disk, tape or chip, to identify its contents.

external store. *n.* a term for BACKING STORE, showing its peripheral nature.

externally specified index (ESI), *n.* a feature which allows a computer to act as the switching centre for messages between a number of other systems. It provides automatic routing through the system for each message, without interrupting the computer's own work.

extraction indexing, *n.* perhaps the most common method of machine indexing. Under the control of an **extraction index program**, the system scans the document in question and builds up a list of all the most common non-trivial words and phrases. Some programs give extra weight to highlighted terms (e.g. bold or italic) on the grounds that these are more important.

F

face, *abbrev. for* typeface, a particular design of type (size not being relevant: compare with FONT).

face to face (FTF), see TELECONFERRING.

facsimile or **facsimile telegraphy** or **facsimile transfer,** *n.* obsolete terms for FAX, the transfer through the phone network of copies of documents. In printing, a **facsimile platemaker** is a high-quality fax system able to produce printing plates direct from fax signals.

fact finding, *n.* an important early stage in SYSTEMS ANALYSIS: it usually includes research into current practice and people's views and ideas about it.

factory, *n.* a place for the manufacture of goods from raw materials. Factories are fertile fields for IT; using COMPUTER INTEGRATED MANUFACTURE and the ROBOT, for instance, some factories are now almost fully automatic. To maximize their efficiency is the subject of many research projects round the world.

fail-safe, *adj.* designed to return to a safe condition in the event of a failure or malfunction. It can be used of, for instance, a robotic system that drops to a safe state if something goes wrong.

fail-soft, *adj.* describes an IT system that can keep working at a basic level if something goes wrong.

false code, *n.* a character code that is not part of a system's character set, e.g. one received from a remote terminal. Most systems replace false codes with a standard character code (a false code flag character, such as |); either software or the user can then search for the flags and delete or try to replace them.

A **false drop** (**false retrieve**) is a record found in a search that does not meet the user's criteria because of an incorrect definition of the search.

family, *n.* group of related objects, e.g. type faces, files, software packages, or IT hardware systems, perhaps from a single source.

fanfold, accordion fold, concertina fold or **zig-zag**, *adj.* used of continuous printer paper, i.e. not in single sheets, but folded as the name implies. It is normal for fanfold paper to have holes along the edges so sprocket wheels can pull the paper through the printer. See also FRICTION FEED.

fast access, *n.* a relative term used of storage; e.g. main store has faster access than backing store, but slower access than cache. See ACCESS TIME. The **fast modes** offered by some fax systems are non-standard methods of cutting down transfer time; being non-standard, few work unless sending to a similar model of fax machine or card. Some modems have fast modes of the same type.

Fast picture search is a feature of some videotape recorder/players; it allows the user to scan quickly through a tape to the desired point.

FAT, *abbrev. for* FILE ALLOCATION TABLE.

fatal error or **catastrophic error** *n.* an error (in most cases in software or its use) that leads to a crash; i.e. the system stops working.

father, *n.* see GENERATION, sense 1.

fax, *n.* a system for the transfer of images of documents through the telephone network. Fax systems (cards and machines) come in four groups. Groups 1 (analog) and 2 (digital) are no longer made, while Group 3 (also digital, and able to communicate with Group 2 systems) is the norm. At the start of the 1990s no official standard for Group 4 faxing existed, but some firms have produced machines they claim will fit that standard when it becomes official. Those machines transfer data at 64000 bits per second (Group 3's limit is 9600) and cannot use standard telephone lines.

Also in the fax field, **group calling** is the use of a single key press to poll, or to broadcast to, a group of machines in sequence (the user will have entered the numbers of the other machines in the store for that key, the **group code** being the key's code).

Despite the fast spread of this technology, there is still a place for the **fax bureau**, a firm that provides a faxing service for others (e.g., in a copy shop). The originals of the documents may be on paper (scanned into a **fax machine**) or computer-generated (sent via a **fax card**, or **fax board**, in the computer). In either case they may be any mix of text and graphics. At the other end must be a compatible fax system (machine or card) put permanently or manually on line to the telephone network.

There are several world-wide standards, or GROUPS, for fax

systems. Most modern systems are in Group 3 but are downwardly compatible with Group 2.

The faxing process involves:

(a) dialling through the network;

(b) handshaking (in which the two systems exchange details about themselves);

(c) transfer of the image, with some degree of ERROR DETECTION and maybe ERROR CORRECTION;

(d) storage (fax card, or machine with a large store) or printout (standard fax machine) of the received image.

FD, *abbrev. for* FULL DUPLEX.

FDM, *abbrev. for* FREQUENCY DIVISION MULTIPLEXING.

feasibility study, *n.* the consideration by a systems analyst of the pros and cons of possible solutions to an IT problem. This is an important stage in SYSTEMS ANALYSIS.

feature extraction or **pre-processing,** *n.* a process whereby a system seeks and extracts from a signal the features of interest, and rejects the rest. It is important in, for instance, speech recognition and optical character reading (OCR).

feed, *n.* **1.** any line into or out of a circuit or system, including one that supplies power (**power feed**) as well as one that carries a signal.

2. a method of passing paper through a scanner or printer. In the latter case the system may, for instance, use a (single) **sheet feed** method (perhaps using a SHEET FEEDER), pin (or sprocket) feed as with continuous FAN FOLD paper with sprocket holes down the edges, or **friction feed** (using rollers). **Line feed** involves moving the paper into a position where it is ready to be printed with a new line: lf (ASCII 10) is the signal that causes this to happen, while **form feed** (ff, code 12) moves the paper to the start of a fresh page.

There are also systems to feed media into drives, e.g. a magnetic tape into its path in a tape drive, or a compact disc from a 'jukebox' into the disc drive.

feedback, *n.* the return of part of an output signal to the input of the circuit concerned. The effect is to increase the input signal (**positive feedback**, also increasing GAIN), or to reduce it (**negative feedback**, reducing gain). The former is a crucial aspect of CONTROL, while the latter applies to self-correcting systems.

feeder (line), *n.* a line that carries power or signals into or out of a system. See FEED, sense 1.

FEP, *abbrev. for* FRONT END PROCESSOR.

FIBRE OPTICS

FET, *abbrev. for* FIELD EFFECT TRANSISTOR. See also MOS.

fetch, execute/reset or **cycle,** *n.* the cycle of actions in a processor in which the system fetches from store a single instruction, carries it out, and prepares for the next instruction. See MACHINE CYCLE. The **fetch phase** is the first part of that cycle.

FF, *abbrev. for* **1.** form FEED.
2. FLIP-FLOP.

fibre optics, *n.* the science and technology of carrying information or data on light waves, often in a highly transparent glass cable. A single light wave travels through the fibre by a series of internal reflections, as shown below, the process being the same even if the fibre bends through a sharp curve. This makes it easy to transfer a signal over a long distance. By 1990, the longest system planned is to link Japan and Europe via Russia (560 million bits per second over 17 000 km). However, one special technique had achieved sending data at 2.5 thousand million bits per second over a 2000 km route without amplification.

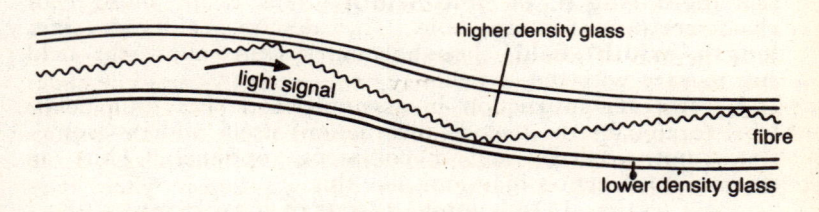

fibre optics.

The fact that a light wave has a very large band width compared to, say, a radio wave is just as significant as the transfer method. This means that it can carry a vast quantity of information. MODULATION is the process of adding a signal bearing information (or data) to a carrier wave, there being a number of ways to do this.

Moreover, by MULTIPLEXING, it is not hard to make the single carrier wave carry a number of signals at the same time: multiplexing ensures they remain distinct, so the reverse process at the end of the line can separate them again. By such means, a single light wave may carry dozens of video signals and hundreds, perhaps even thousands, of telephone conversations and fax and data transfers.

It is crucial that the source of the light wave should produce a tightly parallel beam of single frequency light. The laser (including the LIGHT EMITTING DIODE, a semiconductor laser) is able to do this; such light sources are simple, reliable and inexpensive.

The received signal does show some effect if the fibre suffers a distortion at some point. This effect is used in weighing machines and surveillance systems (e.g. those used for taking traffic censuses).

fiche, *n.* a type of MICROFORM in which the images lie in two dimensions on the surface of a rectangular sheet. See also SUPERFICHE and ULTRAFICHE.

field, *n.* a space for one item (or in certain cases, a block) of data. In a data base, a field is the space within the record of an entity (person or thing) for one attribute (characteristic) of that entity, e.g. part number, gender, half-life. If the field is the basis for a search of a file, it is called a **key field**; in any event, all fields in a data base have **field names** by which we can refer to them. Also, in most cases, each field has a given size (**field length**, or **field width**). This is the number of characters (bytes) it can hold. That describes a **fixed (size, length, width) field**, though some systems allow the field size to vary with the contents.

A computer instruction in assembly code has four fields: label (optional), the opcode (instruction) itself, address (sometimes not needed), and a comment (optional). Thus an assembly instruction may look like this:

```
          start   LDA    numb1    'start of main loop'
fields:   label   op     address  comment
```

A **video field** is one single screenful; in most cases, this is not the same as a frame (one single complete picture) as, to improve quality (by cutting FLICKER), a frame consists of two separate fields interlaced together. See TELEVISION.

field effect transistor (FET), *n.* a type of TRANSISTOR with three terminals: source, gate, and drain, with the gate current in control of the current in the channel between source and drain. See also MOS.

field flyback, see FLYBACK.

FIFO, *abbrev. for* FIRST IN, FIRST OUT.

fifth generation, *n.* the newest type of computer (and its software) based on parallel processing and machine intelligence. See FUTURE and GENERATION sense 2.

file, *n.* **1.** a data structure which can be viewed as an array whose fields do not have to be the same data type or size. It is perhaps the most important data structure. See also DATA BASE.
2. any adequately organized set of data in an IT system (main store or backing store). The term program files is therefore used as well as data and picture files. In the case of backing store, a **file allocation table (FAT)** is the system's directory of the store's contents (not the same as the directory the user can access, as the FAT includes, as well as the **file names**, a wealth of storage address details and codes). File control (**filing**, **file maintenance**, **file management**) is how the operating system organizes the files available, including storage, access and transfer. In practice the organization methods tend to depend on a file's characteristics, for they imply certain methods of storage and management. The main file characteristics are:
(a) size;
(b) GROWTH rate;
(c) ACTIVITY, measured by hit rate, the fraction of the records accessed or processed in, for instance, a day;
(d) VOLATILITY: the number of new and deleted records in a day.
File conversion involves changing a file from one storage medium to another, or from one type (format) to another.
File interrogation is the use of a program, perhaps within the operating software or a separate utility, to study the contents of a given file. **File inversion** is the process of making an INVERTED FILE, one with the same information as the main one, but sorted and ordered to make specific types of searching simpler.
A **file mark** is an end of file (EOF) marker. See END MARKER. **File protection** includes a number of methods to ensure nothing changes a file's contents in error; a **file protection ring**, for instance, is a ring attached to a magnetic tape to write-protect it (prevent any erasure or change). **File security**, on the other hand, includes methods of limiting access, such as the use of pass words and secure areas.
film recorder, *n.* **1.** a COMPUTER OUTPUT ON MICROFORM system (see also FOSDIC).
2. a camera used to take photographs of a screen, to give a form of hard copy.
filter, *n.* **1.** an electronic circuit or other system which passes

signals only if their frequencies are within a certain range. The range is the filter's pass band.
2. a similar device for passing only a certain band of frequencies of light (**colour filter**) or other such radiations
3. See MASK, sense 3.

fine index, *n.* a highly detailed index. See INDEXING. If an indexed file covers the surfaces of a number of disks, for example, a coarse index will tell you (or the system) which disk contains the record of interest; that disk will then have a fine index to point to the actual sector.

fine mode, *n.* a process for sending a fax image in more detail than the norm. Fine modes are not standard, but many systems now offer them. A few in fact now offer a superfine mode.

firmware, *n.* a jargon term for programs (software) stored on chips (hardware), i.e. part way between software and hardware. The first firmware involved HARD WIRING the system using real wire circuits rather than those in the surface of chips. Firmware is still described as hard-wired instructions.

first generation, *n.* the computers of the 1940s and 1950s, whose logic circuits were based on valves (electron tubes). See EDSAC, EDVAC and GENERATION sense 2.

first in, first out (FIFO), *adj.* describes how data items enter and leave a QUEUE data structure. Compare LAST IN, LAST OUT.

fixed field, *n.* a field able to store a fixed number of bytes. Compare FIXED LENGTH field.

fixed head, *adj.* denoting a disk drive unit with one head for each track, rather than one per surface. This is more complex, and less reliable; on the other hand, the arrangement much reduces access time. Fixed head systems are, however, now rare.

fixed (or **constant**) **length** (or **size** or **width**)**,** *adj.* (of a field or record in a data base, or of an IT system's word) unchanging in size whetever the circumstances. Working with fixed length makes life a great deal easier for the programmer, but leads to much loss of flexibility in handling data and instructions. Fixed length working is the current norm, however.

fixed-point number, *n.* a number held in a standard form, with the binary (or denary) point always in the same position. To do this means breaking the number into two parts (ignoring sign): the mantissa, which holds the actual value, and the exponent, which gives the size. A standard form in the case of denary (decimal) numbers has the mantissa always in the range

0.000...1 to 9.999...9. In that case, we give the distance between Earth and Moon (384 400 km) as 3.844×10^5 km).

IT systems often hold binary numbers in the same way (but with the binary point at the extreme left). Doing this increases the range over which stored numbers can lie, but reduces precision. See NUMBER. Compare FLOATING-POINT NUMBER.

fixed record, *n.* see FIXED LENGTH record.

flag, *n.* an indicator of a special situation or condition, sometimes called *marker, pointer, sentinel* or *tag.*
1. an indicator attached to a data item to show it as something special. It is, in effect, a subsidiary field (one-bit if the flag is binary, i.e. two-state).
2. a special character indicating that the next character does not have the normal meaning. The **flag code** is the same as the escape code (ESC).
3. a binary (i.e. two-state) cell in a **flag register** which when set to 1 by some action or event tells the software to do something out of the ordinary to cope. If the register has eight cells, the system can detect and handle eight such situations (e.g. arithmetic overflow, interrupt from a peripheral). At the start of each MACHINE CYCLE, the operating software checks the value of the flag register. If this is zero, no flags are set, which means there are no problems, so the cycle proceeds. If the register's value is not zero, its value codes the event that set the flag, so the system can take the correct action.

flatbed, *adj.* (of a scanner, e.g. in a fax machine, or copier) denoting a situation where the object to be scanned is placed face down on a flat glass sheet which then moves across the scanning array. Flatbed systems can cope with the pages of books and magazines and even solid objects; roller systems (the alternative) cannot.

In a **flatbed plotter** a sheet of paper is fixed and the pen moves over it by travelling up and down a track that itself moves to and fro. See also PLOTTER.

flexible manufacturing system (FMS), *n.* a system of making objects in a factory under full computer control using robot machine tools and robot transport systems. The approach is particularly suited to making prototypes, one-offs and objects in small batches (runs), because the flexibility it offers is very important. Such systems are also easy to build into a COMPUTER AIDED DESIGN AND MANUFACTURE system for the same reason.

flicker, *n.* a visual sensation produced by a low frequency var-

FLIP-FLOP

iation in brightness. If the variation is small, or if the frequency is high (above about 30 Hz), the brain does not register flicker consciously (though subconsciously it may still do so). Subconscious flicker can lead to headache and similar problems. Also, certain low-frequency flickers can induce epileptic fits in some people.

To reduce flicker to an acceptable level, many visual display systems, rather than showing a whole frame at 25 Hz or 30 Hz (the normal display frequency), INTERLACE two half frames (fields) at twice the frequency (see also TELEVISION).

flip-flop (FF), bistable or **toggle,** *n.* a device or system with two stable states. The system flips from one state to the other on a suitable input, and stays there until another suitable input makes it flop back. Such circuits form the basis of semiconductor storage, with a flip-flop for each bit. The Figure shows a typical flip-flop of this type, with each output fed back to the other input. Note, however, that there are other designs, and also that circuits with somewhat different behaviour may also have the same name.

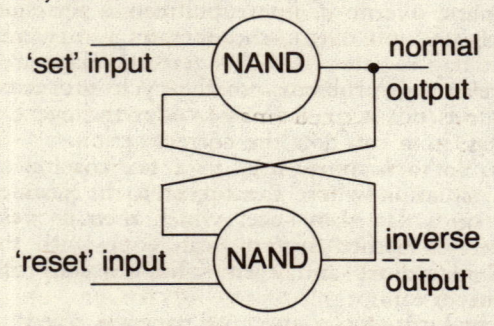

flip-flop. A simple (set-reset) flip-flop circuit.

flippy, *adj.* or *n.* a type of floppy DISK which can be turned over to allow the drive to access the second side.

floating-point number, *n.* a number held or shown in true value ('normal') form, with the decimal (denary) or binary point in its correct place. Compare 1500.56 (floating point form) with 1.50056×10^3 ('standard' form; see FIXED-POINT NUMBER). In the case of binary numbers in an IT system (where the space for a number is limited), floating-point numbers have higher precision than the fixed-point form (thus to use our denary example we would perhaps have to write 1500.56 as 1.500×10^3); on the other hand, they cover a lower range. See also NUMBER.

flooding, *n*. **1.** the filling of an enclosed space on screen with the current ink (foreground) colour or pattern, a common feature of paint (art) software.
2. the sending of a number of copies of a single packet through a packet-switched network to ensure speedy transfer to the other end (but at the cost of overloading the network).

floppy or **floppy disk,** *n*. a magnetic DISK made by coating thin sheet plastic, which the user can remove from the drive. Floppies come in various sizes (normally between 5.25 in (134 mm) and 3 in (76 mm) and can hold a few hundred kilobytes. However data storage densities are rising fast, and small floppies able to carry ten or 20 MB are likely soon.

FLOP, *abbrev. for* floating-point operation. See FLOPS.

floppy tape, or **stringy floppy** *n*. a type of backing store for micros that consists of a continuous loop, maybe a few metres long, of narrow video-quality magnetic tape. This gives very compact, cheap, high density, fast access storage; even so, such systems are now rare, as small discs and cheap chips have appeared.

FLOPS, *abbrev. for* floating-point operations per second, a measure of processor speed (mainly as megaflops or gigaflops). See also MIPS.

flow chart or **flow diagram,** *n*. a method of showing an algorithm or process (or a structure) in block form. The shapes of the blocks show the nature of each action or part. There are several standards that apply.

In IT, flow charts are common for showing the processes involved in a program (also, of course an algorithm). Compare STRUCTURE CHART. For SYSTEM FLOW CHART, see SYSTEM.

The Figure shows the main standard box shapes in each case. The normal flow of time in a chart of this type is shown as down and to the right (with arrows on the linking lines to show other flows).

flush, *adj.* level or even; straight-edged, or blocked (in word processing and such contexts). Most texts are **flush left** (blocked left, left justified), with all lines starting on the left at the same distance from the margin but ending on the right wherever the word lengths happen to take them (ragged right). The reverse, ragged left and straight at the right

FLUTTER

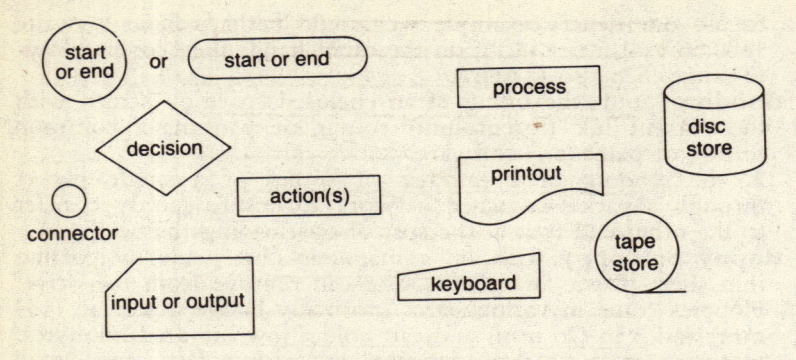

flowchart. Some program and system flowchart symbols.

margin, is **flush right**. Fully justified text is flush both left and right.

flutter, *n.* a fairly high frequency (above a few hertz) variation in the running speed of a tape, often caused by uneven wear in the drive. This can cause major problems if the tape is analog (e.g. audio). See also WOW.

flyback, *n.* in a cathode-ray tube display, the rapid return of the spot to the start of the next line (**line flyback**) or to the start of the next field (*field flyback*) or frame (*frame flyback*). The Figure shows a frame of an interlaced eight line display. The full lines are the displayed lines (spot switched on): the others are flyback lines (spot switched off): very short dashes indicate line flyback, short dashes indicate field flyback, and long ones show frame flyback.

flying spot, *n.* a (now rare) form of scanning, with a cathode-ray tube producing a fast moving spot of light, a lens system then focusing this on the sheet being scanned.

FM, *abbrev. for* FREQUENCY MODULATION.

FMS, *abbrev. for* FLEXIBLE MANUFACTURING SYSTEM.

folio, *n.* (*printing*) a single printed page and/or its page number.

font or **fount** *n.* the complete set of characters (including spaces) of a given typeface (style, design) in a given size. A **font disk** is a disk that carries one font for use in a phototypesetting system, or a disk that carries a face for use in a range of sizes in a particular computer printer. A **font chip** is a chip with the latter function (in fact much more common

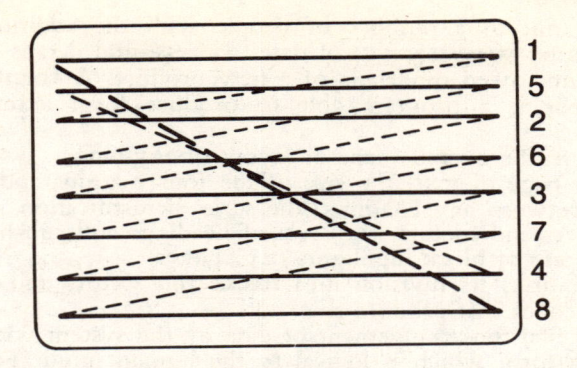

flyback. Flyback and interlacing on an eight-line display.

than a disk in recent years).

footing or **footer,** *n.* a message giving, for example, details of title, author, and/or page number, which can be set to appear automatically at the bottom of each page of a document.

footprint, *n.* **1.** the amount of worktop space taken up by a computer or other IT unit; a small footprint means you have to make less room available.
2. the area of the Earth's surface to which a satellite can send signals or from which it can receive them. See SATELLITE.

foreground, *n.* the text or graphics on a screen, as opposed to the screen itself (the background). Most systems allow the user to choose the colours of foreground ('ink') and background ('paper') to suit current needs.

forgiving, *adj.* describes a hardware and/or software system flexible enough to allow errors without crashing. See FRIENDLINESS.

formant, *n.* a unit of spoken sound, e.g. either a pure vowel or a pure consonant. Each formant consists of the pattern of **formant frequencies** that gives it its unique nature; analysis of each pattern is important in SPEECH RECOGNITION, while **formant synthesis** is a common approach to SPEECH SYNTHESIS.

form feed (FF), *n.* the process of feeding paper through a printer to the start of the next fresh sheet. A **form feed character (FF)** is a code (ASCII 12) sent to a printer that can obey such codes to produce this action.

form letter, *n.* a standard letter used in an organization for

FORMAT

sending out to a number of people with the addition only (perhaps by MAIL MERGING) of date, address, and details such as an amount owed or details of a new product. A **form letter generator** is a program able to produce form letters very easily.

format, *n*. the overall shape or layout of anything.

1. (of a page of text) the size of the four margins and of the gutter between any columns, the style of justification, the use of headers and footers, the style of headings and sub-headings and the use of block highlights (e.g. boxes).

2. (of a disk) its division into tracks and sectors and the recorded codes that produce this.

3. (of a file) the arrangement of data by the system within the file in a form which is logical to the human mind. **Formatting** is the process of preparing the format of disk, text, or file and subsequent layout within that pattern.

A **format character** (**format effecter**) is a code in a signal sent to an output unit (e.g. a printer) that controls the format of the data that follows.

Forth, *n*. a high-level program language which stores all data items in a stack. This makes it fast and very compact, and suits it to control. On the other hand coding is less straightforward than with most other languages; for example, arithmetic instructions must use reverse Polish (postfix) notation, with each operator after the operand concerned:

$$5\ 4\ +\ 4\ *\ 7\ +\quad \text{for}\quad 7+4\times(5+4)$$

Forth was published by Charles Moore, a US astronomer, in 1968. He designed it for telescope control, and named it as a 'fourth generation' language, but had to call it Forth rather than Fourth as his computer could not accept names of more than five characters. A Forth program consists of separate 'words' (instructions), each defining an action. The system compiles each word straight after entry, so flags errors at once.

Fortran, *n*. the first high-level program language, produced by John Backus and others in the mid-1950s, and still very common in science and engineering because of its great numerical processing power. (The name comes from 'formula translation'.)

Fortran's only data structure is the array (or matrix), and the data types include double-precision and complex numbers. This structure and the data types are declared as follows at the start of a program:

```
DIMENSION array1(17,6), freqrange(50)
DOUBLE PRECISION pi, resonance
COMPLEX accurrent, acvoltage
```
Fortran coding and compilation are very efficient operations. Indeed the compiler can translate sub-routines (procedures or modules) individually, and Fortran sub-routine libraries are common and important. On the other hand, the language is weak at handling input/output and files.

forward chain, *n.* a style of knowledge base searching in an EXPERT SYSTEM. The system scans through the knowledge base for rules that relate to the current query (search), and applies the rule(s) found in order to reach an answer. Compare BACKWARD CHAIN.

forward channel, *n.* a channel in telecommunications that carries control signals in the same direction as the main signal. The control signals may include codes for error handling or general supervision. Compare BACKWARD CHANNEL.

FOSDIC, *n. acronym. for* Film Optical Scanning Device for Input to Computers, a system for scanning film images (originally of punched cards, now of microform) for specific data, and copying the records to main store (originally to a card punch); a method of COMPUTER INPUT FROM MICROFORM.

fount, *n.* an alternative term for FONT.

Fourier analysis, *n.* a system of breaking down a complex wave form into a set of pure waves (harmonics) of different frequencies and amplitudes.

fourth generation, *adj.* (of IT systems, from about 1970) based on very large-scale integration of components in chips, and correspondingly powerful software. See GENERATION, sense 2.

fox message, *n.* a standard signal that contains a whole character set, used to test an IT system (e.g. a keyboard or a communications channel). A simple form is 'a quick brown fox jumps over the lazy dog'; but a real fox message should use ALL available characters (e.g. digits, symbols, and shifted characters as well as letters).

frame, *n.* **1.** a set of bits lying across a paper or magnetic tape (equivalent to a column of a punched card).
2. one screenful of video data, with a frame built up of two FIELDS in most cases. **Frame control** is a feature of video tape players that provides the synchronization needed for them to play tapes made on other machines. A **frame grabber** is a circuit able to accept and store a single frame for continuous

display (specially in videotex systems) or for access and processing by computer. For **frame flyback**, see FLYBACK.
3. one screenful of videotex data (with a page perhaps having a number of frames). A **frame code** is a signal sent to synchronize the display with the data.
4. part of the opening synchronizing signal of a packet in a packet switching system.
5. a packet of data in a PACKET RADIO system.

free indexing, *n*. INDEXING, i.e. text data base searching, without restriction on the search terms used.

free running, *adj*. denoting a system that allows a number of users access to a data base at the same time.

freedom of information, *n*. the availability of information on IT systems. This is protected by both national and international laws. The British Computer Misuse Act of 1990 makes it a criminal offence without permission to:
  (a) access data held in an IT system;
  (b) modify stored data by adding, deleting, amending, or in any way;
  (c) cause the disruption of software operation;
  (d) cause stored data to become unreliable.

A further aspect of such laws may be the de-regulation of telecommunications, e.g. to remove restrictions on the use of frequencies and cable systems.

frequency, *n*. the number of events of a given type in a given time. In most cases it is the number of waves (cycles) of an analog signal in a second; the unit is the hertz (Hz). Frequency is the most common way to distinguish between signals or their carriers (see SPECTRUM, for instance).

  Frequency division multiplexing (FDM) is a form of MULTIPLEXING; the different signals in a wide band channel have carriers that differ in frequency. **Frequency modulation (FM)** or **frequency shift keying (FSK)** is a type of MODULATION that involves the changing of the carrier's frequency to represent the signal carried: see Figure.

  Frequency re-use is the use of the same frequency for signals passing through it in very different directions (rather than a different frequency band for each). It can much increase the signal handling capacity of a satellite.

friction feed, *n*. a method of pulling paper through a printer or scanner by using rollers that press on it rather than pins (sprockets) that pull on holes in the paper's edges. See FANFOLD.

FULL DUPLEX

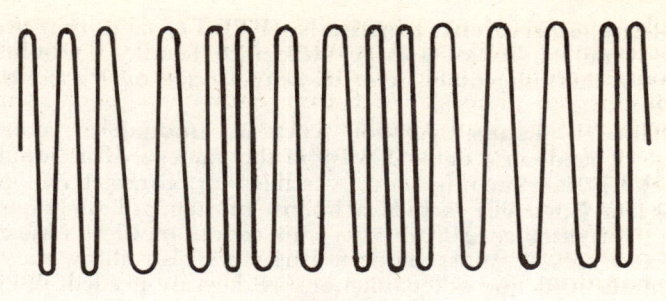

frequency.

friendliness, *n.* any aspect of a system that can reduce the user's fear or uncertainty. Friendly systems are forgiving, reliable, easy to use, and consistent in the instructions the user must follow. A friendly screen display is well laid out and uncluttered, uses colour and other highlighting effects with care, and always shows what to do next. Friendly systems have friendly manuals (if they need manuals at all); these are also well laid out and uncluttered, easy to follow, and highlighted with care.

The design of friendly systems always involves discussion with typical users, rather than relying on hardware or software experts who may have forgotten what it is like to be inexperienced in computer use.

front end, *n.* another term for USER INTERFACE, e.g. a terminal of a mainframe. A **front end processor (FEP)** is an input/output processor designed to handle (e.g. format) input and output data. A **front end system** is a micro-computer with a similar task, but even more able to relieve the main processor of the need to take care of aspects of the user interface.

FSK, *abbrev. for* FREQUENCY SHIFT KEYING.

FTET, *abbrev. for* FULL TIME EQUIVALENT TERMINALS.

FTF, see TELECONFERRING.

full adder, *n.* an ADDER with three inputs, for the two bits to be added and a carry bit from a previous addition. A full adder may consist of two half adders linked. See ADDER, fig. 2.

full connection, *n.* a system of networking in which each node links directly to each of the others.

full duplex, *n.* a term for DUPLEX communication, which can involve signals both ways at the same time.

full-time equivalent terminals (FTET), *n.* a measure of the overall ability of a large system to handle a number of users at the same time, or of its actual usage over a period of time.

function, *n.* **1.** any operation where the (output or returned) value depends in a defined way on the value(s) of its input independent argument(s) (i.e. variables or parameters). Most program languages include a library of standard functions (to give, for instance, square root and trigonometrical ratios like sin and arctan); most modern languages also allow the programmer to define other functions as they are needed.

Functions, defined suitably, can act on any data types; the value returned may differ in type from that of the argument. Thus the Basic function LEN acts on a string argument and returns a number (the number of characters in the string); it is called a numeric function on the basis of the type of value returned.

As a good program language allows the user to define functions in the same way as procedures, procedures are also sometimes called functions. However, strictly, a procedure causes an action while a function returns a value.

2. a specific action in a system. This is controlled by a **function code** or CONTROL CODE, or by pressing a **function key** (a keyboard key whose action is defined by software or the user rather than being fixed).

functional, *adj.* denoting anything concerned with one specific task or duty, or a small set of them. Thus an IT system's **functional element** (or **functional unit**) is a circuit or unit with just one function. A **functional program language** is a DECLARATIVE PROGRAM LANGUAGE where the mathematical actions involve recursion. In such a language, a program consists of a set of equations (mathematical statements) in no special order; these define values in terms of other values, and functions in terms of recursion, other functions, and values: 'running' the program involves setting the system to solve all those equations.

future technology, *n.* those aspects of IT whose future development we can attempt to predict from our standpoint in the present. In the field of information technology, it is particularly hard to predict even the near future, however well recent trends are understood. Thus, the industry over recent decades shows highly constant trends in improved and more flexible hardware, miniaturization, and the purchase price,

FUZZY LOGIC

power, and running costs of IT systems. Recent predictions have been made suggesting that, not long into the 21st century, each person will have a wristwatch style PC to talk with that has more power than the currently largest supercomputer and can communicate with any other wrist PC in the world. This is be no means certain, however. In the same way, we cannot expect to successfully make predictions by extending current trends in software, machine intelligence, or robotics. See also IT GENERATIONS, ELECTRONIC COTTAGE, GLOBAL VILLAGE.

fuzzy logic or **fuzzy theory,** *n.* a form of computer logic based on present knowledge of human thinking processes. It attempts to link a degree of truth with its statements (perhaps by giving their probability as a number between 0-fully false- and 1-fully true), rather than making purely binary statements, i.e. ones that can only be true or false. Fuzzy logic presently occupies a central role in research into machine intelligence, particularly in relation to expert systems and neural networks.

A **fuzzy set** contains data items where each of the values can lie anywhere between 0 and 1 (rather than being just 0 or 1). If each data item represents a probability, a fuzzy logic system is in place. As well as being crucial to knowledge based machine intelligence, uses of such an approach range through image analysis (as in **fuzzy video**), power station control, and running transport systems.

G

g, *symbol for* gram, a thousandth of a kilogram (unit of mass).

G, *symbol for* **1.** GIGA, unit prefix for 1 000 000 000 (10^9), as in 10 GB, ten thousand million bytes.
2. (*telegraphy*) a six-bit word.
3. (*electronics*) conductance, a measure of how well a circuit or line passes current.

GaAs, *symbol for* GALLIUM ARSENIDE.

gain, *n.* **1.** the ratio of the output strength, i.e. power P_2 (or voltage V_2 or current I_2), of a circuit or system to the input value (P_1, etc.) a measure of amplification (the efficiency of an amplifier).

Being a ratio, gain has no unit. However, even if the output is less than the input (attenuation rather than gain), we tend to quote it in DECIBELS (dB), the ratios being as follows:

$$10\log(P_2/P_1) \quad 20\log(V_2/V_1) \quad 20\log(I_2/I_1)$$

A power gain of 3.010 dB is the same as a doubling in signal strength; −3.010 dB denotes halving. (Most people use the value 3).

A **gain control** is a device used to vary a system's gain, as with the volume control of a television set. It is often a variable resistor.

2. (*telecommunications*) the efficiency of a directional aerial compared to that of a simple (an omnidirectional) one.

gallium arsenide (GaAs), *n.* a semiconductor material used for making chips (integrated circuits), with a number of advantages over silicon. It has a gap width of 1.4 V, and transistors made from it work at up to 400 °C. Gallium arsenide chips are likely to replace those made from silicon because:

(a) they can work at a higher temperature;

(b) they can be smaller (so use less power and act five or six times faster);

(c) they can link much better to microwave and fibre optic systems;

(d) they can survive high radiation levels.

On the other hand, they are harder to produce and to work

with and more costly than silicon chips. Despite these problems, however, the Cray-3 super-computer uses GaAs chips.

Gallium phosphide has an even higher maximum working temperature (870 °C); on the other hand, its gap width of 2.4 V is too large to allow easy use at present.

game paddle, *n.* an input unit rather like a joystick. See PADDLE.

game theory, *n.* a branch of mathematics (first worked on in 1921, and named a few years later by VON NEUMANN). It deals with the best choice of action in cases of conflict of interest. The aim is to help a player best oppose the effects of chance or an opponent, so it concerns strategy rather than tactics. It involves statistics and solutions obtained by LINEAR PROGRAMMING.

Game theory is the basis of many kinds of SIMULATION run on computers (e.g. for training), and MACHINE INTELLIGENCE. It is, in essence, an important field that involves statistics and probability.

Gantt chart, *n.* a method of showing a project (e.g. as the output of a CRITICAL PATH ANALYSIS program) as bars for the different activities on a time chart.

gap, *n.* **1.** the space between two blocks of data in backing store. The term is most common in the case of magnetic tape, where the **gap width** is fixed, often at 19 mm). See also GUARD BAND.

2. the energy difference between the top of the valence band of a substance and the bottom of its conduction band. The Figure shows two typical cases with, for the n-type semi-

gap.

conductor, the DONOR levels that add electrons to the substance. The **gap width** measures this, and is normally quoted in electron volts or volts rather than joules, 1 eV being about 1.6×10^{-19} J. The value is a crucial factor in how effective a substance is as a semiconductor (see, for instance, GALLIUM ARSENIDE).

3. the space between the head of a storage reading/writing unit and the surface of the medium concerned (e.g. magnetic disk), **gap width** being the distance concerned. On the other hand, the **head gap** is the distance between the two poles of a magnetic read/write head: the smaller the gap, the higher the data transfer rate (frequency) the drive can handle.

gap bit, gap digit or **gap character** *n.* a parity bit, check digit or check character: a unit of data used for error detection that does not carry any fresh information.

garbage, *n.* any unwanted or meaningless data. An IT system's store is always full of data; as well as that involved in current work, there is garbage left from random currents at switch on, from tasks now finished and from deleted files. The CHARACTER FILL and **garbage collection** (also known as *housecleaning*) deal with this in two ways. Good modern systems carry out both actions regularly and automatically. The garbage is data that may be of interest to other people. For security reasons it is therefore best to erase it properly. A character fill will replace each byte of garbage with a random character or with, say, 0 or X.

If the garbage is spread through the store between chunks of data the system still needs, access to that data will be slow, files will be split into separately stored sections, and there is a danger of running out of storage space. The garbage collection process brings together at the start of the store all the data still required, leaving all the garbage in one large space at the end. See also GIGO.

Note also the slogan **garbage in: garbage out**. This warns that input errors must lead to errors in results.

gas-plasma display or **gas panel** or **gas tube,** *n.* a type of flat-screen system. It consists of an array of electrodes in a flat oblong gas-filled tube; changing the voltage of a set of electrodes ionizes the gas at those points, thus making the gas discharge and emit light. The colour of the display (monochrome only available at the moment) depends on the gas; in most cases this is neon, with an orange output. Different designs provide text-only displays or allow text and graphics.

GATE

Current plasma displays cost more than LIQUID-CRYSTAL displays (lcds); they do not, however, use more power, and they do not need a separate light source.

gate, *n.* **1.** the control electrode of a field-effect TRANSISTOR.
2. a basic logic circuit (element), the value of whose single output depends on the input value(s). Truth tables are used to show the output value for each possible set of inputs. Here we use the binary values 0 and 1 throughout, though in IT systems the values are two levels of voltage, while in logic (Boolean algebra) they are False and True. The three main gates are shown in Fig. 1.

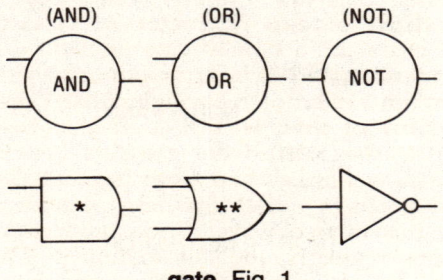

gate. Fig. 1.

The two-input AND and OR gates shown are common; so too are gates with more than two inputs. The NOT, on the other hand, has only one input. Other important gates are shown in Fig. 2, again shown for two inputs only:

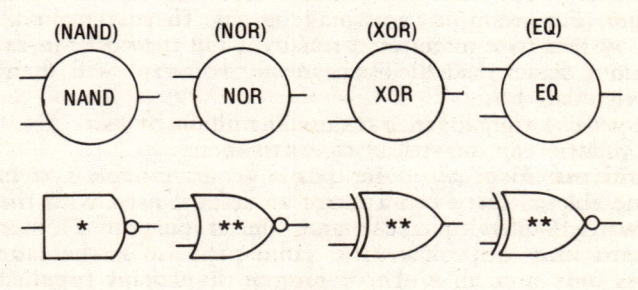

gate. Fig. 2.

The six two-input (strictly multi-input) gates shown provide

GATEWAY

all input/output patterns required of logic circuits. There are other possible patterns; working back from truth tables, one can design a set of basic gates to give any effect.

Indeed, some sets of NAND gates alone can produce any desired effect. NAND logic systems use only NAND gates. While NAND logic often makes elements more complex than when using basic gates, it is much cheaper. This is also the case with NOR gates. Fig. 3 shows how to link NOR gates to produce any basic output pattern.

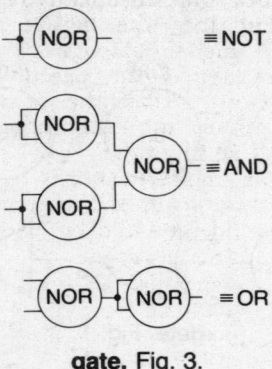

gate. Fig. 3.

All the functional elements in the processors of all IT systems consist of sets of gates. See, for example, ADDER.

gateway, *n.* an electronic link between two differently organized networks that allows users of one to enter the second. For example, you may be able to pass from a viewdata system to a mainframe run by a rail network, in order to find out travel details. The gateway software will then be in the viewdata host.

GB, *symbol for* gigabyte, a thousand million bytes.

GDT, *abbrev. for* GRAPHIC DISPLAY TERMINAL.

general purpose, *adj.* describing a programmable system, that is one able to carry out a range of tasks if used with the right software. General purpose and special purpose IT hardware systems may both have the same processors; the latter can access only a small range of programs, perhaps supplied on a ROM chip, while the former will have backing store and therefore access to an almost unlimited range of applications. A **general purpose** program is applications software with a

GENERATIONS

single field of action, but whose users can input values (parameters) to restrict it to a more narrow task. A **general purpose language** is a high-level program language able to work in more than one broad field (e.g. science, commerce and data file handling). Basic is of this type.

generations, *n.* **1.** (file) the hierarchy of day-to-day master files produced and used in an office. A master file is one that contains current data for searching and sorting by the users. Each working day, however, there are a number of new transactions (e.g. sales, staff changes, changes of product data) the firm must merge into the master file to make a new master. In that merging process (also important to provide backup), the old master is the parent (father) of the new master, the child (son). After the next merge, the parent becomes the grandparent, the child becomes the parent, and there is a new child (see Figure).

For security reasons, it is the norm to store each past generation in files separate from the current master (child) and from each other. Should the child be lost for some reason, the firm can then re-create it.

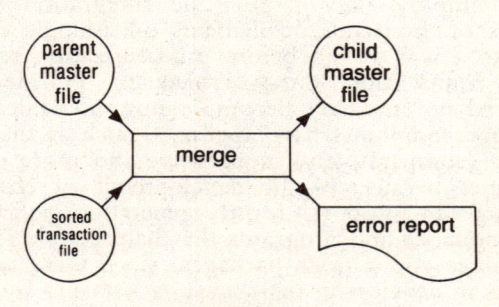

generations.

2. (IT) the hierarchy of IT hardware design types, and of the software they can handle. The five generations are shown below (though people differ in the details). The systems of each stage have offered, compared to the previous generation:
  (a) reduced size;
  (b) increased speed;
  (c) reduced purchase cost;
  (d) reduced power and cooling need;
  (e) reduced running cost;

GENERATIONS

(f) increased reliability;
(g) more potential for standardization.

First generation (i.e. from the 1940s and 1950s, such as ACE, EDSAC, EDVAC, ENIAC, LEO). The hardware used electron (vacuum) tubes (called valves) for switching, arithmetic and logic. VON NEUMANN's stored program concept appeared in 1946, with systems after that being the same in principle as those of today. Hardware standardization in detail did not follow until ten years later, however, and programming was only in machine code.

Second generation (late 1950s, early 1960s, e.g. ATLAS). The TRANSISTOR (invented 1948) came to replace the electron tube, and computers with a modular design appeared. Fortran, the first high level language, came out in 1957, and very many others followed in the next few years.

Third generation (1964-late 1980s): more and more transistors were packed into integrated circuits (chips), first patented in 1953. System size and cost fell so much that the micro (personal computer) was born in the early 1970s.

Fourth generation (late 1980s-): the chips in current systems employ very large scale integration (VLSI), with hundreds of thousands of elements on a single chip. There is still quite a way to go before miniaturization reaches current physical limits (the QUANTUM BARRIER). Full feature pocketbook-sized systems have become common, while, on the other hand, supercomputers have appeared, such as the Cray-3. The latter are (comparatively) inexpensive and more powerful than mainframes because of the development of effective parallel processing. In support, fourth generation software involves data dictionaries and programs that help people specify, design and produce applications packages, since there are now many problems in developing HIGH-LEVEL PROGRAM LANGUAGES.

Fifth generation systems are still being developed, but they are expected by the mid-1990s. Rather than continuing the trend to miniaturization (although that remains constant at present), designers are looking at quite novel styles of working. Parallel processing (and data-flow architecture) will be the hardware norm of the fifth generation, while progress in machine intelligence should produce software that can learn by experience and with which users can work in natural (human) language. LISP, OCCAM and PROLOG are relevant program languages of today. Highly complex relational database systems and effective image recognition (machine vision, very significant in robotics), speech recognition and synthesis for the user interface can also be expected. Thus a real fifth-generation system will be a personal SUPERCOMPUTER. See also FUTURE.

Fifth generation concepts first became widely discussed in 1981 when Japan invited other countries to join a major research and development programme. The invitation was turned down, and various single countries and groups started similar programmes. In the early 1990s the race is between Japan's ICOT, Europe's Esprit, MCC (civil) and Darpa (military) in the US, and the successors of Alvey in Britain (though there is a good deal of cooperation between the developers of these programmes). The British Alvey programme of 1983–88 had the aim of aiding education, training and product development in the IT industries. However the training component was dropped, as was direct support of industry by Government purchase. The project budget was £350 million; success was mixed.

generic, *adj*. denoting off the shelf (i.e. generally available), or not specific. **Generic coding/mark up** involves adding codes to a document in store (e.g. with a word processor) so any database management or typesetting system can work with it. **Generic software** is classes of software. It could be spreadsheets or software for physics teaching rather than any specific example.

geographical data base, *n* a database used for storing many types of geographical data such as weather and climate details, pollution levels of various kinds, land cover and usage, and species of plants and animals. The largest such data base is the United Nations' GRID (Global Resource Information Data base); this contains over 60 GB of data.

geostationary, *adj*. unchanging with respect to a point on the Earth's surface. Thus a **geostationary orbit** is one in which satellites move round the Earth at the same rate as the Earth rotates: the orbit must be in the same plane as the Equator and be about 35 700 km in radius. A **geostationary satellite** (or **geosynchronous satellite**) is one in such an orbit; its FOOTPRINT on the Earth's surface is fixed, so that ground aerials, once set up, point always in the same direction to send to, and receive from, it. Satellites for broadcasting and/or communications require such an approach; satellites used for survey are more effective in a polar orbit of much smaller radius because they cover a wide area.

GHOST

Because the Earth (and therefore its gravitational field) is not perfectly regular, geosynchronous satellites in fact cycle slightly about their fixed position. As long as the movement is very small (a tiny fraction of a degree) there is no problem in use.

ghost, *n.* a faint image sometimes seen when watching television pictures, slightly shifted with respect to the main image, that is caused by reflection of the broadcast signal from, for instance, a large building or steep hill.

GHz, *symbol for* gigahertz, a thousand million hertz (cycles per second). The frequencies of radar and uhf (L-band) radio signals are of this order.

giga-, (symbol **G**) *unit prefix* for 10^9, a thousand million. A video disc can store several **gigabytes** (GB) of data. A modern supercomputer may be able to work at the rate of several **gigaflops**, i.e. several thousand million floating point operations a second. Radar waves are in the GHZ region. **Giga-scale integration** is the design and production of chips that contain a thousand million elements. This has not yet been achieved (see INTEGRATION).

GIGO, *abbrev. for* 'GARBAGE IN: GARBAGE OUT', a warning that you cannot expect an IT system to output correct data if you do not input correct data (or instructions).

GKS, *abbrev. for* GRAPHIC KERNEL SYSTEM.

glass fibre, *n.* a hair-thin strand of pure glass used to carry signals on light waves; see FIBRE OPTICS.

global, *adj.* denoting comprehensive, able to apply to a large range of cases or objects, if not a complete set. In word processing, for example, **global editing** involves using just one command to make the same type of change throughout a whole document (or a marked section), e.g. changing to right justification or using a **global search and replace** action. In a program, you may call a **global function** from, and use a **global variable** in, any part of the program, rather than just (locally) within one procedure.

global village *n.* a phrase coined by Marshall McLuhan to describe a future world brought about by universal cheap electronic communications. In this world, all people (i.e. over the whole globe) have ready contact with all others, and can access vast amounts of up to date information. Other people later enlarged the concept to include further aspects of village life IT could influence on a large scale, such as mutual help, friendliness, security. See also ELECTRONIC COTTAGES.

glossary, *n.* a list of specialized words and phrases with notes on meanings, A **glossary command** (or **glossary function**) is the name given by some word processors to a form of global search and replace. Here you type, say, <a for one common complex phrase (e.g. your firm's name), <b for a second, and so on. When you have finished the document, you then command the system to replace all such codes with the full phrases. In some cases a simple program approach can automate this. A **glossary package** is an electronic glossary kept in main or backing store for users of word processors or database managers to call on for the meanings of words when needed.

golfball printer, *n.* a now rarely used printer with a whole character set embossed on the surface of a sphere-shaped print head. The golf ball twists and turns to bring each character to be printed in contact with the ribbon.

grandparent or **grandfather,** *n.* the second (and usually oldest) reserve master file in a system of file GENERATION (merging, backup).

graph, *n.* a pictorial representation of a set of numeric data. Modern **graph drawing software** can display on screen very many types of graph in two or three dimensions, with full effective use of colour and shading to aid communication: line graphs, bar charts (histograms), pie diagrams and pictograms, for instance. Suitable hardware (graphics printers and plotters and film or video units) can transfer the screen images to paper, negative or video tape, in the last case perhaps with animation.

A **graph follower** is an input device able to scan a graph on paper and transfer an image to screen and computer store for editing and/or insertion into a document. For **graph pad** and **graph tablet**, see GRAPHICS PAD.

Graph reduction is a style of parallel processing likely to be significant in fifth-generation systems. Software translates ('reduces') each task into a tree-like graph, each node in the tree then going to one of the processors.

graphic, *n.* or *adj.* any pictorial representation of a structure or concept, e.g. a line diagram or flow chart. **Graphic data reduction** is the changing of graphic material into a digital form an IT system can handle (e.g., using a scanner). A **graphic display terminal (GDT)** is a terminal or work station where users can see and work with high resolution graphics. The **graphic kernel system (GKS)** is a major standard for

GRAPHICS

graphics handling software; it defines almost 200 functions and specifies hardware features and links with software. **Graphic structure input (GSI)** is a method of searching a data base which contains graphics (e.g. chemical structures); the user sketches the design of interest as part of the input process. A **graphic user interface (GUI)** gives the user a desktop-like environment to work in, and thus is more friendly than a text-based system; see also WIMP.

For other types of **graphic hardware** (input and output units able to accept or display graphics), see GRAPHICS PERIPHERAL. For other **graphic software**, see GRAPHICS SOFTWARE.

graphics, *n.* the whole field of handling pictorial material in IT, with hardware and software aspects. The crudest systems may display and print low-resolution pictures (**block graphics**) as strings of **graphics characters.** These are part of the system's **graphics character set**. To enter these, the user may be able to put the keyboard in **graphics mode**, or may have to use complex combined key presses.

There are many special designs of **graphics peripheral** (an input or output unit able to accept or display non-text data). A **graphics pad** (or **graphics tablet**) is an input unit on which the user can draw or write, with the design displayed on screen and held in store for editing or some other form of processing. There are many designs of pad, but all have a sensing system (e.g. pressure, electric, light, infra-red, acoustic) able to detect the pointing device from moment to moment. Cruder pointers include JOYSTICK, MOUSE, PADDLE, TOUCH SCREEN and TRACKER BALL; see Figure.

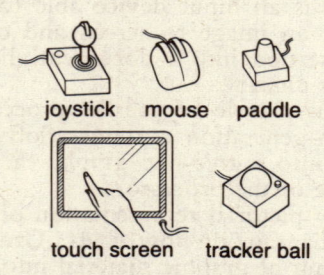

graphics peripherals. Pointing devices.

On the output side, units able to display graphics on a screen are needed (the higher the RESOLUTION, the better), or to put

GRAY CODE

pictures on paper (dot printer or plotter), photographic film (e.g. COMPUTER OUTPUT ON MICROFORM) or video tape/disc. Output on film as a 35mm slide or overhead projector transparency or on video tape/disc (with, in this case, the possibility of animation) is now part of the popular field of PRESENTATION GRAPHICS. This combines high-resolution graphics software (see below) with drivers for suitable output units. The aim of such systems is to produce materials that improve the presentation of data at conferences and in sales meetings, for instance.

Apart from presentation graphics and COMPUTER AIDED DRAWING (CAD), **graphics software** is of two types: **business graphics**, for the design of graphs of data (see GRAPH DRAWING SOFTWARE), and ART SOFTWARE (or painting) programs. The latter make the sketching, editing and polishing on screen (using a mouse) of freehand pictures and designs very straightforward. The user can call on a number of standard shapes and line styles, various sizes and shapes of text character, a range of foreground (called ink) and background (called paper) colours and patterns, and block features such as move, transform (e.g. stretch, rotate, shear) and copy.

Gray code, *n.* a code for binary numbers. The four-bit version is as follows:

denary	binary	Gray	
0	0000	0000	
1	0001	0001	-
2	0010	0011	
3	0011	0010	
4	0100	0110	-
5	0101	0111	
6	0110	0101	-
7	0111	0100	
8	1000	1100	
9	1001	1101	-
10	1010	1111	
11	1011	1110	-
12	1100	1010	
13	1101	1011	
14	1110	1001	-
15	1111	1000	

Invented by Elisha Gray in the 19th century, this is a 'reflected

GRAY SCALE

binary code' as, apart from their most significant bits, the words are symmetrical about the centre (see the dashes on the right of the table). It is also a unit code because each value differs from its neighbours in only one bit; this is of great value in error detection.

Gray coding is commonly used in analog-to-digital units and telemetry (measuring at a distance). Telemetric data (e.g. from remote weather sensors) tends to change value slowly, in this case from one word to its neighbour; so, if more than one bit value changes, it is easy to detect a possible error. For much the same reason, it is also often used to code the cell-by-cell output of video cameras and other kinds of output which involve a GREY SCALE.

Gray coded wheels are common for reading the position of a shaft as it turns. One example might be a wheel using four bits (with an angular resolution of 360/16 = 22.5 degrees) and an array of four light sources and sensors. Other systems can read position by electrical or magnetic means. It is easy (if costly) to increase resolution by using more bits.

gray scale, see GREY SCALE.

grey, *adj.* denoting part way between black (no light) and white (full light). A **grey document** is one not published in the normal way (i.e. it is not fully available to the public), such as an internal report or a samizdat (underground news sheet). Document data bases that include grey documents are of much more value than those without as they hold more information.

A system's **grey scale** is the number of shades (including black and white) it can work with. For example, some fax machines and cards can send and receive an image with 16 greys, and so can handle multi-tone pictures (especially photos) very well. This is costly, for the scanner and the printer must be able to handle this level of resolution, and the transfer takes four times as long at a given bit rate. However, newspapers have worked with such grey scales for decades, and some office fax machines and cards now offer them.

grid, *n.* **1.** a set of lines (like those on graph paper) some art programs offer the user to help in layout, or the same kind of feature in other systems.

2. a pattern of dots that make up a character on screen or as output by a dot printer, or which a character reading system checks as it goes through the process of trying to identify a character.

GULP

3. the layout of a spreadsheet (rows, columns and maybe pages of cells).
4. the current-control electrode of a cathode-ray tube (and of a triode, the electron tube the simple transistor replaced): so called as it is a mesh of fine wire through which the electrons pass.

gross index, *n.* a broad-ranging but poorly detailed index in a hierarchical INDEXING system. After using the gross index to find the right section (e.g. the disk that holds the part you want of a file), a fine index gives the exact place (e.g. sector). Some reference books work in the same way.

group, *n.* a set of related objects or systems. **Grouping** data means putting the items in related sets. This is a method of sorting a file, for example. The word 'group' can also be used as an equivalent for FIELD. A **group mark** is a code used to show the start or end of a set of data. See FAX for Group 1, Group 2, and Group 3. See also MARK READER.

growth, *n.* a measure of the rate of increase of data in a file (e.g. number of records per month). Planners must take account of this characteristic of a file (along with its size, activity and volatility) as it affects the storage method, for instance.

GSI, *abbrev. for* GRAPHIC STRUCTURE INPUT, a method of searching a data base which contains graphics (e.g. chemical structures).

guard band, *n.* an unused space to prevent interference between two data stores or carriers; a strip between two tracks on a tape or frequency band between two channels.

GUI, *abbrev. for* GRAPHICAL USER INTERFACE.

guide, *n.* a method of showing the user the path of tape in a tape machine or of film in a camera or projector.

gulp, *n.* an alternative term for a double byte, a 16-bit item in an IT system with an eight-bit word length.

H

half adder, *n.* the simplest binary ADDER, with two inputs and two outputs. One possible design appears in the Figure, but whatever the design may be, the truth table immediately below the Figure shows the outputs for all inputs. If the outputs are labelled O2 and O1 as S(um) and C(arry), the table gives the correct results of two-bit binary addition (as this appears at the end of each line).

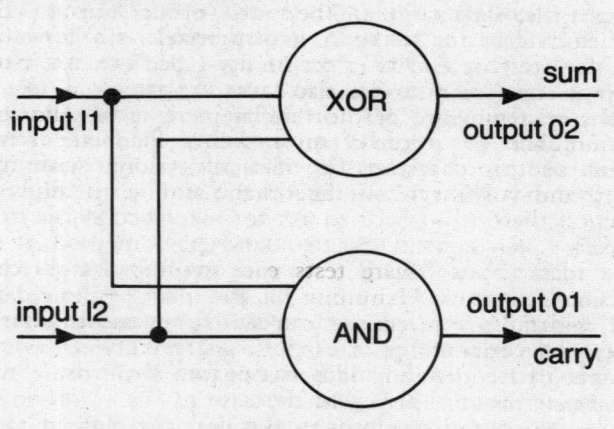

half adder.

```
I1 I2 O2 O1
 0  0  0  0    0+0=00
 0  1  0  1    0+1=01
 1  0  0  1    1+0=01
 1  1  1  0    1+1=10
```

Such an adder is too simple to be of any use as it stands; joining two half adders to make a full adder allows a third input, and if this is a carry bit from a previous addition, the system can now add binary numbers fully.

half duplex (HD/X), *n.* or *adj.* denoting communication through a channel which can be either way, but only one way at a time. Compare SIMPLEX and (full) DUPLEX.

halftone, *n*. or *adj*. denoting a picture with parts other than pure black and pure white, i.e. with a GREY SCALE. Traditionally, all print media printed such pictures as a grid of black dots on white paper. The larger the dots, the darker the image at that point. Now there are many ways to produce halftone (grey scale) pictures, for example by using different sizes of dots.

half word, *n*. a data unit in an IT system (i.e. a set of bits it can handle as a unit) that is half the system's standard word length. Using half words on occasion can speed up processing, but to do so is complex, so the approach is rare.

Hamming code, *n*. a method of coding binary numbers before transfer, to allow both error detection and error correction, devised by Richard Hamming (a US mathematician). Take the case of four-bit data words: adding a PARITY bit means one redundant bit for each word. That allows error detection, and the receiver must then request the sender to transmit the word again. The Hamming code involves three extra (redundant) bits: on the other hand, as it allows error correction there is no need to ask for incorrect words to be repeated.

The receiver's software tests each word with three parity checks, one for each Hamming bit and a set of three data bits. If the test fails, the receiver can work out which data bit is wrong, and correct (flip) it.

Simple parity checking fails if two bits flip during transfer: the receiver flags no error. In the case of the Hamming code, the receiver can detect that two bits have flipped, but not which ones. In this case, it can request a repeat. Thus the Hamming system is 'single error correction, double error detection', whereas simple parity checking is 'single error detection' only.

hand(s) free phone, *n*. a form of telephone which the user does not need to hold continuously to operate. The term is used to describe systems anywhere along the spectrum between a telephone you can call from without picking up the handset (but you must pick it up when you want to speak) and a light headset with earpiece and throat microphone. None are fully hands free: there will be at least some manual method of 'dialling' until truly effective speech recognition by machines has been achieved.

HANDLER

handler, *n.* the special part of some operating software systems that deals with the needs of peripherals.

handshake, *vb.* to exchange setting up signals before a data transfer takes place. In a **handshaking** process, the sending unit calls and the other responds; the two then exchange necessary information, such as of maximum data transfer rates and error detection methods. When the two units are ready, if they are compatible, the transfer will begin. Fax systems need to handshake; so do many other types of communications unit.

hanging indent, outdent, or **negative indent,** *n.* an indent where the line starts to the left of the text's normal left margin rather than to the right. See INDENT.

hangover, *n.* a jargon word for patches of poor contrast in a printout or received image (e.g. fax output).

hard copy, *n.* a term used to describe printout on paper (a soft copy of a document or graphic being the one on screen).

hard disk or **platter** or **plate,** *n.* a rigid magnetic disk used for backing storage. Floppy disks become fairly rigid as they spin, but a hard disk can work with much closer tolerances. This means it needs far more careful handling: hard disks are therefore either permanently fixed in their drives or, if removable, are very well packed. Most hard disks are made of aluminium coated with fine magnetic dust.

Modern systems tend to use a set of several, up to about 11, hard disks which are co-axial (on a common central spindle), forming a **hard disk pack**; there is a read/write head for each surface in use. The Winchester 'disk' (really a disk pack) is a common type, but there are many others. In use, the disk spins all the time, normally at 60 turns a second. This cuts access time a great deal compared with that of floppy disks (which spin only on demand).

A formatted hard disk surface may have 200 tracks, with perhaps 20 sectors (blocks) with gaps between. A set of tracks at the same distance from the spindle of a pack forms a cylinder (see the Figure). It is normal practice to address data by cylinder, surface and sector number; furthermore, to keep head movement (and therefore access time) as low as possible, systems store the records of a file in the same cylinder rather than on the same surface.

hard sectoring, *n.* a method of fixing the sectors of a disk permanently by punching holes through the disk. This makes the disk less flexible in use than a soft-sectored one; on the

HARD WIRING

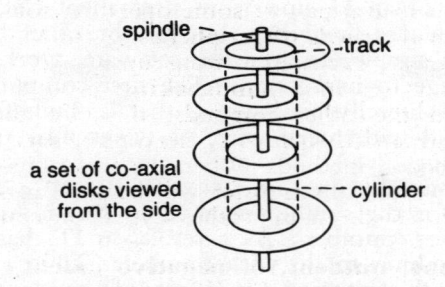

hard disk. A hard disk pack cylinder.

other hand, hard sectoring provides for more storage space.

hardware, *n.* the set of physical parts of an IT system, i.e. the ones you can touch, as opposed to the software (operating instructions) that makes the system work. A typical digital computer has a number of hardware units: the central processor (which includes the clock and control unit), with the arithmetic and logic unit (ALU) and the main store possibly being separate, and various peripherals, e.g. input and output units and backing store. In many modern systems (such as a pocket computer) it is hard to see the joins between the different hardware units. However, the ones mentioned (and shown in the Figure) are conceptually distinct.

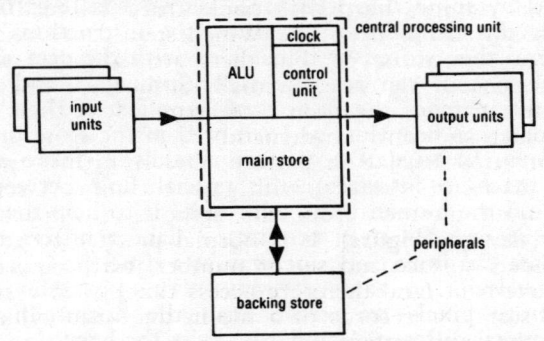

hardware. The main parts of a digital computer.

hard wiring, *n.* the formation of the control, arithmetic and

HASH

logic systems of an IT unit from permanent electric circuits. This much reduces flexibility, but on the other hand, means the unit needs simple, or even no, software, works faster, and loses no storage to instructions. The first computer operating 'software' was literally hard-wired, that is, built from discrete elements linked with metal wire; FIRMWARE now provides that kind of working.

hash, *n.* **1.** sometimes used for GARBAGE.

2. the name for the symbol #, used in North America as an abbreviation for 'number'. As a result, in IT, hash has come to mean something to do with numbers. Thus a **hash algorithm** (or **hash function**) is a set of steps a system can follow to produce a number, **hashing** being the actual number generation process.

For example, if you need to hold for DIRECT ACCESS a number of records in a certain space (e.g. disk surface), each record has a key field, and each part of the space has an address. The programmer designs a hash algorithm which can spread the records evenly throughout the space. Then, for each record, the algorithm acts on the key to give the storage address. The algorithm also lets the system find a given record quickly, knowing its key field value.

A **hash table** is a storage space in main store with hashing giving direct storage and access of data. An example is the label table (list of variables) of a program.

A **hash total** is used for verification. It is a number produced by some algorithm on a set of data (e.g. the records of a file, the elements of an array, the instructions of a program), and then stored or transferred with the data set. At any stage the system can run the algorithm again and check the new result matches the hash total supplied; if there is a mismatch, data has been lost or corrupted in the store or transfer.

HCI, *abbrev. for* HUMAN COMPUTER INTERFACE (more accurately, human machine interface), the crucial link between an IT system and the human users who want it to help them.

HD(X), *abbrev. for* HALF DUPLEX, a data transfer channel in which data can flow only one way at a time.

HDTV, *abbrev. for* HIGH DEFINITION TV, i.e. television with many more pixels on screen than the norm. In the early 1990s, several different 'standards' exist for hdtv.

head, *n.* any device for storing (writing) and/or copying (reading) and/or wiping (erasing) data to/from a storage medium. Thus a laser or LED is part of the head of an optical disc,

HEAD

stripe or tape drive; paper tape and card heads (see PUNCHED MEDIA) punch or detect holes. There are many other types.

The magnetic head of a magnetic data storage system (disk, stripe or tape) is a tiny electromagnet, i.e. one or more coils round a core with two pole pieces (see Figure). To store (write) data on the magnetic surface a tiny distance away, the system sends a signal (current) through the coil. The electromagnetic field between the poles (see GAP) affects the iron oxide dust to give it a record of the data in the signal. As long as the surface is well treated the records remain for ever.

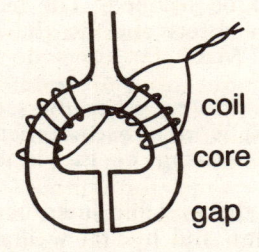

head. The electromagnetic structure of a magnetic read/write head.

At any time the head can work in reverse to read the data stored, i.e. to capture a copy as an electric current to send back to the system. Electromagnetic induction is the process involved: as the head moves over the surface, the magnetic fields in the dust induce a signal (current) in the coil.

A magnetic head can erase data too. If the coil carries a high frequency electric current, the high frequency magnetic field between the poles will shake the dust at random, so it loses the stored pattern.

A **head crash** is a hazard for magnetic HARD DISK users. For the reading/writing to work properly, the head must stay very close to the magnetic surface. A common description compares it to a jumbo jet flying a couple of centimetres from the ground. Vibration, or a tiny speck of dust in the way, may cause the head to collide with the surface. This is likely to scratch the surface and also perhaps harm the head. A crash can cause much damage, making the disk useless in some cases. Even a small scratch may cause great loss of data.

In a VIDEO recorder or player, the **head drum** is the unit that holds the turning heads. The **head end** of a CABLE televi-

HEADER

sion system is the central control and distribution point.

header, *n.* **1.** the same as HEADING, a brief title or other message at the top of each page of a text.

2. a set of data (also called **header block**) at the start of a signal, program or data structure, giving basic information such as amount and type of data and where it should go (address). A **header label** is the header of a file at the start of a tape; it includes details of the tape and of the file, and when/how it was written, to help identification.

In an optical character or mark reading system (OCR or OMR), the user feeds a **header sheet** through the scanner before the sheets to be scanned. The header sheet defines the format of the main sheets and (in the case of OMR) where marks may appear. Many fax users do much the same thing before sending.

heading, *n.* a brief title or other message at the top of each page of a text. Most word processors let their users define the content, style, and placing of the headings (or headers) of documents.

health hazards, *n.* the possible links between IT systems and danger to the physical and mental wellbeing of those who use them. Despite many claims and much research, it is not known how much danger IT systems pose to users' health. Some may produce toxic gases (e.g. copiers that emit ozone); hazardous radiation (e.g. X-rays from cathode-ray tube (CRT - non flat) screens); toxic waste (the drums of some copiers and page printers); and strong electric fields (CRT screens also) which can attract dust and lead to skin problems. While there is no clear proof of sickness caused by such aspects of IT as these, it is wise to avoid excess exposure.

In particular, if you use a computer with a CRT display, you should:

(a) sit at least half a metre from the screen;
(b) restrict keyboard work to six to eight hours a day;
(c) take a break each hour or so;
(d) avoid doing so when pregnant.

Breaks also give you a chance to exercise and reduce strains and aches. See also REPETITIVE STRAIN INJURY.

helical, *adj.* shaped like a helix, a 3D spiral like a cylindrical spring. **Helical scanning** is how many video recorder heads cover the surface of the passing tape. The tape moves fairly slowly in a helix round a drum; inside the drum one or more heads rotate at very high speed. The signal tracks are helical, therefore, so that the tape can hold much more data per unit length.

A **helical wave guide** is a design of metal tube for the transfer of superhigh frequency (SHF, or W band) MICROWAVES. Using NARROWCASTING, ultra-high frequency waves (UHF, L band) can pass a long way through air. Higher frequencies cannot, because the air attenuates (weakens) them too much; people then use WAVE GUIDES (special metal tubes) to transfer them. Rectangular section guides are fine up to a certain frequency; then circular ones take over. Helical guides, circular tubes with copper wire wound in a helix on the inside surface, can transfer waves up to about 100 GHz.

help line, *n.* a telephone number on offer to users of hardware and/or software by the makers or suppliers. People having problems with hardware or software then face less trouble finding solutions. The cost of the service is part of the purchase price in some cases; in others it is an optional extra, making the service like a club or user group.

Some programs offer **help screens**. These are pages of information and instructions that can be viewed by typing a certain command or pressing a certain key (PC software widely uses the F1 function key for this). **Context sensitive help** is now quite common: the help screen you obtain refers to your current context (e.g. searching a file or trying to print). The help screens in other cases are either general (you have to scan through to find what you want) or menu-driven (pressing the help key gives you a list of topics).

hertz (Hz), *n.* the unit of frequency for waves and other cyclic actions. One hertz is a cycle per second. It is not good practice to use the hertz as the unit for the rate of irregular events.

heterogeneous multiplexing, *n.* a form of MULTIPLEXING in which different signals pass through the system at different speeds.

heuristic, *adj.* or *n.* denoting 'self teaching' or trial and error. To solve a problem non-heuristically, you apply an algorithm (set of steps) you know will work. If there is no such algorithm, try a heuristic approach. Many machine-intelligence programs involve some degree of heuristic working. For example, a knowledge-based expert system may include a set of **heuristics** (in effect, rules of thumb rather than facts) in its knowledge base. A **heuristic program** (or **heuristic routine**) is one which tries several ways to reach a solution and then

HEX(ADECIMAL)

judges which gives the most useful result.

hex(adecimal), *adj.* in the base 16 number system. The (16) hex digits are 0 1 2 3 4 5 6 7 8 9 A B C D E F; hex F has the same value as denary ('decimal') 15; 16 is 10 in hex. A hex number is a set of hex digits, the normal rules of place value making these worth units (16^0), sixteens (16^1), 256s (16^2) ... moving left from the **hex point,** and 1/16 (16^{-1}), 1/256 (16^{-2}), 1/4096 (16^{-3}) ... moving right from it. Thus the hex number 4F.A3 has the same value as denary 79.6367... .

Because 16 is a power of 2, hex working with (binary) microprocessors is more efficient than denary working, and simpler for humans than binary. While people had to program the first computers in binary machine code, they soon found **hex code** would make life easier for them. The operating software, on the other hand, had to translate each hex digit into a set of four bits (a nibble or half byte). Some microprocessor systems have a **hex keyboard or hex pad**, with 16 hex keys and a couple of others such as <RETURN> for this purpose.

hidden lines, *n.* any lines that are part of a 3D design or object, but do not appear in a screen view or printout when other parts are 'in front'. It is not hard to set up a graphics program that allows a 3D object to be designed and to appear on screen. For the program to 'decide' which lines to hide as you view from new angles is much less simple. It is even more difficult to keep light and shade patterns correct as the viewed object rotates.

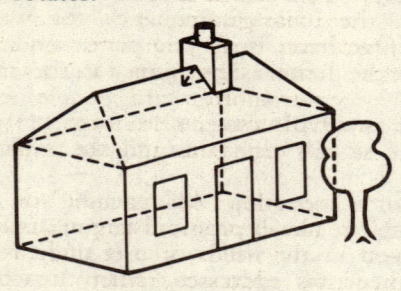

hidden lines.

hierarchical data base, *n.* a data base in which information is stored in a structure with varying levels of importance. Thus, to access information of very minor importance (in terms of

HIGH-LEVEL PROGRAM LANGUAGE

the structure of the data base itself), it is necessary to reach it via the upper (more important) levels first. Compare RELATIONAL DATA BASE.

hierarchy, *n.* a relationship between objects or people which describes clearly different levels of importance. It is normal to have the most important level at the top. Hierarchies tend to be like a pyramid in shape (think of the staffing of a large computing department). However, as they also tend to involve branching from level to lower level, we mostly view them as trees (like family trees). Indeed the data structure called a tree is exactly like this. A DATA BASE is a tree-like hierarchy too, with files, records and fields in the lower levels.

A **hierarchy chart** is a STRUCTURE CHART, a hierarchical block diagram of all or part of a program as used in program development and documentation.

high definition TV (HDTV), *n.* television with many more pixels on screen than the norm. Several standards exist for TELEVISION systems with sharper pictures than the norm. All have many more pixels on screen, and some offer other useful features. At the time of writing, it is not yet clear which standard will become worldwide. See also RESOLUTION.

high density, *adj.* describing the ability to store more data in a given space than usual. This is a relative phrase. Thus a high-density floppy magnetic disk of the early 1990s for a PC can store 1.44 MB (megabytes), given a suitable drive. People have, however, produced prototype magnetic disks the same size able to carry ten or fifteen times as much data.

high-level program language, *n.* a program language in which each instruction may translate to more than one machine code instruction. The higher the level of a program language, the more straightforward people find it to work with; however, it will also be less able to cope with the specific features of the hardware, and the translation process is more complex.

Compared with lower-level languages (such as machine and assembly codes) high-level program languages tend to be:

(a) more suited to the needs of user and programmer (they relate to the problems addressed rather than to the hardware used);

(b) more portable; i.e. easier to transfer to a different hardware system (but note that in most cases there are many DIALECTS);

(c) more open to structured coding techniques.

HIGH-LEVEL PROTOCOL

On the other hand, high-level program languages (sometimes called 'third-generation software') are still quite close to the hardware they work with rather than to the user's needs: programming with them is still a complex, skilled task, so is therefore costly, slow and prone to error. Programming with so-called fourth generation software should overcome these problems.

Fourth-generation software includes program development tools, such as program generators and author languages. On the whole, in the early 1990s these are still crude, but they show great promise for the speedy production of efficient and effective programs by less skilled staff.

high-level protocol, *n.* a set of conventions for running a network that relate to the network's functions rather than to its actions (i.e. to purpose rather than to method, the latter being LOW-LEVEL PROTOCOL).

highlight, *vb.* or *n.* showing part of a text (e.g. headings, keywords, safety notes) in a different form from the body of a text to attract attention. Common systems are **bold**, *italic* and underlined.

high resolution, *adj.* denoting output (screen or paper) with a higher density of detail than is normal. This is a relative term. No doubt future generations will call the high-resolution graphics of today low resolution. The same applies to HIGH-DEFINITION TV (HDTV): high definition and high resolution are much the same.

high-speed, *adj.* working at a greater rate than the norm, a relative term the meaning of which changes with time. **High-speed memory** (HSM) is main store with unusually short access times. High-speed peripherals (e.g. modems, printers, readers) work faster than others, but still much more slowly than an IT system's central processing unit.

highway, *n.* an alternative term for BUS or TRUNK, i.e. a major data transfer path linking a number of close units and devices, with the data passing in parallel to increase transfer rate.

history of IT, see INFORMATION HANDLING, HISTORY OF.

hit, *n.* the retrieving of a record in a file as the result of a successful search. This happens when the record's data in the field(s) concerned matches the specified search terms. **Hit rate** is the ratio of records retrieved in a search to the number in the file. See also ACTIVITY. (In much the same way, it measures the success of a CACHE.)

A **hit on the fly** printer is one with embossed type (i.e. not

HOME INFORMATION SYSTEMS

a dot printer) where the type does not stop moving to form each character. This makes for faster printing.

HOBS, *abbrev. for* HOME and office banking: a facility which allows account holders to access a bank's computer via a micro in the home or office.

Hollerith, Hermann (1860–1929) a US engineer who in 1889 developed the concept of storing data for processing on punched cards. This was done to allow the work on the data from the 1890 census to finish before the 1900 census. Using the **Hollerith code**, patterns of holes punched in cards (a card for each record) coded the data. The system used card punch machines for the data storage, and punched card readers (called tabulators, i.e. machines for making tables) to read data and thus process (e.g. sort and search) it. See also PUNCHED MEDIA.

It took eight years to process the 1880 census data (50 million people); and only three for the work on the 63 million records of the 1890 census. Hollerith's system led to many important developments: his firm, the Computing Tabulating Recording Company, later became IBM, the world's largest computing firm in the early 1990s.

hologram, *n.* a 3D light image stored in the surface of photographic film (or a metal or plastic copy). Laser light scans the scene and the film captures the pattern caused by interference between the direct waves and those reflected from the various parts of the scene. When you look at the image behind the hologram, you obtain different views from different angles. After a quarter century of research, however, there is little progress toward holographic (i.e. true 3D) television. All the same, people expect that by the early 21st century, holography will have major uses in many IT fields, such as demultiplexing, scanning, optical computing and pattern recognition.

Holographic storage of data is a system of growing importance. As a hologram stores, in effect, a large number of separate images, it has the power to store large amounts of data. Holograms, being hard to copy, are in wide use for security (on, for instance, credit cards and bank notes). There are, however, other systems that are cheaper and just as good in this context.

home information systems, *n.* IT systems developed for use by only one person or a small group. They are much the same in principle as those growing in importance in the office and school. They allow effective access to large amounts of data, stored on hard, compact or video disc, or elsewhere via the telephone network, broadcast signals, cable and satellites. See also TELECOMMUTING, GLOBAL VILLAGE, ELECTRONIC COTTAGES and SMART home.

home, IT in the, see CONSUMER IT.

homogeneous multiplexing, *n.* a type of MULTIPLEXING where all the signals carried transfer at the same rate.

horizontal resolution, *n.* the number of dots per unit that a scanner can resolve (i.e. distinguish between) or a printer can print across a sheet of paper. The usual units are dots/mm or dots/inch (DPI), figures of 12 dots/mm (300 DPI) giving adequate results for many systems.

host, *n.* **1.** the central computer in an on-line data base and/or electronic mail network.

2. an alternative term for **host processor**, the central computer in a network or other distributed processing system.

hot line, *n.* see HELP LINE.

hot spot, *n.* the brightest central part of a projected image (e.g. in a microform display). It can cause data reading problems because of poor contrast in the hot spot.

hot zone, *n.* a band a few characters wide to the left of the right margin of documents in some word processors. If a word starts in the hot zone but goes past the true margin, the system asks the user whether it should leave the word as it is, hyphenate it, or move it to the next line.

housecleaning, see GARBAGE COLLECTION.

housekeeping, *n.* the general care of an IT system. As well as cleaning and maintenance, however, this includes tasks such as listing files and disks, and backing up. In other words, housekeeping involves all non-specialist work needed to keep a system running effectively and safely.

HSM, *abbrev. for* HIGH SPEED MEMORY (store).

hub, *n.* the powerful central fax machine in a fax network. A fax network is a set of linked compatible machines (including fax cards in computers), each with a specific range of tasks (and therefore features). The hub machine(s), however, are even more feature-rich than the others (the slaves); in particular they are likely to be the only ones able to broadcast or relay, so the slaves feed broadcast and relay tasks to the hub.

Huffman, see MODIFIED HUFFMAN.

human-aided, *adj.* denotes a system designed to refer

problems to a human operator. This means an expert has to intervene sometimes when the machine cannot cope with a problem or decision. **Human-aided machine translation**, for example, is the use of software that at least 'knows' when there may be unclear meaning, so refers to the user for rulings as necessary.

The **human computer interface (HCI)**, more accurately 'human machine interface', is the crucial link between an IT system and its human user(s). At no stage should a user be unsure what to do or be bothered by trivial tasks; at no stage should the machine act in a way that is less than efficient and effective as far as concerns its work. Often the design of the HCI is a major aspect of FRIENDLINESS, but it is more than that: it concerns a good partnership between the machine and its user.

A **human language** (natural language) is one used for normal communication between people. The structures and syntax (grammar) of even a primitive human language are far more complex than any modern IT system can handle. It is, however, the hope of information technologists that progress toward human-machine communication using natural language will be swift.

A **human window** is jargon for the power of some knowledge-based expert systems to 'explain' how they reached a certain conclusion. Most will just list the relationships and probabilities that led to the conclusion.

hybrid, *adj*. describing anything made out of two or more different forms. A **hybrid computer** is one with a digital central processor and analog input/output, whereas a pure ANALOG COMPUTER has an analog central processor to deal with the inputs and produce the outputs. It is not possible for an analog computer to be general purpose. Someone must design each one for a certain range of tasks. A hybrid system, on the other hand, can be programmable, even if it is less accurate in what it does.

A **hybrid interface** is the link between an analog system and a digital one; it must be able to convert data between the two types. There are various types of **hybrid network**. A hybrid computer NETWORK combines sections with a ring or cluster design and a bus. People also use the phrase to denote a network of hybrid computers. A hybrid cable network offers various services other than television (for example, telephone links and services such as data transfers).

HYDRAULIC

hydraulic, *adj.* powered by forces in a trapped liquid. The parts of many robot systems that provide the action in the system are hydraulic (or PNEUMATIC, where the forces come from a gas under pressure). A motor moves a piston in a master cylinder, linked by valves to the slave cylinder currently in use. The changes of pressure in the slave cylinder cause its piston to move in one of two different ways.

hypermedia, *n.* any computer-controlled system which allows the user to interact with a number of media, e.g. text and graphics on film, on CD-ROM, and on magnetic disk. Interaction should be very flexible, so users pass through any part of the material by any paths they wish. See also INTERACTIVE VIDEO and MULTI-MEDIA.

Hypertext is a simple type of hypermedia. A hypertext system gives access only to text (and perhaps very simple graphics). Even so, access can be very flexible, with the user reading the text as a linear book, or moving round in any way one may imagine. The index is electronic, and there is often a dictionary and/or glossary on call too. A true hypertext package also allows any reader to add notes at any point and export chunks of the material into a word processor.

hyphenation, *n.* a feature of many word processors whereby they hyphenate long words that do not fit on a line rather than wrapping them round to the next line. As the rules of hyphenation are complex in most languages, only advanced systems will be able to hyphenate correctly all the time. **Discretionary hyphenation** is a version of the feature where the user can override the decision to hyphenate and/or the position of the hyphen.

Hz, *symbol for* HERTZ, unit of frequency.

I

IAR, *abbrev. for* INSTRUCTION ADDRESS REGISTER.
IAS, *abbrev. for* IMMEDIATE ACCESS STORE.
IBG, *abbrev. for* INTER-BLOCK GAP.
IC, *abbrev. for* INTEGRATED CIRCUIT.
icon, *n.* a graphic symbol for an action or object. Thus many WIMP user interfaces use a dustbin picture as an icon to represent the action of deleting a file. This approach has become so popular that now many modern software systems use icons to show the actions which can be taken at any stage when using the software.
i-cycle, *abbrev. for* INSTRUCTION CYCLE. See also MACHINE CYCLE.
ID, *abbrev. for* 'identity (code)', i.e. the string a user of a secure system must enter to identify who s/he is and find out whether the system can allow access or not.
IDA, *abbrev. for* integrated digital access. See ISDN.
IDD, *abbrev. for* international direct dialling, a system which allows a phone user to call people in other countries without the assistance of the operator.
identification, *n.* **1.** the name of a data item (more often called label or variable name).
2. the process of logging on to a secure IT system using a series of passwords etc.
3. a block (or 'division') in any Cobol program used as a header, to give basic information such as program and author names, and version date.
identifier, *n.* the name or label of a data item, as defined in a program, for example.
idle character, *n.* a type of null character used to cause a delay in a process.
idle time, *n.* a period during which an IT system is ready for use but is not in fact working on any task.
IGFET, *abbrev. for* insulated gate field-effect TRANSISTOR. See MOS.
IKBS, *abbrev. for* INTELLIGENT KNOWLEDGE-BASED SYSTEM.
illegal code, *n.* any set of bits an IT system cannot recognise as valid.
illegal operation, *n.* any instruction an IT system cannot carry out.

IMAGE

image, *n.* in IT, a character, line and/or shape. This can be a single letter of the alphabet, a word, or a complex visual image such as a photograph or drawing. As with text, people need to input, store and output images. **Image dissection** is the process of analysing the image of a scanned character in an optical character reading system. **Image printing** is much the same as page printing, i.e. sending a copy (image) of a complete page in coded form to a suitable printer for output.

Image processing is a major field of modern IT. In some way or another it involves a computer's enhancing (improving) an image by going through a series of standard steps.

Image separation is a standard method for reproducing colour pictures. The picture is separated into various images, as viewed in different lights, which are recombined when reproducing (i.e. printing) the picture. In colour printing the picture is separated into four colours (black, cyan, yellow and magenta). Some colour graphics programs output colour images in this way.

immediate access store (IAS) *n.* **1.** a section of memory which holds data that is likely to be needed often or soon (e.g. current program instructions).
2. core or MAIN STORE.

immediate address, *n.* the actual address in store where the system can find a data item or to which it should go, as quoted in the address field of a program instruction. See ADDRESSING.

immediate mode, *n.* an ENVIRONMENT in which a user can give an instruction to an IT system for it to carry out at once (rather than storing it as part of a program). Many operating software systems offer an immediate mode for housekeeping purposes.

immediate processing, *n.* a way to handle input data as each item arrives rather than holding it to deal with later. Immediate processing is the same as demand processing, a crucial part of real-time working.

impact printer, *n.* any printer where there is actual contact with the paper being printed on between the printer head through a ribbon. Ink jet and page printers are not contact printers, while daisywheel and dot matrix (pin) printers are.

imperative language or **procedural language,** *n.* a program language in which any algorithm sets out how to reach the desired solution without stating the solution's properties (compare DECLARATIVE PROGRAM LANGUAGE). Order of instructions is crucial in an imperative language, the von Neumann model being the basis. Most common program languages are of this type.

implementation, *n.* the putting into action of (usually) the main stage of a system life cycle. Here the systems analysts and designers, having defined how to meet a given problem, instal the necessary hardware and software. System testing and documentation are involved at this stage too, as will be the training of the staff who will work with the new package.

incompatibility, *n.* a major difference between how two systems handle data, so that they cannot share programs or data sets. An important aim of systems designers, even of different manufacturers, is to ensure their products are compatible with international standards and/or with systems from elsewhere (without meeting problems of patents or copyright).

increment, *n.* or *vb.* an increase or decrease in value by a given amount. The concept of **incrementation** is crucial to most loop structures; the system must increment some variable from a starting value to a final value, perhaps doing other things during each cycle. Basic's FOR ... TO .../NEXT ... structure is most obviously of this type, but in fact many looping algorithms involve the same idea.

Incremental compilers can compile an unfinished program; they will then be able to compile new statements and add the result to the object code without re-compiling the whole program. This is of great value for interactive program development. An **incremental plotter** is one able to draw graphs and other line designs (which are in principle analog in nature) from input digital data. To run the pen from point to point on the paper (with or without drawing) involves moving pen and/or paper by a number of small stages; these increments are often in the range 0.125 - 0.05 mm (1/200 - 1/500 inch). See PLOTTER.

An **incrementer** is an electronic circuit (logic unit) with the task of adding 1 to the value held in a register. An important example is for a processor to increase by 1 the value held in the sequence control register (program counter), so the next MACHINE CYCLE can deal with the next instruction.

indent, *n.* or *vb.* to format a block of text (e.g. a list or the first line of a paragraph) so that the left margin differs from the norm. In most cases, indented text starts at the right of the standard left margin, but see HANGING INDENT (outdent).

INDEX

index, *n*. **1.** an alternative (and better) name for the SUBSCRIPT of a data item (element) in a data set (e.g. array). If the data set has the name sample, the items are sample(1), sample(2), sample(3) ... sample(n); here the value in brackets is the item's index (or subscript). If a store holds the data set, the index of each item quickly leads the system to it.
2. in general, a table of data items (in the widest sense) with identifiers for each, so a system or user can find the items in a store. In the index the order of items is such as to suit the needs of the system. For example, the order is alphabetical in the case of a book index.

Indexing is the task of labelling data items (e.g. parts of a text) and setting up an index table for ease of access. People have devised many kinds of index for information retrieval purposes; see, for example, ASSIGNED TERM INDEX and DERIVED TERM INDEX; FREE INDEXING; PRE-COORDINATE INDEX and POST-COORDINATE INDEX. Some indexes are hierarchical, with a narrow, detailed FINE INDEX below a wide, coarse GROSS INDEX. An **index term** (or head word) is a term used to classify an item in an indexed set (e.g. a text in a document data base).

Indexed addressing is a form of ADDRESSING in program instructions, in which the address field contains a value from which the system derives the actual address by relating it to the value in the **index register**. A common form of this applies when a sequence of address cells contains a set of data items. The index register then holds the address of the first of these and each instruction's address field contains the offset, the number of the element in the set.

Indexed sequential access is a way to relate the items in an ordered (sequenced) data set to their addresses in store. The **indexed sequential access method (ISAM)** is an important approach to the indexing of stored data to aid access. An **indexed sequential file** has the records held in order, with an index at the start of the file or in a separate file. The index contains the address (cylinder, surface, sector) of each record; this allows DIRECT ACCESS, so applies only to files held on disc or in chips.

indirect addressing, *n*. a form of ADDRESSING in which the instruction's address field gives the address of the cell that contains the address for the data. This slows down processing (in that such an instruction needs two accesses to store rather than one); on the other hand, it allows the system to address a larger store.

INFORMATION HANDLING

inexact (plausible) reasoning, *n*. a FUZZY LOGIC feature of many knowledge-based expert systems that lets these work with statements that are neither fully true nor fully false.

inference engine, *n*. the part of an EXPERT SYSTEM package that relates statements and concepts from the knowledge base in order to produce results.

infinite loop, *n*. an algorithm loop that will never come to an end, the result of an error in coding. For example, the Basic loop shown will be infinite: the coder used the name 'lable' rather than 'label'.

```
LET label := 0
REPEAT
LET label := label+1
PRINT label
UNTIL lable=10
```

infix, *adj*. describing the process where the arithmetic operators appear between the operands concerned, rather than being after them as in POSTFIX (e.g. reverse Polish) notation. Though infix is the standard human way to think of arithmetic expressions (and therefore is the norm in program languages), it is less straightforward than POSTFIX when an IT system works on it.

infomatics or **informatics,** *n*. a fairly common term throughout Europe for information technology.

information, *n*. that which adds to human knowledge. In an IT system (when during transfer, under process, or in store) the coded representation of information has no meaning as such; we then call it DATA. Thus information becomes data when it enters an IT system; at the output side, it becomes information again when a person has access to it. People widely use data and information as the same, however.

An **information channel** is the set of hardware and media between two stations in a data transfer line, while **information feedback** is the transfer of data received by a station back to the sender to allow checking.

information handling, history of, *n*. the history of how people have learned to manage information. We are now in the fourth information handling revolution:

FIRST	writing	4000–3000 BC
SECOND	arithmetic	2000–1000 BC
THIRD	printing	1000–1500 AD
FOURTH	information technology	1800–present day

In each case, a very significant advance took place in the

INFORMATION HANDLING

storage, transfer and processing of information. Between times, there has only been progress in applying existing ideas more efficiently.

Information technology (IT) has, since the early 20th century, utilized electricity and/or magnetism and/or electromagnetism (and more recently electronics and microelectronics) for information handling. Progress in IT has allowed us to reach what many call the second industrial revolution. While the first industrial revolution was in energy processing (which made physical living conditions better), the second has been in information processing, which improves facilities for our minds.

It is common to trace the history of computing technology back to the mechanical calculating aids of the 17th century. These became more complex and cumbersome as calculating needs grew, particularly with the development of ballistics, astronomy and navigation. BABBAGE designed the most complex pre-electricity system of all. The design was good, as was the concept of programming that it involved (see also LOVELACE). It was not possible, however, to machine the parts of the system with adequate procision.

Programming a machine (and thus moving towards automation) was not an entirely new idea at that time. Various people devised techniques for automating textiles machines, in particular, in the 18th and 19th centuries. Joseph Jacquard (French, 1752–1834) was most important in this context. His concept of punching program instructions as holes in something like card was in very wide use in many types of machine by the middle of the 19th century.

The punched card (see PUNCHED MEDIA) was the approach used by Herman HOLLERITH in his automation of the processing of the US 1890 census data. IBM can trace its history directly back to Hollerith's firm. The main significance of Hollerith's work was that it was the first to use electricity successfully as an integral part of the automation process.

From the IT point of view, the most significant aspect of the 20th century has been the use of electronics and microelectronics to handle data (including program instructions) more effectively, and with more speed and reliability, finally giving Babbage's ideas a chance to become reality. By the middle of the 1930s, people in several countries were working towards electronic computers. See GENERATIONS for more recent detail. See TELEGRAPH and TELEPHONE for their history.

information processing, *n*. in IT, an alternative term for data processing, but seen from the user's point of view (e.g. from that of the firm that owns the data processing system). An **information provider (IP)** is a person or group responsible for a number of videotex pages. The IP may rent these from the videotex host or have them free; in any event, the ip must keep the information contained up to date, as well as legal, decent and honest.

information retrieval, *n*. in IT, data retrieval seen from the point of view of the user. An **information retrieval language (IRL)** is a set of rules by which a non-expert user may interact with a data base in order to access required information accurately and with as few problems as possible.

information science, *n*. the field of handling information in any form of value to people. It therefore closely relates to the work of libraries in the modern multi-media sense, and includes such theoretical aspects of information technology as information cataloguing, INDEXING and access. An **information spinner** is the same as the HOST of a videotex system. **Information storage and retrieval** are aspects of information processing (see above, and see also information retrieval, above).

information technology (IT), *n*. the handling of information by electric and electronic (and microelectronic) means. Here, handling includes transfer, processing, storage and access, IT's special concern being the use of hardware and software for these tasks for the benefit of individual people and society as a whole. Until recently, the field described carried the name **new information technology** (NIT); this was to keep it distinct from library technology and such areas as filing in cabinets and boxes, the postal service, and printing.

information theory, *n*. the mathematical study of information handling and concerns the actual information content of a message (information item), as this relates to REDUNDANCY. To some people, information theory includes the study of coding techniques; strictly, however, that is communication theory. An **information vendor** is a videotex host.

infrared (IR), *adj*. or *n*. electromagnetic radiation close to the low-energy (red) end of the visible SPECTRUM, with frequencies in the range 5×10^{11} to 7×10^{14} Hz (approx). There are many uses for infrared beams to carry short range signals (e.g. for TV remote control units and to form a wireless link between

IN-HOUSE

a keyboard and a micro). Infrared is also as commonly used as light in fibre optic systems.

in-house or **in-plant,** *adj.* an organization's existing staff and resources rather than those bought from a specialist firm. Thus many large firms have an in-house systems analysis section, so have less need to call on outside analysts.

initialization, *n.* the setting up of a program variable to a starting value before use, perhaps as part of a declaration. Some program languages default to initial values for new variables (e.g. 0 for numerics and "", the null (empty) string for strings), but the default value may not be the one you want; other programs require the programmer to initialize them.

inking, *n.* a jargon term for drawing a line on a graphics screen by moving a pointer across it, e.g. by moving a mouse with a button held down.

ink-jet printer, *n.* a quiet fast matrix printer which builds up characters and graphics as sets of dots formed by firing tiny drops of ink at the paper. The print head has a vertical row of small nozzles fed by tubes from the ink reservoir. Coded electric pulses from the computer act on electromagnetic pumps.

Another style of ink-jet printer has a single nozzle. The ink drops are charged electrically as they leave the nozzle and a changing electric field between head and paper directs them vertically to the correct position.

The ink is wet for a few moments after reaching the paper, so can smear before it dries. A related system overcomes this by using semi-solid plastic ink, heated as it leaves the nozzle; this dries at once to form a slightly raised, embossed-like, trace on the paper. All types of ink-jet printer are easy to design for colour printing.

in-order traversal or **symmetric order traversal** *n.* the use of a recursive algorithm to work through (or tour) the nodes of a tree data structure. The algorithm concerned is:

                    traverse left sub-tree
                    visit root node
                    traverse right sub-tree

Other traversal methods are: *pre-order* and *post-order*.

in-plant see IN-HOUSE.

input, *n.* the transfer of data into the store of an IT system, perhaps for processing and for later access. Peripheral hardware, such as an input unit, is necessary. This can either access data automatically (see MACHINE READABLE INPUT) or requires a person to operate it. See input unit (below).

INPUT/OUTPUT

No input unit, automatic or manual, can transfer data to store as fast as the IT system can process it. This is mainly because all input units have some mechanical moving parts. An **input bound** system is one where the speed of the input unit is the main factor in the speed of the system as a whole: almost all the time, the rest of the system is waiting for input data to process.

When the data input system is manual, there is always a danger of **input error**. For instance, the human user may not understand properly the required format of input data, or may make simple typing slips (e.g. transposition error, as in typing 132 rather than 123). Most software systems therefore include some degree of **input checking**. There are two main types:

(a) VALIDATION ('mug trapping'): the program checks that each input data item is valid, e.g. of the correct type (numeric rather than string, for instance), length, and format (as with the entry of the date);

(b) VERIFICATION: the user enters the same set of data twice (or two people do so once); the program compares the inputs and, if it finds any difference between the two versions of a given data item, asks for it again.

An **input device** is the same as an input unit (see below).

input/output (I/O), *n.* **1.** the part of an IT system which both accepts data from, and outputs data to, its peripherals. There is often little actual difference in the way the input/output element in a syste treats data, regardless of whether it is being input into the main processor and store, our output from them.

The **input/output bus** (I/O bus) of a processor is a parallel data channel which acts as the main link between the store and its communication with the peripherals. **Input/output control** (I/OC or IOC) is the input/output controller in these cases, a unit designed to speed input/output processes. The **input/output control system** (I/OCS or IOCS) is the set of hardware and software that routes each packet of data the right way along the bus, by opening and closing gates.

An **input/output device** is the same as an input/output unit (see below). An **input/output instruction** is an instruction for an IT system that concerns the transfer of data either way between a peripheral and store (or between a peripheral and a register); it is now rare for a program language to offer such a general purpose instruction. On the other hand, general **input/output symbols** are still common in flow charts; the

INPUT UNIT

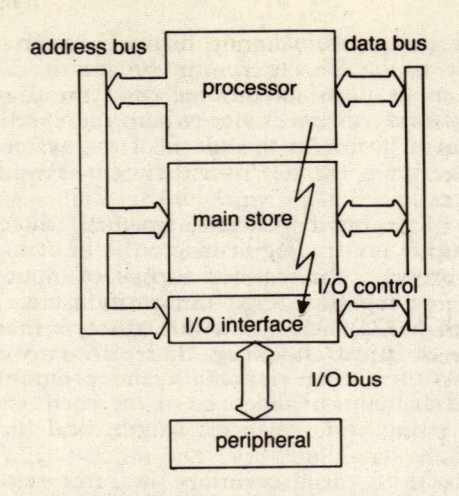

input/output. Input/output transfer.

reader has to judge from the context whether the symbol means input or output (though most people drawing flow charts write the action inside the box). The Figure shows two common input/output boxes.

An **input/output unit** is an item of hardware able to work either for data input or for data output (e.g., microphone/speaker and paper tape punch/reader). The term can also be used for a single box that contains both input and output units, such as a dumb terminal.

2. data transfers between main and backing store only.

input unit, *n.* a hardware item which has the task of accepting data in one form from outside, coding it into electrical pulses of a form that suits the processor, and passing it on to the processor. For automatic types, see MACHINE READABLE INPUT. There are many manual types:

(a) A *keyboard* or keypad is the most common (though there are many layouts and designs). This has a number of press-button switches on a panel; the switches link a 2D matrix of wires, so that each key-press has a different electric effect. An ENCODER converts each electric effect to the corresponding pattern of electric pulses (bits); the bit pattern then passes as a digital signal to the processor.

(b) Many *keyboard* users have come to rely more and more

INPUT UNIT

on a mouse as a speedy pointing device (i.e. one that controls a cursor on screen). The user rolls the mouse over the work surface; sensors monitor the movement of the large ball underneath. Two or three buttons have the same action as major keys (such as <ENTER>), and the effect of rolling with a button pressed often differs from that of rolling without. The mouse is near essential for work with graphics screens, but is also part of the standard WIMP user interface. The upside-down mouse (or *tracker ball*) is quite common.

(c) the upside-down mouse (or *tracker ball*) is quite common, because rolling a mouse over a surface means the user needs a clear area (perhaps 200 mm × 300 mm), and not all users have that much empty desk top. Indeed, some keyboards include a *joystick* or tracker ball. Not all users find it easy to roll the ball with the palm of the hand.

(d) Other pointing devices include the *paddle* (a type of joystick), *touch screen* and *light pen*. The touch screen lets the user point directly at the display surface and detects the finger tip. This may be by picking up the change of electric capacitance at the point on the screen below the finger, or by noting which of the many narrow infrared beams in the grid over the surface the finger breaks.

(e) As with the touch screen, a light pen allows the user to point straight at the display. This is more intuitive than keeping the pointing surface and display surface apart. Thus with either approach, you may make your choice from a menu by touching the screen at the right point, sketching out a design, or writing something. The light pen has a photocell in its tip. This detects the FLYING SPOT that makes up the display; timing the resulting electric pulses that pass down the lead from the pen lets the processor work out where the pen tip is from moment to moment.

(f) However, for sketching on screen, the GRAPHICS PAD is more common than the light pen and touch screen. Indeed, the graphics pad is simpler to use in that it involves much the same action as pen on paper; but the user must all the time glance up at the screen.

(g) Of growing importance as a manual input unit is the *microphone*. Linked to an effective SPEECH RECOGNITION program, this lets the user talk in normal voice and fair speed to the system. Most current packages cannot work with more than a few hundred words (and there would be major problems of noise in an office, for instance, if many people

INSERTION

were to input data this way). All the same, such input systems are widely used where people need to keep their hands free.

insertion, *n.* the adding of a new data item between two existing ones. Thus the **insert mode** of a word processor allows the user to add extra words in the middle of a text, and the insertion of new data items in a list is a crucial feature of that data structure. An **insertion sort** is a SORTING routine in which the program moves a data item that is in the wrong place straight into its correct place, rather than stepping it between them.

instruction, *n.* a code or keyword and associated data, all in a form an IT system can accept, that tells the system what operation to carry out next. If the system is to carry out the instruction without delay, it is called a command (and the system must then be in command mode); a statement is an instruction within a program, i.e. it is not carried out until the program runs.

It is now unknown to give instructions to IT systems as sets of binary digits (bits, 0s and 1s). However, that is the only form these systems can recognise. There must therefore be a translation process, provided by a program or other language.

Standard IT systems run their programs in a linear fashion, instruction by instruction (though parallel processing is starting to change this). In turn, the system fetches each binary instruction from store at the address held in the **instruction address register (IAR)**, decodes it, and carries it out. This sequence of actions is the system's MACHINE CYCLE, sometimes called **instruction cycle** or I-CYCLE. During the cycle, the instruction concerned sits in the **current instruction register (CIR)**. It is the task of the **instruction decoder** to set to work the correct circuit for each instruction's bit pattern (see also DECODER). The cycle's **instruction phase** is not, however, the stage of decoding, but a name for the instruction fetch.

The decoder has a link to an action circuit for each instruction it can handle. The more instructions it can handle, the larger the system's **instruction repertoire** (or **instruction set**), and the easier for the programmer. On the other hand a large instruction set means many decoder links and action circuits, a complex and costly processor, and reduced speed. Hence the growth of interest in **reduced instruction set computers** (RISC machines).

As noted above, an instruction consists of a code or keyword and associated data. The details depend on the **instruc-**

INTEGRATED

tion structure. This is most clear in the case of assembly language; here an instruction may have up to four FIELDS: label (optional), opcode (essential), address field or data (essential with most opcodes), and comment or remark (optional part of program documentation).

instrument, *n*. an input, output, or input/output unit in a tele-communications system, e.g. a phone instrument (handset).

insulated gate field effect transistor (IGFET), see MOS.

integer, *n*. a whole number data type, one with no fraction part, whereas a real number can have a fraction part. It is much harder for a computer to store and process real numbers than integers, so systems based on **integer arithmetic** can be cheap and fast. See also ARITHMETIC.

Many program languages offer both integer data types and integer arithmetic, and reals and flowing point arithmetic (plus functions to convert between integers and reals). Programmers using such languages can choose numeric types to suit their needs, therefore.

integrated, *adj*. denoting parts linked into a whole unit. Thus an **integrated circuit (IC)** is a circuit where the elements (components) and links all lie in the surface of a CHIP of semiconductor material. See also INTEGRATION.

An **integrated data base** is one able to hold data without redundancy. Schema integration applies to DISTRIBUTED DATA BASES; its concern is to minimise the need for users to know which physical part of the whole they are working with at any moment. Here 'schema' means the logical view or structure of the data base at local or global level; view integration aims at ensuring the same schema at each local host.

An **integrated device** is an integral part of a hardware unit. Many stand-alone micros now come with hard disk drives, and some have fax. In those cases, the drive and fax unit are integrated. For **integrated digital access**, see ISDN.

Integrated processing describes the building of an efficient system from a range of separate data handling processes. One of the major aims of systems analysis and design is to create such systems for large organizations, as they allow hardware resource sharing and the free exchange of data.

At a more local level, **integrated software** is a package of several logically separate programs that work the same way and can exchange data as appropriate. The programs may include word processor, spreadsheet, and database manager.

INTEGRATION

Working the same way means they have the same screen layout and special key presses (the same user interface) so it is easy for a user to move between them. Data exchange would allow, for instance, a word-processed text to include parts of spreadsheet tables and database records. For the **integrated services digital network**, see ISDN.

integration, *n.* **1.** setting up a data base with a minimum of redundancy. See INTEGRATED DATA BASE.
2. the linking of hardware units and software systems to increase the efficiency and effectiveness of data processing. See INTEGRATED PROCESSING and INTEGRATED SOFTWARE.
3. the linking of communications systems to form a versatile single whole. See ISDN.
4. the concentration of more and more electronic circuit elements (components) and their links into the surface of a small CHIP of semiconductor material (in most cases, silicon), to make an integrated circuit. Packed for protection into a case with pins that seat into sockets on printed circuit boards, chips are robust and cheap, use very little power and need very little cooling, and offer extremely high-speed working. They are the basis for a very wide range of hardware design.

The basic circuit elements of IT systems are diodes and transistors (switches or gates). The integration of several transistors into one chip in the early 1950s saw the start of the third IT GENERATION. That process was one of small-scale integration (SSI); we have since moved through medium-scale integration (MSI) and large-scale integration (LSI) to the current very large-scale integration (VLSI), with around a million transistors on a chip. The rate of growth of integration scale goes on without slowing (but see QUANTUM BARRIER), towards giga scale integration (GSI).

integrator, *n.* a logic circuit whose output is the integral of the input with respect to time. It consists of a capacitor in the feedback loop of an amplifier. A **summing integrator** combines a summer (summing amplifier) and integrator so that the output is the sum of the input integrals with respect to time (see Figure).

integrity, *n.* a resistance to change of stored data as a result of hardware and/or software errors and/or malice. There is no way to avoid errors corrupting data from time to time; the prudent system manager therefore maintains an approach to backing up (dumping) files. Then, if an error causes a problem, the software will detect the change and copy into

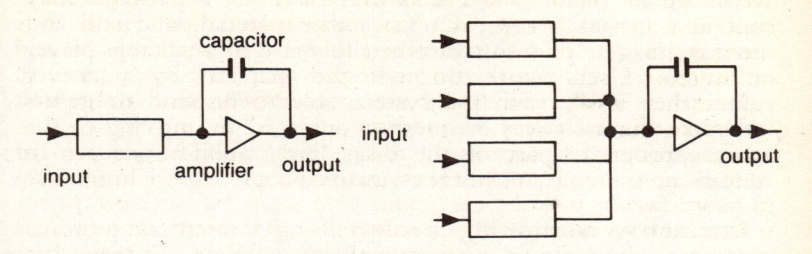

integrator. Integrator and summing integrator.

the master file the backup versions of the corrupt data items.

The process of VALIDATION helps maintain the integrity of data as it passes from one form through an input unit to an IT system's store. See also PARITY.

intelligence, *n.* a feature of a machine that would be called intelligent if exhibited by a person. See MACHINE INTELLIGENCE.

intelligent, *adj.* (in IT) showing some signs of MACHINE INTELLIGENCE. An **intelligent device** (e.g. copier or peripheral) has some local processing power (whereas a dumb one has none). This allows a degree of programmability and, in turn, a degree of decision-making power. In the case of a computer peripheral, the more the intelligence (local processing power), the less it needs to call on a processor elsewhere (e.g. in a network). The end result is a device (a computer) able to stand on its own.

An **intelligent home/office** uses IT for a great range of automation applications; for example, for such tasks as automatic meter reading, computer control of all electric items, communications with the outside world (e.g., for the user to phone in and switch the oven on and the heating off).

For **intelligent knowledge-based (expert) system**, or IKB(E)S, see EXPERT SYSTEM.

Typical of the progression from dumbness to intelligence is the spectrum between a dumb terminal (with input/output only), through an **intelligent terminal** linked to a mini or mainframe and a network station, to a full feature micro able to stand on its own (but sometimes link into a network).

interactive, *adj.* allowing two-way communication (normally between an IT system and a human user). **Interactive compact disc (CDI)** working is a mix of the styles of inter-

INTERACTIVE

active video (below) and CD-ROM. A CDI package may contain a COMPACT DISC of text, audio material, and still and moving images, plus software to allow use in a suitable player or micro. Users work through the material by whatever routes they wish, with the system able to respond to inputs (whether menu choices or question answers) by moving to the most appropriate part of the disc. Early applications are in education, training and libraries; many people expect home use to grow fast.

Interactive computing involves using a micro or terminal in some dynamic conversational way; thus, **interactive graphics** software lets the user produce and edit pictures on screen. The system must be in **interactive mode** to allow this (e.g. running an **interactive program**). The user can choose courses of action and respond to, and even ask, questions. Computer games are, of course, interactive; so too are word processors and, indeed, most programs met by 'ordinary' computer users.

Professionals often work with interactive computing too. For example, an **interactive program language** is one that allows programmers quickly to test and edit instructions and move in and out of command mode. (Most modern interpreted versions of Basic are highly interactive.) On the other hand, an **interactive routine** is a procedure whereby the computer passes through a loop (a repeated set of instructions) until some condition becomes true. For **interactive software**, see interactive computing above.

Interactive television is a system which allows cable television viewers to take a more active part than usual. For instance, at a point in a play, the station might screen a menu of choices of endings. The ending shown is the one most viewers have chosen on their keypads. (This approach is much more effective, and cheaper, than the use of phone-in votes, but it does need a two-way cable link between studio and home.) **Interactive video (IV)** is much like interactive CD (CDI, above). At the centre is a store of information: text, still and moving graphics and video, and sound. With suitable software and hardware, the user can move very flexibly through the disc material. The information store in this case, however, is on video tape or video disc (the latter giving faster access to any part but being more costly). Interactive video is widely used in training and public information systems; the Figure shows typical hardware.

INTERFACE

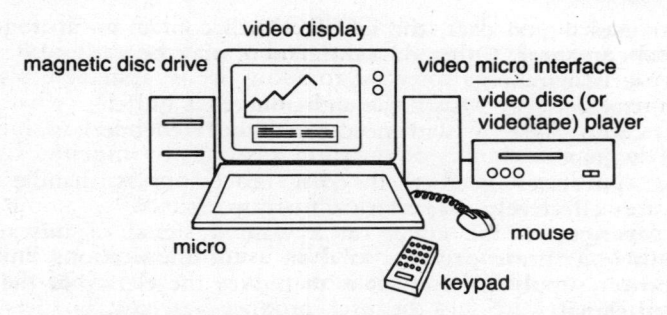

interactive video. Interactive video hardware.

    Interactive videotex is the formal name for viewdata, a system linking micros in offices, shops, schools and homes with a central data base on a host computer. The link is through the phone network, and so is two-way. This makes it interactive in that users can request particular screens of information, can place orders (teleshopping), and have access to electronic mail.

inter-block gap (IBG), *n.* the gap between two blocks (physical records) of data stored on magnetic tape or disk (in which latter case the blocks are sectors). The gap may be quite clear or may partly contain markers for the beginning and end of the two blocks. In the case of tape, the gap allows the drive to accelerate and decelerate as it reads each block. Disk drives do not start and stop in the same way as tape, however; the block gap is needed to hold the markers.

inter-com(m), *abbrev. for* internal communication system, a local private voice network with a small number of stations and no switchboard. There are various systems; often the most effective has the inter-comm units plugged into mains power sockets. The mains current then carries the control and voice signals. (This use of mains to carry signals is widely used by electric power companies for internal messaging; it is also of growing interest as an approach to computer networking.)

interface, *n.* the physical and electronic link between two hardware units. The physical link may be a simple socket and plug, or it may carry the data by light, infrared, microwave, or radio. The electronic aspect of the interface must take account of differences between the data handling systems on the two sides. Thus, if one side supplies analog data and the

INTERFERENCE

other uses digital data, the interface will contain an analog-to-digital converter. Other data differences may be:
(a) serial/parallel;
(b) transfer speed (so the interface needs a buffer);
(c) coding system (with need for decoder/encoder);
(d) voltage.
Some interfaces need their own processors to handle the transfers effectively. See also USER INTERFACE.

interference, *n.* the effect on a wanted signal of unwanted signals (e.g. noise or cross talk) in a communications link or its power supply. The effect is to reduce the clarity of the received signal.

Natural interference follows lightning flashes; human sources include mains hum, signals on nearby channels, car ignition systems, and electrical equipment. Digital transfers are much less open to interference than are analog ones. Other ways to reduce the effects of interference are, as appropriate, using directional aerials, careful siting of hardware, putting a filter in the mains supply, and fitting suppressors to noisy ignition systems and electrical machines.

interlace, *n.* a technique of alternating two (or sometimes more) (FIELDS) in the display of a television set or monitor frame in order to reduce flicker. The lines of each field are slightly offset from those of the previous field.

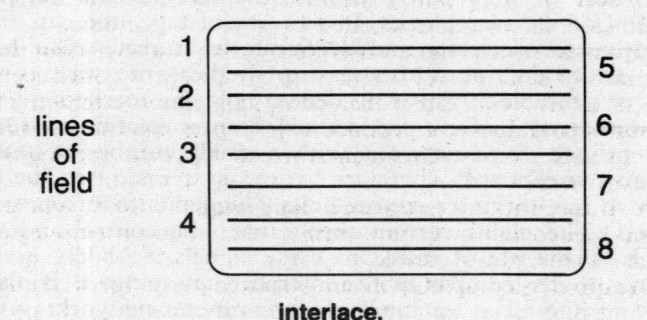

interlace.

interleaving, *n.* **1.** a method of accessing data from two stores in order to process it at the same time.
2. a method of inserting blocks (segments) from one program into a second program so the processor can run both at the same time, in a simple form of MULTI-PROGRAMMING. The order

of insertion is designed to maximize the use of processor time: i.e., a processor-hungry segment of one program runs at the same time as the other deals with input or output.

3. a method of storing the blocks of a file on alternate (or even each third) sectors of a disk surface. As the disk spins fast, after reading sector 1, the system will find that sector 2 has gone past: so, to access data on that sector next, it must wait a whole disk revolution. Interleaving avoids that delay.

interlock, *vb.* **1.** to use flags, for example, to prevent a system starting a new task until the current task is finished. See also PRIORITY.

2. to prevent unauthorised access to data, e.g. by inserting a password.

intermediate store, *n.* a part of the main store used for data currently being processed.

internal, *adj.* denoting the inside of an IT system. Thus a system's **internal character code** is its own method of coding data if it does not use a standard one such as ASCII. The **internal label** of a storage medium (e.g. disc or tape) is a machine-readable header giving basic details of contents. In the program language PL/1, an **internal name** is a local label.

Internal store is an outdated term for read-only memory when used for holding programs (i.e. for firmware), or for main store.

interpreter, *n.* **1.** a unit that reads a punched card and prints on the card the characters coded by the hole patterns.

2. a machine-code program used to translate and carry out the instructions of a high-level language program one by one according to need. Interpreting rather than compiling allows interactive programming and does not produce object code. On the other hand, the interpreter must remain in store all the time the high-level program runs.

An **interpretive program language** is one where the design makes interpretation rather than compilation essential (or, at least, highly suitable).

inter-record gap (IRG) *n.* an outdated term for INTER-BLOCK GAP.

interrogation, *n.* the process of sending a signal that will produce a response.

(a) Processors interrogate peripherals to check on status, e.g. to find out if they are ready to send or receive data. See also POLLING.

(b) Users interrogate (i.e. search) data bases in order to find

INTERRUPT

suitable stored information.

interrupt, *n.* a signal to a processor to report the need for special action. The processor suspends (interrupts) its current program, saving all register contents on the stack, and jumps to the routine to handle the special action. After that, it restores the register contents from the stack and resumes what it was doing.

Various kinds of interrupt may occur. To allow for this, it is common for each interrupt signal to set a bit in the FLAG REGISTER. At the start of each MACHINE CYCLE, the processor checks the value stored in that register. If this is not 0, there has been an interrupt, and the actual value shows the action needed. A PRIORITY system deals with cases where more than one interrupt occurs during a single cycle, or where a second interrupt appears while the system is dealing with the first.

Interrupt masking involves suppressing low priority interrupts for the time being while the system deals with a higher priority task. Interrupts include:

(a) notice of impending power supply failure;

(b) operator action;

(c) timed interrupts (ones that take place automatically after a certain number of cycles to allow special checks);

(d) peripheral interrupts (e.g. to announce an empty buffer or the need for more printer paper);

(e) program actions such as calls to the supervisor;

(f) errors during program runs.

inter-satellite link (ISL), *n.* a channel for signal transfers between communications satellites (rather than between one satellite and a ground station). Links between geostationary satellites are rare as they increase the delay between message and response too much; a delay of more than a quarter or half a second causes major problems.

intruder detection system, *n.* an IT system that detects intruders in a space and allows appropriate action. A simple intruder alarm system consists of a number of sensors (e.g. pressure pads and infrared beams) linked to a simple or complex processor and one or more warning units. Human guards may use intruder systems sometimes in conjunction with access to monitors in a CLOSED CIRCUIT TELEVISION network.

invariant field, see FIXED FIELD.

inventory, *n.* **1.** a type of disk directory used with some large computers.

2. a term for STOCK CONTROL software.

inverse, *adj.* denoting anything reversed in some way compared to the norm. Thus some fax cards offer an **inverse image** (white on black rather than black on white) to make it more readable on screen. In any IT screen display, **inverse video** text has foreground and background colours swapped as a method of highlighting. Some desktop publishing programs offer a similar feature for printouts.

inverted file, *n.* a type of index file offered by some database management systems. In those systems, each record in the main file includes a name and a number of attributes (characteristics, e.g. topics in the case of a file of abstracts). The inverted file has a record for each attribute which includes the names of all main file records with that attribute.

inverter, *n.* an electronic circuit with the same truth table as a NOT GATE.

I/O, *abbrev. for* INPUT/OUTPUT. In an **I/O bound** system, most of the actions and time concern input and output rather than processing. An **I/O buffer** is a single store for input or output data in transit between peripherals and the system's main store.

I/O bus, *abbrev. for* INPUT/OUTPUT BUS.

I/OC or **IOC,** *abbrev. for* INTPUT/OUTPUT CONTROLLER.

I/OCS or **IOCS,** *abbrev. for* INPUT/OUTPUT CONTROL SYSTEM.

I/O hardware, see INPUT UNIT, OUTPUT UNIT.

I/O port, *n.* an interface for linking input/output units to a central processor.

IP, *abbrev. for* INFORMATION PROVIDER, a person or group responsible to the management of a videotex system for providing pages of information and keeping them up to date. An **IP terminal** is a terminal link to a videotex host computer used by an information provider (who then does not need to transfer information on disk or some other way).

IPC, *abbrev. for* (industrial) PROCESS CONTROL.

IR, *abbrev. for* **1.** INFRARED, radiation on the low energy side of light.

2. INFORMATION RETRIEVAL, the process of gaining access as required to information stored in a data base. An **IRL** is an INFORMATION RETRIEVAL LANGUAGE, one designed to make that access simple even to the non-expert.

IRG, *abbrev. for* inter-record gap. See INTER-BLOCK GAP.

ISAM, *abbrev. for* INDEXED SEQUENTIAL ACCESS METHOD.

ISDN, *abbrev. for* the INTEGRATED SERVICES DIGITAL NETWORK, the

ISDN

major international standard TELEPHONE communications system coming into widespread use. It employs digital links from end to end (whereas most digital networks of today have analog lines between the actual users and their exchanges). The system allows channels to handle digitised voice and all kinds of data traffic (including video) at the same time. It therefore opens the way to such features as:

(a) video phones (these use slow-scan monochrome television at present, but full-colour and full-speed methods are being developed);

(b) simultaneous voice and data communication, i.e. talking to someone on the phone while their computer screen shows the data that is on yours;

(c) multiplexing several phone channels (e.g. voice, fax, computer data, intruder alarm), each with a different number on a single line;

(d) the display on a phone handset of the incoming caller's number (though there is much contention about this);

(e) video conferring between participants in several different locations;

(f) high-speed fax (e.g., Group 4) and viewdata access;

(g) transferring data without the use of modems and low traffic local area networks;

(h) automatic telemetering.

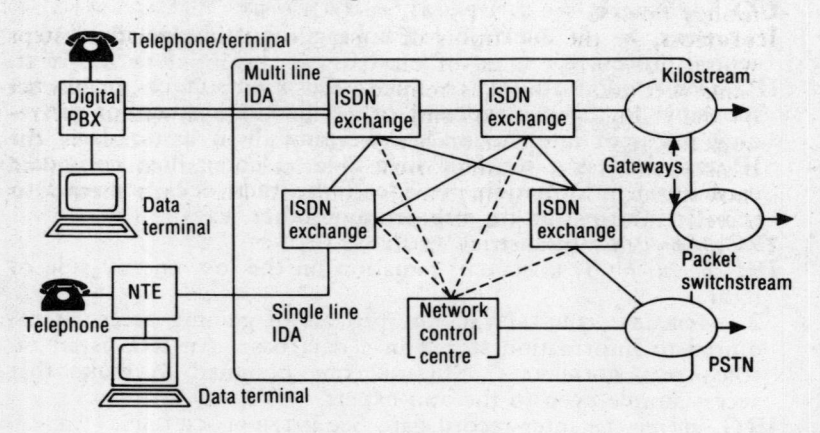

ISDN.

The aim of the system is to integrate:
(1) user access;
(2) voice and data transfer;
(3) terminal interfaces;
(4) packet and circuit switching;
(5) private and public networks.

Britain's IDA (integrated digital access) system opened as a pilot of ISDN in 1985; it offered two channels (B and D) with a total capacity of 80000 bits per second. The Figure shows its structure when extended the next year. By the end of the 1980s, ISDN links between Britain and the rest of Europe were in place and the system was spreading rapidly. Singapore was the first country to have a full ISDN service, however (in 1989). The current standard (2B + D) offers 144000 bits per second.

ISL, *abbrev. for* INTER-SATELLITE LINK.

ISR, *abbrev. for* INFORMATION STORAGE AND RETRIEVAL.

IT, *abbrev. for* INFORMATION TECHNOLOGY.

item, see DATA STRUCTURE, DATA ITEM. **Item size**, or length or width, is the number of bytes (characters, digits) the item takes up.

itemized billing, *n.* the system of sending a report to a phone user with the details of each call made (and even, in some cases, received) rather than with just the total amount of money due.

iteration, *n.* the repetition of a set (loop) of algorithm steps where the output value of one pass is the input to the next. Thus the value sought is refined. This process goes on (as set by the calling program) until either the value is within the required range or its size changes no longer. Iteration is the basis of many algorithms for the solution of mathematical (and thus scientific and engineering) problems. Newton's method is a well known example of iteration.

IV, *abbrev. for* INTERACTIVE VIDEO.

J

J, *symbol for* joule, the standard unit of energy. In microelectronics, where energies are often extremely small, people sometimes use the (electron)volt: 1 eV = 1.6×10^{-19} J.

jacket, *n.* a transparent plastic strip envelope for holding a short length of microfilm.

jack plug or **jack socket,** *n.* a physical link which conducts electricity. The socket contains two or more spring contacts along its length. When you push the long thin jack plug home into the socket, the springs press on the plug's contacts. It is also possible to arrange a contact to break when the jack enters the socket.

A **jack panel** is a board that holds a number of jack sockets into which the user can put jack plugs linked to different channels. Old manual telephone switchboards were like this.

jam, paper, *n.* a malfunction in a printer's paper feed system as a result of paper becoming stuck in it. This is common in some designs of printer (and can happen in all types if a sticky label comes adrift inside). Most good fax machines warn senders if a paper jam means they cannot print out inward faxes: there is a **paper jam warning**.

JCL, *abbrev. for* JOB CONTROL LANGUAGE, a command language used by computer operators to give instructions on how to handle jobs.

jitter, *n.* any sudden irregular departure from the norm or the effect of these. For instance, jitters in television signals can cause jitters such as loss of synchronism and erratic movement in the received picture.

job, *n.* any specific piece of work given to a computer, e.g. a program to run and the data it needs. Most large computers process jobs in batches. The operator will then use a **job control language** (JCL) to tell the operating software how to deal with each job. A JCL program (command file) will tell the system such things as:
    (a) the code for the job's owner (i.e. whom to bill);
    (b) the job name;
    (c) the program language used;
    (d) the drives that contain the program and data files;

(e) the printer to use;
(f) the job's priority.

A **job-oriented language** is not the same; it is a program language very well-suited to a particular kind of job or application. In the same way, a **job-oriented terminal** is a terminal designed for one kind of job (e.g. for work at the checkout of a shop or on an airline booking desk). A **job queue** is the queue of waiting jobs in a batch or multiprogramming system.

Josephson junction, *n.* a very thin oxide junction between two superconducting films. The junction is so thin that electrons can 'tunnel' through it. When immersed in liquid helium, a Josephson junction offers extremely high switching speeds. Brian Josephson, a British post-graduate student, discovered this tunneling effect in 1962, for which he was awarded a Nobel prize in 1973. Claims of developing the first computer using Josephson technology were made in Japan in 1990, quoting a speed of a thousand million instructions per second.

joule, *n.* the standard unit of energy. See J.

journal, *n.* a timed list of items with details, e.g. of messages received by and sent from a terminal or fax unit, or of users gaining access to a mainframe. A **journal file** is a permanent record, such as a journal on tape.

joystick, *n.* an input unit able to act as a pointing device. You push the central lever in any direction to move the screen cursor that way, and have one or two buttons to represent different key presses. A **proportional joystick** is one which also measures how hard you push, perhaps moving the cursor at a corresponding rate.

While joysticks are best known for games playing, they can be of great value as part of a graphics user interface or even for word processing. Some keyboards therefore have integral joysticks.

judder, *n.* a vibration, e.g. in fax scanners or paper feeds leading to distortions in the printouts.

jukebox, *n.* a store for a large number of discs with a single drive into which a robot arm can move any disc required. While access time is long if there is need to change a disc, this approach is still much quicker and safer than a manual one.

jump, *n.* or *vb.* a move within a running program to an instruction out of the normal sequence. Almost all programs gain much value from branching (and looping, which is in essence the same); this needs the power to jump unconditionally (i.e. always) or conditionally (if a set condition is true).

While all assembly program languages must have a jump instruction, this is not true of structured high level program languages. All the same, most of them do have GO TO or a similar instruction, although it is rarely good practice to use it.

junction, *n.* the interface between different types of semiconductor material, where diode action takes place. A **junction transistor** consists of two junctions back to back. See TRANSISTOR. See also JOSEPHSON JUNCTION.

junk, *n.* anything unwanted and not asked for. IT equivalents of postal junk mail include **junk email** (where the receiver suffers in having to pay for extra time on line) and **junk faxes** (more annoying as the recipient loses telephone line access time and must pay for the paper).

justification, *n.* a straight rather than ragged margin to a piece of word processed text. It is normal for text to be left-justified (to have a straight left margin), so justification often means right justification (setting the right hand margin to be straight). Centred text has neither margin justified.

Most word-processing systems produce fully justified text lines (i.e. justified right and left) by padding the gaps between words with extra spaces. A processor's **justification range** is the greatest number of extra spaces it will add for this purpose. Justification is a lot easier (and has much less ugly effects) when applied to proportionally spaced text and/or when the processor and printer allow micro-spacing. A **justification routine** is a program that adds justification features to a system.

K

k, symbol for KILO-.

Kansas City, *adj.* a standard for holding data on audio tape cassettes, very common when cassettes were the normal backing store for home and school micros. The name comes from Kansas City USA, where the standard was devised.

Karnaugh map or **Veitch sketch** *n.* a method of setting out in graphic form the contents of truth tables. M. Karnaugh first published the scheme in 1953, having slightly changed the ideas of E. Veitch. Properly used, Karnaugh maps make simplification of logical expressions much more straightforward than other methods.

kb, *symbol for* kilobit (1000 bits), a unit of storage chip capacity. As some people use k rather than K for 1024, and some use b rather than B for byte, kb may also mean:

      1024 bits
      1000 bytes (8000 bits)
      1024 bytes (8192 bits)

Clearly, therefore, it is best not to use kb at all.

KB, *symbol for* kilobyte (1000 bytes), or, to some, for 1024 bytes.

KBES, *abbrev. for* KNOWLEDGE-BASED EXPERT SYSTEM.

kcs or **kc/s,** *symbol for* kilo-cycles per second, the unit of frequency now called KILOHERTZ.

kern, *n.* (*printing*) that part of a character that lies outside the main body of the character. This may lead to the need to overlap the kern with part of an adjacent character. Printers working with metal type used to be able to do this; therefore the best of modern desktop publishing programs and their printers offer **kerning**, the overlap between parts of adjacent characters, such as in the Figure.

key, *n.* **1.** a data item which identifies a set of related data items. In most cases the set of data items makes up a record in a file, and the key value is in the **key field**. If the file's key field values are not unique, there may be a need for a **secondary key** in a second field. The key field in all files is not

181

kern. Kerned characters.

always the same; if users search a file for different types of data the key may well change.

2. a marked button switch which, when pressed, will produce the corresponding character code. A **keyboard** (large) or keypad (small, perhaps with numbers only) is an input unit, a surface on which there are a number of keys. IT system keyboards and keypads include various keys for special effects; in particular, <RETURN> (or <ENTER>) marks the end of a data item. <SHIFT>, <ConTRoL> and <ALTernate> keys, when pressed with others, change the effects of those others; function keys have special effects, which the user may be able to program.

There are many designs of keyboard, with different styles of key, different layouts of keys on the surface, different orders of keys. In the last case, the standard in Britain and elsewhere is QWERTY, while AZERTY is standard in many other countries.

Keyboarding, or (more accurately) **keying**, is the action of using a keyboard or keypad: typing, in other words. **Keyboard lock out** means that an operator cannot send data from a keyboard if the channel required is not available. A **keyboard operator** (sometimes called data preparation clerk) is a person whose job is to enter data full time into an IT system. See STAFF.

As noted above, a **keypad** is a small keyboard: either a board with many small keys (as in the case of a calculator) or, more often, one with a small number of standard size keys (as in the case of a **numeric keypad**, one for typing numbers only). Many modern keyboards have a numeric keypad to the side, to allow ease of use when the user has to type many numbers (e.g. when doing accounts).

A **key phone** is one with keys rather than a dial for calling out. A **key telephone system** is a private branch telephone network with key phones at the extensions; it offers such features as audio conferring, call transfer and grouping without

KILO-

the need to contact the switchboard.

A **keypunch** (now rare) is a machine with a keyboard, pressing the keys of which punches corresponding holes in cards (see PUNCHED MEDIA). **Keystrokes** are key press actions, a measure of data entry speed (as monitored automatically by many systems) being **keystrokes per hour (KPH)**. For **keyboard verification** see VERIFICATION.

Using a key punch for off-line data entry was the standard method of data preparation in the first generations of IT systems (when processor time was very costly). Clerks would key the data to cards and verify this input. The packs of cards would then pass through a card reader, the processor's main input system. The modern equivalent is to offer off-line data entry by a **key to store** approach. Versions of this are **key to disk** and **key to tape**. In each case, as the clerk keys the data it passes directly to backing store (still with verification) without troubling the main processor. A small processor can handle the needs of such a system, and the main processor, no longer INPUT BOUND, can access the new file as required.

keyword, *n.* a word or phrase that gives access to a record (like the key words, or head words, in this dictionary). A **keyword in context (KWIC)** index is an index of, for instance, titles, arranged in key word order with the key words aligned vertically:

                    Fax cards and machines
                    Faxing made easy
         The facsimile (fax) system
            Managing with fax
                Office fax working
               Using fax machines and cards

In each case here the key word is fax. See KEY, sense **1**.
2. one of the set of strings a program language translator will recognize and translate, such as, in Basic, REPEAT, TO, ELSE. In some languages keywords are reserved: programmers cannot use them as labels in programs, or, sometimes, even include them within labels (as with sTOpvalue).

kilo-, *prefix for* thousand, symbol k. Thus 3 kW is 3000 watts (perhaps the power usage of a communications satellite). The **kilohertz**, kHz (1000 Hz), is a common unit of wave frequency.

In IT, kilo (better **Kilo**, symbol K) is the prefix for a multi-

KIMBALL TAG

ple of 1024 (2^{10}). Thus **kilobaud** = 1024 baud (data transfer rate), and **kilobyte** = 1024 byte (data item or storage unit size, for instance).

Kimball tag, *n.* a small punched card (see PUNCHED MEDIA) attached to an item of clothing in a shop to carry basic details about the item in machine-readable form. Its uses at the point of sale and for stock control are much like those of the bar code on items of goods in other shops. The same technique is now widespread for hotel room keys, the lock having a slot to accept and read the card.

KISS, *jargon abbrev. for* 'keep it simple', advice to programmers that implies that a simple algorithm is less trouble than a complex one that solves the same problem.

kludge, *n.* a jargon term for a set of hardware units or software routines that just about manage to solve a problem but are not designed to work together.

knowledge, *n.* the set of facts, skills, theories and experiences of a person or group of people. A **knowledge base** is such a set in a particular subject area (domain) when stored in an IT system.

A **knowledge-based (expert) system (KBES)** is a group of software tools that work with a knowledge base to provide answers to a user's questions (if put in a suitable form). The system can attach degrees of certainty (probability levels) to the answers and display the reasoning behind its conclusions. This may make it seem INTELLIGENT. In that a knowledge base can contain more knowledge of a domain than any single human expert (when entered there using the special skills of a **knowledge engineer**), an EXPERT SYSTEM can be of great value. Applications are common in medicine, law, engineering.

Knowledge engineering is the work of knowledge engineers. They are skilled in the working of expert systems and in how to formulate a human expert's set of facts, skills, theories and experiences in a given domain to form a knowledge base. Knowledge engineering also includes the design of the interface between knowledge base and human user; the inference engine. See EXPERT SYSTEM.

KPH, *abbrev. for* KEYSTROKES per hour, measure of the speed at which a keyboard operator or checkout clerk works.

Kurzweil machine, *n.* a reading machine for the blind. The machine links a text scanner and optical-character reading program with speech synthesis.

L

label, *n.* **1.** the header of a file, with its name and other main characteristics. An **internal label** is stored on the tape or disc as part of the file itself; an **external label** sticks onto the outside, and can be checked by eye.
2. the name given in a program to a constant, variable quantity, instruction or procedure. It is easier for the programmer to refer to any of these by name than by value or by storage location: the translation program takes care of the details, such as by building up and referring to a **label table** (compare HASH TABLE). Below are examples of the four different uses of labels (the labels themselves are in square brackets on the left, but note that within any line a mixture of constant, variable, instruction or procedure labels can be found).

[pi]	LET pi := 3.14159 ... PRINT pi
[radius]	INPUT "Give the radius/mm" radius ...
	PRINT "Diameter - " radius*2 "mm"
[mainloop]	mainloop
[value]	STO value...JIN mainloop
[instruct]	PROCEDURE instruct ...
[answer]	IF answer = "Y" THEN instruct

The line numbers in older versions of Basic are all labels, with the extra function of ensuring order.

The most important use of labels is for variables. As a program language offers several different data types, it may require the programmer to code labels correspondingly. Thus labels for Basic's three data types are:

data type	label	example
real	no label	radius
integer	%	count%
string	$	name$

LAN, *abbrev. for* LOCAL AREA NETWORK.
land line, *n.* a cable (or, sometimes, radio or other wireless link) that carries telephone or telegraph signals between two points (in most cases overland). Normally the phrase refers to a trunk line (i.e. one between exchanges) or to a rented line

LANGUAGE

between a single client and the local exchange.

language, *n.* a system (set of rules and structures) for expressing ideas in spoken or symbol form. All human languages (NATURAL LANGUAGES) are very rich and complex, having developed over thousands of years in most cases. The languages used to give instructions to IT systems (PROGRAM LANGUAGES) are far simpler, with far smaller vocabularies (sets of KEYWORDS) and far fewer and more rigid rules (the syntax, or grammar).

A **language translator** is a program that takes in statements in one language and converts them to statements in another. While there are more and more effective programs for translating text between pairs of human languages, the phrase mainly refers to the programs (ASSEMBLER, COMPILER, INTERPRETER) that translate program instructions to machine language.

laptop, *n.* or *adj.* a micro that falls in size between a desktop system and a pocket computer. Laptops are very portable (up to about 10 kg). A laptop has a full size keyboard, a flat screen (LCD or plasma) able to show ten or more full length lines of text, effective backing store (microcassette, disc, or chip), and internal power supply able to keep the system fully working for a number of hours. Most laptops come with a good range of software and methods for the transfer of data to and from desktop machines; a few offer modems for fax and/or data communications.

large-scale integration (LSI) *n.* the INTEGRATION of hundreds or thousands of microelectronic circuit elements in the surface of a single semiconductor chip.

laser, *n.* (originally, *acronym for* Light Amplifier by Stimulated Emission of Radiation) a source of a tightly parallel beam of very pure light (or other electro-magnetic radiation, in IT mainly infrared). The waves in the output are also coherent (in step with each other); this makes them easy to work with. Being of very high frequency compared with radio, for instance, pure 'light' waves can carry a huge density of information. Hence the use of lasers in FIBRE OPTICS systems.

Light waves can also pass through each other with negligible interference, so one mirror or lens can handle hundreds of beams at the same time. This is a major feature that leads to OPTICAL PROCESSORS. These are compact and fast-working IT systems that use light beams from lasers, instead of electric currents, to carry all control and data signals. In all these cases, the laser light comes from the surface of a small piece of treated semiconductor: i.e. a chip.

There are many other uses of lasers in IT. In a **laser com** (COMPUTER OUTPUT ON MICROFORM) system, it is a laser that traces the image on the film (rather than the more traditional electron beam). A **laser line follower** is an automatic graphics scanner (input unit); the laser beam follows continuous lines on the original to produce an image on screen and in store. A **laser platemaker** is a type of fax machine in which a **laser scanner** scans a sheet, with the reflected light (picked up by a photo-cell) making an image in the form of a pulsed electric current; at the receiver, the current modulates a second laser to produce a printing plate.

Laser printers are a major type of page printer (i.e. a printer that builds up an image in its store of a whole page before printing it, in very much the same way as a photocopier). Many so-called laser printers in fact use light-emitting diodes (LEDs) rather than semiconductor lasers as the light source, but the principle is the same. The most recent advance in this field is to make images from dots of different sizes; this improves resolution without added cost or reduced speed.

The process is electrophotographic (xerographic). The light beam forms the image (any mix of text and graphics) of the page on a sheet of sensitive paper; plastics powder ('toner') then sticks suitably to the sheet, and a hot roller bakes it on to form the final image. Colour laser printing is only now beginning to appear, however; rather a mystery as colour copying is common and uses very much the same technology.

Laservision is the trade name of one kind of VIDEO DISC system; in fact lasers are very common in the write and read heads of optical (including compact) disc drives. To write, a high power laser burns or melts holes in the disc surface in a pattern that corresponds to the data to be stored; to read, a low power laser scans the patterns, with a photocell picking up the reflected light and sending the information on as a digital signal.

last in, first out (LIFO) *adj*. describes the order in which data items enter and leave a STACK. A **lifo list** is a stack. If a processor includes a hard-wired stack, this is sometimes known as a LIFO.

last in, last out (LILO) or **first in, first out (FIFO),** *adj*. describes the order in which data items enter and leave a QUEUE.

last number re-try, *n*. a feature of many modern telephone

LATCH

and fax systems that automatically calls an engaged number repeatedly.

latch, *n.* a simple FLIP-FLOP able to store a single bit for a short time.

latency, *n.* the same as SEARCH TIME, a significant part of ACCESS TIME.

lateral reversal, *n.* the flipping of a picture left to right (i.e. round a vertical axis) to make a mirror image.

layout, *n.* the same as FORMAT, the design of pages (for instance) in terms of margins, columns, headers, footers, boxes.

LCD, *abbrev. for* LIQUID-CRYSTAL DISPLAY.

leader, *n.* **1.** a blank length at the start of a tape (vulnerable to damage when being threaded into the drive, and not used to carry data).
2. the first field in a record used to identify the record (i.e. a KEY).

leaders, *n.* dots (or, sometimes, dashes) used to fill a row to lead the eye across the page. Leaders were once common in printing, but are rare now; they were frequently used in contents lists:

    hypermedia...................................185

leading, *n.* (pronounced 'ledding') the space between lines of text, in most cases measured in points.

lead-in page, *n.* the routing page in a videotex system.

leaf(let), *n.* the terminal node of a TREE (i.e. one with no descendants).

leased line, *n.* a telephone or telex line used only by the leasing firm (for security, or to prevent problems of other users taking too much capacity). See also ACCESS LINE. **Leasing** is in fact common for IT hardware (as for cars and for other items of office equipment). It is much like renting, but tends to be for a fixed fairly long period.

least cost routing, *n.* the choice of the cheapest and most efficient route for a packet of data between sender and receiver. Often there are very many possible routes; from moment to moment computers decide the best route, also taking into account how busy each route is.

least significant bit (LSB) *n.* the rightmost bit in a binary number, that with the least (place) value (for example the 0 in 11111110). In the same way, in denary (decimal), the **least significant digit** is the rightmost digit.

LED, *abbrev. for* LIGHT-EMITTING DIODE, a semiconductor junction diode which gives out light of a pure colour (often red) when passing a current. An **led display** is a rectangular grid of closely packed LEDs, able to switch on under computer control to display static or moving text and/or pictures. An early use on a small scale was in calculators and watches; here the LEDs produced a far better (i.e. brighter) image than LCDs, but their high power demand has made them now very rare in this context.

LEO, *acronym for* the Lyons' Electronic Office, the first commercial computer (started 1947, working 1953). The owners were the British catering firm of 'Joe' Lyons, who used the system for routine clerical work. LEO had a very large mercury delay line store and highly effective semi-autonomous input/output units.

Leo Computers, founded as a result in 1954, designed and made two further highly successful models of commercial computer, both as advanced for their time as LEO (I) itself.

letterpress, *n.* the traditional method of printing since the earliest systems in China and Europe (Gutenberg), but now rare. Letterpress involves inking a plate of raised characters and pressing a sheet of paper on the plate.

letter quality (LQ), *adj.* output from dot printers that is of such high quality that it is very hard to distinguish it from the output of daisy wheel and other such machines.

letter shift, *n.* the main SHIFT key on a keyboard and the effect of pressing it. The key allows the user to shift between the lower and upper CASES of type, i.e. between two CHARACTER SETS. Many IT keyboards have other shift keys for much the same purpose; e.g. <ConTRoL>, which then depressed while pressing other keys gives access to the set of CONTROL CHARACTERS, and <ALTernate>, for access perhaps to a graphics character set.

lexical analyser, *n.* a program which breaks input instructions into units it can recognize (i.e. handle, such as key words, labels, operators) as part of the process of assembly and compilation (translation of program code into machine code). The analyser also carries out such tasks as removing unwanted spaces, and changing lower case to upper case, **Lexical analysis** is the process which the analyser goes through to perform its various tasks.

librarian, *n.* in a computer centre, the person (**data librarian** or **file librarian**) whose job is caring for the centre's data tapes and disks, etc. As a computer centre may have many thousands of tapes and disks, the librarian's task is much the

LIBRARY

same as that of a book librarian; cataloguing, ordering, dealing with issues and returns. In addition, however, there are security aspects to bear in mind; the librarian must ensure that a tape/disc goes out only to authorized people, and will organize backing up. See also STAFF.

library, *n.* in IT, an ordered set of related items one or more people can call on when needed. See LIBRARIAN for **data library** (**file library**). A **program library** is a user's set of programs and packages, e.g. translators, utilities, statistics software, ready for access as required. A **routine library** is a similar set of procedures (sub-routines) available to be 'plugged into' any program under development as appropriate. Many program languages come with a library of standard routines.

Other specialist users of IT systems may have their own libraries. For instance, someone working with a computer aided design package will expect access to a library of standard shapes and designs.

life cycle, *n.* the series of steps and actions between recognising that a problem exists in a system and having a chosen solution in place and fully working. See SYSTEMS ANALYSIS. The mains steps are:

(a) systems analysis as such, and feasibility study;
(b) choice of solution;
(c) design of solution;
(d) implementation (which includes testing and staff training).

The process tends to be cyclic in that, after some time, the new system will show problems as the work load grows or other circumstances change.

LIFO, *abbrev. for* last in, first out.

ligature, *n.* two or more characters joined together in letterpress printing (or the link(s) between them), a rare feature in desktop publishing.

light, *n.* visible radiation in the electromagnetic SPECTRUM, with wavelengths defined to lie in the range 400–900 nm (1 nanometre = 10^{-9} m). As well as human eyes (which vary in the range they can in fact detect), light sensors include photographic emulsion and various photocells. Light waves have much higher frequencies (shorter wavelengths) than radio waves; this allows them to carry far higher densities of information when used for communication. See also FIBRE OPTICS (the use of '**light pipes**'), LASER and OPTICAL PROCESSOR.

A **light conduit** is an obsolete name for light pipe; a bundle of optical fibres each carrying its own set of signals along a trunk line.

A **light-emitting diode (LED)** is a semiconductor junction diode which gives out light of a pure colour (often red) when passing a current. See also LED. In use, the LED is forward biassed, and this applied voltage forces minority carriers across the junction; here they recombine with majority carriers and release energy as light photons (and heat). The name of the process involved is electro-luminescence. The wavelength of the photons produced depends on the size of the energy GAP in the semi-conductor. Various compounds of gallium produce output in the infra-red region (900 nm), red (660 nm), orange (610 nm), yellow (590 nm), and green (560 nm). Other colour effects follow mounting two LEDs back to back with an alternating supply.

The brightness of an LED depends directly on the size of the current; too large a current will, however, overload the device and cause it to fail. It is normal, therefore, to mount a current limiting resistor in series with an LED.

A **light gun** (or, more often, **light pen**) is an INPUT UNIT with which you can interact directly with a cathode-ray tube screen. The pen includes a photo-cell able to detect the screen's flying spot as it passes the pen's head. As the spot takes a certain short but known time to scan the screen, software can thus 'know' where the pen is pointing. By this means, a person can use the pen to select a choice from a screen menu, and to write and draw on screen with a suitable graphics program. Though this is a very natural way to interact with a screen display (especially if the screen is near horizontal), there are problems due to the thickness of the glass (leading to parallax errors) and to the size of the pen's tip. It is not strictly correct to call a bar code reader (or other such device with light source as well as photo-cell) a light pen, but the usage is common.

Light stability concerns how well OPTICAL CHARACTER READING can 'read' a document as the brightness and colour of the light change. Some systems require very precise lighting.

LILO, *abbrev. for* LAST IN, LAST OUT. Compare FIRST IN, FIRST OUT (FIFO).

limited distance modem, *n.* a modem designed for data transfers over short distances, up to about 50 km.

limiter, *n.* **1.** a device used to keep the power of a signal within a set range.

LINE

2. any device that keeps some value within a set range (including a software device to restrict the range of a variable).

line, *n.* **1.** a narrow continuous mark, for example, part of a screen design. A **line drawing** (**line illustration**) is one made entirely of lines, there being in particular no tones (greys); a **line drawing display** is a form of monitor, maybe linked with graphics pad or light pen, designed to show line drawings. A **line follower** is a robot's hardware/software system that helps it move from place to place without danger; a light source and sensor assembly with feedback to the steering wheels keep it on the line. The user can, of course, 're-draw' the line to provide a new route. A **line generator** is a device for producing full, dotted or dashed lines between the points on a screen.

2. a channel (or circuit) through which signals can pass, within an IT unit or between two. Perhaps the most common form physically in the latter case is the 'twisted pair', two copper wires for current and return. A line adapter is an old name for MODEM. A **line analyser** is a unit for testing the characteristics of a line electronically or otherwise. A **line concentrator** is a device with more input lines than output lines: the latter carry data at a higher speed, though most have a buffer to smooth out overloads. A **line driver** (same as bus driver) is an amplifier that can drive several hardware units linked to the same line (or bus). In a cable television network, a **line extender** is an amplifier that makes up for loss of power at a spur.

Line level is the strength of a standard signal in the line in question, while **line load** is the line's load factor: the fraction (as a percentage) in use compared with its capacity.

Line noise is the existence in the channel of unwanted signals (e.g. from interference and cross-talk) that make the wanted signal harder to receive. **Line speed**, often measured in baud or bits or bytes per second, is the rate of data transfer through the channel. **Line status** concerns whether the line is ready to transmit or receive, for instance.

A **line switcher** is:

(a) a system for linking inward and outward telephone lines into a single duplex circuit (i.e. for circuit switching),

(b) the same as line concentrator (above), or

(c) able (manually or automatically) to switch inward calls between voice handset and fax or email system.

A **line termination unit** sits at the interface between a

computer and a modem to aid data transfers either way between them. See also DELAY LINE.

3. a row of text on screen or printout. In word processing, a **line counter** displays the number of lines of a text (and you may be able to control the number on a printed page). The **line end zone** is the region near the right hand margin of a text in which a new word when started will automatically jump to the next line (same as hot zone). A **line feed** sends the cursor or print head to the next line; the **line character**, or **line feed code**, (ASCII 10) causes this to happen under software control. A **line finder** is of value when printing onto forms; with it, the printer moves to the correct line for the next print item.

On screen or printout, **line misregistration** is any form of distortion that causes it to deviate from the proper position. A **line printer** in effect prints a line at a time, in that the system sends it the whole line to process at once (compare character printer and page printer, see PRINTER). The main types are the BARREL PRINTER (drum) and the CHAIN PRINTER (belt). People measure printer speed in **lines per minute (LPM)** in these cases.

4. a row of pixels of a visual display. In the case of a cathode-ray tube, the **line flyback** is the very rapid return of the flying spot to the start of a line after reaching the end of the one before.

5. a single input, command or set of program instructions ending in the <RETURN> code. In the case of program lines, a **line editor** is software for editing a program a line at a time. Some program languages label each line with a number (as do most forms of Basic, for instance); the **line number** is therefore the label, of use for keeping the instructions in order and for calling lines for editing, as well as for the usual benefits of instruction labels.

linear, *adj.* logically in one dimension only. Thus a **linear program** (or program section) has no branches (and therefore no loops or other structures that involve decision). **Linear programming** is not closely related; rather it is an optimization procedure, for finding the greatest or least value of a function where the variables involve linear (in)equalities. A **linear search** is a sequential (or serial) search: a search that starts at the beginning of a set of items and checks one by one until finding the target, or passing where it should be (sequential), or coming to the end of the set (serial).

LINK

link, *n.* **1.** (or **linkage**) an instruction, call, or software that joins two or more machine code routines into a full working object program. A **link(age) editor** is a program able to do this and resolve problems that may arise.

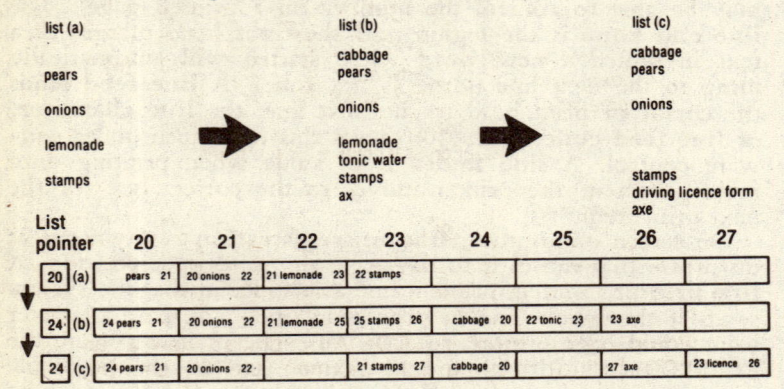

list (a)	list (b)	list (c)
pears	cabbage pears	cabbage pears
onions	onions	onions
lemonade	lemonade tonic water	
stamps	stamps ax	stamps driving licence form axe

List pointer	20	21	22	23	24	25	26	27
20 (a)	pears 21	20 onions 22	21 lemonade 23	22 stamps				
24 (b)	24 pears 21	20 onions 22	21 lemonade 25	25 stamps 26	cabbage 20	22 tonic 23	23 axe	
24 (c)	24 pears 21	20 onions 22		21 stamps 27	cabbage 20		27 axe	23 licence 26

link (Sense 2.) A linked shopping list.

2. another term for POINTER, in the case of pointers between the logically adjacent members of a linked list or ring data structure. A **linked list** is a logically linear (1D) structure to which you can add, and from which you can remove, data items (elements) at any point (see Figure, where (a) (b) and (c) show three different stages of a linked list). There is a pointer (link) to the head of the list in the system's label table; the head carries a pointer to the next item, and so on to the tail (the last item). Some linked lists allow each element to carry a second pointer, the address of the item before it in the list. Amending the list is simply a question of changing the pointers. A **linked ring** is a linked list, the tail of which points to the head.

3. (*communications*) another term for channel or circuit. A **link protocol** is the set of rules that govern data transfers through it.

liquid crystal display (LCD), *n.* a flat visual display unit that needs outside light but otherwise uses very little power. The LCD is the main type of display used in portable IT hardware (digital watches, calculators, pocket and laptop micros, radio phones, and so on); it is also very common as a flat clear display for mains powered units such as fax machines, copiers and printers.

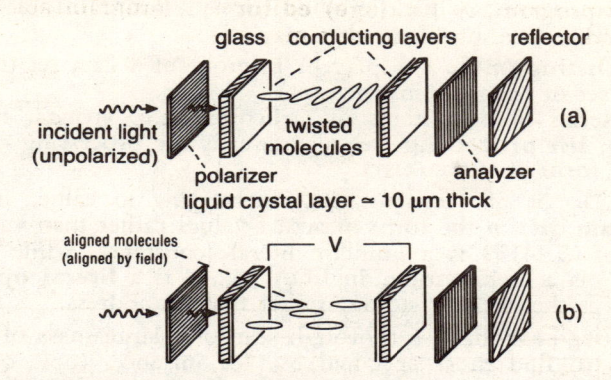

liquid crystal display (LCD). An exploded view of an LCD cell (a) showing light (normal) and (b) showing dark (field applied).

The structure is as shown in the Figure. The 'liquid crystal' particles, which are long and thin (though in the liquid state), cluster as in a crystal; a voltage between the conducting glass plates makes them polarize light that passes through; the light does not then return from the reflecting back plate, so that part of the display appears dark. To produce an image, each cell (pixel) needs separate wiring to carry the switching voltage. This has made LCDs complex and costly; until the last few years, too, they suffered from poor contrast, slow image changing speeds, and a small viewing angle. Active matrix LCDs, with a transistor to control each pixel, improve matters. Now, prototypes of bright 16-colour high resolution LCDs have appeared, with 250 mm screens; though very effective, these need rather a high power level (around 15 W; twice what is acceptable in a portable computer).

Lisp, *n.* a compact, functional program language designed for LISt Processing by John McCarthy at Massachusetts Institute of Technology (US) in the late 1950s. The language treats both programs (sets of instructions) and data sets as LINKED LISTs of so-called atoms, putting the lists in brackets. It also offers effective recursion and a versatile set of symbols for users' purposes. Lisp is now common in machine intelligence

LIST

systems, where its strength in handling non-numeric data gives it much potential. In Lisp, (Abdul Bessy Chris) is a list of three atoms, while ((Abdul) (Bessy) (Chris)) is a list of three lists.

list or **listing,** *n.* **1.** a display or printout of a data set (including a set of program instructions).
2. a series of data items or structures (e.g. strings, file records); **list processing** (see also LISP) is the processing of data in the form of LINKED LISTS.

literal, *n.* or *adj.* constant, i.e. unchanging in value, such as program data in the form of actual values rather than variables (labels). 3.14159 is a numeric literal (constant), while "Welcome" is a literal string. In LDA 14, 14 is a **literal operand** if that is the data for storage rather than an address.

literature search, *n.* a thorough scan of a large mass of documents to find those specified by, for instance, topic or keyword(s). The output is a set of references and/or abstracts and/or key quotes. Computer-based literature searching, which is fast and accurate (accurate specification assumed), is now very common; it is an important aspect of information retrieval.

liveware, *n.* a jargon term for the STAFF who run a large IT system (i.e. viewed as a resource or as an expense in the same way as hardware and software).

load, *vb.* **1.** to add inductance to a channel in order to cut down AMPLITUDE distortion.
2. to enter data, e.g. a program, into an IT system. A **loader** (or **loading program** or **loading routine**) carries out the final stage of assembly or compilation; it puts into main store an executable program ready to run (or copies an object program from backing store to main store). An ABSOLUTE LOADER will always load a given program at the same (absolute) address, while a **relocating loader** will store it at the most suitable address each time. **Loading on call** is loading data (or programs) automatically into store as required, a major feature of batch processing software.

lobe, *n.* an angular extent over which an aerial transmits or receives strongly (see Figure). A polar graph (strength against angle) shows how an aerial's signal strength depends on angle. Sometimes the pattern is complex, but there are always one or more lobes.

LOCATION

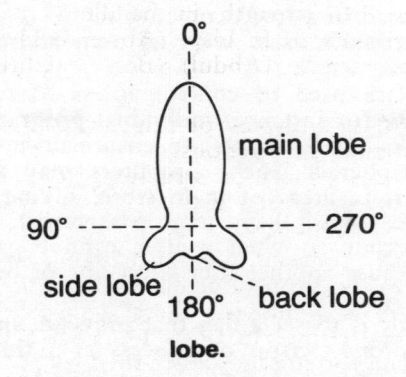

```
            0°
            |
         main lobe
            |
  90° ------+------ 270°
            |
 side lobe  |  back lobe
          180°
```
lobe.

local, *adj.* denoting nearby, e.g. in the same building or on the same site. A **local area network (LAN)** is a network where the most distant stations are no more than a kilometre or two away from the central server; the largest LANs now may be university campus-wide, with several thousand stations served by a number of main frames; strictly such systems consist of a number of true LANs linked together. See also NETWORK.

In a telephone network, a **local exchange** (switching centre) serves all the telephone lines in an area (e.g. suburb, or village and nearby farms), there being one line (**local line** or loop) to each telephone. Each local exchange links to one or more others by trunk lines.

Using a network station or mini/main frame terminal in **local mode** is using it as a stand alone machine; this means the station or terminal must be INTELLIGENT (have **local intelligence**), and have its own processor and backing store, as well as input and output units. A **local network** is the same as a local area network (above).

In a cable television network, **local origination** describes programmes made in the area (in a local studio or with simpler indoor or outdoor hardware), rather than being an import from some outside service.

To a programmer, a **local variable** is a variable with a label recognized only in one part (procedure) of a program; a global variable plays a part throughout the program's procedures.

local viewdata, see MICROVIEWDATA.

location, *n.* **1.** in television, a programme made on location is

LOCK

one not produced in a studio or on a set.

2. A single STORAGE CELL, with its own address, in main or backing store.

lock, *n.* a device used to control access to something. In a large computer, for instance, individual programs and routines may have locks (or **lockouts**) to ensure un-interrupted access to certain peripherals. Such computers may also have locks (codes) for certain areas of main store, giving access only to users with the correct keys (e.g. passwords). In a telephone system, a lockout is when a user cannot gain access to a shared line because another user is on line or because of excess noise.

To lock a file is to set a flag that prevents any change to its contents; only one person or process at a time can access a locked record.

A hardware system has **locked up** if some software or user error prevents any access at all; the only way to work with it again is to carry out a hard reset (or switch off and on again).

log, *n.* a journal or usage report produced automatically by, or on demand of, an IT system (e.g. multi-user computer or fax system). See CALL LOGGER, DATA LOGGING. In computing, a **log file** or **log tape** is a transaction file (or tape): a record of all transactions as described above, or of all the user's most recent business transactions for later merging into the master file (see file GENERATION).

To **log in**, or **log on**, to a multi-user computer (or network) is to start a user session by giving identity codes and/or password. At the session end, you **log off** or **log out**.

logic, *n.* a branch of mathematics which involves the analysis (with no regard to meaning) of the patterns of reasoning which lead from premises (input data) to conclusions (output). The binary digital mode of working of almost all IT systems relates to **Boolean logic** (see BOOLE); here all logic statements have only two values, called TRUE or FALSE.

A **logic analyser** reads, at certain times, the logic states of a digital system and records the results for later display. See also DATA LOGGING. A **synchronous logic analyser** takes readings at times set only by the outside system (e.g. when changes take place); an **asynchronous logic analyser** does so at pre-set times.

A **logic bomb** is a routine hidden within software set to act at some time in the future; in almost all cases it then causes damage (e.g. wiping out files) or carries out some

LOGIC

criminal act (e.g. the transfering of data elsewhere).

A **logic card** is a printed circuit board that can be added to an IT system to give it some extra special function; for instance, a fax board for use in a micro or network.

A **logic circuit** is any circuit whose action we can describe in terms of binary (Boolean) logic, **logic design** being the design of such circuits starting from principles of logic. See also GATE.

There are various kinds of **electronic logic**, ways to describe a circuit in terms of its elements (components) and the signals that pass between them. The main types are:

(a) CMOS, the second most common in the early 1990s with voltage controlled metal oxide semiconductor (MOS) transistors; valued for the low power demand.

(b) current mode logic; same as ECL, below.

(c) DCTL, direct coupled transistor logic; good, but with problems if the transistors differ even slightly in how they behave.

(d) DTL, diode transistor logic; now very rare despite being fast.

(e) ECL, emitter coupled logic (or current mode logic); very fast but with a high power demand.

(f) LS-TTL, low power schottky transistor/transistor logic; widely used in large scale integration (LSI).

(g) RCTL, resistor/capacitor/transistor logic: same as RTL, but with capacitors in parallel with the resistors to increase the switching speed.

(h) RTL, resistor/transistor logic, now very rare, but the first commercial system: same as DCTL, but with resistors in series with the transistors to overcome the problems of DCTL.

(i) SITL, static inductive transistor logic, used mainly in high power circuits.

(j) TTL, transistor/transistor logic (with many varieties): much the same as DTL, but with multi-emitter transistors rather than diodes; most common and important, but on the whole replaced by LS-TTL circuits (one of many variants).

(k) TTTL, transistor/transistor/transistor logic, a major variant of TTL aimed at higher efficiency and better immunity against noise.

All these comprise the so-called **logic families**. A **logic element** is the same as a GATE. For **fuzzy logic**, see FUZZY LOGIC. A **logic gate** is the same as a logic circuit, see GATE. A

LOGICAL

logic operation is a defined logical operation on input data, while **logic programming** is a form of functional programming; a common program language that provides this is PROLOG.

A **logic symbol** is a symbol used in **logic diagrams** to show the effect rather than the structure of a logic element. See the Figure.

traditional

AND OR NOT NAND NOR XOR

JEC 617: 12
(BS 3939: 12)

& ≥1 1 & ≥1 =1

logic.

For **logic unit**, see ARITHMETIC AND LOGIC UNIT: that part of a processor which carries out arithmetic operations and comparisons following the standard rules of logic.

logical, *adj.* related to some aspect of **logic**; thus a **logical structure** is one seen from the human point of view rather than from any physical aspect such as tape or disc format. This applies to a **logical data base**, **logical file**, or **logical record**, for instance.

In programming, a **logical error** follows a slip in the programmer's thinking. For instance, coding IF this > that THEN ... instead of IF this < that THEN ... will lead to logical errors when the program runs.

A **logical shift** is an operation on a binary value which involves moving each bit one place left or right, wrapping to the other end any bits that fall off as a result. Thus a logical shift left of 1101 gives 1011. A **logical type** in programming is a data item, with no more than two values, called, for instance, 0 and 1, true and false, or no and yes. In the Basic instruction IF flag THEN ..., flag is a logical with only two possible values (set or not set).

Logo, *n.* a high-level, logic based, interpreted program language devised by Seymour Papert and others at the Massachusetts Institute of Technology in 1967, and aimed at learners of programming. Logo's turtle graphics aspects are best-known (those being accessible to very young learners); all the same, it has much more potential and power than for that alone, and has applications for business and science as well as for learning.

look-up table, *n.* data set in easy to access form, such as the label table used by a processor to hold the storage addresses of data items and structures.

loop, *n.* a set of instructions in a program an IT system may pass through a number of times. There are three kinds of loop ALGORITHM; in Basic the structures are:
- DOTHIS/.../TIMES n, where n. is a number: for when the programmer knows how many times the system should pass through the loop instructions.
- REPEAT/.../UNTIL ...: for when the system must pass through the loop instructions at least once, until the stated condition becomes true.
- WHILE .../.../ENDWHILE: much the same, except this time, if the condition is true at first, the system does not pass through the loop at all.

A **loop back check** is a test for data transfer errors in which the data bits received go back to the sender for comparison. A **loop network** is a network with a single channel between each pair of nodes, all the nodes being linked in a closed path.

loss, see ATTENUATION.

loudspeaker, *n.* see SPEAKER: a unit giving a sound wave output.

Lovelace, Ada (Ada Augusta Byron, daughter of the poet Lord Byron, the Countess Lady Lovelace, 1815–1852) a close working colleague of, and translator for, Charles BABBAGE, and often called the first programmer. Part of her work with Babbage involved devising programs for his 'analytical engine'. The program language ADA (1979) carries her name.

low activity processing, *n.* working with a data base or file but with a low ACTIVITY (hit rate).

low level, *adj.* close to the way an IT system works rather than to the way a human thinks (high level), a **low-level program language** being one the system can follow without further translation (i.e. machine code). A **low-level protocol** is a set of rules about the use of a system (e.g. network) that takes more account of how the system works than about how people use it.

LOW POWER

low power schottky transistor/transistor logic (LS-TTL), see LOGIC, (ELECTRONIC LOGIC).
low resolution, *n.* crude graphics rather than smooth (high resolution) ones. Low-resolution graphics involves working with large pixels, even with character blocks as shown, rather than with small dots. See also RESOLUTION and DEFINITION.
low speed, *adj.* a relative term that describes a fairly low data transfer (or access) SPEED. Thus a low-speed printer will print more slowly than other machines.
lower case, *n.* or *adj.* text that does not use CAPITAL (upper case) letters or symbols accessed with a <SHIFT> key. See CASE.
LPM, *abbrev. for* LINES PER MINUTE.
LQ, *abbrev. for* LETTER QUALITY.
LRC, *abbrev. for* longitudinal redundancy check, a form of parity checking that works on block rather than character level. It is a widely used system for checking for errors in programs after storage or transfer.
LSB, *abbrev. for* LEAST SIGNIFICANT BIT.
LSI, *abbrev. for* LARGE SCALE INTEGRATION.
LS-TTL, see LOGIC (ELECTRONIC LOGIC).
luminance, *n.* brightness, in particular that part of a television signal that handles the monochrome (black and white) aspect of a picture.
Lyons' Electronic Office, *n.* see LEO, the first commercial computer (started late 1940s).

M

m, *symbol for* milli-, a thousandth, as in mW: milliwatt, a thousandth of a watt.

M, *symbol for* mega-, a million (or, in IT, strictly 1048 576), as in MB: megabyte, a million bytes.

machine, *n.* any single stand-alone unit or system, in particular a computer (whether special purpose or general purpose). However, see also TURING MACHINE and VIRTUAL MACHINE. For **machine-aided translation (MAT),** see COMPUTER-AIDED TRANSLATION. A machine, i.e. a computer, is a complex of electronic circuits designed to carry out some range of tasks under the control of one or more programs. Those programs must be in **machine code** with all instructions as sets of bits (0s and 1s) the system can accept.

A **machine code instruction** held in store for action has, in most cases, two parts: the opcode (sequence of bits in the machine's instruction set that defines the action it should take) and the operand (sequence of bits that defines the data with or on which it should act).

Machine cognition is, to some, any aspect of machine intelligence (see below). Its main concerns, however, are 're'cognition, i.e. the automatic reading of data (see machine readable input, below) and/or PATTERN RECOGNITION, an aspect of machine VISION. All the same, in that cognition concerns knowledge and learning, machine cognition means many things in the field of machine intelligence to different people.

machine cycle, *n.* the sequence of actions by which an IT system carries out a single instruction in a program held in main store. There are three main phases. Each involves opening and closing gates between different parts of the system so that only one data item can move, and that only one way. The phases are as follows, the parts of the central processor mentioned can be seen in the Figure.

(a) Fetch: in which the system prepares to accept the next instruction, and transfers a copy from its cell in the main store to the processor's *logic unit*. For this to happen, the cell address must be in the memory *address selection register*

MACHINE CYCLE

machine. Central processor and machine cycle.

MACHINE CYCLE

(MASR). The copy of the instruction passes from that cell through the *storage buffer register* (SBR) into the control unit. During this stage, a copy of the contents of the ASR pass to the *sequence control register* (SCR, or program counter, PC). The two parts of the machine instruction (see above) split; the opcode goes to the *operation register* (OR), and the system stores the operand (address part) in the now free ASR.

(b) Execute: in which the system carries out the new instruction. The system uses a decoder on the value of the opcode (in the OR) to activate the correct sub-circuits of the *control unit*. There are various groups of opcode as far as concerns possible effects:

(i) data transfer (either way) between peripheral and main store cell, or between processor register and cell (which includes actions that involve the *arithmetic and logic unit*): in which case the ASR contains the address of the cell in question, and the data will pass through the SBR to/from that cell as required.

(ii) un-conditional or conditional jump out of the normal program sequence: now the ASR holds the address of the next instruction.

(iii) stop: in which case control returns to the operating software and the contents of the ASR have no meaning.

(c) Reset: when the system prepares to handle the next program instruction. In case (ii) above, the ASR holds the address of the cell that carries that instruction, so now there is no need for further action. For instructions in case (i), on the other hand, the system calls on the contents of the SCR; this is because the next instruction it needs is the one that follows the current one in sequence in the store. The incrementer adds 1 to the contents of the SCR and the new value passes to the ASR.

Thus, whether the system is to jump or not, the ASR now contains the address of the storage cell that holds the next instruction, and the cycle can start again.

A **machine error** follows a fault in the hardware of the system (a hardware bug). **Machine independence** concerns how well a peripheral or program can work with a range of systems rather than with just one type. It is (or should be) a major aim of all hardware and software developers to maximize independence, though full independence is impossible at the moment. See also COMPATIBILITY.

MACHINE INTELLIGENCE

machine intelligence or **artificial intelligence (AI)** *n*. any aspect of a machine's actions that we would call intelligent if observed in a person. The main fields of current interest are problem-solving, learning, knowledge-based EXPERT SYSTEMS, interaction with human (natural) languages, and machine vision (below). Human intelligence involves reasoning and is not easy to describe in terms of simple logic and yes/no answers. IT systems, on the other hand, offer great speed, so a common approach to machine intelligence at this stage in history is to apply brute force to problems. All the same, there is good progress in working with FUZZY LOGIC, and this is likely to be the best way forward. See also TURING.

For **machine language**, see machine code (above). A **machine oriented language** is a program language where the features relate closely to those of a particular hardware system (processor in particular); this makes programs written in it much less portable than those in an applications-oriented language.

A major field of development in machine intelligence is that of **machine-readable input** methods. As well as being a source of error, the manual (human) input of data to an IT system is, to many firms, the most costly aspect of processing. They may employ hundreds of data preparation STAFF for this work. Automatic input, in which a device reads the data straight into the computer, will produce vast savings when fully set up. At the point of sale, bar codes and Kimball tags, for instance, passed over or through suitable readers, speed up input, reduce errors and the chance of theft, and make the operators' work simpler and more pleasant. Here, however, there are still operators, though various systems to automate the process more are under development. Stripe cards (magnetic and optical) and smart cards also need people to present them to the reader.

Data preparation departments tend to work with vast numbers of documents, such as objective test answer sheets, cheques, payment slips, application forms, abstracts, and meter reading cards. If the relevant data here is machine readable, the only need for staff is to bundle the papers the right way up and feed them to the reader. The systems involved tend to be optical scanners (e.g. for mark reading and character reading) or magnetic units (as in magnetic ink character reading), though there are other approaches. PUNCHED MEDIA (cards, tape) were once the only approach to machine readable input, also used for backing storage. Like such modern equivalents as the Kimball tag, they suffered by not being also human readable.

Once the data is in the computer, in some kind of data base file, it should be **machine searchable**. This involves coding it so searches can quickly find the information needed.

For **machine translation**, see COMPUTER-AIDED TRANSLATION; for **machine vision**, see VISION.

macro, *adj*. on a larger than normal scale, or *n*. in assembly coding, a single instruction that translates to a number of machine code instructions. This saves time and trouble in coding, and brings the assembly language to a higher level. For example, a language may offer the macro INC, for adding 1 to (incrementing) the contents of the storage cell with address a. The assembler would translate this into instructions for these steps:

(a) copy current accumulator value to the stack;
(b) load the value 1 into the accumulator;
(c) add to the accumulator the value stored in cell a;
(d) copy accumulator contents to cell a;
(e) pop the stack value back to the accumulator.

An assembly language with this feature bears the name **macro assembler**, while a **macro code** is the same as a macro.

In data processing and high level coding, a **macro element** is a data structure that contains a number of data items (elements). It has a single label (name, identifier) and a method (e.g. the use of subscripts) to allow access to any item.

In documentation, a **macro flowchart** is the same as an outline chart i.e. one that gives an overview of the system or program in question. A single detailed flow chart or a number of micro charts then expand on it as required. A **macro instruction** is the same as a macro, with a **macro library** being the set of macros a programmer can call on when using a given macro assembler. **Macro-programming** involves writing assembly language code mainly in terms of macros. This may make life simpler for the programmer, as noted above, but has the danger that the translated object program may become very long.

A useful aid for finding program bugs is a **macro trace**. This keeps a log of all major steps taken during a program run, rather than one of each single instruction carried out (see TRACE).

MAGAZINE

magazine, *n.* **1.** a removable box that contains a backing storage medium, e.g. a hard disk pack, a set of magnetic stripe cards, or a compact or video disc.
2. a related set of videotex pages, in most cases fairly small (no more than a hundred or two).

magnetic, *adj.* of, producing, or operated by (ferro)-magnetism. This is a property of some substances that gives them, when suitably treated, two opposite poles (points or surfaces, called north-seeking and south-seeking); there is then a magnetic field around and between the poles. This is a region of space that affects magnetic materials.

Magnetic materials consist of tiny magnetic regions, called domains, each with a pair of poles. In some cases, it is possible to isolate the domains as permanent **magnetic bubbles**; in **magnetic bubble storage** these domains, in trains of thousands held in loops in the surface of the substance, store bits of data. See BUBBLE.

A **magnetic card** is the same as a magnetic stripe card (below), with a **magnetic card file** being a set of stripe cards, accessed with a **magnetic card reader**, to form a **magnetic card store**. This is a fairly rare form of backing store.

A **magnetic cartridge** or **magnetic cassette** is the same as a magnetic tape cassette (below). A **magnetic cell** is the basic unit of storage on a magnetic disk, stripe or tape, and is able to carry one word of data as a set of domains. For **magnetic character**, see magnetic ink character (below).

Magnetic core was a rare name for a **magnetic core store**. Now never used, this was an array of very small ferrite rings (called cores) mounted on a grid of fine wires; these carried the write currents that set the polarity of each ring (causing it to store one bit) and the read currents that accessed the stored data. The stores, though non-volatile, were very bulky, costly and slow. However, as 'core' also means 'centre', the name core store lives on as an alternative for main store.

A **magnetic delay line** is a form of DELAY LINE; its action depends on the fairly slow speed at which magnetic waves pass through a substance. For **magnetic disk** (floppy, hard) see DISK; for **magnetic (disk) drive/unit**, see DRIVE.

Magnetic drums were the first effective form of direct access magnetic backing store; until disks appeared, they were popular, though very bulky and costly (see Figure).

Magnetic film is very thin (just a few tens of micrometres) and

MAGNETIC

magnetic. Fig. 1. A magnetic drum store.

has sometimes been used for main storage on the surface of a glass plate although it needs a tight packed array of heads to keep access time short.

A **magnetic head** is a device for reading data stored on, and writing data to, the surface of a magnetic backing storage medium, such as drum, disk, tape, stripe. It consists of a tiny electromagnet that floats on a cushion of air over the moving surface, or actually touches it. See HEAD.

Printing data using **magnetic ink** is common in some contexts, e.g. cheques and similar documents. The standard system (E13B) has the set of 15 **magnetic ink characters** shown in the Figure. The approach of **magnetic ink character reading** (MICR) or **magnetic ink character scanning** is a form of MACHINE READABLE INPUT (and the characters are human readable too); this gives **magnetic ink character sorting** the speed and reliability needed for clearing cheques.

magnetic. Fig. 2. The magnetic ink character set.

MAGNITUDE

In IT, **magnetic media** include all magnetic methods of data storage: disk, stripe and tape in the main, but also drum, film and MICR. In each case, a fine magnetic powder (with very small domains) covers the surface smoothly. At each point a north-seeking or a south-seeking pole may be exposed, giving the potential of bit storage (but see DISK and VERTICAL RECORDING). As with audio tape, the magnetic media used in IT provide a non-volatile store that can, all the same, be erased and re-used. This makes it very cheap as well as effective.

A **magnetic printer** is a fast page printer that uses magnetism to build up the image on the drum for transfer to the sheet. **Magnetic storage** is any use of magnetic media (see above) for holding data for later access. It includes the **magnetic stripe card**, although the common form of this that appears with credit and atm cards carries very little data. The stripe is a film of magnetic powder with a number of tracks. As the card passes through the reader, a set of read/write heads scans the stored data and changes it as appropriate.

Magnetic tape is a very common backing storage medium. It is fairly cheap, and offers fairly fast (though only serial, not direct) access. Wound on open reels (or, far less often) spooled inside a **magnetic tape cartridge** or **magnetic tape cassette**, one tape may store a hundred or more megabytes, with the bits of each byte (plus a parity bit) running across its width, one bit per track. The **magnetic tape drive** (see DRIVE) needs a read/write head for each track. Standard open reel tapes are 12.5 mm wide and 365 m, 730 m or 1095 m long; storage density is high, in most cases in the range 25 to 300 byte/mm. See also GAP. A **magnetic tape encoder** is a key-to-store unit: a data entry device with a keyboard from which data passes directly to a tape. For **magnetic thin film**, see magnetic film (above).

magnitude, *n*. size, the magnitude of a number being its value with no account taken of sign. See ARITHMETIC. Many program languages have a function, ABS (for ABSOLUTE) in most Basics, that returns the magnitude of its denary argument.

mailbox, *n*. a data store in an EMAIL host computer or large memory fax system, for access by one person or a small group (also a deprecated contraction for **mailbox message**, a message left in a mailbox). A **confidential mailbox** needs a password before the user can see the contents.

mail merge, *n*. a process whereby select data from a file can enter a second text file automatically at the correct place(s). A common use is to 'personalize' standard letters, e.g. for junk mail. At each place where data is to enter, the letter contains a code. Thus, in 'Dear @mge1', the code tells the system to replace the code with the first field (in this case, full name) of each record in the data file as it prints out each letter.

main, *adj.* central and/or most important. **Mainframe** is an old (and now very rare) term for central processor, that part of the system fitted into the main one of a number of large circuit storage frames. Mainframe is now a rather vague term for any standard type of large computer, i.e. other than personal computer, mini and super-computer. All mainframes have large main and backing stores (perhaps hundreds and thousands of megabytes respectively), and very fast processors with a large word length (e.g. 64 or 128 bits); they work with a range of different types of peripheral, including (in most cases) a large number of terminals.

In a videotex system, the **main menu** (or **main index**) is the first one seen, giving the broadest links to the rest of the system. People also widely use the term for the first (most general) menu (index) offered by any software package driven by a hierarchy of menus (indexes).

In an IT system, the **main store** holds the data (which includes program instructions) needed by the processor at a given moment; it is therefore the store most intimately linked with the processor, as part of the central processing unit. See also STORAGE.

mains data transfer, *n.* the use of the mains cable network of a site to carry higher frequency data signals between hardware units in a local network. The units simply plug into normal mains sockets. In the interface between each unit and the main cable, however, must be a chip that adds the unit's unique code (network address) to each outward signal. It must also recognize that code when heading any passing signal, so it can divert it into the unit.

The approach is more costly than it should be; however, it is of growing interest for linking:

(a) intercomm units and telephone handsets in a local network;

(b) the various parts of intruder and fire alarm systems;

(c) lamps, heaters, electric motors for curtains and blinds, and other such items in an 'intelligent' (i.e. computer controlled) home or office;

(d) computers to each other and to printers in simple local computer networks.

MAINTENANCE

On a somewhat larger scale, the same technique links:

(e) meters for services (e.g. gas, water, power) to central readers in an area;

(f) nationwide communication units of electric power companies (who use the high voltage trunk cables the same way).

maintenance, *n.* in IT, the activity of ensuring that programs and equipment operate efficiently. This is important not just for hardware (in the normal sense), but for software: keeping files current and backed up, and keeping programs up to date with changes in the users' needs. The latter is the main task of a **maintenance programmer**.

make up, *n.* or *vb.* preparing a page of separate text and graphics items for reproduction. Many people prefer to call desktop publishing programs page makeup (or page layout) software.

Maltron, *n.* perhaps the most common of many keyboards designed from ergonomic principles. Standard keyboards are not well shaped for human hands, nor are their keys fully suited to comfortable healthy keying action. Ergonomic keyboards address both problems; they also group the keys for fast accurate action. Their designers also claim that users suffer much less from REPETITIVE STRAIN INJURY.

MAN, *abbrev. for* medium (or metropolitan) area NETWORK, one with stations perhaps tens of kilometres apart.

management, *n.* any process concerned with human control, as among the senior STAFF of a computer department (or of any organisation). A **management information system** (MIS) is a software package aimed at the precise handling of the information needs of management; such a package may include various planning and statistical programs, as well as routines to deal with budgets.

Manchester I, *n.* the first electronic stored-program computer, first run at Manchester University (UK) in 1948 (a year before EDSAC), design having started two years before. Clearly this was a first GENERATION machine, a major feature being the use of an electrostatic main store. The system became the world's first commercially available computer, sold from 1951 as the Ferranti Mark 1.

mantissa, *n.* the magnitude or value part of a number expressed in standard form. Thus, in denary, the number 123456 in standard form is 1.23456×10^5; here 1.23456 is the mantissa and 5 is the exponent. For the binary version, see ARITHMETIC.

manual, 1. *n.* a handbook, i.e. a printed guide to the usage of an IT system. Some manuals are on a rather larger scale (coming in a number of volumes); on the other hand, it is becoming more and more common to offer instructions and guidance to users, at least in the case of software, on disk.
2. *adj.* of anything carried out by people rather than by machines. IT systems with **manual control** have an operator with the power to over-ride the machine's decisions. **Manual (data) entry** involves human keyboard operators rather than automatic (machine readable) input. Cheaper fax machines have only **manual receive**; the user must press a button to accept an inward fax, rather than having the machine receive calls automatically.

map, *n.* a two dimensional graphic representation of a system, sub-system, or concept. A **bit map** is an image of the screen display held in main store, with one or more bits per pixel. If there is only one bit per pixel, the display is purely monochrome (i.e. just black and white); the more bits per pixel, the more levels of grey or colours can appear on screen. A **Karnaugh map** (or Veitch sketch) shows the action of a gate (logic circuit). See KARNAUGH MAP. A **memory map** shows how a system shares its main store between different types of program and data.

marker, see FLAG.

mark reader, scanner or **sensor,** *n.* an input unit that accepts sheets of paper with marks in certain places and passes the coded data to the central processor. This is a form of MACHINE READABLE INPUT, common for objective test answer sheets, market survey response forms, and meter cards. In the reader is an array of perhaps 40 or 80 light sources and sensors (photocells), and a set of rollers to pass the sheet through quickly but in a straight line. The light reflects differently from the marks than from the rest of the sheet; suitable software interprets the marks as data.

mark/space ratio, *n.* the ratio of the lengths of the positive to the negative pulses (1s and 0s) in certain kinds of data transfer (Morse code is one example).

mark up, *vb.* to add suitably coded data at the head of a word-processed document to control the printed layout (format).

mask, *n.* **1.** a word-processed form on screen for the user to complete.
2. a part of the process of making a ROM, a read only data

MASR

storage chip, used in making each layer. The mask is a chemical layer placed temporarily on the upper surface of the WAFER (large semiconductor disk that contains many chips during manufacture); the system deposits the new layer of junctions and links only through gaps in the mask, and this is then removed.

3. a logical operation (also called **masking** or FILTERING) carried out on a data item to disable, identify, or amend part of it. The word also applies to the bit pattern the system generates to do this, the mask being the same length as the item to be masked, and stored in a **mask register**. In this four bit example, the aim is to find the value of the left-most bit: the mask is 1000, this being ANDed with the test data, say 0101. ANDing gives the result 0000. In fact, whatever the value of the test data, ANDing with 1000 will produce 0000 if the test data starts with 0 and 1000 if it start with 1. Thus the other three bits are **masked** (disabled, have no effect).

Much the same kind of masking will check for high priority flags in a flag register, set certain flags to 0, and separate the opcode from the address part of a machine instruction.

4. a device used in rather the same way to identify optical characters in OCR systems, the process being **mask matching**.

MASR, *abbrev. for* memory address selection register. See MACHINE CYCLE.

massaging, *n.* changing the structure of input data to fit a desired pattern.

mass, *n.* or *adj.* large scale, as in **mass data**, a larger amount of data than the main store can hold, and **mass storage**. See BACKING STORE.

master, *n.* the file in current use for searching and sorting, etc. At the same time as it is in use, new transactions make it more and more out of date. Every so often (in some cases once or twice a minute, more often daily) the master and transaction files are merged to produce a new master. See file GENERATION and MERGING.

MAT, *abbrev. for* machine aided translation. See COMPUTER-AIDED TRANSLATION.

match, *n.* the state of two data items being exactly the same. To check this in the case of single bits, a match GATE (equivalence gate) will do: its output is 1 only if the inputs are the same. A COMPARATOR checks whether sets of bits (and therefore any pair of data items) are identical.

MEDIUM (METROPOLITAN) AREA NETWORK (MAN)

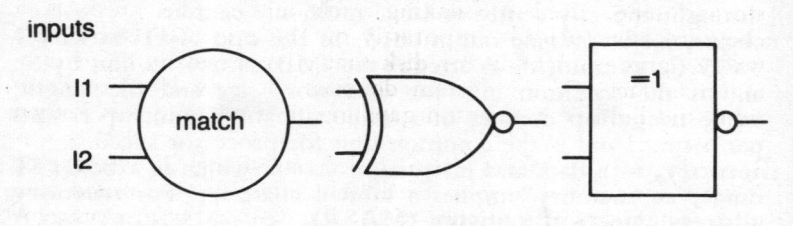

match.

maths processing, *n*. **1.** a feature of some word processors that allows the user to carry out calculations and incorporate the results in the text.
2. a function of extra processing chips available for some computers. They concentrate on heavy calculating, thus letting the main processor work on other tasks.

matrix, *n*. **1.** the mathematical equivalent of a two dimensional array.
  Matrix processing is a form of array processing offered in some program languages.
2. a rectangular grid, or array, of points or cells (including pixels). Thus each character on a display screen consists of a pattern of light and dark dots, as does the output of a **matrix printer**, e.g. dot matrix printer and ink jet printer. See also MAGNETIC INK CHARACTER READING.

MB, *symbol for* megabyte, one million (strictly 1 048 576) bytes, the unit of store size and file length.

MBR, *abbrev. for* memory (storage) buffer register, the gateway between main store and processor. See Figure, MACHINE CYCLE.

MCR, *abbrev. for* MAGNETIC (INK) CHARACTER READING.

mean time before failure (MTBF), see MTBF.

mean time between maintenance checks (MTBM), see MTBM.

mean time to repair (MTTR), see MTTR.

medium, *n*. (plural **media**) **1.** a material used for data storage, and thence any object that carries such a material, e.g. disk or tape, and thence chip. See, for instance, MAGNETIC MEDIA and PUNCHED MEDIA.
2. a material that carries signals, and thence any system for public information transfer.

medium (metropolitan) area network (MAN) *n*. a NETWORK with stations perhaps up to tens of kilometres apart, e.g.

215

MEGA-

throughout a city centre or large multi-site campus.

mega-, *prefix denoting* one million (in the case of IT, strictly 1 048 576), symbol M. A **megabyte** (MB) is one million bytes, and is the common unit for data store size and file length, while **megaflop** denotes one million floating point operations per second, and is the common unit for processor speed.

memory, *n.* a data and instruction STORE, which is a better IT usage, as 'memory' implies a human character. For **memory address selection register (MASR),** see MACHING CYCLE. A **memory card** is a type of SMART CARD that contains a bank of storage in the form of flat eproms; current capacities range up to 2 MB. Such cards have a number of uses as personal information stores, e.g. in medicine and education. A **memory phone** has several registers (small data stores) for frequently used numbers, the last number called, and so on. Much the same is true of a large range of IT hardware (such as copiers, modems, fax machines).

menu, *n.* a list of options on display as offered by a program; the users make their choices by moving the cursor or pressing keys. As at many stages in many interactive programs where there is a number of options, a menu is a good way to make the options clear. **Menu-driven** programs are more FRIENDLY than command-driven ones, but slower in action. Often, therefore, a program will try to combine both in such a way as to appeal to naive and expert users alike.

merging, *n.* the process of linking parts, or the whole, of two files. A major task of file maintenance in a large system involves merging the current MASTER file with the latest transaction file (which the program must first sort into the same sequence as the master). The process (see the Figure) produces a new master for the users to work with (and an error report showing on which transactions merging failed). The old master is called the parent (or father) of the new one, which is the child (son). For security reasons, it is common to keep safe both the father and the transaction file that was merged with it, and to do the same for the GENERATION before. See also MAIL MERGE.

mesh, *n.* another term for NETWORK (but now rare in most contexts).

message, *n.* a signal, often fairly short, between one person and another through an IT system that does not offer direct real-time interaction. The word also applies to short coded signals between hardware units as part of their HANDSHAKING

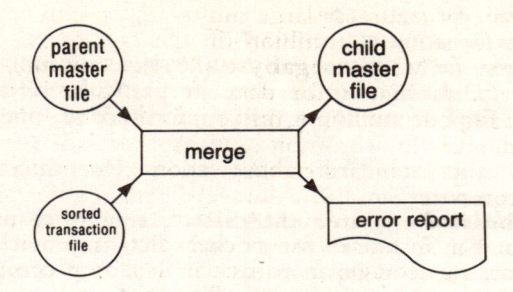

merge. The file merging process.

techniques.

A **message control flag** is a code sent with a machine message to indicate whether the signal is data or a set of control codes. A **message header** is a short set of codes at the front of a message to indicate its source, starting time, nature, destination, and so on.

Message routing is the process of passing a message (or a packet, part of a message) from stage to stage through a **message-switching system** (e.g. a telephone network). In such a network, a **message-switching centre** is a place (node) where such switching takes place (perhaps an exchange).

messaging, *n*. any form of data transfer in which a message passes at once from source to destination, rather than being held in a centre (e.g. email host or voice bank) for later access.

metal oxide semiconductor (MOS), *n*. a common type of transistor (strictly the substances from which its junctions are made). See MOS.

metal oxide semiconductor field effect transistor (MOSFET), see MOS.

metafont, *n*. any FONT design program, such as T_EX, where users can define characters by exact shape (rather than as a fixed size and aspect ratio MATRIX of dots). The output is digital and able to drive suitable printers and typesetting hardware with high quality output.

metropolitan area network (MAN), *n*. a NETWORK with some stations perhaps tens of kilometres apart. See MEDIUM AREA NETWORK.

MFLOP

Mflop, *abbrev. for* MEGAFLOP.
MH, *abbrev. for* MODIFIED HUFFMAN.
MICR, *abbrev. for* MAGNETIC INK CHARACTER READING.
micro-, *prefix denoting* small size, in particular a unit prefix (symbol µ) for one millionth, as in microsecond, one millionth of a second.
micro, *n.* the standard abbreviation for microcomputer (personal computer).

A **microcassette** is an audio cassette smaller than the usual size (made, for instance, for pocket dictating machines) and used for backing storage, in particular in laptop computers and small robots. DIGITAL AUDIO TAPE, also used to some extent for backing storage, comes on microcassettes too. A **microchip** is a small piece of semiconductor holding a complex **microcircuit** with thousands of elements, see CHIP. **Microcode** is a set of microinstructions (see below), the whole or part of a microprogram (also see below).

microcomputer, *n.* (universally called micro) a personal computer, one used mainly by one person at a time. Strictly, the term includes all systems smaller than a desktop machine (although these tend to carry such names as nanocomputer, laptop, pocket computer, wrist watch computer). At the centre of all micros is a single microprocessor, although more and more often others support this. Indeed, many people use the term microcomputer either for microprocessor or for a single chip that contains both processor and main store.

microelectronics, *n.* the science and technology of circuits that carry very small currents (a few milliamps or less), and of the elements that make up such circuits. Now it tends to be restricted to microcircuits, those on chips, and in particular to the design and use of microprocessors (see below).

For **microfiche**, see microform (below) and ULTRAFICHE, STEREOFICHE, SUPERFICHE. **Microfilm** is a second common type of microform, but with the images next to each other in one dimension rather than arrayed in two dimensions on a sheet. Both systems have cameras, printers and readers.

A **microfloppy** is a magnetic DISK smaller than the normal size. This is a relative term, in that the standard size of floppy disks falls over the years. The standard size is now changing from 133 mm (diameter, 5.25 inch) to 89 mm (3.5 inch). The latter formed the group of microfloppies in recent years, but now the term tends more and more to mean floppies 50 mm (2 inch) across.

MICROPHONE

A **microfolio** is much like a microfiche, but consists of a number of short strips of microfilm sandwiched between two sheets of plastic film. All are types of **microform**, a microform being one or more very small projectable photographic images in some usable format. The most common types are microfiche and microfilm (above), but some firms use jackets: cards with a central hole to carry a single microform image. Various types of **microform camera** exist to produce the images (normally from sheets of paper) in quantity and at speed, while a microform printer will produce hard copy of a single sheet from a microform image. In fact, in most cases a printer is part of the more costly ranges of microform reader, a projector that throws a fairly bright image of a microform page onto a ground glass screen. Readers range from small, compact, portable units (with which people on the move may read, for instance, magazines on microform) to bulky desktop machines with complex control systems and high quality printers. The concern of **microform management** is storage of, and access to, large numbers of images (often under computer control). Most microforms are monochrome text images, but **microform in colour** is of growing interest, especially for illustration. **Micrographics** is the technology of producing microform images with a suitable camera.

microinstruction, *n*. a single instruction in microcode (whole or part of a microprogram, see below). It is one of a set of control steps that allows a system to carry out a single machine instruction (see MACHINE CYCLE).

micro-mainframe, *n*. one of a number of semi-jargon computer names invented by suppliers, and therefore best avoided. It describes a machine somewhere between a micro and a main frame in price and power (but not the same as a mini). **Micron** is also a non-standard but fairly widely used term for micrometre (one millionth of a metre).

microphone, *n*. an input unit that takes in sound waves and converts them to (analog) electric signals; for these to enter an IT system, there must be an analog to digital converter. Microphones are important input units in audio systems and video cameras, public address units, telephones and intercoms. They are, of course, essential in computer systems that accept SPEECH input. There are many types, with different methods of changing the sound waves to electric current; the most common involve electromagnetic, electrostatic and capacitative TRANSDUCERS.

MICROPROCESSOR

microprocessor, *n.* a complex microcircuit (integrated circuit), or set of such chips, that carries out the functions of the processor of an IT system, i.e. it contains a control unit (and clock), an arithmetic and logic unit, and the necessary registers and links to main store and to peripherals. Microprocessors differ in architecture (design), instruction set, speed, and word length; the instructions may be fixed ('hard wired', although no wire is now used) or supplied by microprograms (less common). The architecture determines such factors as registers available, stack processing power, addressing modes, and basic data types. These data types are bit, perhaps nibble (four bits), byte (eight bits), and internal word (the number of bits carried by the internal buses). However, practical systems commonly include slave (or co-)processors to carry some of the load and extend the features and power of the processor.

The first microprocessor was a four-bit, four-chip set produced for calculators by Intel in the US in 1971. The four chips were processor, ROM, RAM, and shift register; the system had 45 instructions in its set and could address 4.5 kB of main store. Twenty years on, many microprocessors exist, most able to handle 16 or 32 bits and address half a megabyte or more.

The **microprograms** mentioned above are sets of very low-level instructions that allow a microprocessor to carry out its machine instructions. As explained under MACHINE CYCLE, for a microprocessor to carry out a single machine-code instruction involves a number of steps.

Thus for the system to carry out even a straightforward instruction, such as to copy a word of data from a given storage cell to a register, in fact involves a large number of microinstructions in the relevant microprogram. A **microprogrammer** is expert at writing these programs **(microprogramming)**; they are very highly specific to the processor in use.

Micro-Prolog is a widely used version for micros of the machine intelligence program language PROLOG. **Micropublishing** is the production and distribution of documents (books and serials, such as magazines and catalogues) as microform (above).

Microrecording involves copying an original to make a much smaller image; as well as microform technology, it includes card **(microcard)** and paper **(microprint) versions. Microrobotics** is the technology of design and use of small

MILLI-

robots and such systems, either for control by micros, or on a microscopic scale. In the latter case, there are now electric motors and devices of that nature on chips.

In word processing, some kinds of software and printers have a **microspacing** feature that allows very precise horizontal control of the spacing between characters (as in modern typesetting). The use of microspacing allows fully justified text (i.e. text with straight left and right margins) without ugly extra spaces between words. It is thus a development of proportional spacing.

microviewdata, or **local viewdata,** *n.* viewdata on a single micro or over a local area network, rather than involving costly links to a remote host. A microviewdata data base is likely to be fairly small, but offers much in libraries, exhibitions, schools and offices.

microwaves, *n.* short length (high frequency) electro-magnetic waves; they bridge the SPECTRUM between the radio waves used in television and the infrared region, and include the radiations used for radar and microwave cooking as well as those involved in microwave communications links. Microwave frequencies are of the order of 10^9 - 10^{12} Hz, with wavelengths from around 0.5 m down to 1 mm. A **microwave relay** is a signal transfer station in a microwave communications network, whether the network involves the use of waves through open air (with high dish aerials) or through wave guides.

Microwriter, *n.* a keyboard with only six keys: one per finger plus <RETURN>. It can therefore be operated using only one hand. This is particularly valuable for the disabled, and for those who need to work in secret or in a small space. Each character is a set of one or more key presses. In some versions the keyboard comes with processor and main store to allow the unit to hold word processed text for later entry to a micro.

midicomputer, *n.* a rare term (and one best avoided) for a computer, fitting somewhere between mini and mainframe in power, features and speed.

milking machine, *n.* a portable unit able to extract data stored in a stand-alone unit (e.g. meter or monitor) for later transfer to a computer for processing.

milli-, *prefix* denoting a thousandth, as in millimetre (mm, a thousandth of a metre) and millivolt (mV, one thousandth of a volt).

MINI(-COMPUTER)

mini(-computer), *n.* a now fairly rare term for a computer with enough storage, power and speed to support up to ten or twenty terminals. In general, local area networks or small main frames have replaced minis. A **minidisk** (or **minifloppy**) is a smaller disk than the standard (which itself is falling in size); see also MICRO-FLOPPY.

miniature, *n.* anything on a small scale, with **miniaturisation** being the process of reducing the size of systems and components.

MIPS or **Mips,** *abbrev. for* million instructions per second, a measure of the speed of working of a processor.

MIS, *abbrev. for* management information system(s), software package(s) designed to aid MANAGEMENT.

mnemonic, *n.* an assembly language opcode (often of three letters) that is fairly easy to remember as it relates to the function. For example, LDA = LoaD into Accumulator a copy of the data item stated.

mobile phone, *n.* a portable (i.e. wireless) handset able to link with a public telephone network. See CELL. A **mobile switching centre (MSC)** is a station near the centre of a group of cells and linked to a standard telephone exchange. A land line joins it to the base station that serves each cell in the group.

mode, *n.* any style of action. Thus a computer may be working in batch or interactive mode (as the software dictates) with a screen display mode of colour or monochrome and a given resolution.

modem, *n.* a hardware link (interface) between a digital IT unit (e.g. computer, fax machine, viewdata terminal) and an analog phone line to a local exchange. The name comes from MODULATION/demodulation, the two main functions of a two-way link between digital and analog channels (though the term 'line adapter' was once common). As with any interface, the modem's function is to match the signals on the two sides; it may also be able to store frequently used numbers as well as access and data transfer codes. Modems on single chips are now common, and, as communication between remote IT units grows in importance, more and more computers have modems fitted. Most (if not all) modems now offer at least one international data transfer standard.

modified, *adj.* anything changed in some way to suit given circumstances. For **modified address**, see ADDRESSING; for **modified frequency modulation**, see MODULATION. **Modified Huffman (MH)** is a data compression standard for

MODULATION

fax systems. The other main one is **modified Read (MR)**; good systems offer both. Named after David Huffmann, the technique involves encoding long sets of black or white bits in short form. **Modified NTSC** video players are PAL machines that can work with NTSC tapes or discs. See TELEVISION.

modifier, *n.* a code or quantity used to modify the address of a data item in modified ADDRESSING.

Modula, *n.* one of a set of related program languages (the main one being **Modula 2**) designed in Switzerland by Niklaus Wirth. He also designed Pascal, and there are many common features. (Indeed, some people view Modula as an extension of Pascal.) Modula offers separate but linkable modules (hence the name), the ability to handle concurrent processes, low-level machine access, and separate compilation. It is an object-oriented system of great value in real-time work.

modular programming, see MODULE.

modulation, *n.* the process of adding a signal to a carrier wave in order to allow more signals without interference. There are many styles. The main ones involve letting the carried signal modify the carrier's amplitude (strength), frequency (wavelength) and phase, AMPLITUDE MODULATION (AM), FREQUENCY MODULATION (FM), and PHASE MODULATION (PM): see the Figure for the first two.

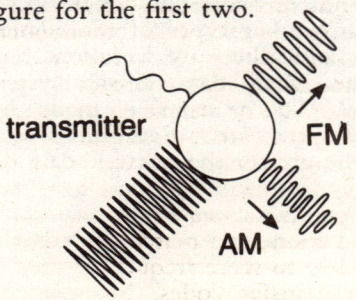

modulation. Fig. 1. Amplitude and frequency modulation (AM) and (FM).

Modified frequency modulation, however, is a method of raising the data storage density of a magnetic disk by modulating (adding a high frequency wave to) the write signal at the write head.

In **pulse amplitude modulation (PAM),** the amplitude of

MODULE

the pulses in a digital train depends on the input (carried) signal. **Pulse code modulation (PCM)** is the main method of carrying analog information in digital form. At set intervals (see Figure 2), the modulator reads the size of the analog signal and codes it as a binary number between 0 and the value of the word length. The signal then transfers as a set of binary words.

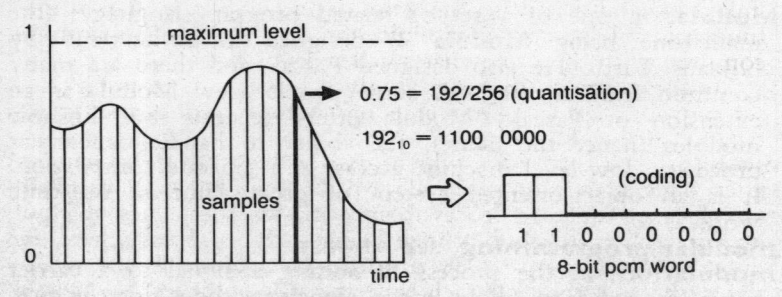

modulation. Fig 2. Pulse code modulation.

$0.75 = 192/256$ (quantisation)
$192_{10} = 1100\ 0000$
8-bit pcm word

Pulse duration modulation (PDM) is rather like PAM, but in this case it is the length of the pulses rather than their height that depends on the input signal.

There are many other types of modulation, some different from the above, and others are variations on one or the other. In each case, the overall data transfer system is as shown in Figure 3 below. The transfer is made by electromagnetic waves in empty space, air, wave guides or fibres (the higher the frequency, the greater the possible data density).

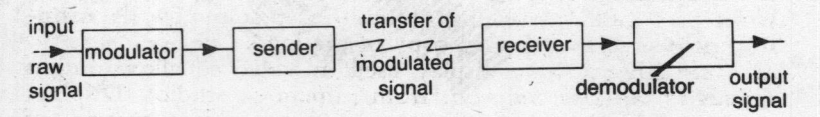

modulation. Fig 3. The transfer of a modulated signal.

A **modulator** is a device in any such system for mixing the two signals; at the far end, a demodulator separates the two and removes the carrier.

module, *n.* **1.** a single peripheral or other unit one can plug into an IT system to add to its features.

2. (now rare) a unit of main store with 20000 cells, originally the standard number of cells in a single board of MAGNETIC CORE STORE.
3. a chunk of a program that relates to a major single part of the outline algorithm, and so has a major but single function. A module stands alone to a fair degree, therefore it can be coded independently of other parts of the program, only being linked to, and tested in, the whole at a later stage. It is sometimes possible to set up module libraries, though this is more common with the somewhat smaller procedures.

Modular programming involves treating a program as a set of modules, to allow ease of coding, testing and maintenance. See also BEAD.

modulo, *n.* an operation which gives as a result the remainder after integer division, thus 25 MOD 3 gives 1. A **modulo check** is a validation process that works on the values of input key presses, **modulo-N check** being such a process where the diviser (**modulus**) is N. A **modulo-N counter** is one where the output returns to 0 each time the value reaches $N-1$, so a modulo-10 counter shows 0 1 2 ... 9 0 1 ... .

molecular wire, *n.* a current-carrying 'wire' consisting of a single long molecule of polymer in a zeolite (a substance with an open molecular structure). If such wires are used within computers, circuits a hundredth the size of the present ones would be possible.

monadic, *adj.* having only one argument (**monadic function**, e.g. SIN) or operand (**monadic operator**, e.g., as in -5).

monitor, *n.* **1.** a program, normally part of operating software, that observes, checks, and, if need be, modifies the actions of the system.
2. a software/hardware system that supervises and logs the work of a multi-processing or multi-user computer. A **monitor printer** provides hard copy of the log.
3. a cathode-ray tube display used in video to allow output signals to be observed (e.g. from camera or studio). Displays were widely used as computer output devices instead of normal television sets because they offered better quality results.

monochrome, *adj.* in IT, denoting a screen display or hard copy with only two BRIGHTNESS levels, though now widely used for any display or hard copy without colour (i.e. including those with a grey scale). Amber and green screens, deemed to be more restful than black/white displays, are

MONOSPACING

common monochrome units.

monospacing, *n.* a screen or hard copy output of text in which all the characters have the same horizontal extent. Compare PROPORTIONAL SPACING.

Morse code, *n.* an early American MARK/SPACE RATIO code invented by Samuel Morse (1791–1872), a telegraph inventor, still very widely used in (radio)telegraphy. Each character appears as a sequence of one or more dots (short pulses) or dashes (long ones). Originally, human operators sent signals using this code, generating the patterns with a sprung switch (**Morse key**), although by the end of the last century, automatic methods of generation based on keyboards had started to appear.

MOS, *abbrev. for* metal oxide semiconductor, a very widely used class of TRANSISTOR, also called metal oxide semiconductor or insulated gate field effect transistor (MOSFET or IGFET). In a field-effect transistor (FET) the input electrode (gate) links the channel between the source and the drain (see Figure). The device controls the current in the channel by voltage rather than by current (as in a bipolar transistor). The main advantage of FETs is their low power demand.

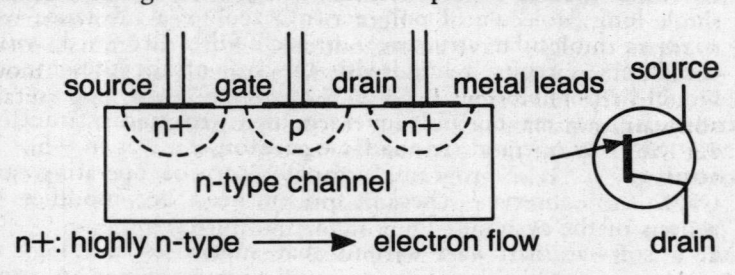

MOS. An *n*-channel junction gate field effect transistor (NJUGFET).

The Figure shows an n-channel FET, one using **NMOS** technology. The base material is p-type in a **PMOS** transistor. The most important type is, in fact, **CMOS**, complementary MOS technology. This overcomes the main problem of FETs, which is their slow speeds compared to those of bipolar systems. It also offers (as well as low power demand) the ability to work with unstable and weak power sources, e.g. throughout the range 3 – 18 V, and high immunity from noise.

most significant bit/digit (MSB/D) *n.* the left-most bit/digit in a binary/denary number, i.e. that with the highest place value.

motherboard, *n.* a printed circuit board into which one can plug one or more subsidiary circuit boards, and a slot to carry the edge connector on each *childboard*.

motor, *n.* an electromagnetic (or, more rarely, electrostatic) unit that converts input electric current into mechanical (rotary or linear) force. Motors are very common in large robots, though smaller ones may use hydraulic or pneumatic methods of control of forces. See also STEPPER MOTOR. Motors have almost no upper limit on size; people build the smallest ones into the surface of chips.

mouse, *n.* an input unit used as a pointing device, i.e. one that controls the movement of a cursor on a screen. With it, a user can very quickly move the cursor (with fair but not high accuracy) to any part of the screen, e.g. in games playing, to choose from a menu, or to edit part of a word-processed text.

The mouse itself consists of a ball set in the base of a unit that fits the palm of the hand. Sensors in the base detect how the user rolls the mouse over a work surface, while two or three buttons give the effect of key presses. (Some newer models, though, have many buttons, either to emulate many keyboard functions or to provide a calculator.) The mouse links to the IT system by cable or infrared beam, and suitable software translates its motion to cursor control.

MP/M, *abbrev. for* MULTIPROGRAMMING control program for micros, a version (never common and now very rare) of CP/M (also now rare), an operating software system for micros that gives them support for multiprogramming.

MPU, (rare) *abbrev. for* microprocessor (unit).

MR, *abbrev. for* MODIFIED READ, a standard for compressing fax data which works in much the same way as modified Huffman.

MSB/D, *abbrev. for* MOST SIGNIFICANT BIT/DIGIT.

MSC, *abbrev. for* MOBILE SWITCHING CENTRE.

MS-DOS, *abbrev. for* Microsoft's DISK OPERATING SYSTEM, the world-wide standard operating software for IBM compatible micros.

MTBF, *abbrev. for* mean time before failure, a (usually vague) measure of the reliability of a component or system.

MTBM, *abbrev. for* mean time between maintenance checks. An alternative term for MTBF.

MTTR, *abbrev. for* mean time to repair.

mug-trapping, *n.* a widely used jargon term for input VALIDATION, checking that inputs to a program are of the right type and in the right range.

multi-, *prefix* to denote applicability to a number of people or objects, rather than just to one. Thus a **multi-access** system is one to which more than one user can link at the same time: the processor has the power, speed, and storage to share its time and resources between all users, each of whom should feel as if he or she is having its complete attention. Most minis and main frames offer the feature, with the users working at terminals. See also NETWORK.

multi-addressing, *n.* a feature of many processors which allows more than one operand (ADDRESS) for most opcodes (instructions). While one address working is common, two address and three address styles are widespread. Multi-addressing is also a term for fax broadcasting. **Multidrop** refers in various ways to communications links:

   (a) multi-addressing as in fax broadcasting;

   (b) a single (shared) line that connects two or more subscribers to an exchange;

   (c) a star network with one or more intermediate nodes (switching centres) between a station and the central node.

multifrequency pulsing or **multitone phoning,** *n.* a technique for coding each signal from a push button telephone as a pair of tones from the five available (700, 900, 1300, 1500 and 1700 Hz). A **multifrequency receiver** is a demodulator that can separate the various frequencies in the **multifrequency signals** that result. A **multifunction system** is an IT system somewhere between a single-purpose (dedicated) and a general purpose one.

multilayer, *adj* describing more than one surface layer, as in a multilayer (printed) circuit board (one with more than one layer of printed links). A multilayer microfiche is one with two layers of images viewed in differently polarized light, or with four using holography for viewing. A **multipage file** has more than one page (as may happen in word processing and fax messaging), while **multiple access** describes any sort of polling or broadcasting method in data transfer. This includes **multiple broadcast** in fax. See BROADCAST.

multiple key retrieval, *n.* different techniques of data retrieval that depend on more than one search key: as well as the primary key, there are one or more of secondary keys.

MULTIPLEXING

multimedia working, *n*. the linking of video (including from cameras, tape and disc) with sound, still images, and computer generated screens. The approach has potential in training and teaching as well as for presentations and entertainment. The demand comes mainly perhaps from the media world, who appreciate the cheap, effective power of the modern micro. See also HYPERMEDIA. For **multiple polling**, see POLLING.

multiplexing *n*. treating a number of signals to allow them to pass through a single channel at the same time. (Compare SIMPLEX, HALF DUPLEX, DUPLEX and DIPLEX.) In **frequency division multiplexing (FDM),** each signal modulates a carrier of a different frequency. The transferred signal combines all the carriers and their carried signals, with a means of separation at the far end. **Space division multiplexing (SDM),** better called **time division multiplexing (TDM),** involves sharing the signals between different time slots. Figure 1 shows TDM used to fit three PULSE CODE MODULATED signals into a single channel.

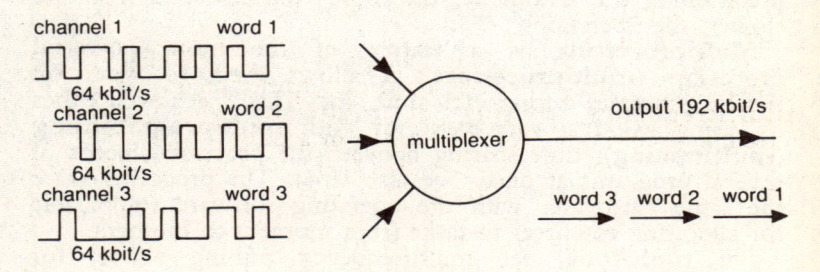

multiplexing. Fig. 1. Time division multiplexing of three 64kbit/s signals.

There are several other methods of multiplexing a number of signals down a single line. Figure 2 shows the basic technique. Clearly, the channel's bandwidth must be at least as great as the sum of those of the signals carried: the higher the frequency of the channel, the more signals it can bear, hence the use of OPTICAL FIBRES or MICROWAVES rather than radio for voice phone and cable television traffic. In **adaptive multiplexing**, however, the allocation of signals to channels depends on demand.

Multipoint is, in most cases, the same as multidrop (see

MURRAY CODE

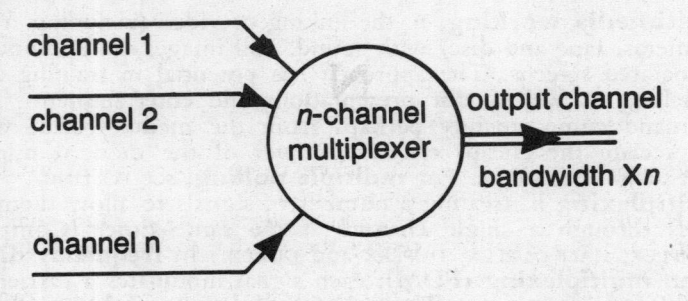

multiplexing. Fig. 2. The basis of multiplexing.

above), while **multipolling** is the same as multiple polling (also see above). A **multiprecision** system is one that can carry out arithmetic operations to different degrees of PRECISION as appropriate; this feature is of value as the higher the precision of the arithmetic, the more complex, and therefore slower, the operations.

Multiprocessing is a feature of the more powerful processors (**multiprocessors**); it allows them to work on several processes during each time slot. This is achieved either by using PARALLEL PROCESSING or with **multiprogramming** (**multitasking**), time sharing between the processing needs of several programs at once. See also MP/M. The programs share the same hardware, with the operating software responsible for allocating resources to tasks from moment to moment.

For **multitone**, see multifrequency pulsing above; for **multiuser**, see multiaccess above.

Murray code, n. (Donald Murray, 1900) an improved version of the BAUDOT CODE produced for Murray's punched paper tape telegraph. His aim was to minimize the number of holes across the tape for each character code (so the paper would not tear). A number of versions of Murray code appeared in the next few decades, but in 1931 they were brought together in the International Alphabet number 2.

music synthesis, n. the creation of musical tones (pure ones with correct pure overtones) electronically, as in an electr(on)ic organ or synthesizer.

mux, n. a common term, mainly in charts, for MULTIPLEXING.

N

naive, *adj.* non-expert, as in **naive user**, a person not used to the hardware or software in question.

NAK, *abbrev. for* negative acknowledgement, a hand shaking signal from a data receiver to the sender to indicate that the last block sent failed in a check.

name table, *n.* a symbol table, HASH TABLE, or LABEL TABLE; where a system stores the labels and storage addresses of variables and other data structures.

NAND, *n.* (= not and) a type of GATE, with an output unless all inputs are 1.

nano-, *unit prefix* for 10^{-9}, as in nanosecond, a thousandth of a millionth of a second. Some people use **nanocomputer** for a machine smaller than a micro (e.g. a laptop), but it is best to avoid this usage.

narrow band, *adj.* describing a channel with a small band width, and so able to carry only one signal. Compare BROAD BAND, where many signals can pass at once by some form of MULTIPLEXING.

narrowcasting, *n.* a method of working with data transfers in rather the same way as broadcasting, but with a tight (directional) beam, so that few receivers can intercept the signals.

natural language, *n.* the same as HUMAN LANGUAGE.

NCR, *abbrev. for* no carbon (paper) required, a technique for making simultaneous copies of a printout without carbon paper. At the back of every sheet except the last, a coating of tiny spheres holds the ink until broken by pressure.

needle, *n.* one of the pins in the head of a dot matrix printer, sometimes called a **needle printer**.

negative acknowledgement, SEE NAK.

negative numbers, *n.* those with value less than zero. In binary, there is no way to code the minus sign (−) as such; in sign and magnitude format (see ARITHMETIC), the first bit therefore carries sign information, in most cases with 0 for positive and 1 for negative.

NEQ, *abbrev. for* NON-EQUIVALENCE GATE.

nest, *vb.* to embed one block or structure within a second, larger one, as with:

NETWORK

(a) a loop within a loop in a program or ALGORITHM.
(b) an open SUB-ROUTINE in a program, rather than a separate (closed) one (procedure).
(c) a data block within a larger more general block.

network, *n*. a number of IT units linked by communications channels, as in the telephone network and a network of computers. In the latter case, see LOCAL AREA NETWORK, MEDIUM AREA NETWORK, and WIDE AREA NETWORK, which relate to the scale of the system. The Figure shows the three main network architectures: star (cluster), bus and ring. They each have advantages and disadvantages as regards speed, reliability, and cost. **Hybrid networks** (which combine features of more than one kind of network) are common at all scales as a result.

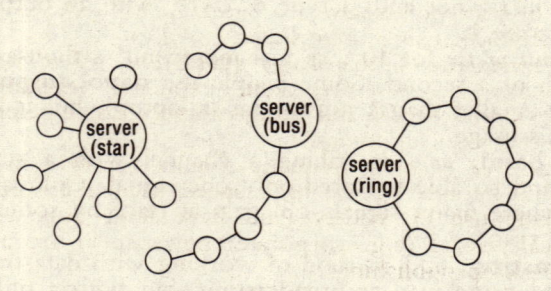

network. The three main network styles.

The aim of a network is to link the individual (work) stations so they can share data and hardware and software resources; this makes the approach much cheaper than having the same number of separate stand alone machines, even if intercommunication is not essential (as it is in the case of the telephone network, for instance). Networks differ in the intercommunications load factor, and consequently in the intelligence of the stations and the data transfer speed of the links.

A **network chart** is a map, or block diagram, of a network, while **network planning** concerns design for individual needs. **Network topology** describes the layout of a network in terms of star, bus and ring. See also NEURAL NETWORK and OFFICEWARE.

neural, *adj*. used in IT in any context where a system tries to approach the complexity and power of an animal's nervous system, as in **neural computer** (a powerful parallel system) and **neural network** (a network with high complexity and power). One approach to a neural network which has been developed is to link hundreds of processors on a WAFER; designing and maintaining the links remains a considerable barrier to success, however. Many people predict that by the end of the century the 'normal' micro will be an effective working combination of neural hardware and expert system software, able to work with natural language (including speech and printed input), and thus be the system of the true fifth GENERATION. A **neuristor** is a single processor in a neural computer. See also BIONICS.

neutral transfer, *n.* **1.** a binary (two-state) digital method of transfer of teletype signals.
2. polar transfer using three states.

new information technology (NIT), *n.* often the same as INFORMATION TECHNOLOGY, but explicitly excluding such systems as print media and filing cabinets: i.e. it refers only to systems that use electronics.

newspaper, *n.* a high frequency, and therefore high speed, periodical. Because of the high speed needed for publication, newspapers use IT widely (and have long done so). On a small scale, local (e.g. corporate) newspapers are a standard use of desktop publishing.

next instruction register (NIR), *n.* the register of a system's control unit that stores the address of the next instruction to be carried out. See MACHINE CYCLE.

nexus, *n.* a point of interconnection in a system or network, e.g. where a number of channels meet.

nibble or **nybble,** *n.* a rare term for half a byte, i.e. a set of four bits treated by a system as a single unit.

NIR, *abbrev. for* NEXT INSTRUCTION REGISTER.

NIT, see NEW INFORMATION TECHNOLOGY.

NMOS, *abbrev. for* negative channel metal oxide semi-conductor. See MOS and TRANSISTOR.

node, *n.* a NEXUS in an network where channels converge (come together) or diverge (spread out). In the case of a telephone network, an EXCHANGE (switching centre) is a node.

noise, *n.* any signal in a channel that makes it harder to read the wanted signal. See INTERFERENCE. In data retrieval, **noise factor** measures the number of items retrieved in a search that are not in fact relevant to the searcher. A channel's **noise**

NON-DESTRUCTIVE

factor or **noise level** is a measure of how much interference a signal may experience (see also SIGNAL TO NOISE RATIO). A **noise killer** is an electronic unit aimed at keeping a channel's noise level low.

non-destructive, *adj.* describing any action or access which leaves the data item concerned the same as before. In particular, a **non-destructive read** is a reading access which leaves the data read untouched. Few systems now involve destructive reading.

non-equivalence (NEQ or XOR), *n.* a GATE (circuit, element) with an output only if the inputs differ; the opposite of match, and the same as exclusive-or.

non-impact printer, *n.* any printer which does not involve some mechanical part striking the paper through a ribbon. Examples are ink-jet and laser printers. Not only do such machines suffer less wear, but they are likely to be much quieter when working; having fewer moving parts also makes them faster.

non-volatile store, *n.* a (main) storage system that does not need a power supply in order for it to retain the data stored. The magnetic core stores of early computers were of this nature, as is modern day read only memory (ROM) (the same, in essence as hard wired store). Most forms of read and write memory (RAM) are volatile; systems that need to retain the data they store when the mains supply is off use a battery of cells to provide the power required to refresh the data from moment to moment.

NOR, *n.* (= not-or) a type of GATE, with an output only if no input is 1.

normalization, *n.* a process that converts numeric data to the system's standard form (e.g. a floating point of a given type, in most cases that giving the greatest precision, see ARITHMETIC). In many relational data bases, data items (string as well as numeric) must be in a suitable **normal form** before the system can work with them.

NOT, *n.* a GATE whose output is the opposite of its single input.

NTSC, *n.* the US National Television System Committee. The NTSC television standard (the number of scan lines, colour representation, and frame frequency) is used in Japan, South America, and North America.

n-type, *adj.* denoting an extrinsic semiconductor material with more free electrons than holes. Thus current passes through it mainly as a flow of negative charge. See also DONOR.

null, *adj.* denoting no intrinsic value. The **null character** (ASCII 0) has uses such as to fill time in a signal or space in a store. A **null pointer** points at no true address, so marks the end of, for instance, a LINKED LIST. A **null string** is one with zero characters; often strings are initialized to the null value when declared (thus giving them a place in the system's label table).

number, *n.* a set of digits expressed in a positional system (e.g. denary, decimal, or binary) which gives the set an overall value. Each digit (bit in the case of binary) has a place value. See ARITHMETIC.

There are various types of number that relate to work with IT systems:

(a) natural numbers: the non-negative integers;

(b) integers: those with no fraction part (integer arithmetic in computers is fast, and so is widely used);

(c) reals: integers plus numbers with a fraction part;

(d) complex numbers: each of which has a real part and an imaginary part (a real multiple of the square root of -1). Some program languages can handle these, and they are important in certain areas of science and engineering.

There are also various ways to show number values:

(a) fixed point: with the decimal/binary point in its 'true' position;

(b) floating point: with a MANTISSA and an EXPONENT (as in the denary 1.23×10^4), there being several standard forms for different fields of work;

(c) postfix, such as reverse Polish notation which cuts out the need for brackets in expressions.

numeric, *adj.* describing number values, whether denary (decimal) or binary. **Numeric control** involves the use of digital computer techniques to control machines and industrial processes; the steps appear in terms of values for such factors as the position of the head of the machine. A **numeric (data type)** has a purely numeric value, being, for instance, an integer, real, or complex number. A **numeric keypad** has keys only for the digits in the system used (denary or hexadecimal), with a special symbol or two, <DELETE>, and <RETURN>.

nybble, *n.* a rare spelling of NIBBLE.

O

object, *n.* **1.** the product of a process. **Object code** is a ready to run machine-code program output from a translator (assembler or compiler). **Object language** is the same as machine code, and an **object program** is a program in machine code.
2. a data item or structure which can be treated indiscriminately as a unit by suitable software. An object involves both properties (data) and behaviour (procedures); however, the user can access and manipulate the properties only through the behaviour, i.e. by sending the object a message and observing the effect. Unfortunately, **object-oriented** is a 'buzz' adjective of the late 1980s and early 1990s, applied to almost any kind of software to add a degree of respectability and modernity.

An **object-oriented data base** is a DBMS which can handle any object in the same way; it therefore has more power (from the searcher's point of view) than a relational data base, though offers much the same type of flexibility (see DATA). A good program of this nature can also 'explain' its actions, so has elements of machine intelligence. The power of **object-oriented programming** is that the software produced can more realistically mirror the real world, but without troubling the user with unnecessary complexity.

objectives, *n.* the precise aims of a process that the designer or user can assess at the end of the project.

Occam, *n.* a concise fifth GENERATION program language, with only 28 reserved words (key words), designed for use with systems based on transputers (i.e. parallel processing systems). William of Ockham (*c.*1285 - *c.*1349, English philosopher) is particularly famous for his principle of economy in logical argument now known as 'Ockham's razor'. Written in Latin as *Entia non sunt multiplicanda praeter necessitam*, it is perhaps best translated as 'keep it simple' (see KISS).

OCR, *abbrev. for* optical character reading, **OCR-A** and **OCR-B** are standard type faces designed for the purpose, but a good modern system can cope with a very wide range of printed and typed faces.

octal, *adj.* and *n.* involving the number base 8, i.e. that with which one counts 0 1 2 ... 7 10 11 ... . **Octal code** is a form of machine coding (now rarely, if ever, used); in it each octal digit (opcode and data item) translates to three bits: this makes coding simpler than with binary ('real' machine coding), but less convenient than coding in hex(adecimal) and harder than in denary.

octet, *n.* a set of eight; this is an old term for byte, still sometimes used for a set of eight bits in a system with a greater word length (e.g. an octet is half a word in a 16-bit system).

odd-even checking, *n.* the same as PARITY CHECKING, a method of using one check bit per word to detect errors.

odd parity, *n.* PARITY in which each word+parity bit contains an odd number of 1s.

OEM, *abbrev. for* ORIGINAL EQUIPMENT MANUFACTURER.

office, *n.* a place for business, professional or clerical work; a central site for information handling. **Office automation** involves the large scale use of IT to aid information handling (input, storage, processing, searching and output), an ELECTRONIC OFFICE being one with a high degree of automation in that sense. A MANAGEMENT INFORMATION SYSTEM is a combination of hardware and MANAGEMENT information software (MIS), while the **paperless office** (see PAPER) and the **office of the future** are jargon terms (with little real meaning) for the electronic office. **Officeware** is jargon for integrated desktop business software: not only integrated from the point of view of an individual user but, via the office network, integrated for all users. For example, the users can access the overall office diary or just the parts that concern them individually. Allied with effective internal EMAIL, this approach to a joint diary makes setting up meetings, for instance, much more straightforward.

off-line, *adj.* or *adv.* denoting a peripheral or terminal working to an internal program, but not linked or needing access to the main processor. An **off-line system** needs some (local) intelligence (processing power of its own); to allow this. Off-line data input and off-line printing are common cases; each is an I/O BOUND process that would badly tie up the central processor if carried out ON LINE.

ohm, *n.* the unit (symbol Ω) of electric resistance (the opposition of a conductor or circuit element to current).

omission factor, *n.* the fraction of the number of records retrieved in a search to the number that should have come up had the user defined the search properly.

OMR, *abbrev. for* OPTICAL MARK READING, a fairly common type of MACHINE READABLE INPUT.

on-hook calling, *n.* obtaining access to a telephone line and calling a number without lifting a handset: a useful feature of many fax machines as well as of many modern telephones. Normally, lifting the handset closes a switch, so to get a line while leaving it 'on the hook' means the user must press a switch instead.

on-line, *adj.* working under the control of, or linked to, a central processor. An **on-line search** is data retrieval where the user's input/output unit is a terminal or network station, the data searched being in the central store. If the network is wide area, on-line searching can be very costly (and hard to access without expertise); on the other hand, the data is up to date. OFF-LINE searching, where the data is on a local disk (e.g., compact disc) is far cheaper and simpler, but is best for data that does not date quickly.

on-screen viewing, *n.* the accessing of inward faxes with a micro and fax card (rather than by using a fax machine); inward faxes go to store, from where the user can display each one, taking a printout only if needed. On-screen viewing with current systems is slow (as is the printout after); on the other hand, a few fax machines with large stores now also offer the feature.

one-address instruction, *n.* an instruction that takes only one address, or a machine code system in which no opcode can have more than one address part. See ADDRESSING.

one gate, *n.* the same as OR gate.

ones (1s) complement, *n.* (*of a binary number*), the form obtained by flipping the bits (making 0s 1s and 1s 0s). See ARITHMETIC. In general, each digit is arrived at by subtracting it from 1 less than the radix (base) of the number system (i.e. from 9 in the case of denary). Hence 1s complements also bear the name *radix-minus-one complements*.

opamp, *abbrev. for* OPERATIONAL AMPLIFIER.

opcode, *abbrev. for* OPERATION CODE, the (three letter, in most cases) mnemonic code for a machine instruction in an assembly language. After assembly, the opcode is the corresponding binary form in the object code. A language has one opcode for each instruction in its instruction set.

open, *adj.* ready for access; **open access** is unrestricted ACCESS, i.e. any access which needs no pass word. An **open file** is one readied for reading and/or writing. **Open learning** is a way

OPERATIONAL AMPLIFIER (OPAMP)

to deliver learning (in education or training), where the learners may drop in to a learning centre at any time and pick up work where they left off. IT is almost essential for the management and presentation of open learning systems. Compare COMPUTER-AIDED LEARNING.

An **open subroutine** is a chunk of a program with a single clear function, but kept as part of a larger piece of code rather than being made separate as a procedure (closed sub-routine). **Open System Interconnection (OSI)** is an approach to CONNECTIVITY (linking IT systems based on different standards), being developed by IBM and the International Standards Organization (ISO). The OSI model has seven layers (aspects) of connectivity, from the physical (electronic etc.) to the applications layer (communication within applications software).

operand, *n.* a data item on which an instruction (opcode or key word) acts. In the case of machine and assembly code instructions, the **operand field** is the place (ADDRESS FIELD) for the operand or its address.

operating software/system (OS) *n.* the program or suite that controls all the resources of, processes in, and detailed action of, a processor in an IT system. There are many kinds of operating systems, as each machine needs its own particular types for the various types of usage (e.g. batch, multi-user, parallel). See also DISK-OPERATING SYSTEM.

operation, *n.* any single action on data in an IT system, controlled by a machine code INSTRUCTION: **operation code** (opcode) and data details. In each MACHINE CYCLE, the **operation register (OR)** holds the current opcode. In a flow chart, an **operation symbol** is a box (in most cases, oblong) that stands for any operation without a specific symbol.

operational amplifier (opamp), *n.* an integrated circuit that works on an input signal to produce a desired output. The first opamps were high performance dc amplifiers for use in analog computers; they could add, subtract, integrate and differentiate the input(s) to form the output. Modern versions do that and much more, in digital as well as analog systems.

The ideal opamp has infinite gain, linearity, band width and input impedance, and zero size, price, noise level, output impedance and temperature drift. No opamp is ideal, of course, but many very good devices now exist. The Figure shows the standard symbol; other leads carry power and control signals.

OPERATIONAL RESEARCH (OR)

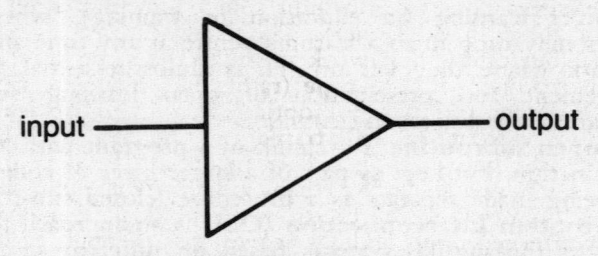

operational amplifier. The op amp symbol.

operational research (OR), *n.* the analysis by mathematical models of systems of working (often now done using a micro). It is an aspect of systems analysis, and is a technology in its own right.

operator, *n.* **1.** a symbol or character for an operation, which may be monadic (having one operand) or dyadic (with two). The arithmetic operators are + − * / and ^.

2. a person with a role in looking after a large computer system (where there is often a need for several in each shift). The **chief operator** works at the **operator's console** (terminal) and communicates with the system to give commands and react to messages. See also STAFF.

optical, *adj.* describing visible light and, by extension, infrared and ultraviolet (both being near light in the SPECTRUM). Optical systems use light as a tool or method of data transfer. An **optical cable** is a bundle of one or more optical fibres (see below), used for high density, mainly digital, data transfers; see FIBRE OPTICS. **Optical character reading (OCR)** is a method of MACHINE READABLE INPUT in which a light source and photo-cell (or an array of these in a scanner) detects the pattern of light and dark on a sheet; suitable software interprets the output signal. **Optical discs** store data in the form of pits in the surface of a suitable medium, a laser and photo-cell in the head reading the data. See COMPACT DISC and VIDEO DISC. An **optical fibre** is a single fine strand of very pure glass, treated so that an input light signal cannot escape. See FIBRE OPTICS.

Optical mark reading (scanning) (OMR) is a cruder form of MACHINE-READABLE INPUT than OCR, the scanner being able to detect only straight marks in given places on the sheet (and their absence). **Optical media** are data stores read

OPTICAL

by a head that consists of a light source and photo-cell (or an array of these in a scanner). The COMPACT DISC is a major example, but others that work in much the same way are the larger VIDEO DISC, **optical tape** (rather like magnetic tape, but with a number of tracks of optical data), and **optical card** (stripe card with an **optical strip**).

An **optical processor** is a chip where all the data transfers are on light waves, rather than involving electric currents. There is no need for fibres to carry the light the small distances concerned, and, as light waves pass through each other without effect (unlike electric currents), optical processing has the potential of being much cheaper and faster than microelectronic systems. The logic circuits involve laser (or LED) light processed by liquid crystals. The first working systems of this kind were announced in 1990 (one using parallel optical processing, with 32 optical processors working together), though research in the field has a long history. See also OPTOELECTRONICS.

Optical publishing involves producing data stores of one of the above kinds for distribution to people with suitable **optical readers**, i.e. with heads as described above under OPTICAL MEDIA (see the Figure also).

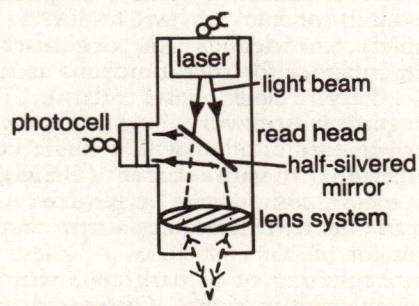

optical. An optical read head.

An **optical scanner** has a row of such heads, as many as ten or more per millimetre to give fairly high resolution. In an OCR reader or fax machine input, for example, rollers feed the sheet for scanning past the head. For **optical stripe**, see optical card above. **Optical transfer** is the transfer of data as signals carried on light waves, either through empty space or through a fibre. The main advantage compared with radio,

OPTOELECTRONICS

say, is that the very much higher frequency of light provides a huge band width; this allows the channel to carry at the same time a very large number of signals multiplexed together. Both people and scanners can read text in an **optical type(face)**; a good system can now handle a wide range of printed and typed faces (but see OCR). For **optical video disc**, see VIDEO DISC.

optoelectronics, *n.* the science and technology of optical data transfer; the efficient production of the light carriers and their modulation by the signals in question, the transfer methods themselves, and the detection and separation of the two at the other end. By the early 1990s, integrated optoelectronic gallium arsenide chips, with photodevices (cells and LED lasers) linked with electronic ones in the surface had reached towards 10000 elements. See also FIBRE OPTICS and OPTICAL PROCESSOR.

OR, *n.* **1.** a type of GATE, with output only if at least one input is 1.
2. *abbrev. for* operation register. See MACHINE CYCLE.
3. *abbrev. for* OPERATIONAL RESEARCH, often part of systems analysis.

organization and methods (O&M), *n.* a field that requires many of the skills of the SYSTEMS ANALYST, but much less detailed technical knowledge. An **organiser** is a pocket computer with software for such functions as simple data base management, diary, clock (and alarm), calendar, and calculator. **Organiser software** in a computer provides the user with much the same, often with a single key press.

original equipment manufacturer (OEM), *n.* any firm that buys in major components (e.g. drives) to put in IT systems that carry its own label, i.e. a firm that buys elements in bulk but not for re-sale as such.

orphan, *n.* the beginning of a paragraph, word or line at the bottom of a new page in a word processed text. This looks ugly, and a good system will prevent it. Compare WIDOW.

OS, *abbrev. for* OPERATING SOFTWARE/SYSTEM.

OSI, see OPEN SYSTEM INTERCONNECTION.

outage, *n.* a non-working state, or breakdown.

outdent, *n.* a hanging indent, that is, a line that starts to the left of the normal margin (as with the first line of each entry in this dictionary).

output, *n.* any data passed from a program or system to the user or to a second program or system. An **output bound/**

limited program is one which has so much output to handle that the processor becomes non-available for other tasks for a large proportion of the time. An **output device/unit** is an item of hardware designed to produce or present output (e.g. microform, plotter, printer, robot device, screen, speaker, video tape or disc recorder).

overflow, *n.* the result of a process that gives a number (or, less often, a string or file) that cannot fit the space available; in the case of numeric data, when a number is too large for the system to handle. Such a number may carry an **overflow bit** set when it is out of range.

In a direct access data store, an **overflow block** is space set aside for records that cannot fit the block assigned by the hash algorithm. During a search, the system will first look in the assigned block, then move to the next overflow block if it fails to find the record.

An **overflow flag** is a bit in a flag register that is set when arithmetic overflow occurs. This is likely to cause an interrupt to the normal process taking place so the system or the user can take action. An **overflow routine** is the process described above when a search for a record fails to find it in the assigned block.

overhead, *adj.* denoting the same as check or parity in **overhead bit**.

overlay, *n.* a section of a program loaded from backing store into main store, replacing the section already there. Programmers employ the technique of **overlaying** as a form of controlled memory management, in cases where the whole program is too large to fit the space available in main store. Thus some word processors will carry the spell checker as an overlay routine; when the user calls the checker, it overlays part of the word processor, this being retrieved at the end of the check.

override, *vb.* to interrupt one task with another of a higher priority. The operator of a large computer can override earlier instructions to ask the system to carry out a new task. An **override function** is one with a higher priority than others with which it may be found; in arithmetic, brackets serve this purpose.

overwriting, *n.* the storing of data so it takes the place of data there already, as for example, when you re-use a magnetic tape or disk, or work with a word processor in overwrite rather than insert mode.

P

PABX, *n.* (out-dated) *abbrev. for* PRIVATE BRANCH EXCHANGE (PBX), the 'a' standing for automatic.

package, *n.* a box of computer software ready for use, and manuals (documentation) ready for distribution.

packet, *n.* a chunk of data of standard size and format for transfer through a network. In a wide area network, any signal larger than the packet size passes to a **packet assembler/disassembler (PAD)** in the local exchange (switching centre); here the packet switching system breaks it into packets and adds the header each needs (with destination, order number, time, etc). The packets then pass to the PAD nearest the destination via a trunk. As each follows the most convenient path (see ADAPTIVE ROUTING), they are likely to arrive out of order; the PAD uses the headers to re-join them before passing the signal on to the recipient (see Figure).

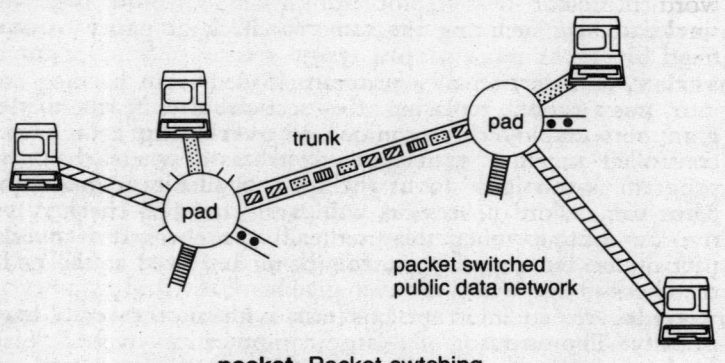

packet. Packet swtching.

Packet density is:
(a) the number of bits a store can hold per unit length of track;
(b) the number of logic circuits per unit area of surface of a chip.

Packet radio is much like the **packet switching system**

PAGINATION

(PSS) described above, but uses radio waves for the transfer rather than wires. In effect, the sender transmits in short bursts (called frames) rather than a continuous signal. There are three types of frame: information (the most important), supervisory (control), and unnumbered (for general broadcast).

packing, *n.* data compression (compaction). **Packing density** is the same as packet density (both meanings, see above), while a store's **packing factor** measures the fraction of the store size that contains current data.

PAD, *abbrev. for* the PACKET ASSEMBLER/DISASSEMBLER unit in an exchange.

paddle, *n.* a type of crude joystick used mainly for computer and video games.

page, *n.* **1.** a fixed size unit of storage (compare the page of a book). See PAGING.
2. a fixed unit of a word processed text or other such document, that appears as a printed page. A **page footer** is the information repeated at the foot of each page of printout (e.g. reference and page number); a **page header**, in much the same way, is the data item repeated at the top of each page (e.g., subtitle). A **page (at a time) printer** accepts data (e.g., word processor output) for printing as a whole page in a single action. Such printers can produce high quality output; they also make **page layout** (**page makeup**) simpler for the user, though they tend to be costly.

A **page reader** is a type of optical character reader that can work with pages that differ in size. **Page scrolling** is the same as the vertical screen scrolling many systems offer to allow users to scan what would printout as a whole page of data. A **page view terminal**, on the other hand, avoids that need by having a portrait (upright) format display rather than the standard landscape (horizontal) one. Indeed, many such screens have a display area that is A4 in size, and some even give black text and graphics on a white background. On these, screened documents should appear exactly as in printout.

pager or **bleeper,** *n.* a portable radio-controlled alarm unit. Pagers vary in the range at which they can work (local, metropolitan, wide) and in the features on offer. Some have LCDs to screen a brief message; a few allow the owner to respond to a call.

pagination, *n.* the setting out of a lengthy document into pages for printout, the term generally meaning the use of running page numbers.

PAGING

paging, *n*. **1.** the setting out of a lengthy document into pages for printout.
2. calling someone by way of a PAGER system.
3. a timesharing technique whereby pages of data cycle between backing and main store, **paging rate** being the data transfer speed in this context.
4. viewing a document on screen page by page, with keys to let the user move up or down a page at a time. A **paging terminal** has such keys.
5. working with data batched into pages for transfer between backing and main store. The operating software treats the main store as a set of pages (segments), perhaps each of 256 B. It can then move data (in a file or program; in the latter case, see also OVERLAY) into and out of main store in chunks as required.

paint, *vb*. to fill an area of a screen graphics image with a colour or shading effect. This technique is one aspect of **paint programs**. See ART SOFTWARE.

PAL, *abbrev. for* phase alternate line, one of the world's three broadcast television standards used in the UK, parts of Europe, Australia and Southern Africa.

palantype, *n*. a keyboard for working with phonetic characters, sometimes for processing by computer.

PAM, *abbrev. for* pulse-amplitude MODULATION.

pan, *vb*. to scroll horizontally, necessary with certain word processors if the text line length is greater than the screen can display. The same technique moves a camera's field of view horizontally.

paper, *n*. the medium that carries the output of a printer; some programs also use the term for the screen background. In printers and in scanners, the **paper advance** system moves the paper through the machine smoothly and correctly. Some fax machines have a **paper cutter** on the output: at the end of each inward fax, this will detach the printout from the roll. Poor paper advance design tends to increase the danger of a **paper jam**; the paper no longer feeds through properly and may even accumulate inside the feed. (Paper jams may also follow poor cleaning or leaving a sticky label on a feed roller.) Most fax machines and some printers have some **paper jam warning** method; perhaps the machine bleeps to tell the user of the problem. A few fax machines tell the sender of a message of this kind of problem to prevent loss of data.

A **paperless office** (jargon) is one where IT is so much

PARALLEL

used that there is no need for paper, although it is unlikely that such an office exists. A **paper out warning** is a feature of most fax machines; in almost all, the thermal paper that carries the inward messages is on a roll, perhaps 30 or 100 m in length. A well used fax machine therefore runs out of paper fairly often, so a warning is needed both for the owner and for people trying to send faxes.

Paper tape is a form of PUNCHED MEDIA, very widely used until the late 1970s for telegraphy and computer data storage. Across the width of the tape with its small central sprocket holes are nine tracks, for a byte of data and a parity bit. The tape held 1s and 0s as holes or no-holes in the tracks. A **paper-tape punch** would have a keyboard, each key press leading to the punching of a byte across the tape. A **paper-tape reader** with an array of nine small lamps and photocells scanned the tape and transferred the data to the computer or to a printer.

parabolic dish, *n*. an aerial able to receive low-power radio signals or to transmit a narrow beam (narrowcast). At the focal point of the dish is either the receiver or transmitter; the parabolic shape allows full use of the whole area of the dish.

parallel, *adj*. in IT, describing working in step at the same time. In a **parallel computer**, the operating software allocates tasks to the many slave microprocessors (SEE TRANSPUTER) for them to carry out at the same time. This is of great value where the computation involves large numbers of similar calculations (as in array processing or dealing with fluid flow), but parallel processing has potential in all areas once people overcome the problems of nonlinear programming.

Parallel data transfer involves each bit of a word passing along a channel (bus) in step at the same time. It is much faster than serial transfer (where the bits pass one at a time). On the other hand, in a parallel line the bits soon lose step (data SKEW); this means that parallel transfer (also more costly) is of value only for runs of less than a few metres. An IT system can therefore have a **parallel interface** to link it to only a short parallel cable (e.g. to a close printer); in other cases, the interface must be a serial one, with translation between parallel and serial modes of transfer. For **parallel processing**, see parallel computer above.

Parallel running often forms part of the implementation stage of a system life cycle: a new system is in place, and to check it (as well as to cope if it breaks down), the staff run it

PARAMETER

in parallel with the old system. In other words, all inputs pass to the two systems, and the staff can compare the outputs. This is more costly than the more usual PILOT RUNNING. In a **parallel search** the system queries one or more parts of each storage cell at the same time. See ASSOCIATIVE STORAGE. Some database management systems can also carry out parallel searches of the stored data, looking for different things at the same time or for the same thing in different parts of the file; this is not truly parallel, however, unless it uses parallel processing. For **parallel transfer**, see parallel data transfer above.

parameter, *n.* a value (or label) passed between a procedure (closed subroutine) and its calling routine, or the reverse.

parent, *n.* a data item or other object which leads to others. Thus a parent node in a network is closer to the centre than its child nodes or stations. See also GENERATION sense 1, and TREE (indeed any context with a hierarchy).

parity, *n.* a simple method of data checking by pairing, in which a **parity bit** is a type of CHECK BIT. If, in transfer, the data word has eight bits, at the sending end the system adds an extra bit. In the case of **even parity**, the value of the extra bit will be such as to make the set of nine contain an even number of 1s; **odd parity** aims for an odd number of 1s. At the other end, the system checks that parity has not changed in each word received; if it has, there has been an error, and the receiving system can ask for that word again (see NAK). The receiving process is that of **parity checking**. People use such a system in all cases where there is a significant chance of data corruption: almost always in data transfer, therefore, but also sometimes in storage.

parsing, *n.* the process of analysing syntax (grammar). A **parser** (syntax analyser) has the task of working out whether an input line has overall meaning in the language in question and whether there are any syntax errors which make it ambiguous. Parsing must take place whenever a system has to find the value of a numeric or string expression, or to carry out an instruction in a high level program language. It is also crucial in computer-aided translation software. In all cases a **parse tree** is implicit in the parser's approach to an input; this is a hierarchical map of the allowed cases.

partition, *n.* a section or segment of a large block, especially of main or hard disk store, allowing easier handling. In some cases of storage partitioning, the segments are highly independent so that data transfers between them are rare; these may not share programs and data.

party line, *n.* a telephone (or other such) line shared between more than one station or usage.

Pascal, *n.* a compiled high-level program language widely used in teaching and training, and therefore for general purpose use. The language is named after Blaise Pascal (1623–62), a French mathematician, scientist and philosopher who in 1647, invented an important calculating machine used for keeping accounts.

The program language was invented by the Swiss programmer Niklaus Wirth between 1968 and 1971. He based it on Algol, and it now has many dialects. Its major features include a very strong block structure (of procedures with parameters); it is hardly possible to produce unstructured code with Pascal. Even so, it compiles well, being fairly close to machine architectures in its philosophy. A Pascal program consists of a heading and a block of declarations and statements that may call on procedures and functions; these in turn are also blocks. The programmer may add to the data types and structures available, and the features include set operations (operations on sets). Pascal offers all three types of loop ALGORITHM.

pass, *vb.* to work through something. Most assemblers are **two pass**: they work through the source code twice before being able to produce complete object code. The first pass translates the code (and carries out syntax checking), and lists the labels used. In the second pass, the assembler translates the labels and the jumps into addresses.

A **pass-band** filter is an electronic circuit that allows through signals of a certain frequency range (band) but blocks all others.

passifier, *n.* a feature of a communications link that allows users to decide how many times and how quickly to repeat corrupted signals. This is somewhat like the auto re-try feature of some modern telephones and fax systems.

passive, *adj.* in IT, describing an electronic element which contains or demands no source of power. This means it cannot produce power or amplify a signal. Examples are resistors, diodes and capacitors.

password, *n.* a code a user must enter into a system before gaining access to protected hardware, systems, software, or data. For greater security there may be several levels of password, either with a new password giving access to a more secure level, or with different passwords letting users into different sections.

patch, *n*. **1.** a small routine added to a program to overcome a bug or problem.
2. a changeable link between communications channels. A **patch panel** is like an old fashioned switchboard.

pattern recognition, *n*. a major aspect of various areas of machine intelligence (in which software must attempt to detect and build on patterns within data), of optical character recognition (which here includes MICR), and of machine vision. Except in the first case, the system must have suitable sensors for input as well as suitable software.

PAX, *abbrev. for* private automatic exchange, now in effect the same as PBX.

pay cable, *n*. a type of local cable television system for the use of which viewers pay as they view (rather than paying a fixed rental).

payroll, *n*. a major type of file processing software. Its inputs are the details of staff work hours, etc., and changes to the staff list (transaction file); the outputs are pay slips, a file of payment orders for the bank, and so on.

PBX, *abbrev. for* PRIVATE BRANCH EXCHANGE.

pc, *abbrev. for* PERSONAL COMPUTER.

PC, *n*. **1.** a personal computer 100% compatible with IBM's PC and related families, though strictly 'PC' is reserved for IBM machines alone. **PC-DOS** is the DISK-OPERATING SYSTEM of IBM PCs, MS-DOS being that of compatible and near-compatible machines.
2. a program counter (see MACHINE CYCLE).

PCB, *abbrev. for* PRINTED CIRCUIT BOARD.

PCM, *abbrev. for* pulse code modulation. See MODULATION.

PD, see POTENTIAL DIFFERENCE.

PDM, *abbrev. for* pulse duration (width or length) modulation. See MODULATION.

peek, *vb*. to obtain a copy of the contents of a stated main store cell. In most program languages that use it (there are not many of these), this is a function: i.e. in use it has the form LET result := PEEK(address). See also POKE.

PEL, *abbrev. for* PIXEL.

perceptron, *n*. a form of NEURAL NETWORK.

perforated tape, *n*. an alternative term for punched tape. See PUNCHED MEDIA.

PERSONAL IDENTITY DEVICE (PID)

perforator, *n.* an alternative term for a PAPER-TAPE PUNCH, a device or machine for putting the holes into the tape that code data.

perigee, *n.* the point of closest approach to the Earth in the orbit of an Earth satellite.

peripheral, *n.* any hardware unit that is not part of an IT system's central processor (CPU). The peripherals of most systems include input and output units and backing storage hardware. A **peripheral interface** is the physical and electronic link between the CPU and a peripheral (see INTERFACE). A **peripheral transfer** is a data transfer between a peripheral and the CPU, in either direction. In most cases, it passes along the I/O bus as set by the I/O control. A **peripheral unit** is any peripheral as described above.

permanent file, *n.* any file with a longer life-time than a temporary one (e.g. than a scratchpad file).

permanent storage, *n.* a term for NON-VOLATILE STORE, such as read-only memory (ROM).

permutation index, *n.* an index used in document searching which lists in order all the words of the title of each document, each word in turn coming first. Thus a paper called 'Professional fax procedures' would appear in the index as:

    fax procedures professional

    ...

    procedures professional fax

    ...

    professional fax procedures

persistence, *n.* the measure of the time for which an image on a visual display lasts after REFRESHING stops. Applied mainly to cathode-ray tube displays, this relates to observed flicker and smoothness of animation. See also PHOSPHOR.

personal computer (PC), *n.* any stand-alone micro for use mainly by one person at a time (and now, more and more, for sole use by one person). The term was first used in 1976 (in the US magazine *Byte*).

personal data, *n.* any filed data about a living person. If the data is in an IT system, it may be easy to access. This has implications for privacy and security; thus many countries have laws to protect personal data. These laws express the rights of the individual (the data subject) and the duties of the holder (the data holder). See also DATA PROTECTION.

personal identity device (PID), *n.* an item without which a person cannot gain access to an IT system (whether or not

PERSONAL IDENTITY NUMBER

there is a password such as a PIN too). Pids include stripe and smart cards of various kinds.

personal identity number (PIN), *n.* a type of password, usually consisting of a numbers sequence, widely used with public-access data bases (e.g. bank autoteller machines).

personnel, *n.* the staff of a firm or organization. For the personnel of a computer department, see STAFF. **Personnel software** are programs designed for handling effectively the needs of personnel departments (see also PAYROLL).

PERT, *abbrev. for* Programme Evaluation and Review Technique, a major CRITICAL PATH ANALYSIS (PROJECT SCHEDULER) system.

petal printer, *n.* another name for a DAISYWHEEL PRINTER; the wheel consists of a set of characters, each on a radial petal.

phase, *n.* **1.** a stage in a lengthy process, e.g. that of the system's life cycle, with analysis, design, and implementation phases. During implementation, there is likely to be a **phased transfer** (i.e., a step by step one) from the old system to the new one; see PARALLEL RUNNING and PILOT. There are also three main phases in a MACHINE CYCLE.

2. (symbol ϕ, unit radian or degree) applied to a cyclic measure (e.g. a wave or carrier signal), the part of a period which the measure has reached at a given instant. The phase change in a complete cycle is 360°, a half cycle being 180°, and so on. The phase of each wave in the Figure changes from point to point. There is always a **phase difference** (symbol Δ) of 90° between them. The horizontal axis in the Figure is the 'phase axis'.

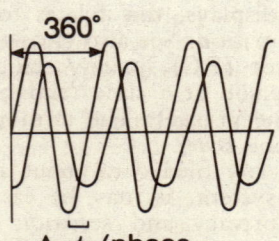

$\Delta \phi$ (phase difference): 90°

phase.

Phase encoding or **phase modulation recording** is a method of holding digital data in a magnetic medium. Each storage cell contains a pair of opposite poles (north and south seeking), with their order showing whether the cell contains 1 or 0. **Phase modulation** is a form of MODULATION in which the input signal modifies the phase of the carrier.

phone, see TELEPHONE.

phoneme, *n.* a unit of spoken language, the phonemes in 'phoneme' being f, oa, n, ee, and m. Many SPEECH SYNTHESIS systems base their work on phonemes.

phosphor, *n.* a substance that gives out light while it receives radiation of some suitable kind (e.g. 'cathode-rays', or electron radiation, in a CRT) and for a short while after. The delayed light radiation is known as **phosphorescence**. See also PERSISTENCE. Tiny **phosphor dots** cover the inside of a cathode-ray tube: for a colour display they are in groups of three, one dot for each primary colour. See TELEVISION.

photo by wire, *n.* a fax-like system widely used by news media to transfer images of photos at speed from place to place. See PICTURE BY WIRE.

photocell, *n.* a sensor for light (and, by extension, related radiations in the ultraviolet and infrared regions of the spectrum). There are various types, based on the various photoelectric effects discovered since the 1880s. All give an electric output that depends in some way on the input radiation; most are, therefore, analog light sensors, needing an analog-to-digital converter when used for input to an IT system. The **photo-diode** and **photo-transistor** are very common now, e.g. in scanners (a major use of photo sensing in IT). See the Figure for the standard symbols.

photocopier, *n.* a machine that uses some process (now very often using XEROGRAPHY) to make paper copies of an original sheet or object. See COPIER.

photonics, *n.* a rarely used term for either FIBRE OPTICS or OPTOELECTRONICS.

photooptic storage, *n.* a type of store based on some optical medium (often an optical film).

photosensor, *n.* a light sensor, or PHOTOCELL, as used in many IT systems.

photosetting, *m.* the creation of a positive (black) image on a negative (white) background by the use of a light projected onto light-sensitive materials. Photosetting can be a form of TYPESETTING, but this is not always the case.

PHOTOTYPESETTING

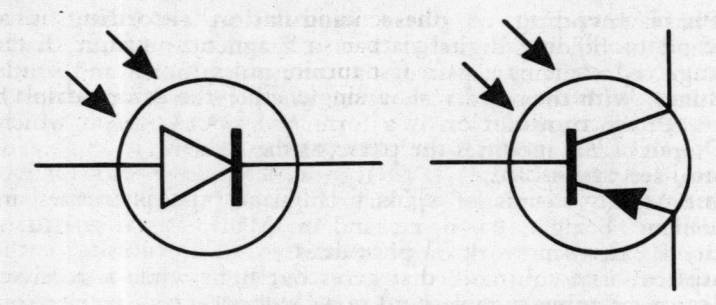

photocell. Photodiode and phototransistor.

phototypesetting, *n.* the creation of typeset characters using optical or electronic means. The most sophisticated typesetting systems in current use generate type electronically from data stored on disk or in computer memory, and output using laser technology. Earlier systems created type by PHOTOSETTING.

phototelegraphy, *n.* an obsolete term for FAX (normally a public fax where the sender takes the document to a central office, perhaps run by a PTT).

physical structure, *n.* the actual layout of a file, for instance, in a store, e.g. in blocks rather than in records (an aspect of logical structure). It is for the operating and applications software to take account of the physical structure of stored data; the user may not even need to know about the logical structure and certainly should not find the USER INTERFACE changed if the physical structure changes. This last aspect is **physical data independence**.

pi character, *n.* any special character not found in the standard character set of a modern typesetting system. If there is a need for such a character (e.g. a Greek letter such as pi, hence the name), the text must include a **pi-code** for it.

pica, *n.* a widely used type size system, with characters set at ten to the inch. Strictly a pica is 12 POINTS, i.e. 4.2 mm.

pickup, *n.* any transducer in general, but the term is generally restricted to denote a head able to detect data stored on a disk and to convert it to an electric signal.

pico-, *prefix denoting* 10^{-12}, a millionth of a millionth, symbol p.

picture by wire, *n.* a fax-like system widely used by news media to transfer images of photos and other pictures at speed from place to place. At the sending end a head (light source and photocell) moves along a bar so it scans the surface of the picture, which is fixed to a fast turning drum.

picture element (PEL), *n.* a single unit of a screen display; see PIXEL (picture cell).

PID, *abbrev. for* PERSONAL IDENTITY DEVICE.

piece identity number (PIN), *n.* an alternative term for BAR CODE; strictly, the term stands for the information in the bar-coded label.

pilot, *adj.* denoting on trial or under test. **Pilot running** is the testing of a newly installed system by using it with a small set of sample inputs. Compare PARALLEL RUNNING.

PIN, *abbrev. for* PERSONAL IDENTITY NUMBER or for PIECE IDENTITY NUMBER.

pinfeed, *n.* an alternative term for TRACTOR FEED: using sprockets and holes to feed printer paper.

pipe, *n.* a wide data channel; a name for bus in some hardware units and for data storage channels in, for instance, a bubble device. **Pipe-lining** speeds up processing by using a technique whereby a machine cycle starts on an instruction before the previous one has ended; thus instructions are 'in the pipe line'.

piracy, *n.* the theft of software by selling illegal copies.

pitch, *n.* **1.** the frequency aspect of a sound as perceived by the human ear.

2. the measure of character size and spacing in a printout; the number of characters per inch is the norm. PICA is a ten-pitch type face, while Elite is twelve pitch.

pixel, pixcel or **pel,** *n.* a picture cell, the smallest unit of a screen display the system can address. Pixel size affects image RESOLUTION; the smaller the pixels, the greater the resolution (detail). Often, a given hardware/software package may offer several screen display modes with different resolutions. A **pixel pattern** is a grid of pixels of standard size (for the given system), from which each screen character is devised. Figure 2 under MAGNETIC shows the principle, though for a very different context.

PL/1, *n.* 'Program Language number 1', a high-level program language of value in both business and science contexts. When devised by IBM in the 1960s, the aim was to make it so flexible that there would be no further need for other program languages. This did not prove to be the case, however, and PL/1 is not widely used (even though better versions were devised).

PLASMA DISPLAY

plasma display, *n.* a flat screen system using light radiation from a current in a low pressure gas. See GAS PLASMA DISPLAY.

plate, *n.* a rare term for PRINTED CIRCUIT BOARD.

platen, *n.* the main paper roller in a printer, that behind the paper and below the print head.

plausible reasoning, *n.* much the same as INEXACT REASONING, an important aspect of MACHINE INTELLIGENCE.

plotter, *n.* an output device for giving hard copy of a graphic image. As regards physical structure, there are two main designs. In the **flat bed plotter** (**x/y plotter**), the paper rests on a flat table, and the pen moves to and fro on a carrier which itself moves up and down. The paper passes round a drum in the **drum plotter**: while the pen moves to and fro on a fixed rod, the drum moves the paper up and down (see Figure).

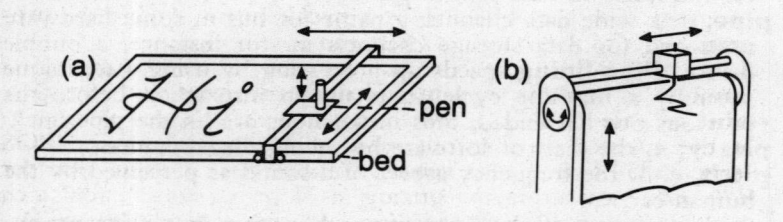

plotter. A flat bed (a) and drum plotter (b).

plug compatibility, *n.* a sales term for such a high level of compatibility between hardware units that the new owner can simply plug one into the other for them to work together.

PMOS, *abbrev. for* positive channel metal oxide semiconductor; see MOS and TRANSISTOR.

pneumatic, *adj.* denoting driven by (compressed) air or some other gas, and used in various types of robotic drive. Pneumatic systems are cheap, quiet and reliable.

pocket computer, *n.* a computer small enough to fit into a pocket or bag. Such a machine has a fairly small liquid crystal display and keyboard (not, in this case, always with a standard, e.g. QWERTY or AZERTY, layout), and is battery powered (though it may also have a mains transformer socket). In most cases backing store on chips supports the fairly small main store, and there are ports for links to a desktop machine and/or modem and/or printer. Because of the small keyboard size, a pocket computer is not likely to include a word processor program: although simple database, diary, and clock software tend to be standard. It is not easy to state how a computer like this differs from a programmable large screen pocket calculator, or from a pocket electronic organizer: a computer is generally more versatile. See also PORTABLE COMPUTERS.

point, *n*. **1.** a widely used measure of distance in printing, e.g. 0.351 mm, twelve points making a PICA.

2. a sharp end: a **point contact** diode was an early type of diode (e.g. the 'cat's whisker' wire used to form a junction with a semiconductor crystal in home-made crystal radio sets).

3. a station in a network, with a **point-to-point** communications line linking only a pair of stations (compare MULTI-DROP line).

4. a stage in a program run: e.g. a **branch point** (where the program flow may branch), or a **break point** (where the program is set to stop during a test run for checking).

5. a marker between the integer and fraction parts of a number, as in **binary point** and **decimal point**.

point of sale (POS), *n*. where a sale actually takes place, e.g. at the counter or checkout desk of a shop. IT in the POS terminal till linked to a central computer is of value here for data entry and automatic pricing (as with bar codes), for stock control, for credit-card checking and EFTPOS, and for measuring the rate of work of sales staff.

pointer, *n*. **1.** the address of a given data item stored so as to 'point' to the location of that item. Thus the index of a file is a list of data item labels and pointers, as is a label table. Some data structures, e.g. linked list and tree, have pointers attached to each data item to link it to parent and child(ren). See also FLAG.

2. (or **pointing device**) an input unit with which the user controls the position and movement of the screen cursor (also often called pointer), in, for instance, an art program. The main pointing devices are joystick, mouse, paddle, tracker ball; keyboards exist with any one of these, apart from a mouse, built in.

poke, *vb*. to change the contents of a specified storage cell while working in a high-level program language. High-level program languages normally do not allow access to storage cells (for that would make them harder to use); those that do may use an instruction like POKE *N* 'C' to put the code for

POLAR TRANSFER

C into the cell with address n. See also PEEK.

polar transfer, *n.* a data transfer technique sometimes used in telegraphy with a three-state code (e.g. 0 1 2) rather than binary. In fact two of the states represent two different mark/space signal units, with the third for no unit. The name is unfortunate, in that polar strictly refers to two state contexts (as in the north and south seeking poles of a magnet). Thus a **polar signal** in telegraphy is more often one where current one way stands for 0 and current the other way for 1. However, see LOBE, an effect in a 2D **polar graph**.

polarization, *n.* a characteristic of waves in the electromagnetic spectrum (radio and light), which relates to the angle of the plane in which the waves travel. Normal (unpolarized) waves travel in all planes at random; polarized ones are restricted. However, radio waves and microwaves are polarized at the sending end; aerials must align with the plane of polarization for good reception.

Polish, *adj.* denoting notation for numbers that avoids the use of brackets in expressions. See REVERSE POLISH NOTATION, its modern form in IT, a type of postfix notation.

polling, *n.* **1.** interrogating peripherals in turn to check status (e.g. whether each is ready for a data transfer) and to avoid clashes. Polling is central to a multiuser system; the processor must poll the terminals continuously.
2. inviting remote stations in turn to send data. It is common to program a fax system to do this automatically; for instance, during the night, a firm's fax machine may poll the systems of the sales staff to collect the day's orders from each one.

pop or **pull,** *vb.* to remove the outermost data item from a structure, in particular a stack. Note that access of this nature to data items does not produce copies as in normal reading: after popping, the items no longer exist in the structure.

port, *n.* an interface at the edge of a central processor for links with a peripheral. To port data or programs is to transfer copies from one system to a second (generally incompatible) one.

portability, *n.* **1.** (of a program) a measure of the ease of transfer from the host machine to a second (generally incompatible) one. It should be the aim of programmers to produce highly portable code, to maximize usage; on the other hand, different machines offer different features and functions (which is how they differ), so a richly featured program may have to remain specific to the original system. **Porting** is the transfer process.

2. (of a computer or other item of IT hardware) a measure of how easy it is to carry from place to place. The first **portable computers** (early 1980s) tended to be called transportable, or luggable: they were still very bulky and heavy. Now laptops (1 kg or so, but with full size keyboard and fair display) and POCKET COMPUTERS are highly portable. The ideal machine would be:

(a) able to fit in a bag but still have a near full sized usable keyboard (or other suitable form of data entry);

(b) tough and very reliable as regards its power supply (see, e.g., BATTERY);

(c) supplied with full-feature business software that is fully integrated and fully compatible with standard desktop systems;

(d) powerful enough to transfer data to and from desktop and other systems (including email and fax).

In the late 1960s, Alan Kay (the DYNABOOK designer) noted that the ideal computer is woven into one's clothes, i.e. should be completely integrated with human needs. Attempts are being made to make this concept an actuality.

POS, *abbrev. for* POINT OF SALE.

post, *vb.* **1.** to enter a new item of information into a computer record.

2. to log some important event, i.e. to enter details into a LOG file.

postfix, *adj.* denoting a method of showing numeric expressions with the operator after each operand, so that each operator acts on the previous intermediate result: as in '2 + 3 +' to give 5, rather than '+2 + 3 ='. See also REVERSE POLISH NOTATION. Compare INFIX.

posting, *n.* the logging of events in a large computer system, a normal role of the operating software as well as of the operator. A **posting dictionary** is a directory of index terms and related record numbers in a bibliographic file. **Postings** are the numbers of related records in each case (and also the number of records a search retrieves).

post mortem dump, *n.* a dump of storage contents to paper (or screen) after a program run, a tool in testing. A **post mortem program/routine** has the task of analysing the way a program under test runs. **Post mortem time** is how long it takes a system to recover after it fails for some reason.

post-order, see IN-ORDER TRAVERSAL.

post processor, *n.* a system or program that accepts and

POTENTIAL DIFFERENCE

further processes the output of another system or program; compare PRE-PROCESSING.

potential difference (PD), *n.* the 'force' that sends an electric current through a circuit. When there is a current in a circuit, there is a PD between the ends of each part of the circuit. We can view a signal as a varying current through a circuit, or as a varying PD between two points in it. *Voltage* is used as an alternative term for PD.

power, *n.* 1. a measure of the complexity of the data handling tasks which a system can cope with at acceptable speed. A typical unit is Mflops (a million floating-point operations per second), but there are few standards here.

2. the number of times to multiply a value by itself, the number being the index or exponent. Thus in 10^3 ($10 \times 10 \times 10$, i.e. 1000), the power/index/exponent is 3. Most program languages (but far from all) have a function to produce this type of result.

3. an energy supply to a system (strictly, the energy supply per second, measured in watts, W). Some systems can cope with a **power failure** and they may have a backup supply (batteries or a generator, although the latter takes time to come on line), or an emergency data dump routine that can rescue crucial data while the power decays. **Power line data transfer** is the passing of signals through a power cable rather than through a special channel. See MAINS DATA TRANSFER.

PPS, *abbrev. for* PULSES PER SECOND, a unit of data transfer rate.

precedence code, *n.* a signal in a data stream that the characters that follow differ in meaning from the usual; compare SHIFT, sense 2. See also PRIORITY.

precision, *n.* the measure of the number of significant figures of a value, e.g. 3.14 is less precise than 3.14159. Working with higher precision in an IT system involves extra processing power and storage; it also cuts down the range of numbers the system can handle. Compare ACCURACY.

A **precision laser** has a tightly focussed beam which allows use for high precision cutting, etc. In making chips, precision lasers (and electron beams) help work the surface.

pre-order, see IN-ORDER TRAVERSAL.

pre-process, *vb.* to work on data to prepare it for the actual processing. A **pre-processor** is a program that does this. EMULATION may need a pre-processor to convert data from one format to another. Pre-editing involves suitably amending data and re-formatting it before input. Compare with POST-

PRINTED CIRCUIT BOARD (PCB)

PROCESSOR.

presentation graphics, *n.* graphics designs aimed explicitly at presentations of ideas to others, perhaps on screen or as hard copy: but more often as transparencies for overhead or slide projection. Presentation GRAPHICS SOFTWARE has features to aid this; it will also link with the special output units required (e.g. a slide-maker).

primary, *adj.* denoting first level, or most important In a file of records, the **primary key** is the field for the data on which the system sorts and searches the file. The records' values in this field should be unique; even if they are, there may still be a need for one or more secondary keys. In a multi-processor, the **primary processor** links the system with outside control.

print, *vb.* to use a PRINTER to present output on paper (hard copy form) rather than on screen (soft). A **print buffer** is a store for data in transfer to the printer. To prevent the processor being occupied with printing rather than getting on with other work, modern systems often have very large print buffers (able to hold hundreds of thousands, or even more, bytes of print data).

A **print drum** carries on its surface the sets of embossed print characters in a drum (cylinder) printer. A **print hammer** is a bar with a single pair of characters (shifted and un-shifted) at its end, as in a daisy wheel printer (where it is a petal) or in a conventional typewriter. **Printout** is the hard copy obtained from a printer, while a **print run** is the complete process of producing a set of printouts (e.g. of bills). The **print wheel** of a daisy printer is the daisy itself. The **print width** of a printer is the maximum number of standard characters (in many cases, PICA characters, ten per inch) it can put in a line. This depends on the size of the carriage (platen); standard printers have print widths of eighty characters per line, while wide carriage machines may offer perhaps twice that.

printed circuit board (PCB), *n.* a plastic board (sometimes called card or plate) of standard size designed to carry a pattern of 'printed' metal tracks and the holes for mounting the chips and other circuit elements. Thus a complete board can carry a large complex circuit; if there is a fault, it is normal practice to replace the whole board and take the failed one for detailed testing. The first use of PCBs was for the radio proximity fuses of the German V1 'doodlebug' flying bombs of 1944. The technique was so successful that within a

PRINTER

few years the US authorities decreed that all instruments in aircraft should have a PCB base.

It is not in fact printing that makes the metal tracks (which appear on both sides of the board in most cases), but etching. The most common method is to coat the board with a metal layer and put a wax layer in top. The wax is removed to expose the metal that is not required on the final board. The etching bath contains acid that dissolves the exposed metal; after this, the wax layer is removed.

PCBs need not be flat. With the advent of SURFACE MOUNTING, it is now quite common to make any plastic part of a system double as a board to carry surface mounted elements (e.g. the inside door panel of a car).

printer, *n*. a machine for putting the data output by an IT system onto paper as a hard (permanent) copy. There are many **printer types**; we can class machines according to:

(a) whether they (in effect) print a character, a line or a page at a time;

(b) whether they involve impact between a moving part and the paper (through a ribbon) or not;

(c) whether they can work with plain paper or need some special type; and

(d) the nature of the process that gives an image on the paper.

As well as the actual print mechanism (likely to involve some kind of print head), a transport system based on a stepper motor moves the paper through the machine (in some cases in either direction). Despite having complex and high precision moving parts, most printers break down rarely. All the same, they may be noisy and may present quite high running costs for consumables such as paper.

Printer faces are the typefaces offered by printers. Machines using embossed characters (e.g. daisywheel and the various line printers) can, in theory, offer any typeface; on the other hand, the user will have to buy each print wheel or drum needed, and change them often during a print run. Modern printers of other types (such as dot matrix machines, whether using pins or ink jet, and page printers) tend to offer at least two or three different faces; with many of these systems, the user can buy extra chips that provide extra faces. Access to all these tends to be under software control, although is some cases the user can code his or her needs by pressing the front panel buttons.

In a **printer bound/limited** process, the processor is likely to find itself under-used, as it has to devote so much time to printing. Printing off line (spooling) or using a very large PRINT BUFFER are two common solutions.

Printer plotter is an obsolete name for a printer that, as well as being able to form characters, can make hard copy of graphic data. All printers other than those with embossed characters can do this now, however. A **printer switcher**, a manual or automatic switch that links any of a set of small IT systems (e.g. micros) to one printer, provides a crude (but effective) approach to simple networking. As few users need to have printing take place for more than a small fraction of usage time, the switcher provides clear savings.

printout, *n.* the HARD COPY, data dumped to paper for more permanent storage than if dumped just to screen. **Printout capture** involves going through the actions of printing; but sending the print file to store rather than to a printer. In this form, the user can keep the file for later printing or for transfer to a second system. Much the same process is on offer by some fax cards: they can send a printout captured file as a fax signal.

priority or **precedence,** *n.* the degree of importance of an operation, file or process in a hierarchy. All program languages assign priority to arithmetic processes (and most do the same for logical actions), with * and / having higher priority than + and -, for example. 'Importance' as defined above is not always from the point of view of the user. Thus in a MULTI-PROGRAM system, the programs to run during a given period have priorities as regards processor access in inverse order to their processor demand; an I/O bound program has a higher priority than one that needs the processor a lot.

A **priority queue** is a LINKED LIST in which the order of the elements (items that relate to jobs or tasks) reflects their priority for attention. At the head of the list is always the item with the highest priority.

privacy, *n.* any restricted access, in particular to PERSONAL DATA and data a person or firm thinks is of high value (e.g. a trade secret).

private branch exchange (PABX, PBX, PAX), *n.* a local switchboard that controls the links between the one or more exchange lines and the various internal lines (to extensions); or the switching centre for a private telephone network with no links to the public system. Most modern PBXs (in the first case) allow extension users to 'dial' out without going through a human operator (though a log may keep details of all calls made). There are various approaches to automating the connections for inward calls, but, in general, there is still a need for human operators.

private line, *n.* a communications channel set aside for only a single user.

problem-oriented program language, *n.* a high-level program language designed very much from the user's point of view rather than with machine needs in mind. All high-level program languages are problem-oriented to a degree. This is true almost by definition, in that some people regard level as relating to the degree of problem orientation. The more problem-oriented a language is, the less machine-oriented it must be, and therefore the harder to translate.

procedure, *n.* that part of a program which is viewed as a whole as handling a particular task within the overall algorithm, and which is kept separate from the main program. The main program, or a second procedure, calls on the procedure as required; at its end, program control returns to the calling point. Two features of a procedure not found in all closed subroutines are:

(a) naming: it can carry a long meaningful label which can act much like a key word;

(b) PARAMETER-passing.

A program language that offers procedures is likely to allow more structured (efficient) programming than otherwise. To many, this is the value of **procedural program languages** (**procedure-oriented program languages**) such as Pascal.

process, *vb.* to carry out a set of actions on input data in order to give an output that is of more value to the user, a **process** (*n.*) being that set of actions. See also PROCESSOR.

Process control is the use of automatic input, data processing, and feedback in industry (abbreviated as IPC) in order to control automatically the flow of raw and processed materials and goods. Most applicable to industrial processes that involve continuous flow (as in mining, large scale transport, and chemical plants), this is a crucial area of industrial automation.

processing, *n.* the passing of stored or input data through a set of actions that makes up an overall process. See also DATA PROCESSING.

processor, *n.* the central part of any IT system, with:

(a) a control unit to handle all the data flows inside and outside the processor;

(b) an arithmetic and logic unit to carry out the various arithmetic actions that all processing entails, and also the logical comparisons involved in branching;

(c) a clock to keep all these actions in step.

For further details, see MICROPROCESSOR, a processor made of one or more chips (as all are nowadays).

program, *n.* a set of instructions in suitable form, so that, when translated, an IT system can carry them out to complete a given task. (See also ALGORITHM, but note that not all programs are linear in that the instructions are steps the system should follow in order; see FUNCTIONAL program.) A **program-coding sheet** is a piece of paper ruled to help the programmer keep instructions to the correct format; such sheets are now of use mainly with assembly language work. A **program counter (PC)** is a processor's sequence control register (SCR); see MACHINE CYCLE. After a **program crash**, the program halts without reaching the proper end; this is the result of a bug (fatal error) of some kind in the coding. A severe crash will so affect the operating software that it cannot take over; the machine locks up and must be re-set, or even switched off and on again, before it will work.

The process of **program development** is in many ways like that of systems analysis, stretching, as it does, from initial concept and definition (specification) to delivery of a fully working, documented package. In between, the main stages are planning, coding and testing, though all should overlap to a significant extent. Structured program development, aided by use of a structured program language (e.g. a procedural one), is a careful thoughtful approach to program development. It involves good planning and step-wise refinement of the concept and, well done, much reduces the chance of error.

program documentation, *n.* the keeping of records throughout program development. This helps ensure the programmer does not stray from the initial concept (design), and leads to final DOCUMENTATION, a crucial part of the package produced.

program execution, *n.* the (translating and) running of a program, i.e. having it work on a set of stored or input data to produce useful results. A **program flow chart** shows in block graphic form the sequence of actions in a whole program (outline chart) or that in a tricky part (detailed chart). See FLOW CHART.

Many people consider programming to be the most costly

part of system development and, in addition, it always involves errors. In an attempt to by-pass these problems, various **program generators** have appeared. These are themselves programs, of the fifth generation; they take in a simple statement of what a desired program should do, and produce working code on that basis. All the same, while the program that results may be complete and correct, no program generator so far can produce compact, inspirational code (i.e. a highly efficient program); program generation is still a major field of MACHINE INTELLIGENCE research. See also AUTHOR LANGUAGE and APPLICATIONS PROGRAM GENERATOR.

program language, *n.* an environment for making programs; a set of rules and keywords designed for tasks within a range of applications. The early programmers had to work in MACHINE CODE; their programs were strings of 0s and 1s the computer could act upon directly. To make coding simpler for the people involved, ASSEMBLERS, and then HIGH-LEVEL PROGRAM LANGUAGES, appeared. Work on MACHINE INTELLIGENCE has, in more recent years, led to various other useful styles.

A **program library** is the set of programs owned and used by a person or group. See LIBRARY. **Programmability** describes:

(a) hardware systems with INTELLIGENCE which allows the user to program them to carry out a range of tasks: a **programmable store** is one whose cells the program counter (above) can address;

(b) whether it is possible for a person to produce a program to handle a given problem (human task): some problems are theoretically impossible to solve with a program; the programs that would handle others would need longer than the life time of the universe to come to an end.

Many modern keyboards have **programmable keys** (function keys): spare keys and associated software so the user can program them to carry special instructions or complex character strings. Indeed, in some cases, every key is programmable. The more costly fax machines have such keys too, each perhaps able to carry the fax and telephone numbers of a firm and perhaps 20 characters of text (e.g. firm and contact names). Then a single key press will set up the desired telephone or fax call. **Programmable read-only memory** is a chip the user can program rather than the maker. See PROM for details and varieties.

programmed learning, *n.* an unsuccessful approach of the

1960s (mainly) to setting out learning tasks as sets of small steps (linear or with branching) so that a machine could deliver them to learners and trainees. In those days, most of the machines were mechanical; even today, few (if any) systems of COMPUTER-AIDED LEARNING have overcome the problems then found. In the field of fax, **programmed transfer** is the same as DELAYED SEND: the user programs the system to send a given fax some time later (e.g. at night when telephone calls cost less).

It is the task of a **programmer** to produce compact, friendly, working programs (and, in most cases, all associated technical documentation) from an initial specification. The work itself is **programming**, and depends on a program language (see above). A good programmer has the right attitude to the work (e.g. to structure planning programming) and a thorough knowledge of several program languages; such a person does not find it difficult to grasp the methods of a new program language within a very short time. See also STAFF.

program relocation, *n.* the moving of a whole machine-code program from one part of the main store to a second. It therefore needs to be coded with no mention of any absolute addresses. Such a relocatable program is of great value in a large computer system, in that the operating software can load it into any part of the main store without problems to suit current circumstances. A **program-report generator** is a routine in a database management system that allows the user to define the REPORTS to produce on any set of stored data. A **program specification** is a design brief: a clear, structured statement of the program's aims, objectives and approach, plus descriptions of the inputs and outputs.

program statement, *n.* an instruction in a high-level language program. Many modern program languages allow multistatement lines, ending in a <RETURN> or other symbol; in that case some special symbol other than <RETURN> (often ':') must mark the end of all but the last statement in the line. For **program structure**, see ALGORITHM, STRUCTURE. For **program structure chart**, see STRUCTURE CHART.

project control, *n.* a major area of human activity that has gained much benefit from IT. Project control involves careful planning of the project (building, industrial process, exhibition) and of the schedule required: and then monitoring progress to keep work on schedule. A **project-control program** (or **project scheduler**) aids project control by:

PROLOG

(a) helping at the planning stage, e.g. to ensure no aspects are left out;

(b) asking for frequent progress reports during development, and then planning the changes to the programme that will keep the project on schedule;

(c) keeping account of hidden costs;

(d) making a wide range of useful reports.

See also CRITICAL PATH ANALYSIS (CPA) and GANTT CHART.

Prolog, *n.* a fifth-generation high-level program language, i.e. one that takes account of aspects of MACHINE INTELLIGENCE. The basic element of this logical programming system is the atom, an expression of a simple relationship between entities (people or things, or labels for them). A Prolog program is a set (in no special order) of atoms and conditional statements. The set sums up a knowledge domain; it thus allows the user to make a query within that knowledge domain and receive an answer the program can 'explain'. MICRO-PROLOG is a widely used version for micros.

Alain Colmerauer and others first produced Prolog, in France in 1972. The main progress since then has been in the hands of Robert Kowalski in Britain and the Japanese ICOT centre (which uses it for the national fifth generation development programme). There has been some use in British schools, mainly for history teaching (i.e. setting up and searching history files), but its rather difficult syntax has proved to be a problem.

PROM, *abbrev. for* programmable read-only memory, a chip programmed by a user rather than by the maker. Programming involves passing current through the chip to melt ('blow') tiny fuses of some kind of alloy in the surface. **PROM-blowing** is the name for this process. Once programmed, the chip is a normal read-only device: there is no way to reprogram it. On the other hand, that is not the case with some other types of PROM. Two major ones are:

(a) EPROM (erasable PROM) programmed by charges fixed in a type of MOS circuit; to erase, shine strong ultra-violet for perhaps half an hour through a window over the chip: you may then re-program with a **PROM blower** as above;

(b) EEPROM (electrically erasable PROM) programming and erasing is purely electrical; we can therefore view this device as a type of non-volatile read and write storage chip (RAM); it is, however, slow in action.

prompt, *n.* a message from a computer that invites the user to make an input (or take some action that leads to an input). Thus, the prompt can also be the same as the cursor many interactive programs use to invite input (though often the program should provide a brief text message as well).

proportional spacing, *n.* the character spacing offered by some printers (and on some word processor and DTP screens); each character has the space it needs, rather than a fixed space, as in monotype.

proprietary, *adj.* denoting copyright, i.e. owned by someone. A **proprietary program** is software owned and sold by a firm, rather than a broad type of program (a generic program, e.g. a word processor, compared to a purchased system).

protected cell, *n.* a storage location that cannot accept a new data item unless it meets some special criterion.

protection, *n.* a system that prevents accidental loss of data, such as deleting or amending a file. Most operating systems allow some method of software protection; e.g. 'locking' a file electronically with a command. Hardware protection involves making some change to the medium itself. Thus, in the latter case, a **protection ring** added to a magnetic tape spool prevents any change to the data on the tape.

protocol, *n.* a set of rules, formats and procedures for using a system (e.g. a communications channel). An international standard governs a good protocol.

PRR, *abbrev. for* PULSE REPETITION RATE.

pseudo-, *adj. prefix* denoting unreal. Thus **pseudo-code** is a method of writing algorithms; it looks like real code in that it uses many real structures and key words, but it is not code any given translation software could handle. (On the other hand, in the past, the word meant assembly code prior to translation; the meaning has changed). A **pseudo-instruction** is a DIRECTIVE in assembly language work: an instruction that does not translate to a single machine code instruction but to a whole set. **Pseudo-random numbers** are a set of numbers that appear random to the human eye, but, being generated by some kind of formula (in a **pseudo-random number generator**), cannot truly be random.

PSS, *abbrev. for* PACKET switching system.

PSTN, *abbrev. for* the world-wide public switched TELEPHONE network, where the hierarchy of exchanges (SWITCHING CENTRES) can link telephones, fax machines, and/or modems.

PSU, *abbrev. for* power supply unit, or power pack, the set of cells (battery) or mains transformer that provides an IT system with the energy it needs.

PTT, *abbrev. for* post, telegraph and telephone supplier, the 'traditional' organization (private or state owned) that provides such services. In recent years, however, changes have led to the services splitting off from each other (and from the transport network they also provided in many countries).

p-type, *adj.* denoting an extrinsic semiconductor with more free 'holes' than electrons. As we can think of a hole as a positive charge carrier, such a substance passes current mainly as a flow of positive charge. See also ACCEPTOR.

puck, *n.* an obsolete term for the pen used with a graphic tablet (though more like a mouse).

pull, *vb.* to remove a data item from, for example, stack (an old name for POP). Compare PUSH.

pulse, *n.* a momentary change in value of an electric current or its equivalent in some other method of data transfer. Pulses are the basis of digital transfers; this includes the control and clock pulses that pass between the units of an IT system to cause programmed actions. Viewing a long series of pulses as a carrier signal leads to various methods of MODULATION (changing it so that it carries information). The main ones are **pulse amplitude modulation (PAM), pulse code modulation (PCM), and pulse duration modulation (PDM)** or **pulse width modulation (PWM).** Any or all of these may bear the name **pulse modulation. Pulse repetition rate (PRR)** is much the same as frequency for such a pulsed carrier, the proper unit being **pulses per second (PPS)**, rather than hertz.

punch, *vb.* in IT, to make a hole in a piece of paper or card. A punch is a device to do this. The process allows data storage in **punched card** or **punched (perforated) (paper) tape** known as **punched media**, (see PAPER TAPE). It is the pattern of holes across the width of the card or tape that carries the actual data. Various codes have been developed to do this to overcome particular problems which the process throws up. However, punched media as above are now rarely found: but see KIMBALL TAG.

purge, *vb.* to delete or erase data (in most cases in a large chunk). The **purge date** of a file is the date after which the user or system may delete the file.

push, *vb.* to add a data item to the open end of a data structure, in particular that of a stack. A **push down/up list** is another name for a stack; pushing a new data item to the stack pushes the others down/up by one place.

Q

QAM, *abbrev. for* QUEUED ACCESS METHOD.

q-band, *n.* a microwave band used in radar, with frequencies in the range 36 - 46 GHz.

QIL, *abbrev. for* QUAD-IN-LINE.

QSAM, *abbrev. for* QUEUED SEQUENTIAL ACCESS METHOD.

QTAM, *abbrev. for* QUEUED TELECOMMUNICATIONS ACCESS METHOD.

quad, *abbrev. for* quadruple, i.e. four-fold. A disk able to store data at **quad density** can hold four times as much as a standard disk. One method involves storing at double density on both sides. **Quadding** involves forming cables and associated hardware from four insulated wires. A **quad-in-line** chip is a dual-in-line chip that carries four similar circuits.

qualification test, *n.* the final test of a program or system, before publication or delivery.

quality control, *n.* a strict (and often automated) approach to testing a product, or, in the case of data preparation, to the completeness and accuracy of input data.

quantizing error, *n.* a loss of precision that results from analog-to-digital conversion. The input analog signal can have any value between zero and the maximum, but the output digital pulses can have only 256 values in the case of eight-bit words (for instance). Thus the conversion cannot be exact for many input values. An everyday example follows from asking for people's ages in years ('digital'); the result is rarely exact.

quantum barrier, *n.* an ultimate limit to miniaturisation, i.e. in chip design. Some effects of quantum physics mean that data transfers will not be consistent and reliable if they involve currents smaller than a certain size in physical channels separated from others by insulators thinner than a certain size. For example, current can 'tunnel' between conducting channels through an insulator if it is too thin. See also JOSEPHSON JUNCTION.

Quantum security involves sending data through a channel with a coding method based on effects of quantum physics. This system (only at prototype stage by the end of the 1980s) offers total security as quantum effects are entirely random.

QUERY LANGUAGE

The developers claim that such systems, which should be able to communicate over a few hundred metres, are the first to pass the theoretical limits of the TURING MACHINE (basis of all current digital computers).

query language, *n.* a natural language subset that allows non-expert users to access a data base (to ask questions). The aim is to allow searches expressed entirely in free form, but no query language is near that goal yet.

queue, *n.* a data structure that works on a first in, first out method, i.e., it is linear and has two ends, one for adding (pushing) new data items, and the other for taking (popping) the next data items for processing. A queue that works like this in main store would, in time, creep through all the cells; it therefore has a certain space available to it, and wraps round when it reaches the end (see Figure).

Keyboard command	Head pointer	Tail pointer	Queue 5	4	3	2	1	Comment
push T R A	3	1			A	R	T	Queue was empty
pop pop	3	3			A			
push E L	5	3	L	E	A			
push F	1	3	L	E	A		F	Head cycles round

queue. Pushing data to and popping it from a queue.

A **queued access method (QAM)** cuts delays in a system's input/output actions by queuing the blocks and synchronising all such data transfers. A **queued sequential access method (QSAM)** is a SEQUENTIAL ACCESS METHOD made more efficient by queuing, and synchronising the transfer of, the input blocks that await processing and the output blocks after processing. A **queued telecommunications access method (QTAM)** handles data transfers between a store and remote terminals. A message control program has the task of synchronising these for greatest efficiency.

Queuing theory involves the mathematical analysis of

human queues. This is important for simulations of service systems (e.g. shop checkouts) aimed at cutting delays.

quicksort, *n.* a major sorting algorithm that involves working on the list first from one end and then from the other in turn. Each time, the size of the unsorted list falls.

QWERTY, *n.* the standard keyboard layout in the English-speaking world, named after the first few letter keys at top left. A common alternative in other countries is azerty, but there have been many attempts to improve typing speed, comfort and accuracy by a complete re-design of layout and key grouping. See, for instance, DVORAK KEYBOARD, MALTRON and MICROWRITER.

R

radar, *n.* a band of RADIO waves in the microwave region (with frequencies around 10^9 - 10^{10} Hz), used for (as it was initially termed) 'radio detection and ranging', i.e. finding the positions of objects on the Earth's surface, in the sky and in space. German scientists explored the concept from 1904 for use with shipping, but used too high a frequency for sky scanning. The first patents on the 'use of television with aircraft' (the inventor's own phrase) came from John Logie BAIRD in 1926, major developments following in Britain a decade later (Robert Watson-Watt, British physicist, 1892 - 1973).

radio, *adj.* describing a range of waves in the electromagnetic SPECTRUM, widely used for local and tele-communications. The radio spectrum has a number of bands (designed for convenience):

code name		band	frequency		wavelength		
ELF	extra low frequency	1	3 - 30	Hz	100 000 -	10 000	km
AF	audio frequency	2	30 - 300		10 000 -	1 000	
VLF	very low frequency	3	0.3 - 3	kHz	1 000 -	100	
LF	low frequency	4	3 - 30		100 -	10	
MF	medium frequency	5	30 - 300		10 -	1	
HF	high frequency	6	0.3 - 3	MHz	1 000 -	100	m
VHF	very high frequency	7	3 - 30		100 -	10	
UHF	ultra high frequency	8	30 - 300		10 -	1	
SHF	super high frequency	9	0.3 - 3	GHz	1 000 -	100	mm
EHF	extra high frequency	10	3 - 30		100 -	10	
-	no name	11	30 - 300		10 -	1	

Band 1 is the infrasonic band, with 2 and 3 for sonic frequency waves, and 4 for ultrasonics. Band 6 carries AM radio signals (amplitude modulated); 7 is for FM radio and television. Higher bands are microwaves; bands 10 and 11 are the radar bands, with sub-bands p, l, s, x, k, q, v and w (up to 300 GHz, merging into the infra-red region). Clearly, therefore, the term **radio frequency (RF)** has a wide range of meanings. Generally it defines waves in the range 10^6 - 10^{11} Hz.

Most radio transmissions are professional, whether from broadcasters, narrow cast, or private (which includes CELL

RANDOM NUMBER

phone, citizens' band, pagers, and such signals as ship to shore). There is also a large amount of amateur (or ham) radio traffic. Users need licences to allow them to transmit; amateur channels now carry more and more digital data as well as voice and signal code.

Radio waves transfer information by adding the video, voice or data signal to a uniform carrier; the process being MODULATION.

All radio transmissions require transmit and receive aerials. These are conductors held parallel to the plane of polarization of the waves; a straight aerial works best if its length is about half the length of the waves concerned.

radix, *n*. a number base ('root' of a number system). It is the number of distinct digits 0...n in the system, n being radix-minus-1 (9 in the case of denary). For **radix-minus-one complement**, see ONES COMPLEMENT. A **radix point** (full stop or comma) keeps apart the integer and fraction parts of a number made up of digits with place values: the decimal point in the case of denary values.

ragged, *adj*. not straight, as in the **ragged right** margin of unjustified text. A **ragged array** has two or more dimensions, but the numbers of elements in the different rows/columns are not equal; viewed as a table, such an array would have ragged edges.

RAM, *abbrev. for* a storage chip holding data in READ AND WRITE MEMORY, sometimes better given as RWM (for it is common to take RAM to denote random access memory, an incorrect usage).

R&D, *abbrev. for* RESEARCH AND DEVELOPMENT, the work needed to bring new products to market.

random access, *n*. an imperfect, but common, term for DIRECT ACCESS, **random access memory** being an imperfect, but common, term for READ AND WRITE MEMORY (RAM or RWM).

random number, *n*. a value produced entirely unpredictably. There are many random processes in nature and in society, and it is crucial for people to model (simulate) them by computer. In fact, no computer can generate random numbers. As soon as an algorithm has been created, it is possible (at least in theory) to predict the next number in the 'sequence'. Instead, the **random number generators** of computers produce PSEUDO-RANDOM NUMBERS; users may take them to be random for most purposes, but they are not really so. A **random variable** can take any value in the range allowed. The

RANGE

chance of any given value being taken derives from its position in the probability distribution concerned.

range, *n.* a set of all the values between a low and a high limit. A **range check** in validation involves testing that an input of the correct type is in the correct range. For example, the range check for inputs to a human age field would reject values outside of 0–120, say. **Ranged left/right** (same as flush left/right) describes a format for text lines that are shorter than the page width (e.g. those in the address of a letter); ranged right, for instance, all the lines press on to the right hand margin.

rank, *n.* the order or level of a number, i.e. its position in a list or hierarchy. To rank data items is to put them in order, i.e. to sort them. The rank of a matrix (array) is its number of dimensions: a two dimensional array is a matrix of rank 2.

raster, *n.* the pattern of close lines that covers a blank monitor display (or a television screen when the station is working but sending no signal). The result is a uniformly grey screen. In IT, the word often means the grid of pixels that makes up such a display (i.e., dots horizontally as well as lines vertically). Then the display's **raster count** is the total number of pixels (the product of the number of screen lines, excluding those not used for display, and the number of dots per line).

In TELEVISION and most standard IT monitors, the signal for display adds to the raster. As the flying spot moves from dot to dot and line to line (see SCAN), it varies in brightness. The image therefore appears dot by dot and line by line. This is so even when the display is of a simple line drawing, the process concerned being **raster graphics**. In such cases, it is more efficient (i.e. faster and with lower storage demand) to display line drawings using VECTOR GRAPHICS; the process here is much like that in a PLOTTER. On the other hand, so-called **raster plotters** do exist; they build up an image dot by dot and line by line, i.e. by a **raster scan**.

raw data, *n.* data as it exists before any form of validation, sorting, pre-processing or processing is done on it.

RCTL, *abbrev. for* RESISTOR/CAPACITOR/TRANSISTOR LOGIC. See LOGIC (ELECTRONIC LOGIC).

reactive mode, *n.* a style of computer usage between batch and interactive (conversational) modes; user inputs cause actions but not necessarily any output.

read, *vb.* to access data stored in an IT system. This type of access tends to imply the data items remain in store (compare with POP, or DESTRUCTIVE READING, where they do not). A **read and write memory/store** (RAM) uses a technique for holding data that allows the user to store (write) data as well as to read it. Compare with ROM, read only memory/store (see below), where this is not the case, but see also PROM. A RAM store (where the data is held on a magnetic medium or in chip in most cases) tends to be volatile: without a constant power supply, stored data will vanish. This too is not the case with ROM.

A **reader** is a hardware unit able to sense and access data stored in some form (in most cases on paper or a plastic card) for input to an IT system. See MACHINE-READABLE INPUT. In a reader, the part that does the actual work (the sensor or array of sensors) is the **read head**.

As noted above, **read-only memory/store (ROM)** holds data permanently. On the one hand, this means the data is not volatile (you cannot lose it); on the other, you cannot erase or change (write) it. This type of store is of great value for holding permanent programs (e.g. all or part of a system's operating software) and for storing programs and other data for sale. To provide ROM in the early days of computing required HARD WIRING the circuits concerned; now chips and optical discs are the standard media. See also PROM (above), i.e. programmable ROM, some types of which have features of read and write memory.

A **read out** is a screen display of data (often of sensed data); it is soft copy, compared to print out or hard copy. In OCR, a **read screen** is a glass sheet through which the scanner views the document in question: the sheet keeps the document flat and the right distance from the head. For **read/write**, see read and write (above): a **read/write head** is a head able to transfer data either way between store and main store. This is the case with, for instance, data on magnetic disk. See HEAD. **Read/write storage** describes any storage medium that is not read only (in particular, magnetic and some types of chip and optical disc). **Read time**, the smallest part of ACCESS TIME, is the time involved in copying the data, once found, between stores.

ready, *adj.* denoting a message (or prompt) that tells the user a system is ready for input (data or command).

real (number), *n.* zero, or any positive or negative number which may include a fraction part as well as an integer part. The integers are a sub-set of the class of reals, but the ways in

REAL-TIME

which IT systems tend to treat them differ. See ARITHMETIC.

real-time, *adj.* describing a system which reacts at once to inputs, i.e., gives output at the same rate as the input. Any control system must be real-time (see FEEDBACK), and so must be an on-line data base (though this does not need to react quite so quickly, so can involve timesharing). A **real-time clock** in an IT system keeps track of elapsed human time (and, in most cases, date); it is not the same as the clock that sends out synchronizing pulses from the control unit of the processor, though some processes may refer to it (e.g., for time-dependent interrupts). A **real-time system** is one which works in real time.

reasoning with uncertainty, *n.* much the same as INEXACT REASONING, important in MACHINE INTELLIGENCE.

recall, *n.* a measure of the precision of a data file search: the ratio of the records retrieved to those that the search should have retrieved.

receive ID, *n.* the identity code for any calling system as recorded by a fax machine. Then the machine may display that code and/or show it in the log. ISDN has the power to offer much the same feature; when your telephone rings, its display would show the number of the caller. There is, however, some controversy about such a feature; indeed, some countries do not allow fax systems to have receive IDs.

receive only, *adj.* applied to a communications unit or terminal that can receive but not send signals or data. Many early teletype units were like this, for use where people wanted to view information (e.g. stock market details and news flashes), but not produce it.

recognition, *n.* the detection and seeing of a pattern in something, e.g. the magnetic ink characters of a MICR string and the letters of a text in optical character recognition (OCR). In OCR, **recognition logic** is the software that attempts to match sensed patterns with stored ones and thus to convert the input from the scanner into digital form. A **recognition unit** is another name for that type of program, or for an OCR scanner as a whole (i.e., hardware and software). See also PATTERN RECOGNITION.

record, *n.* **1.** a data structure which contains a number of fields, i.e. spaces (with labels) for related data items not all of the same type (compare ARRAY). The arrangement of fields in the record is the **record format**. A language that supports such a data structure can operate on the whole record (perhaps part of a hierarchical file (see sense **4** below) or on the data in a given field.

2. a chunk of data treated by a system as a unit, i.e. a **physical record** or BLOCK. In transfer there may be an end of record marker (**record separator**); in store there is an inter-record GAP between each pair of records. A physical record need not be the same as sense **1** or **4**. See BLOCKING FACTOR.

3. any stored data in the widest sense. **Recording** is the storage (writing) process. Here **recording density** is the same as PACKING DENSITY (the amount of data that fits a given space on the medium).

4. the set of data about one entity (person or thing, including a bibliographic entity such as a book or article) in a file of records of many such entities. This **logical record** may, or may not, have a format of fields; it may, or may not, be the same in a given case as sense **1** or sense **2**.

recovery, *n*. **1.** a process whereby a system re-starts normal working after a crash or other fault (e.g., a power failure).

2. a process of re-enabling access to apparently lost data. A **recovery system** is a program that keeps a detailed log of all the computer's activities (data transfers, register contents, etc); it will then use that log to restore the system to its state before the problem.

rectifier, *n*. a device whose design allows it to pass electric current one way only. The most common type of rectifier in current IT is the semiconductor DIODE. There can be hundreds of thousands of these in the surface of a single chip.

recursion, *n*. passing again and again through the same sub-routine (set of program actions) because the sub-routine calls itself. A **recursive function** is a function that calls itself when called. A **recursive program/routine** is one that reaches its results in the same kind of way. Any form of recursion must keep some kind of record of the number of times the call takes place, or, by some other way, set a limit. Though recursion involves a looping process in practice, a recursive routine is not the same as a LOOP because of the internal call to itself.

reduced instruction set, *n*. a smaller than normal instruction set offered by some processors in order to increase speed and make the circuits less complex. A **reduced instruction set chip/computer (RISC)** is one that works in this way.

Most modern processors allow programmers access to a hundred or more instructions yet, in practice, few programs need many of these. In the case of a RISC system, the set is kept small. As each instruction in the set needs a matching process and an action sub-circuit, the smaller the set, the faster the matching and the cheaper the chip. Should there be a need in a given program for an instruction that is not available, the programmer will define it in terms of the instructions at hand.

reduction, *n.* the process of cutting down the size of an image to produce a MICROFORM image. **Reduction ratio** measures how much smaller (e.g. shorter) the final image is than the original.

redundancy, *n.* **1.** the backing up of hardware by having at hand a second system in case the one in use fails.

2. a measure of the extent to which the use of suitable data coding could reduce the length of a signal without loss of meaning; as, for example, with data COMPRESSION systems. If coding could reduce the total amount of data by half, the redundancy of the original signal is 50%.

3. a measure of the fraction of a signal that could be lost without the loss of the message carried. A **redundancy check** involves adding extra (i.e., redundant) data to the signal to allow error checking at the other end; see, for instance, PARITY. The extra data, in whatever form, is **redundant code**. The higher the redundancy, the more effective can be error detection and correction. Thus, each 32-bit word carrying a pixel from the Voyager spacecraft at the edges of the solar system has five data bits and 27 redundant bits: with the signals coming by radio over hundreds of millions of kilometres, the signal-to-noise ratio is very low. That system uses a 'tour 11' error correction code; each word can have up to seven bits wrong and still be corrected. See also HAMMING CODE.

re-entrant program, *n.* a program with unchanging instructions, so it can be called:

(a) by more than one user at a time, or

(b) a second time by one user before the end of the first run.

A better name, sometimes used, is **re-enterable program**.

refresh, *vb.* to apply a suitable signal to ensure stored data does not vanish. There are two common contexts: the content of a volatile store (e.g., the capacitors of many types of RAM chip), and the content of a screen display which needs a new scan tens of times a second. In the former case, there may be need for a refresh only after a read action. The process involved is **refreshing**, based on a **refresh circuit**, and the

RELATIONAL OPERATOR

number of times a second it must be done is the store's **refresh rate**.

regenerative store, *n.* a store which the system must refresh every so often to prevent the contents from vanishing. See VOLATILE STORE.

regenerator, *n.* the equivalent of an analog REPEATER in a digital communications channel. A repeater simply amplifies the input signal to form the output; a regenerator constructs it from fresh again (see Figure). In most cases, a digital (pulsed) signal is binary, having only two values (high and low, i.e., 0 and 1). Even after passing through a channel with considerable noise (interference), it is not hard to tell from instant to instant whether the signal is high or low. The output of the regenerator consists of a number of clean pulses, each generated on the basis of the input. This is the main reason why digital data transfers over very large distances show very little noise.

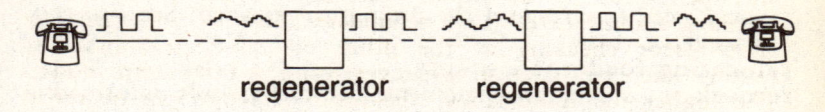

regenerator. Regenerators reconstruct input digital signals.

register, *n.* a temporary store for data being processed. There are many registers in a processor, most being one word length in size; for the details of those in a central processor, see MACHINE CYCLE.

relational data base, *n.* a form of data base management software that allows the user to build up a HIERARCHICAL DATA BASE but with extra links between fields in the different files. This can considerably reduce the need for typing a data item more than once in the input stage; it also allows much more realistic searching and effective updating. On the other hand, setting up a relational data base needs more planning: as well as having to define the files and the fields in each, the user must state the exact relationships between linked fields in the different files.

relational operator, *n.* an operator that has two or more operands and which outputs a binary value (i.e. true or false). Such an operator may be a code (often of two letters, e.g. GT for greater than) or a symbol (>). Thus in value1>value2, the

RELATIVE ADDRESS

operation returns true if value1 is indeed greater than value2, and false in all other cases. Relational operators must appear (or be implied) at a program's branch point and in any conditional statement. It is the task of the logic section of the processor's arithmetic and logic unit (ALU) to evaluate relational operations.

relative address, *n.* the address of a cell in store described as an offset from the current cell, as in JMP−10 (jump back ten places). See ADDRESSING.

relay, *vb.* to pass on an input to the output without any processing other than switching (and perhaps amplification by a repeater or a regenerator). A **relay centre** is much the same as a switching centre (e.g. a telephone exchange). A relay is an electromagnetic switching device; a small input current in a coil switches a larger one in a second circuit.

relocatable code, *n.* a machine code program or routine that works wherever it may be in the main store. This means it must not include any internal absolute ADDRESSES; such values would need to change if the program is re-sited. See also PROGRAM RELOCATION.

relocating loader, see LOADER.

remark, *n.* a program statement that carries only information for readers of the program (e.g. to explain the function of a routine). Such a statement is not an instruction as such, and it therefore needs no translation into machine code during assembly or compilation. It is good programming practice to include many remarks in a program under development. Not only does this help the programmer later wishing to check or test, it is also of great value to other programmers who may want to amend (update or maintain) the program to meet their own needs. See also COMMENT.

remote access, *n.* access to a computer system at a distance from the terminal or work station in question. A communications link of some type connects the station and the central system.

Remote batch processing involves using a **remote batch terminal** to supply the data to the central system for batch processing, perhaps getting the results back at the terminal too.

Many modern systems allow **remote fault finding**. Using a communications link (e.g. the telephone network), an engineer inputs test signals to the faulty unit, and, on the basis of the output that results, may also send correcting signals.

This approach saves much time and cost, and is on offer in more and more computers and fax machines (for example). **Remote job entry (RJE)** is the use of a remote console to send job instructions to a multi-processing computer; it is also the same as remote batch processing (see above). **Remote printing** is a feature of many modern multi-user computers: printout appears elsewhere than at the user's **remote terminal** or work station. This is of great importance for multi-user systems because it means the sharing of costly hardware although, of course, it can be a nuisance.

REN, *n*. the RING EQUIVALENCE NUMBER of a unit (e.g. handset, fax machine, answering machine) linked to a telephone line.

re-paint, *vb*. to re-draw, edit, or REFRESH a graphic design.

repeater, *n*. an electronic circuit with the task of amplifying an input analog signal to form the output. A major problem compared with the use of a REGENERATOR in a digital system is that the repeater amplifies the line noise as well as the required signal. Thus the quality of an analog signal worsens with distance.

repertoire, *n*. the range of actions a processor can carry out by way of instruction types it can accept; i.e. it is the same as a processor's INSTRUCTION SET.

repetitive strain injury (RSI), *n*. a painful condition, which may last a long time, that results from carrying out repeated actions. It follows damage to the tendons and/or joints used in those actions, e.g. at the fingers, hand, wrist or fore-arm in the case of keyboard operators. Avoid RSI by varying the type of work, taking frequent breaks from precise repetitive sets of actions, and by suitable exercise of the part of the body in question. The designers of ergonomic keyboards such as Maltron claim their products much reduce RSI.

report, *n*. an analysis or summary (on screen or paper) of a system or set of actions, or, mainly, some of the contents of a file or database. It is the task of a **report program** to output such reports from a data base or data file, the user, or a **report programmer**, setting up in advance the exact details (content, analysis methods, layout). Many database management programs now include a **report program generator (RPG)**: this helps the non-expert user define the reports required so the system can produce the correct report programs.

re-run, *vb*. to start program execution again, perhaps after a break point or error. In a program, a **re-run point** is a stage at which a re-run may start after a failure (i.e., not at the beginning of the program). **Re-run time** is the time needed after a failure before a re-run can start. See RECOVERY.

rescue dump, *n.* a dump of program data (in most cases from main store to backing store) during a run to reduce RE-RUN TIME after a failure.

research, *n.* the exploration of physical principles or effects with the aim of producing new types of system. **Research and development (R&D)** involves taking the potentially useful results of research to the stage of developing and testing prototypes of new systems.

reserved word, *n.* a set of characters that makes a key word (instruction code) in some program languages that must not appear in any other context in the program (other than in a string constant). In particular, in these cases, no label may be the same as a key word, or perhaps even include that string of characters. Such a language having the key word TO, for instance, would output an error report on finding the label STOPVALUE. In most cases, putting labels in lower case (if allowed) is good practice in any event, and avoids this problem.

re-set, *vb.* to restore a system or value to an initial state. Thus, after dealing with an interrupt, a processor's operating software would re-set that particular interrupt flag back to 0. The **re-set phase** is the part of a processor's MACHINE CYCLE in which the system prepares to handle the next instruction.

resident software, *n.* routines built into an IT system for permanent access on and after switch-on, the same as using HARD WIRING programs or firmware. It is normal for the computer's operating software (or at least the main, central part of it) to reside permanently in the system in this way. Access to such software is much faster than to routines held on backing store or in the read/write part of main store. On the other hand, it is more costly to correct BUGS in (or update) resident software, and less simple to by-pass it.

resistor, *n.* a length of conductor or semiconductor with a higher than usual resistance (opposition) to electric current, thus with the explicit task of affecting the current in some way for some purpose. All lengths of conductor and semiconductor material have some resistance (but see SUPERCONDUCTIVITY); if the lengths are large, the designer must take account of their effect on current.

resistor/capacitor/transistor logic (RCTL), see LOGIC (ELECTRONIC LOGIC).

resistor/transistor logic (RTL), see LOGIC (ELECTRONIC LOGIC).

resolution, *n.* the power of an input system to distinguish between close values or of an output system to record close values, i.e., the fineness of detail the system can handle. A low resolution OCR scanner, for instance, will have more problems than a high resolution device in sensing how two similar shapes differ. A low resolution graphics display or printout is likely to show a staircase effect (jagged stepped lines) on certain lines. The **resolution factor** of a file search is the HIT RATE: the fraction of all the records accessed.

response/action frame, *n.* a screen in a viewdata (interactive videotex) system that allows people making access to respond to its contents by sending a message back to the information provider, e.g. to place a TELE-SHOPPING order or to fill in a questionnaire form. The system knows the date and codes of people using the frame, so this can be an easy way (as well as a cheap one) to fill in forms.

response time, *n.* how long it takes a system to respond to an event with the appropriate action. The response time of a multi-user system should be short enough for each user to feel there is no one else on line; perhaps no more than a second should elapse between pressing <ENTER> at the end of an input and seeing the output on screen.

retrieval, *n.* the obtaining of required information from an IT system, e.g. from a data base file. A **retrieval centre** is the term for the computer (sometimes called host) that holds the data concerned. For successful retrieval, the user must carry out a planned and careful search; otherwise, the results may not be current or complete. See also DATA RETRIEVAL and INFORMATION RETRIEVAL.

retrospective search, *n.* a batch, or other form of non-interactive, search of a data base (particularly a bibliographic data base).

return, *vb.* **1.** to pass an input line to the processor, on pressing the <RETURN> (<ENTER>) key. The name of this button comes from a typewriter's carriage return key, pressed at the end of each line of characters.

2. to jump back to the calling program or sub-routine at the end of the called sub-routine. For this purpose, there must be a keyword, often RETURN. This tells the system to POP the address of the calling instruction from the stack.

3. to pass a computed value back to the calling program or

REVEAL

sub-routine at the end of the called function. As with sense **2**, at the end of the function definition (whether the function is in the library or user-defined), there must be some kind of RETURN effect and stack usage.

4. to send brief signals back to the sender of the main signals in data transfer. See REVERSE CHANNEL.

reveal, *vb.* to show material previously hidden. Many videotex systems allow the use of a reveal feature in a screen, e.g. to show the correct answer to a posed question or puzzle. Some computer aided learning and training programs use much the same technique; it leaves question, user's answer, and correct answer on display at the same time.

reverse bias/voltage, *n.* a voltage which, when applied to a diode or transistor, cuts down the current to very near zero. A **reverse biassed** diode or transistor is in such a state.

reverse channel, *n.* in some forms of DUPLEX system, the channel used for data transfers in the other direction from the main transfers. The main transfer channel is simplex, and the reverse (or background or return) channel (also simplex) has a much lower data transfer rate. A **reverse interrupt** is a signal sent along a reverse channel to request that the main data transfer cease.

reverse Polish notation (RPN) *n.* a POSTFIX form of showing numbers and using them in expressions (named after the Polish mathematician, Jan Lukasiewicz, who devised the concept). The concept is that expressions built from post-fix numbers need no brackets to over-ride PRIORITY. In RPN, we write:

$$
\begin{array}{lll}
x\ y\ * & \text{for} & x * y \\
x\ y\ z\ *\ + & \text{for} & x + (y * z) \\
x\ y\ +\ z\ * & \text{for} & (x + y) * z
\end{array}
$$

A system such as this is essential for STACK-based operations. See also FORTH.

reverse video, *n.* showing strings in background colour on foreground colour rather than the usual way: a method of highlighting. Much the same approach now appears quite often in print as well as on screen.

rewind, *vb.* to spool a tape back to the start. This procedure is always essential with the open reel magnetic tapes used with large computers.

re-writable disk, *n.* a magnetic disk whose stored data the user can access (read) but also write (change). Fully re-writable optical discs have not yet appeared; when they do, there will be massive changes in IT. See READ/WRITE disk.

RF, *abbrev. for* RADIO frequency, in the range 10^6–10^{11} hertz (Hz). An **RF modulator** is a device able to modulate an RF carrier wave, i.e. to cause it to carry a useful signal.

rigid disk, *n.* an alternative term for hard (non-floppy) disk. See MAGNETIC MEDIA.

ring, *n.* **1.** a signal that a person or fax machine is trying to make contact through an exchange line. For **ring equivalence number**, see REN.

2. anything logically circular in format. Thus, a **ring network** is a type of NETWORK arrangement in which the stations link to form a ring. A **linked ring** is a data structure like a LINKED LIST, but with the tail element pointing to the head element.

RISC, *abbrev. for* REDUCED INSTRUCTION SET CHIP/COMPUTER.

river of white, *n.* an occasional effect of text justification without microspacing; inter-word spaces may align vertically over a number of lines to produce the effect of a ragged column break (gutter).

RJE, *abbrev. for* REMOTE JOB ENTRY.

robot, *n.* a programmable mechanical device or machine, from the Czech word for 'work'. The word was first used by the Czech Karel Capek in a play about robots in 1921. Robots tend to be of most value with boring, repetitive, but fairly high precision tasks, e.g. in factories and on farms. They vary greatly in their numbers of DEGREES OF FREEDOM (the different ways they can move), and in intelligence (internal data processing power). Modern styles of COMPUTER INTEGRATED MANUFACTURE often link robots into a network used for COMPUTER AIDED DESIGN AND MANUFACTURE (CADCAM).

Robotics is the study and technology of robot design and usage, particularly, nowadays, the application of MACHINE INTELLIGENCE concepts (e.g. problem solving, machine vision).

robustness, *n.* a measure of how hard it is to cause hardware to fail or software to crash.

rogue (value), *n.* a coded value used to mark the end of a list, e.g., in data input or when read from store. The code must be of the same type as the data items in the rest of the list, but an impossible (yet easy to remember) value. Useful rogue values are -1 to end a list of non-negative numbers and 'zzz' to end a list of names.

ROM

ROM, *abbrev. for* READ ONLY MEMORY, a store where the contents are fixed.

rotation, *n.* an alternative term for the CYCLIC SHIFT of a binary number.

rounding, *n.* an approximation or cutting down of the precision of a numeric value, taking it to a given number of significant figures (from the phrase 'round number'). In IT, this happens if the result of a calculation has higher precision than the system can cope with (see ARITHMETIC). A result of this in turn is a **rounding error**, for the rounded value is not fully correct; rounding errors can accumulate and become significant.

route planner, *n.* a type of software based on a digital map of a transport system. It helps the user plan routes between places with various constraints in mind (e.g. stops on the way, time of day, cost, speed).

routine, *n.* **1.** in systems analysis, the traditional way to handle a given task.
2. sometimes taken to be the same as a small program, i.e. one with a simple task.
3. a part of a program with a given task, i.e. the same as a block, procedure or sub-routine.

routing, *n.* **1.** the assigning of a particular channel between two points in a network for a given signal or packet (block of a signal). In most cases there is a choice of routes between the two points; good software in the switching centres will make the choice on the basis of how busy each route is, as well as how costly. A **routing indicator** is that part of the header of the signal or packet that describes its route to the switching centres it meets. On the other hand, in some systems, the full route is not fixed at the sending end; the message passes from switching centre to switching centre, with, at each stage, the next section of route being decided.
2. moving between the pages or frames of a viewdata tree. A **routing page** carries a menu of options for the user; choosing each one of these will send the system along a different route.

RPG, *abbrev. for* REPORT PROGRAM GENERATOR.

RPM, *abbrev. for* revolutions per minute, a measure of the speed at which a disk rotates in its drive.

RPN, *abbrev. for* REVERSE POLISH NOTATION (using postfix numbers).

RS232, *n.* a world-wide SERIAL INTERFACE standard.

RSI, *abbrev. for* REPETITIVE STRAIN INJURY.

RTL, *abbrev. for* RESISTOR/TRANSISTOR LOGIC. See LOGIC (ELECTROIC LOGIC).

rubber banding, *n.* an approach to building standard shapes in many graphics (or art) programs. The user fixes one point of the shape on screen, using mouse and cursor; then, as the cursor moves, a 'rubber band' outline of the shape appears. The user moves this around, and confirms when the shape is as desired.

ruler, *n.* the calibrated horizontal line on screen in many word processing programs (though some have vertical ones too, especially for DTP). Its function is to show the user (who can, in most cases, edit it) the positions of margins, indents and tab stops, i.e. it helps text layout. Some systems allow a document to carry different rulers at the heads of different sections.

run, *n.* a related set of actions or routines. In word processing, a **running footer/header** is a page footer/header that does not change from page to page (e.g., the title of the document).

Run-time is when a program actually starts to carry out its task (rather than being loaded, or compiled, for instance). A **run-time error** is a BUG that appears at this stage, a mistake or oversight in programming that involves no actual error in syntax. A **run-time system/version** of a program is a compiled (object code) version ready to run, rather than source code the user must first load and compile.

R/W, *abbrev. for* READ/WRITE, as of read and write memory (storage).

RWM, *abbrev. for* read and write memory (storage), a more accurate abbreviation than RAM.

S

s, *symbol for* second, the basic unit of time.

S, *symbol for* siemens, the basic unit of conductance (i.e. of how well a sample of a substance can pass electric current).

sag, *n.* the same as a brownout, a sudden fall in power supply voltage for several seconds or more. An uninterruptible power supply unit at the interface between the power line and an IT system should keep the latter working.

SAM, *abbrev. for* **1.** SEQUENTIAL ACCESS method, a way to store a set of blocks (e.g. records) for access in sequence.
2. SERIAL ACCESS memory, a store where the contents must be accessed and processed in sequence by a system.

sans serif type, *n.* any type face where the characters do not have SERIFS, small side strokes at the ends of the main strokes.

satellite, *n.* a spacecraft in free fall in orbit round the earth (or round any other object in the solar system). To reach such an orbit, rockets give the satellite a speed relative to the earth of around 8 km/s. The craft needs no further power once at the right speed and moving in the right direction as gravity pulls it towards the surface at much the same rate as the surface 'falls away' beneath it. However, to keep a satellite in a perfectly stable orbit, it may need an occasional pulse from its own small correcting rockets.

A **communication(s) satellite** has the task of aiding communications between points on the earth's surface (or between other spacecraft). The standard approach is to put the satellite in a geo-synchronous orbit, one at such a distance, some 36 000 km above the equator, that where it takes the same time to orbit the earth as the earth takes to turn once. Thus, the satellite appears always to be at the same point in the sky. Signals sent in a narrow beam to such a GEO-STATIONARY SATELLITE are amplified and sent back in a wide beam to cover a fairly large footprint on the surface. There, small aerials (dish or flat) detect the signal and feed it to an amplifier and receiver. See also SQUARIAL and TRANSPONDER. Satellite broadcasts for which people must pay to view involve some kind of coding (scrambling); in the receiving set is a decoder that will work only if the owner has paid the current

SCISSORS AND PASTE

subscription. The de-coder therefore has a unique ID so the satellite transmission can control it.

In an IT network, a satellite is a subsidiary or slave station. A more powerful 'master' either controls it or acts as a data transfer link. Such thinking applies in fax as well as computer networks.

SBR, *abbrev. for* STORAGE BUFFER REGISTER. See also MACHINE CYCLE, STORAGE.

scan, *vb.* to pass through or across a 1D or 2D store in a linear fashion. A **scan area** is the area of a sheet a scanning reader can work on, in, for instance, OCR. **Scanning** is the process concerned; a **scanning device**, or **scanner**, is the hardware used.

There are two main approaches. Older systems tend to have a single scan head (e.g. light source and photocell), with the sheet to be scanned fixed to the surface of a fast spinning drum. As the drum spins, the head moves slowly along a bar. This is a **cylinder scanner**. On the other hand, an array of scan heads can produce signals for a whole line of the sheet at a time; the length of the area is the **scan width** of the system (reader).

scheduler, *n.* a program in operating software with the task of control of access to a shared resource. One aspect is to ensure that no process involved can damage others or be damaged by them. The second concerns priorities when more than one process demands the resource at the same time. This latter is the task of a **scheduling algorithm**. Schedulers often need to work at two levels. The higher level concerns the usage of the resource during a period of time, while the lower (the task of a DESPATCHER) handles the sharing from instant to instant.

schema, *n.* (plural **schemata**) a model or structured description of the logical and physical aspects of a data base. Different users may have to bear in mind different schemata of the same data base.

schematic, *n.* a block diagram showing the logic of a data base or any system (indeed, some people use it as a synonym for circuit diagram). It shows the elements and how they inter-relate and interact. See also FLOW CHART and STRUCTURE CHART. **Schematic symbols** are those used in such diagrams and charts.

scissors and paste, *n.* the basic tools of manual page layout, where blocks of text and illustrations are cut from paper and stuck to a sheet as required. Software, e.g. for DTP, using such an approach on screen is often termed CUT AND PASTE.

Scissoring is an old name for windowing, i.e. using the screen as a movable window to display a small part of a large image.

SCR, *abbrev. for* SEQUENCE CONTROL REGISTER. See MACHINE CYCLE.

scrambling, *n.* the encoding of a signal before transfer to keep the contents private. At the other end, it will need decoding (unscrambling). Scrambling and unscrambling tends to be a software process in the case of computer data; a **scrambler** is a hardware unit that does the same for other types of signal (e.g. speech in a phone network).

scratch, *vb.* **1.** to erase data from a backing storage medium.
2. to jot down temporary notes, with, in the IT sense, a **scratch file** acting as a temporary store or work area (sometimes called **scratch pad**). A **scratch tape** is one holding scratch data, and so can soon be erased.

screen, 1. *n.* a visual display. Screens include the cathode-ray tube types (television set or monitor), flat screens (e.g. LIQUID-CRYSTAL DISPLAY and PLASMA DISPLAY), and projection screens. The ideal screen size depends on whether it is for viewing by one person, by a small group, or by many people; whether viewing is to be over a short or a long period; whether the data to display involves colour or not; and the resolution of any graphics. See also ASPECT RATIO.
2. *vb.* to show something as an image on such a display. A **screen (image) buffer** is a section of an IT system's main store set aside for a bit map of the display data. The program sends the data to the buffer which then unloads to the display. A **screen dump** is a transfer of image data to backing store (where some other software may be able to edit it) or to a peripheral (e.g. to a printer to give hard copy, or to a remote machine for display there). A **screen editor** is a program that makes the screen behave as a window onto a program listing; in this case the user may edit the program much as if using a word processor. A system's **screen load** is the maximum number of characters the screen can show at once; this may depend on the current display mode if there is a choice (e.g. some systems can display 40, 60, 80 or 100 characters on a screen line).

scrolling, *n.* a process which can move the data displayed on a screen as if it is viewed through a window. The most common need is **vertical scrolling** as in the case of a word processed document with more lines than the screen display.

Horizontal scrolling (panning) is of value for images wider than the screen (e.g. those in a spreadsheet).

sculpture, computer, *n.* the use of highly complex graphics to produce on screen and colour printout artistic structures in apparent three dimensions.

SCVF, *abbrev. for* SINGLE CHANNEL VOICE FREQUENCY.

SDM, *abbrev. for* SPACE DIVISION MULTIPLEXING.

search, *vb.* to look for a particular record in a given data base. A large file in a data base contains many thousand records. Methods of finding the right one(s) to meet a given need must be fast, effective and easy to use; various approaches have come about in an attempt to make this possible. In many systems, there is some kind of **search language** (command language, or query language): this should allow the user easily to define his or her exact needs. Some search languages are, however, hardly friendly and people wishing to search a costly data base often have to use a specialist human consultant.

In word processing and similar software, the **search/replace** feature allows the user to define a string for the program to look for in a document, and a second string which should replace this. Common options are to do this:

(a) in the whole or one part of the text;

(b) as a global change or a selective one (in which latter case, each time the system finds the first string, it asks the user whether or not to make the change);

(c) with or without account taken of the case of the target string's characters.

Search and replace is a powerful feature but one that can easily lead to mistakes.

In searching a file for given data, as well as using some kind of search language, it is important to have a **search strategy**. This concerns how to define the **search terms** (such as age>21) without error and without causing an inefficient (e.g. slow) search. The user may, in most cases, combine the terms using logical operators such as AND, OR, NOT (age>21 and occup=student or unemployed and not status=married). It is easy to make errors in complex search strategies such as this; the result is that the user retrieves the wrong records for the purpose.

In data transfers between backing store and main store, **search time**, or latency, is a significant part of ACCESS TIME.

SECAM, *acronym* from *Séquentiel Couleur à Mémoire*, one of the world's three main current TELEVISION standards. The major

SECOND GENERATION

regions that use it are the Middle East, eastern Europe, France and Greece.

second generation, *n.* any computer systems using discrete transistors and diodes for the arithmetic and logic circuits. See GENERATIONS sense 2.

secondary store, *n.* a rare name for BACKING STORE.

sector, *n.* the smallest block of backing storage a system can address, in particular on a floppy or hard disk. The system divides the surface of these disks into tracks (the same as cylinders in the case of a disk pack) and sectors; so each track consists of eight or more BLOCKS. Different computer systems work with different numbers of disk sectors. A **hard-sectored** disk, however, has holes punched in it to define where the sector edges are; such a disk can be used only on the range of systems for which it is sectored. On the other hand, a **soft-sectored** disk has the sector bounds marked on it magnetically (during the format process), so it can be re-formatted for any system.

security, *n.* the use of safeguards to keep the data in an IT system safe from accidental or malicious change, loss, or copying. **Physical security** involves techniques such as keys, shields, guards, restricted access to rooms, and so on; suitable operating systems provide **software security** by asking users for ids (USER IDS) and PASSWORDS. Systems need security for data in use and in transit as well as in store.

seek time, *n.* the period of time it takes to move the storage unit's head to the correct place over the medium (e.g. magnetic disk surface), often the major part of ACCESS TIME.

segment, *n.* **1.** a partition in main store, often variable in size, addressed separately by a program (e.g. for a word processor to hold a separate text).
2. the stand-alone part of a program that the system can run without having in store the rest of the program; i.e. a type of procedure or module. Segments of this nature often show a tree structure.

selective calling, *n.* a method by which a sender can address a signal to one of a number of stations on a single line. A **selective sort** involves a so-called ranking algorithm. The program uses this algorithm to choose items one by one from the list that needs sorting; in each iteration, it takes the most important of the items left and puts it at the end of the second (sorted) list.

self-check/test, *n.* a process a user can ask a peripheral to go through to check that a unit is working correctly. Some systems do this automatically on switch-on, e.g. many micros test access to all main store cells as part of their initialization process. **Self-checking code** is a code used in telecommunications that checks all the words in a signal and can then correct the corrupt ones. A **self-documenting** program is either one with full screen help at all times, or one where the programmer has made every effort to explain the code by remarks and other such tools.

self-correcting code, *n*. an alternative term for SELF-CHECKING CODE used in telecommunications to check each word in a message.

semantics, *n*. **1.** that branch of the study of language concerned with meaning.
2. that branch of logic concerned with the truth values of relationships. In computing, truth tables represent these values.
3. the study of symbols and how they relate to what they represent.

semi-compilation, *n*. the process of translating a source code program into machine code that does not, however, include the machine code sub-routines needed by a full object program.

semiconductor, *n*. a substance that conducts electric current to a small extent (much more than does an insulator, but far less well than a metal). At normal temperatures, a number of elements are semiconducting and many insulators join the group at higher temperatures. A substance with semiconducting features at normal temperatures, such as silicon and germanium, is an **intrinsic semiconductor**. Such a substance carries current by the flow in opposite directions of an equal number of electrons and positive 'holes'.

Adding the right type of impurity to an intrinsic semiconductor makes it conduct more efficiently, but now it becomes an **extrinsic semiconductor**. So-called donor impurities add to the free electrons in the substance (most charge carriers are now negative electrons): thus it becomes an **n-type semiconductor**. On the other hand, adding an acceptor impurity in effect adds holes, making the substance p-type (we can view a hole as a positive current carrier). In either case, the nature of the base substance, and the amount and type of impurity, allow the semiconductor designer to select the electrical properties of the product quite precisely. Silicon and germanium are the most common intrinsic semiconductors used in diodes and TRANSISTORS; others have special roles such as that of gallium arsenide in the case of LIGHT-EMITTING DIODES (LEDs).

A **semiconductor diode** is a junction between two types of semiconductor (but see POINT CONTACT DIODE), often p-type and n-type, and has two electrodes (contacts); its functions relate to the fact that it passes current one way only. A **semiconductor disk** (SILICON disk) is a part of main store set aside from the rest and used as temporary backing store. As such, it is far faster than other types of backing store but loses its contents on switch-off. A **semiconductor laser** is, in effect, a type of LED, a junction diode which gives off light as electrons and holes join. In this case, though, the light is of one frequency only, and the waves are in step, as are those of any LASER. Its main uses are in fibre optics and as the light sources used in laser (and compact) disc readers.

sensor, *n.* a transducer with an electric output that relates to its input of some other form of energy. There are many types of sensor, each able to output a signal as a result of some kind of input, e.g. sound and light (very important in IT), and also magnetic field strength, strain, acidity, movement, temperature, and so on. Sensors are crucial in process control and also appear in many types of IT input device. Most have an analog electric output, so need an analog to digital converter at the interface.

sentinel, see FLAG.

separated graphics, *n.* a style of producing very low-resolution screen designs teletext-style from graphics character blocks that have a small space round each. This makes for even less effective designs than CONTIGUOUS GRAPHICS.

separation, *n.* the process of breaking a colour picture into four images, one each for the black, cyan, magenta, and yellow components of the picture. These images (**separations**) can pass through a data transfer link as black and white in each case, to make four plates for printing a colour picture at the other end. This is by far the best way to fax a colour picture for instance.

sequence, *n.* any non-random order, i.e. order with some meaning or value. Thus the records of a file are in sequence if the key field values are in alphabetical or numerical order as appropriate. See SEQUENTIAL ACCESS. A system may need to carry out a **sequence check** to ensure, before processing, that the items in a list or file are indeed in sequence. A processor's

sequence control register (SCR) holds the address of the machine instruction the system's working on at the moment. See MACHINE CYCLE. The SCR sometimes takes the name program counter (PC) or **sequence counter**. A **sequencer** is a sorter; its task is to put input items into sequence. A **sequencing key** is a sort key, i.e. a key field used in sorting.

sequential access, *n.* access to the parts of something taken in the order in which they appear. The term (distinguished from SERIAL ACCESS) implies the order is of some value rather than being random. Thus a file might be in key field value order in which case a search would involve sequential access to the records. The search would stop on finding the required record (as in a serial search), OR once it passes the point at which that record should have appeared.

A **sequential access method (SAM)** for data storage and retrieval involves holding the data blocks (or records) in the best sequence for rapid effective access. The store may be direct or serial access in type. There are various such methods of filing. The records of a **sequential file** are in key field order (sequence); this makes it easier to search than a serial file (random order), whether stored in serial access or direct access media. A **sequential search** involves looking at each record in turn, starting with the first, as described above. There is no better search method for sequential files held in a serial access system (such as tape).

serial, *adj.* working with items as a series, i.e., one by one in the order of appearance. See also SEQUENCE. **Serial access** data storage (as on magnetic tape) gives no address to the individual data items stored; compare DIRECT ACCESS. Thus, any search must start at the first item. A **serial (access) file** is either a file held in such a store, or one where records are in no special sequence (i.e. they are in random order, as are those of a transaction file). See also SAM.

A **serial interface** (such as RS232, and others with similar names) is one that passes data bit by bit (see serial transfer, below). A **serial printer** accepts data for printing bit by bit (but, of course, may have a buffer). **Serial processing** involves carrying out one action at a time: the norm for the IT systems of the early 1990s (but see PARALLEL PROCESSING, an approach that is growing fast in importance). **Serial storage** gives only SEQUENTIAL ACCESS to the data items held (compare DIRECT ACCESS).

A **serial transfer** system passes data one bit at a time down a single channel. This is slower but cheaper than PARALLEL

SERIF

TRANSFER and allows transfers over much greater distances as there is no problem with data SKEW.

serif, *n.* a small mark across or at the end of a main stroke in a printed character. Opinions differ as to whether sans-serif type is more readable, more attractive, or more modern than type with serifs.

server, *n.* a network station (node) that manages a shared resource such as:

(a) a central hard disk: file server;
(b) links to other systems: communications server (gateway);
(c) a costly printer: printer server; or,
(d) the network software itself: network server.

If such a task does not take too much of the station's time, it may double as a user station.

service bureau, *n.* a firm that uses its computers to offer IT services to other firms. There are many ways this may happen. For instance, the other firms may have no hardware of their own so they need a full service. Alternatively they may lack a laser printer, so bring pages on disk for printing.

seven layer (reference) model, *n.* a hierarchy of communications protocols proposed as a standard by the ISO. See OSI.

seven-segment display, *n.* a set of LCDs (or of rows of LEDs) from which one may build up a fairly large range of characters. Such displays are common in calculators and watches and are extremely useful on large-scale displays, for example at sports events.

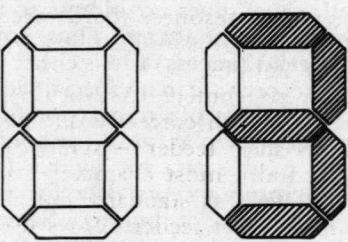

seven segment display. Seven segment display and usage.

Shannon, Claude Elwood, a US mathematician (1916 -) who carried out important work in various IT fields, particularly in communications. **Shannon coding** and the **Shannon-Hartley law** concern coding data for efficient transfer, needed by

Shannon's model (see Figure) of a communication system (1948), and which today remains of great value. This model views the system as:

(a) a communication channel linking an information source and an information destination;

(b) having as a fundamental aim the exact reproduction at the destination of the message that leaves the source;

(c) having problems with noise from some source along the channel (specific or general);

(d) encoding the source message before transfer to produce a signal that suffers least from noise, with a decoder at the other end to reverse the process.

Shannon also devised the first chess algorithm (1950).

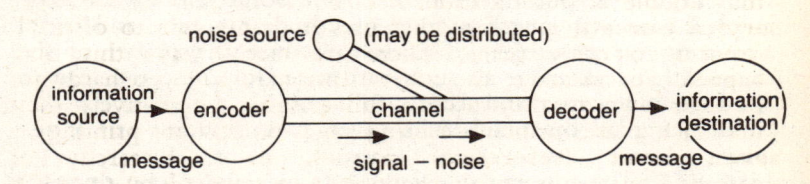

Shannon, Claude Ellwood. Shannon's model of a communication system.

shared logic or **shared processing,** *n.* an alternative term for multi-usage, in which a single processor handles the needs of several terminals and/or tasks at the same time.

shared resource, *n.* any resource (hardware peripheral or software package) on offer in a multi-user system for access by several terminals or stations.

sheet feeder, *n.* an attachment to a printer which allows cut sheet paper to pass through correctly one page at a time. Most page printers have a sheet feeder as standard (and fan-fold feed as an extra or not at all); most character printers, on the other hand, have fan-fold feed as standard and a sheet feeder as an extra or not at all. A sheet feeder allows users to obtain printouts on their normal headed paper; most, on the other hand, tend to have feed problems (such as paper jams) more often than does fan-fold feed.

shelf life, *n.* the lifetime of a product, or until it no longer works as it should. In a market like IT, where obsolescence is a major factor, the term also applies to lifetime in the wider sense: the period for which the product is of value (document)

SHELL

or not out of date (hardware and software).

shell, *n.* **1.** user interface software: a program that accepts user commands, interprets them, and passes them for execution.
2. in general, any program that protects a user at a higher level from the problems of interacting with software at a lower level. This usage is very common in work with machine intelligence.
3. a type of data-sorting program, strictly **shellsort**, the name given by the inventor, Donald **Shell** (1959). This variant of an insertion sort allows data items or records to jump a large distance in the set rather than move step by step.

SHF, *abbrev. for* super high frequency (RADIO), so called decimetric waves, in the range 300 - 3000 megahertz (MHz).

shielding, *n.* **1.** putting IT hardware in some sort of 'Faraday' cage (e.g. a wire mesh around a cathode-ray tube and metal screening on all cables). This is to reduce the power of the signals that leak from all such hardware, for these can lead to breaches of security and danger to users.
2. blanking all the pixels in a given part (window) of a display.

shift, *n.* **1.** The moving of all the bits in a word one or more places left or right. There are three types:

(a) **arithmetic shift**: a shift which moves bits toward the left end of the word, with 0s coming in at the other end. This shift preserves the sign bit and is of value for multiplication;

(b) **cyclic shift**: here bits moved past the end of the word appear at the other end;

(c) **logical shift**: end bits fall off and 0s come in at the other end.

A **shift register** is a register which, when it receives a clock pulse, shifts its contents one place left or right as appropriate.
2. a move, on the basis of circumstances, from a set data transfer rate to a higher or lower one. A **shift down/up modem** (e.g. in a modern fax system) can do this as a matter of routine; the data rate depends on the system at the other end and on the quality of the channel.
3. the SHIFT key by which the output of a keyboard (for instance) is moved to an alternate character set. The traditional alternate character set is lower case and symbols for numbers; on the whole, shift keys now move to upper case and symbols for numbers. A **SHIFT LOCK** key, when pressed, keeps the system in the shifted state until the user presses it again. How-

SIDEBANDS

ever, some shift keys work in a slightly different way. Many modern keyboards also offer ALTernate and ConTRoL keys for much the same purpose; these boards can thus access a very large number of characters and control codes.

4. a whole character set one can access without any shift (sense **3**) action.

short (code) calling, *n.* using a one- or two-digit key code to call a phone number. This is a common feature on modern phone handsets and fax machines. A small store holds the full number linked to each short code; the user programs the system with the numbers most likely to be frequently used.

siblings, brothers or **sisters,** *n.* nodes in a hierarchy (e.g. a tree) with the same parent (and, therefore, at the same level).

sidebands, *n.* the frequency bands above and below the band of a carrier; they appear as a result of an amplitude or angle MODULATION process. The bands consist of a number of **side frequencies** and bear the names **upper sideband** and **lower sideband** respectively.

When a pure signal of frequency f modulates a carrier of frequency F, the two side frequencies appear at $F-f$ and $F+f$. When the carried signal covers the range f_1 - f_2, the lower sideband has the range $(F-f_1)$ - $(F-f_2)$; the upper band starts at $F+f_1$ and goes up to $F+f_2$. This is illustrated in the Figure showing modulation and sidebands.

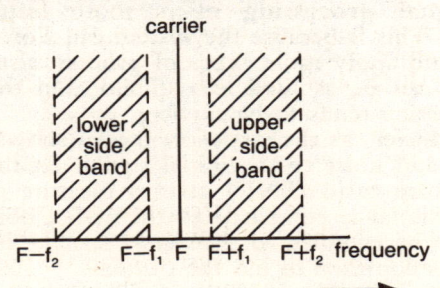

sidebands. Modulation and sidebands.

Sidebands also arise from frequency and phase modulation, but in a more complex way. In all cases, however, it is possible to filter out at least some of the sideband signal without loss; this cuts down the overall signal band, so makes transfer simpler and cheaper. See SINGLE SIDEBAND TRANSFER.

SIGN

sign, *n.* the feature of a number which describes whether its value is less than or greater than zero, i.e. negative or positive. In denary (decimal) working, the unary operators − and + are the symbols for these two cases. In binary, a **sign and magnitude** (**sign and modulus**, or **signed magnitude**) number has one bit (the leftmost in most cases) set aside to carry sign information rather than being part of the value (magnitude). That bit is the **sign bit**, with value 1 for a negative number and 0 for a number greater than zero. Thus in the case of an 8-bit number in sign and magnitude form, only seven bits can carry the value: its range is from 1111 1111 to 0111 1111, i.e. from −127 to +127. In an IT system it is, however, more usual to use 2s complementation to carry the information. See TWOS COMPLEMENT. See also ARITHMETIC.

signal, *n.* a message (or data) in transfer in some coded form; see the SHANNON MODEL. Any signal is a set of values (analog or digital) of some quantity to represent amplitude against time. In most cases the quantity is a form of electric measure.

In the head end of a CATV system, a **signal converter** has a UHF input and a VHF output. The term often appears, however, as any kind of interface. **Signal processing** involves using hardware and/or software to accept a signal and produce a more useful form. Examples are filtering the signal to remove noise, and picture processing to give a clearer image. **Digital signal processing** offers more features than the analog type. This is because the system can store the signal for processing and apply more types of process; also the precision of working can be as high as required. On the other hand, digital processing tends to be slower.

During transfer, as the SHANNON model shows, processes of interference add noise to the initial signal. At the far end, the **signal-to-noise ratio (SNR)** gives a measure of how strong the wanted signal is compared to the added noise. As a ratio (in this case of energies, or powers), strictly it has no unit, although it is common to use the DECIBEL.

silicon, *n.* a chemical element very common in rocks (and therefore sand) in the forms of silica (silicon oxide) and silicates (more complex compounds). Silicon is a SEMICONDUCTOR very widely used as the basis of modern diodes, transistors and chips. A **silicon chip** is a tiny square of very pure silicon with a number of layers of patterns of impurity which build up in the surface a complex circuit of many thousands (even millions) of circuit elements (components).

See WAFER.

silicon disk, *n.* a form of fast accesss STORAGE.

simplex, *adj.* of a channel passing signals one way only; compare with half-duplex (one way at a time), duplex (both ways at once), diplex (two signals the same way at once), and multiplex (many signals the same way at once).

simulation, *n.* a type of computer applications software that models some real life system or process. A simulation allows users to study the system or process cheaply and quickly, and with less risk (compared with trying to study the real thing); a simulation can also be much simpler than real life, in that fewer factors may be involved. Simulations are common in education and training, the social and natural sciences, engineering, and military work (war games).

Sinclair, Sir Clive British inventor and entrepreneur (1940–). He left school at 17 to work for the magazine *Practical Wireless* and to write books, and in 1962 started his own firm, Sinclair Radionics. For most of his career, Sinclair has introduced innovative miniaturized designs cheaply, such as the smallest transistor radio and the first pocket calculator. He designed the Newbrain micro, but sold the design at a time when Chris Curry left to set up the Acorn computer firm.

Sinclair's first micro was the MK14 (1978), the only rival being the Commodore Kim1 (at twice the price). In 1980 followed the ZX80, the first micro below £100, with integer arithmetic, 4K Basic with key words on single keys, and 1K of read and write storage. Later micros, all cheap and innovative and world best sellers, appeared in 1981 (the ZX81), 1982 (Spectrum), 1984 (QL), and 1988 (Z88 portable). Sinclair started the 1990s with a working WAFER scale integrated system. Knighted in 1983, Sir Clive has been involved in many other projects and is still researching the concept of cheap electric cars.

sine wave, *n.* a cyclic action or process that varies with time in a way we can show as a sine curve. This means the measure X depends on time t thus:

$$X = X_0 \sin(2\pi f t)$$

Here X_0 is the amplitude, (the maximum value of X) and f is the frequency.

single, *adj.* lone, or with one part only. A **single address instruction** in a program has one operand or operand address only (see ADDRESSING). A **single address message** is to go to one destination only; i.e. is a point to point transfer. **Single**

SINK

channel voice frequency (SCVF) is a modern approach to TELEX handling, with more power and more features than before. A **single purpose system** is not programmable (general purpose); its single program allows it to work on only a small range of problems (as is the case of a microprocessor-driven sewing machine or a calculator, for instance). **Single sideband transfer** involves passing a modulated signal with only one of the two SIDEBANDS it would normally have. This makes transfer cheaper and simpler, but as the receiver must replace the missing sideband, the situation can become more complex.

sink, *n.* **1.** the point (**data sink**, **message sink**) where data leaves a network to go elsewhere (i.e. much the same as a bridge or gateway).
2. a device which drains energy from a system. Thus a **heat sink** fitted to a high power transistor conducts away excess thermal energy, and so prevents it from getting too hot.

SITL, *abbrev. for* STATIC INDUCTIVE TRANSISTOR LOGIC. See LOGIC (ELECTRONIC LOGIC).

sinusoidal, *adj.* varying in the shape of a SINE WAVE.

skew, *adj.* out of shape or distorted. A **skew character** in a text being scanned by an OCR system is distorted or at the wrong angle for good reading. **Skew failure** is when the problem is so severe that the system cannot recognize the character at all. In parallel data transfer, DATA skew describes how the bits of a word become more and more out of step along the line; this means that a parallel link cannot be longer than a few metres.

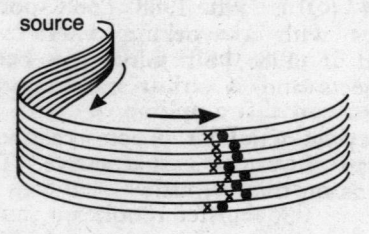

x bits of word 2
● bits of word 1   overlapping, so useless

skew. Data skew in parallel link.

skip, *vb.* **1.** to ignore one or more instructions in a program by

jumping over them. A **skip instruction** causes a jump, conditionally or otherwise, to a point in the program other than the next instruction.
2. to pass over one or more places in a data medium, e.g. to carry out a line feed (**line skip**) action in the case of sheet feed, or a **zone skip** leaving out one of the columns of a table on screen or printout. Skipping is the same as (non-printing) paper advance in a printer.
3. to ignore certain fields in a record during data retrieval.

slab, *n.* 1. part of a word treated as a whole unit in an IT system.
2. the single cylindrical semiconductor crystal from which WAFERS are cut.

slave, *n.* a unit in an IT system with a small number of features, so controlled on occasion by a unit with more power (perhaps called master). This is common in computer and fax networks, where the word 'satellite' may also appear. A **slave display** shows the same as the main screen but has no input unit. Such a display may be used in an exhibition or for a class watching a program run by one person.

SLCI, *abbrev. for* super large scale INTEGRATION, with hundreds of thousands of elements on a chip.

slerexe letter, *n.* a standard A4 typed sheet used to test the transfer speed of fax systems.

slice, *vb.* to cut a thin sample from a larger unit, e.g. to make a WAFER from a slab crystal, a small array from a larger one, or a sub-string from a string. **(Bit) slice architecture** is a hardware design approach to parallel processing. Each slice is a chip with a part of the whole arithmetic and logic unit and associated registers; it works on a slice of the system's word during each cycle. This is the process of **bit slicing** the word (cutting it into chunks of a certain number of bits, e.g. 2 or 4). A **slicer** is a circuit that amplifies one slice.

slow scan television (SSTV), *n.* an approach to video that produces (e.g. with a camera) and transfers a signal at the rate of a frame every few seconds, rather than tens per second as is normal. This means the transfer requires a much smaller band width than in a broadcast. The approach is common with video phones and in security systems.

small scale integration (SSI), *n.* INTEGRATION with fewer than a dozen elements and no more than a hundred in the surface of a chip.

smart, *adj.* having a certain degree of machine intelligence; or, more often, having a certain degree of local processing power and storage. Thus a **smart building/car** involves the maximum amount of computer control of systems and action, including effective navigation systems in the latter case. A **smart card** is a plastic card with its own chip; current systems may contain up to 32 KB of store. The smart card reader provides power and can read data from and send data to the chip. Common uses are for phone cards, cards that contain medical or academic histories, and in security. See also MEMORY CARD.

A **smart device**, such as a **smart terminal**, while having a certain degree of processing power and storage, has less than a so-called intelligent unit. However, the distinction is very blurred. A **smart sensor** comes with its own chip to carry out the analog to digital conversion it needs and to send the output signal safely on its way to a computer (e.g. when the sensor is in use in an area that could add a lot of interference).

s/n, *symbol for* SIGNAL TO NOISE RATIO, a measure of the lack of interference in transfer.

snail mail, *n.* a jargon term for the postal service, when compared in terms of speed to FAX and EMAIL. Both fax and email transfer text, and perhaps graphics, very quickly; the fact that the postal service shows little signs of failing as result of their spread is a reminder that costs, coverage, and technical ease of use are important factors too.

sniffing, *n.* an approach to detecting and correcting errors in computers.

Snobol, *n.* a high level computer program language the main feature of which is its ability to handle character strings.

SNR, *abbrev. for* SIGNAL TO NOISE RATIO.

society, *n.* the set of all groups of people and their organizations that (in this context) an IT system may affect. Indeed the impact of systems on society is part of the field of study of INFORMATION TECHNOLOGY itself. When trying to assess the likely impact of a new IT system on society, it is normal practice to consider these groups:

(a) the owners of the system (or management);

(b) the owners of competing (less up-to-date implied) systems;

(c) the work force at the site of the new system;

(d) the people served by the system (the clients or customers);

(e) local and/or national government;

(f) all other people living in the area.

One must also try to assess the effects of a new development on society in the short term (during and just after implementation), in the medium term (as the new system 'beds down', is taken up by competitors, and becomes accepted by other groups), and in the long term (as regards any potential changes to society as a whole). Only the first of these is in the minds of most SYSTEMS analysts.

socket, *n.* a device into which a plug fits in order to make an electric (or other) link. There are very many types of plug and socket; these differ in the numbers of lines they link, the power of what they transmit and the systems concerned.

soft copy, *n.* a jargon term for what appears on an IT system's screen rather than on paper (hard copy).

soft hyphen, see DISCRETIONARY HYPHEN.

soft key, *n.* a key, the effect or function of which the user can change under software control, and thus the same as a function key. Most keyboards now have a number of function keys, perhaps ten or twenty. Indeed, some now are **soft keyboards** where the user can change the function of every single non-control key to suit current needs. Doing this for more than a short time on more than a few keys creates a demand for caps to fit on the keys; the user can write the function concerned on each of these.

soft sectoring, *n.* a non-permanent method of marking the sectors on a disk. This happens during the formatting process and the disk can later be re-formatted for use with a different system. Compare with HARD SECTORING; here the disk has holes drilled through it to mark permanently where each sector is to start.

softlifting, *n.* a jargon term for the illegal copying of software for internal use (e.g. for use on other machines in the home or office).

software, *n.* the set of one or more programs an IT system needs to carry out a task. It is common to class software as a hierarchy of layers between the hardware (the physical units of processor and peripherals) and the user (who wishes to view the system as a tool). The main layers are (from inside out):

(a) operating software: the programs that actually control the flows of bits around the hardware;

(b) utilities and TSR programs (which offer at a key press a small range of applications from within most higher level environments);

SOFTWARE

(c) program language software (to translate higher level commands and programs into machine code for the operating software to work with);

(d) applications programs (that offer the user the power to carry out tasks of a given type, e.g. word processing and simulation).

It is normal to BUNDLE at least basic operating software with a new hardware system; indeed, the marketing of at least the cheaper micros currently expects bundling of a range of applications as well.

Software documentation is the range of booklets and manuals that the user expects to receive with a software package. This should describe clearly how to install the program and how to use it once installed. See also DOCUMENTATION.

Software emulation allows a given hardware system to work in the same way as another, incompatible, one: it consists of software that translates commands and instructions in the emulated form into the type of machine code the real system will accept. **Software engineering** is the design, development and production of a program to meet a given need; it should include market research and systems analysis as well as coding. On the other hand, a **software engineer** should only advise on documentation as writing this is a very different skill. See also CASE, computer-aided software engineering.

A **software house** is a firm that specializes in software development, either for individual clients (**bespoke software**) or for publication. For **software life-cycle**, see SYSTEM LIFE-CYCLE. A **software package** is a complete finished product: the fully tested program itself (on disk, tape, or chip), the documentation (also fully tested), and the packaging.

Software reliability is the efficiency with which a program carries out its set tasks in the hurly-burly of a user's working day. It is not the same as correctness (for this relates to how well the program matches the design specification); a correct program may be unreliable if the user finds it does not do all that is expected of it. **Software tools** are programs that help software development, maintenance or repair; they range from editors and translators to full feature program generators. However, any program that helps a software engineer (see above) to carry out a given task effectively is now taken as a tool which, for instance, needs analysis, quality assurance, and project management.

solid state, *n.* that branch of physics and electronics which is concerned with how solid matter (in particular metals and SEMI-CONDUCTORS) behaves electrically. For **solid (state) disk (drive)**, see WAFER. **Solid state technology** applies the concepts of solid state physics to real systems; such as to the use of semiconductor materials and transistor design.

son, *n.* a deprecated term for child file (or for any other dependent in a hierarchy). See file GENERATION.

sort, *vb.* to put the elements of a set into groups or into order (sequence) following a particular rule. **Sorting** is a major aspect of data processing, whether applied to a set of single data items or to lengthy records with a large number of fields in a file. For instance, a computer must sort the records of a transaction file into the same order as the master file before merging the two to make a new (up-to-date) master. Again, it is easier to search a file if it is sorted, and easier to compare the contents of two files sorted the same way.

In any case, the sorting rule translates to the use of some key feature of each element in the set. Thus a librarian may wish to sort the records of a book file first into order of title, then into order of author, and lastly into order of class (subject) number. For the three sorts, the same file would be in use, but the key fields (**sort fields**) would differ.

There are many **sort(ing) algorithms** or routines able to carry out such tasks. They differ in speed, efficiency, and ability to handle files in main or backing store. Often, a sorting program is treated as a utility in a system.

sorting, *n.* the putting of the elements of a set into a given order. See SORT.

sound, *n.* energy transferred by pressure waves (**sound waves**) in solid, liquid or gas within the range of frequencies (approximately 20 Hz - 20 000 Hz) the normal human ear can detect. A **sound carrier** is a carrier signal (often in the radio band) used to carry a signal with a sound (audio) bandwidth, as opposed to one working with video. See SPEECH for recognition and synthesis.

source, *n.* **1.** the location from which something has come, e.g. the sender of a signal or message.
2. the point in a network where signals enter from elsewhere (compare SINK).
3. an origin, as in **source code**, a program in a high-level language before translation into the machine code the system can follow. **Source data acquisition** is another term for DIR-

SPACE DIVISION MULTIPLEXING (SDM)

ECT DATA ENTRY, in particular where this occurs at the place where the raw data is generated. A **source document** is an original document from which information is taken to be entered into an IT system (e.g. an article in a journal abstracted for storage in a bibliographic data base). In machine aided translation systems, a **source language** is the language of the original text to be translated (compare with TARGET LANGUAGE). A **source program** is an alternative term for source code (see above).

space division multiplexing (SDM), *n.* a form of MULTIPLEXING in which the different signals pass from sender to receiver down different physical channels.

space segment, *n.* that part in space of a complete satellite communications system: the satellite, its launch, maintenance and so on.

sparse array, *n.* an array most of whose elements are empty (zero or null elements); this may lead to inefficiency in use.

speaker, *n.* a peripheral unit with an analog electric input and a sound output with the same form (in the ideal case). There are many speaker designs which are the reverse of a similar type of MICROPHONE. See also SPEECH SYNTHESIS.

special character, *n.* any keyboard character other than a letter, digit or space.

specificity, *n.* a measure of how close the index terms of a document or file match the concepts concerned and the user's needs.

specific coding, *n.* a rare term for machine coding.

spectrum, *n.* a range of elements with smooth progress from one to the next. In IT, the most important is the **electromagnetic spectrum**: the range of radiations with the following properties:

(a) transfer by waves of electric and magnetic fields;

(b) transfer through empty space at just under 300 000 km/s (and more slowly through matter);

(c) being a wave form, follows the laws of reflection and refraction when meeting the surface of a second medium;

(d) being a wave form, shows interference and diffraction effects;

(e) being a longitudinal wave form, shows polarization effects.

For convenience, the bands within the spectrum carry different names which relate to their uses and/or detection methods. In order of increasing energy content and frequency (number

SPEECH

of waves per second), i.e. in order of decreasing wavelength, the main bands are:

(a) RADIO; involves aerials for sending and reception, e.g. of radio and television signals;

(b) MICROWAVE; involves very small aerials or other special systems, used for radar and point to point communications;

(c) INFRARED; 'thermal waves' (heat) involved in many types of fibre optic system as well as remote controls;

(d) LIGHT; involving waves visible to the human eye, with its own colour spectrum ranging from red to blue (and with hundreds of separately identifiable hues); photocells and photographic film can detect light too (and also detect other nearby radiations);

(e) ULTRAVIOLET; very high energy capacity, but difficult to work with, so not yet in wide use in IT;

(f) X-rays and gamma rays.

speech, *n.* the human faculty of communicating information by speaking, i.e. using the sound waves produced by the voice suitably modulated. Speech is immensely complex in practice, with a given single utterance lasting perhaps less than a second but able to contain a wealth of information. It does so by being a complex pattern of sound waves that differ in amplitude and frequency, and do so from moment to moment. Also, each pattern is almost unique to an individual speaker as well as relating to age, gender, language, accent, and so on.

As speech is the main method of normal communication between humans, there has long been research into ways of making machines recognize and produce it. The complexities of speech make this a very difficult task, however, and, while there has been huge progress in the 1980s, there is still some way to go in the 1990s before we will have translating telephones, voice servers in local networks, word processors we can dictate fully to, speech synthesizers that please the ear and do not stretch the brain, and IT systems with which we can converse normally. (On the other hand, the first two effective commercial dictating word processors each with a speaker-independent vocabulary of 30000 words, appeared in 1990.)

While the thought of every person holding conversations with a wrist computer does not appeal to all, there are many situations where this would be of value: hands-off working in factory, office, and home, and interacting with remote data bases are obvious ones. There are two aspects to the problem:

SPEED

Speech recognition involves the use of a microphone to accept the speech, and software to analyse the signal that results. Analysis involves pre-processing: 'feature extraction', using filters or some other means to break the input down into sounds and pauses; digitising (converting the analog patterns into digital ones); and then relating each set to words and phrases in a dictionary. Once the software has translated the spoken input into its own terms, it can take the appropriate action. Few speech-recognition systems can handle more than a few hundred words, and then, often, only after being trained to work with the voice of a specific person. People, still, therefore, must speak slowly and deliberately, and can use only a small vocabulary and syntax. **Voice recognition** is more than that; it involves the system being able to work out who is speaking as well as what the sounds mean.

Speech synthesis is the reverse process; it is a somewhat simpler one (as shown by its use in toys and talking advertisements for a decade or more). Here, software must translate a message in machine terms into patterns that can pass through to a speaker to make the right sounds. One approach uses waveform digitization: the system learns the patterns it needs by digitising and storing spoken words and phrases; all the software need then do is to put the right ones into the right order to make a sentence. A second is formant synthesis; here the system simulates, in electronic form, all the sounds of speech: again, so it can link them correctly as required.

speed, *n.* usually a measure of the rate of data processing and/or data transfer in an IT system. These are often also measures of the 'value' of a given system. In the former case, common units are millions of instructions or operations per second (MIPS or mops; see also FLOPS), the latter in thousands or millions of bits or bytes per second (see also baud). It is not easy to compare the speeds of working of two IT systems unless they are given identical tasks, and such tasks are benchmarks. Systems with clock speeds around 30 MHz (millions of cycles per second) are no longer rare, and, while some people feel that current technology puts a limit of 50 MHz, others expect systems to reach 150 MHz. Using GALLIUM ARSENIDE chips rather than silicon chips allows one super-computer of the early 1990s to work with a 2 GHz clock rate.

spelling check, *n.* the process of working through a text in store and comparing each word to the contents of a dictionary (really a word list). A **spelling checker** is a program that can do this; modern ones may have dictionaries with about a hundred thousand words and users can add a large number of specialized ones (such as their names and technical terms). All a checker can do is to inform the user of a word it does not have listed; it may offer possibilities from its list, but it cannot detect a correctly spelled word in the wrong place. Thus, a checker cannot pick up 'their' when you mean 'there'. See STYLE CHECKER for that feature.

spike, *n.* a sudden, brief voltage peak in an electric power supply, perhaps rising to several thousand volts. Uninterruptible power supplies should prevent spikes from causing damage. See also SURGE.

split catalogue, *n.* a catalogue with more than one separate listing of keys. Thus a library catalogue may list books by title, by author, and by subject. A **split keyboard** is a type of computer configuration which allows one person to enter and edit data on one keyboard, while a second, working with another keyboard, can carry out searches. A **split screen** is one with two or more WINDOWS.

spooling, *n.* the use of a **spooler** routine or utility to improve the efficiency of usage of input and output units in a multiprocessing environment. For example, such a routine can take a text ready for printing, store it in a buffer, and deal with it without further troubling the central processor. One origin given for the term 'spool' is that it comes from simultaneous peripheral operation on line, but it is more likely to take its name from the process of tape spooling (fast forward or rewind action).

spreadsheet, *n.* a number processing program based on a grid of two or more dimensions with cells arrayed in rows and columns, and possibly pages. Each cell can contain a text string (e.g. a title or label), a numeric value, or a formula that works on values in other cells. The user can enter and edit data, copy and move the contents of cells, save and print the whole or a part of a table, and load stored tables. Major straightforward uses are for laying out neatly and processing the data in tables of accounts or experiment results (for instance). See also WHAT IF?.

sprocket feed, *n.* a way to pass paper (fanfold or roll) through a printer using sprocket holes along each edge. See PINFEED.

spur, *n.* a junction in a network between the main line and a smaller side line, or the side line itself.

squarial, *n.* the name of a flat multi-element aerial used to receive some domestic satellite broadcasts. Each element is a tiny horn antenna linked to the output by co-axial cable in such a way that all the received signals combine.

SRAM, *abbrev. for* STATIC RAM.

SSI, *abbrev. for* small scale INTEGRATION.

SSTV, *abbrev. for* SLOW SCAN TELEVISION.

stack, *n.* a data structure with one open end (called **stack top**). Pushing a new data item puts it onto the stack at that end; popping one takes the outermost item from the stack. A stack is therefore a one-dimensional last in first out (LIFO) list. Compare with QUEUE, a two-ended, first in first out structure (sometimes wrongly called a **FIFO stack**). Many IT systems have a stack implemented in hardware (i.e. hard wired); the structure has great importance in recursion, sub-routine calling, and the handling of interrupts. High-level language programmers may use the system stack or simulate one in a one-dimensional array.

In all cases, the system needs to know only the address of the outermost data item in the stack from moment to moment; a register called the **stack pointer** holds this information.

staff, *n.* the set of people working with a large computer system, other than the actual users. A typical computer department has a *data processing manager* (*DPM*) at the head; this person may be part of the firm's senior management if data processing is a major part of the firm's work. Otherwise a management services manager will be the next step up. Below come separate sections, typically for:

(a) data preparation (with a data preparation manager in charge, and one or more teams of data preparation clerks; keyboard operators; each under a supervisor): handling data entry, editing, transactions;

(b) operations (under the operations manager, with a chief operator, and, for each shift, a shift leader and a team of computer and perhaps communications operators): concerned with the actual running of the hardware and software;

(c) data control (with a data controller in charge, one or more data (or file) librarians to look after the tapes and disks, and one or more data control clerks): responsible for the proper handling of data and data stores within the overall scheme;

(d) programming, if appropriate (with senior and junior

STANDARD

programmers, possibly in teams working on different projects): for the development of required new software and the maintenance of existing programs;

(e) systems (the line being systems manager, senior systems analyst, and junior analysts): the main tasks being the continuous specification, implementation and assessment of new systems.

The above list may not exactly relate at all to the practice in any one firm; however, it broadly indicates common approaches to staffing a data processing department in a large organization. In smaller firms, roles combine, and there is more and more use of outside consultants and/or computer bureaus.

stand-alone, *adj.* denoting anything not needing processor or peripheral support from outside. Thus a network station may have a **stand-alone capability** if it has its own operating software, main and backing stores, and printer. On the other hand, a **stand-alone system** is designed to work as an individual unit (as is a micro).

standard, *n.* any system generally accepted, on a local or wider scale, as the one all should use. Thus a **standard document** is a pre-processed letter or form to which people can add specific details as required. In arithmetic, **standard form** refers to a way of showing numeric values. For instance, one may show the denary value 12345.6 as 1.23456×10^4 (standard form), or as 12.3456×10^3 (scientific standard form, using exponents that are multiples of 3). In computer ARITHMETIC (see also NUMBER) binary numbers are stored and processed in much the same way, with a mantissa and an exponent part.

A **standard function** is a function that comes within a set (library) with a program language. For instance, many program languages offer standard functions to return the sine of a value or the length of a string. Programmers have to write for themselves the code they need to produce the effect of non-standard functions.

Standards comprise the whole set of systems, procedures and protocols a group may apply to one area of IT activity. Nowadays, it is crucial that standards develop quickly and on a world-wide basis because IT is an international activity. On the other hand, haste may mean future developments cannot be catered for; often, therefore, standards develop through an informal process in which powerful firms agree on how to handle a new technology. A **de facto standard** is one that has grown in this way and proved its worth, so that most users accept it. See also COMPATIBILITY.

A **standard sub-routine** (procedure) is one supplied with a program language in a library of useful routines. A **standard system** is hardware or software that meets the standards users expect.

star or **cluster,** *n.* a network layout in which each station (node) has a direct link to the central hardware. This layout is costly on cabling, but easy to control; also, if one station breaks down, the others can go on working in the normal way. **Star networks** are very common in small scale systems (e.g. in a home or small office).

start bit/signal, *n.* a bit/code that marks the start of a data transfer; it comes from the sender to warn the receiver that a signal's ready to come.

state of the art, *adj.* (of a system) fully up-to-date. It is an overworked phrase as far as it refers to current technology and styles of working. Its use needs to be carefully judged to prevent likely users starting to worry about reliability and compatibility.

statement, *n.* a single complete meaningful scene-setting observation or instruction in a high-level program language, or the symbols (code) in which the programmer may express it. Program languages differ somewhat in how they define the concept and what they may expect in terms of labels and separators.

static, *adj.* denoting no change during an action or set of actions (e.g. during a program run). Thus **static buffering** involves setting the size and function of the various buffers at the start rather than on demand. **Static data** is the same as constant data (e.g. the value of π or the name of a firm as it may appear at the top of different screens and printouts); a **static data structure** is one fixed in size before the process (as, in many languages, an array and its dimensions must be initialized).

Static RAM (SRAM) is non-volatile read/write storage: it retains its contents as long as it is supplied with power. Unlike DYNAMIC RAM (DRAM), its contents do not need refreshing every millisecond or so, so the system works faster. On the other hand, a unit of static ram takes up a lot of space in a chip (it consists of several transistors in a flip-flop arrangement); it costs more to fit a system with SRAM chips than with DRAMs, and they take up more space. New SRAM chips seem to be able to overcome these problems, however.

static inductive transistor logic (SITL), see LOGIC (ELECTRONIC LOGIC).

static video, *n.* an alternative term for STILL VIDEO or SLOW SCAN TELEVISION.

station, *n.* an intelligent input/output unit where a single person can work on a network. Much of the time a user will work at the station as if it were a stand alone micro. However, the network offers features such as email and the sharing of data; this means that each station has a unique **station select(ion) code**. All data sent to it must have this code in the header.

status line, *n.* a screen display line that presents the user with useful data (e.g. the current x-y position of the cursor, or the number of words in the current word processed document). A computer, network server, or master fax machine carries out a process of **status polling** every so often: checking the needs of its intelligent peripherals/slaves. See also POLLING. A **status register** is the same as a FLAG REGISTER; its task is to record problems that require an interrupt, including problems and needs at peripherals/slaves. A **status word** is a code passed from such a peripheral or slave to the centre, to indicate its current (or new) status.

STD, *abbrev. for* SUBSCRIBER TRUNK DIALLING.

step down/up, *adj.* denoting a fax or other data transfer system where the hardware can react to line quality by raising or lowering the data transfer speed.

stepper motor, *n.* an electric motor that turns at constant speed in steps of a given angle (rather than continuously). Stepper motors are of great value in many automated control systems, including robotics.

stereofiche, *n.* a type of microfiche in which the small images come in pairs for viewing with a stereo projector to give a three-dimensional effect.

still video or **static video,** *n.* **1.** a process of slow speed transfer of a video signal that comes from a static shot (e.g., of a document). The data transfer speed is slow enough to allow the signal to pass through a phone network. See also SLOW SCAN TELEVISION.
2. a type of camera that records up to fifty shots on a small, e.g. 50 mm across, analog magnetic disc. The disc player can put the pictures on a television set or other display, and normal photos can be made from these before the disk returns

STOCK CONTROL

to re-use. Much the same technique appears in the newer systems with digital storage on chips. These cameras are much more costly than those with a disk, but the digital storage gives far higher picture quality.

stock control, *n.* a major application area for IT. A simple stock control program for a micro will:

(a) allow the user to enter details of each line of stock (e.g. source, size, shelf life, re-order stock level);

(b) allow entry of initial stock level;

(c) process transaction details in order to maintain an up-to-date stock figure for each line;

(d) report after each update on the items that need re-stocking.

More sophisticated software may incorporate:

(e) automatic transaction entry at the point of sale;

(f) a wide range of sophisticated reports, including of relevant accounts;

(g) automatic re-ordering with reference to a suppliers' file.

stop bit/code/element, *n.* a bit/code/element that marks the end of a data transfer. It comes from the sender to tell the receiver that the current signal has finished. In word processing, a stop code in a data stream to the printer tells the printer to pause at that point (while, for example, the user inserts a fresh sheet or changes the print wheel).

storage, *n.* the crucial part of an IT system which holds program instructions and data in binary form (equivalent to 0s and 1s) to allow automatic processing. Storage is also called memory, but this is a less satisfactory term. The system's **storage address register** holds the address of the instruction next to be dealt with; its **storage buffer register (SBR)** is the register at the entrance/exit of main store, through which all data passes, word by word, on its way in or out; for more on both, see MACHINE CYCLE (sometimes called **store cycle**). It is normal to measure **storage capacity** in bytes, one byte being able to store one character (or in kilobytes or megabytes, thousands and millions of bytes respectively). This is the case even where a single **storage cell/location** holds more than one byte.

Over the years a wide range of **storage devices/units** has appeared. It is useful to distinguish between the five common levels of storage, here given in order from the processor:

(a) *registers*: semiconductor stores holding, in most cases, a single word for use in the current sequence of processing actions:

(b) *cache*: a semiconductor store of a few thousand bytes holding program instructions and data the system expects it is likely to need very soon (not all computers have a cache feature);

(c) *main store*: almost always semiconductor based (i.e. built from chips), and ranging in size from a few kilobytes in a small single purpose system to hundreds of millions of bytes in a mainframe or super-computer; used for holding the programs and data in current use;

(d) *silicon disk*: a section of main store set aside as a buffer for data brought in from and sent to backing store during a given session (and thus, in effect, a very high speed but volatile form of backing store); as is the case with cache, this is not on offer in all systems;

(e) *backing store*: non-volatile store for holding programs and data for the long term.

For types of backing store, see MAGNETIC MEDIA, OPTICAL MEDIA, PUNCHED MEDIA; though, again, non-volatile semiconductor systems are fast growing in popularity.

Storage management is an important role for someone on the staff of a data processing department (whether there are programs to help or not); it involves trying to make sure that each part of the store (see above), and holds the right data in the right form from moment to moment. This is to achieve maximum efficiency while the system is working, and also to prevent running out of storage space. A **storage map** can help here; this shows the usage of the major blocks of main store (or of a disk surface). A **storage tube** is a graphics display, based on a cathode-ray tube, that is able to hold an image for a very long time.

store, *n*. the place where an IT system holds instructions and data: in all IT contexts, a better term than memory. See STORAGE. A **store and forward** computer is at the centre of a wide area network used for passing messages and data between the users. The users of a wide area network are very likely not to be on line at the same time, so the chances of setting up a direct transfer are small. The central computer (or host) therefore accepts all such data transfers, and holds them in backing store with the address (mailbox number) of the recipient. When this person logs on to the system, the host can forward all such messages. A **store dump** is the automatic copying of part or all of main store to backing store or to paper. This may be part of an emergency action. The **stored**

STRESS

program concept is central to modern electronic IT; it involves the IT system storing the instructions of the current program and working through them automatically (see, for instance, MACHINE CYCLE). Were this not possible, the user would have to enter the instructions one by one (presumably in binary).

stress, *n.* a sense of strain or difficulty which can be encountered as a health hazard in IT. It may follow trying to cope with too many things at once, a common danger where there are frequent hardware and software failures, and where the systems can work much faster than the people.

string, *n.* a set of any keyboard (or, for instance, ASCII) characters that a system can treat as a whole as regards storage, transfer and processing. **String processing** may involve sorting and searching, or more complex operations that generate new strings from existing ones. Such operations can call on a number of **string functions** in some program languages. However, although handling words and sets of words is a major human task, computer systems are rarely as effective at string handling as at handling numbers. A **string search** is a type of information retrieval approach: the search terms form a string, with or without connectors (such as AND and OR), and the string then becomes the basis of the search algorithm. **String size** means the number of characters in a string (again often given by a function); this may be zero (the **null string**), and some systems impose no upper limit as long as the store can cope.

stringy floppy, *n.* a short fast-moving continuous length of video tape able to transfer data almost as fast as a floppy disk; a useful backing store in some contexts.

stripe card, *n.* a plastic card with, on one side, a stripe of magnetic or optical material that allows a machine to read stored data and (in the magnetic case) to write to the card. A magnetic card can store very little data (e.g. 240 bytes); an optical stripe can hold several megabytes but it is read-only and the readers are (at the moment) more costly, being more rare.

structure, *n.* **1.** a set of data with a logical link, so given a single name and a particular method (e.g. SUBSCRIPT) to refer to each data item in the set. See DATA STRUCTURES.
2. the overall design of a HARDWARE system in terms of the parts and the links between them.
3. the overall design of an algorithm and the program that

STYLE CHECKER

develops from it. A **structure chart** shows program structure in graphic form; it is hierarchical, with each level giving more detail than the one above. Moreover, if you traverse (walk round) the chart clockwise from the root, visiting each box on the way, you have a pseudo-code version of the program. This allows you to produce **structured code**, at least if working with a **structured program language**. This approach of devising a more and more detailed structure diagram for the algorithm, then converting it to pseudo-code and final code, is a top-down approach to **structured programming**. Any approach to structured programming should much reduce the number of errors, and thus produce bug-free and efficient code with a minimum of effort.

The Figure shows (on the left) a small structure chart and (on the right) the main symbols used in these.

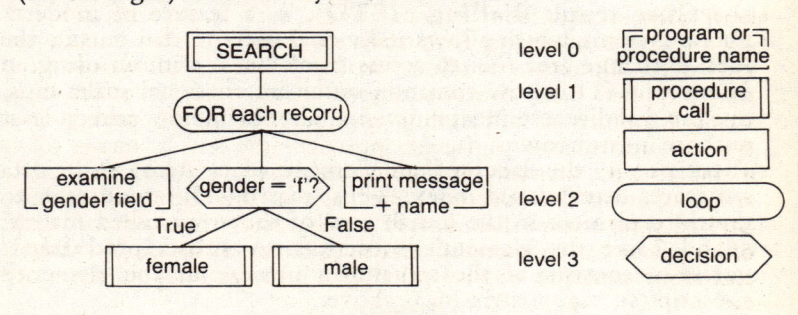

structure.

style checker, *n.* a program used in conjunction with a word processor in an attempt to improve the grammar and style of a text; compare with SPELLING CHECK. A style checker may be able to highlight for the user:

(a) common errors of grammar (e.g. split infinitives, the comma error, singular subjects with plural verbs);

(b) word errors such as 'their' instead of 'there', repetition (e.g. 'showing that this may show ...' and 'come to to work');

(c) jargon that may not suit the anticipated readers (e.g. 'megaproblem', 'all things being equal');

(d) long complex words/phrases where a short word will do (e.g. 'make an effort' for 'try');

(e) sentences that are too long and/or complex;

(f) problems of layout.

stylus, *n.* **1.** a light pen.
2. the pointer used with a graphics tablet.
3. the read/write head used with an optical disc.

sub-, *prefix* denoting a lower level. Thus a **sub-program** or **sub-routine** is part of a longer program with a specific task within that program (see also PROCEDURE). A sub-routine may be open, lying within the main program itself, or closed, stored separately and called by the main program or by another sub-routine. The closed sub-routine is of more value to the programmer, especially when it is likely the program will need to use the sub-routine more than once. (Indeed, frequently used closed sub-routines are widely available to form part of the programmer's collection, or **sub-routine library**). A **sub-tree** is the tree that lies below any node of a tree other than the root node.

subscriber trunk dialling (STD), *n.* a feature of modern phone systems which allows individual users to dial outside the local exchange area (i.e. to access trunk lines) without using an operator. STD is now common on an international scale; thus, one can dial direct to most individual phones in the world, at least to those in large towns.

subscript, *n.* the label of an element (data item) in a data structure, better called index. Thus 'matrix(4,3)' could refer to the third element in the fourth row of the array called matrix; 4 and 3 are the element's subscripts. A **subscripted label/variable** consists of the structure's name plus the element's subscript(s), e.g. matrix (4,3) above.

subset, *n.* **1.** a MODEM.
2. a small group within a larger group.

substitute, *n.* a standard character inserted by software to show it cannot interpret a certain read or received character or control code. Indeed, some software of this type will substitute the standard character for all control codes in case these cause problems with the host system.

substitution table, *n.* a translation table showing the current values given by programmed (soft) keys on a soft keyboard.

suite, *n.* a set of related programs handling related tasks. Thus a modern word-processing suite may include the word processor itself, spelling and style checkers, a thesaurus, and a simple page layout program.

summer, *n.* an OPAMP set where the output is the sum of the two inputs. As the output sum in fact has the opposite sign to the input, when used with just one input the device becomes an inverter (NOT gate). **A summing integrator** is an opamp whose output is the sum of the time integrals of the inputs.

sun outage, *n.* any period during which a communication satellite works less well than it should because of its position relative to the sun. This may be the result of loss of power or overload if the satellite relies on solar cells.

super-computer, *n.* a very fast, very powerful computer with a very large main store, and thus able to address some of the most complex problems. These problems require huge amounts of processing; examples are weather forecasting, the analysis of fluid flows in test tunnels, and census data analysis. The definition of super-computer is vague and ever-changing (especially since parallel processing has become so easy and cheap); all the same, the names of Cray and Cyber still remain supreme. Thus, Cray's super-computer of the early 1990s, based on gallium arsenide rather than silicon chips, has a clock speed of 2 GHz, tens of times faster than others.

The main routes of development, however, involve parallel processing: either the use of a few very powerful processors working together, or that of many tens of thousands of simpler ones. The current problem with the latter is how to program such a system effectively.

At the end of the 1980s, there were just over 400 super-computers in use world wide. The history of computing has shown, however, that 'the super-computer of today is the lap-top of tomorrow'. Thus, Europe's Supernode (1990) super-computer, based on arrays of transputers, has the power of its rivals but costs only a hundredth as much. Intel's iPSC/860 machines are almost as cheap; their approach, however, depends on the first 64-bit micro-processor.

superconductivity, *n.* a process observed in metals and some other materials at very low temperatures in which current can pass with no loss of energy, i.e. there is no resistance. Super-conductors can thus transfer power and data with negligible loss and at very low cost. Although the late 1980s saw much progress in raising the temperature at which superconductivity can be observed, it remains very low (around $-200°C$, needing liquid air for cooling); moreover, super-conductors working at such high temperatures are very hard to use. Thus far, therefore, no practical IT system using super-conductors has come onto the market.

superfiche, *n.* a microfiche with many hundreds of images on the standard size of fiche, instead of a couple of hundred.

superfine resolution, *n.* a non-standard (i.e. proprietary) system for sending and receiving faxes with unusually high detail. As it is a non-standard system, a successful transfer requires the same type of machine at each end.

supergroup, *n.* a set of five 12-channel frequency bands used to form some trunk and international telephone links.

super high frequency, *adj.* of signals in the (RADIO) frequency range 300–3000 MHz.

super large scale integration (SLCI), *n.* a level of INTEGRATION with hundreds of thousands of circuit elements in the surface of a chip.

super scalar, *adj.* denoting a microprocessor that can work on more than one instruction during a single MACHINE CYCLE. One approach is to have two or three instructions passing through the system, reaching the same stage at different moments in the cycle.

supervisor, *n.* that part of the operating software which is mainly concerned with moment-to-moment usage of shared resources. Also called monitor or executive, supervisor is sometimes taken to mean operating software as a whole.

suppressed carrier transfer, *n.* the transmission of a modulated carrier without the carrier. This reduces signal power demand, but means that the receiver must be more complex than usual to cope.

suppression, *n.* stopping something from happening, an alternative term for disabling. Printer suppression is the same as disabling the printer; **zero suppression** involves disabling from display and printout all 0s in any number that have no significance (i.e. leading and trailing 0s).

surface mounting, *n.* a process coming to replace the use of the printed circuit board. Rather than drilling holes through the board to take the pins (legs) of chips and other components, surface mounted elements rest directly on the surface, attached by solder. The approach means circuits need no longer sit on flat boards of a certain size and shape, they can go on any suitable surface (e.g. the curved inside panels of a vehicle).

surge, *n.* a sudden increase in power supply voltage lasting for some seconds. This can damage IT hardware linked to the supply line, unless there is an uninterruptible power supply unit at the interface. See also SPIKE.

surveillance, *n.* the watching of a space for intruders, fire and other problems. IT can assist in various ways, using sensors or slow scan television, for instance.

switch, *n.* **1.** a device used to open and close a current's access to a circuit or sub-circuit. There are very many types of switch for use in different situations. A **switch board** consists of an array of sockets linked to phone lines (for example); plugs linked to other lines can make contact in any socket and thus connect any pairs of lines. See also RELAY and TRANSISTOR, both special types of switch.
2. a decision point in a program with more than two possible outcomes (branches); the CASE structure (or similar) is the best way to provide for this.

switching, *n.* the process of shunting signals or packets through a network so they reach the correct address. This involves a series of one or more SWITCHBOARDS or **switching centres** (phone exchanges in the case of phone signal switching). See EXCHANGE. See also PACKET SWITCHING SYSTEM.

symbol table, name table or **label table,** *n.* a storage system for the labels and addresses of data items and structures.

symbolic address, *n.* the address of an operand given with an instruction in symbol (label) form rather than as a number. See ADDRESSING. **Symbolic code** is a form of assembler that allows this type of addressing (it requires more complex translating than simple assembly). A **symbolic instruction** uses a symbol (e.g. a key word) for the opcode (instruction part) rather than a sequence of bits. A **symbolic language** is any program language higher than machine code, one that allows symbolic instructions and (perhaps) symbolic addressing. A **symbolic name** is the label given to a data item (strictly to its address) by the programmer, while **symbolic programming** is coding in a symbolic language.

sync, *abbrev. for* **synchronization,** making sure different events and actions occur at the right times and in step. Within a processor and associated systems, this is the function of the pulses from the clock. However, synchronization is important in other contexts, especially with data transfer. Here, a **synchronizing signal** travels with the main signal to ensure that the data bits appear and are received in synchronism with a particular clock. The signal may come from the transmitter or from another source.

synchronous, *adj.* denoting a signal in which the interval between successive bits is constant.

syntax, *n.* the grammar of a language: the sets of rules (and, in the case of human languages, the exceptions to the rules) that

SYSTEM

govern its usage for proper communication. In the translation of code from a high level to machine languages, **syntax analysis** is an important stage; it involves checking that the programmer has not made any **syntax errors** (i.e. has not broken any of the syntax rules of the high level language).

system, *n.* any combination of hardware, software, links, procedures and actions that helps people to carry out a task. In particular, an IT system is this kind of combination concerned with the efficient handling of information. A **system crash** is when a system breaks down and can no longer carry out its task; it may result from a hardware problem or from an error in software from which the system cannot recover on its own. **System design** concerns the work of a systems analyst (see below) involved in specification, design and implementation of a new system. Here, and elsewhere, the **system life-cycle** is the sequence of events which runs from recognising the need for a new system to recognising the need for one to replace that in due course. This may last a number of years or just a few months. The main stages are:

(a) needs analysis;

(b) system design: software, hardware, operations and methods;

(c) obtaining and testing the component parts (hardware and software);

(d) linking these into the new system (integration and implementation);

(e) overall system testing and training;

(f) introduction (release);

(g) operation and maintenance;

(h) needs analysis for replacement system.

A **system program** is part of (or the same as) operating software, a **system programmer** being a person who specializes in producing this kind of code. **System recovery** concerns getting back to work after a crash (above), **system recovery time** being how long that takes, on average. A **system resident** program or routine is one that forms an integral part of the system; in other words, it is a low level program in the operating software, maybe as a utility.

The science (or art) of **systems analysis** involves taking a highly professional and expert view of existing systems (whether IT-based or not); the aim is not always to computerize, but it is always to attempt to define and design a better system for the purpose. However, the word 'better' can have

SYSTEM

conflicting applications (see SOCIETY). The tasks of a systems analyst range right throughout system design as set out above, though on a large project different people will specialize in different areas.

A **system flow chart** is a block diagram showing how the parts of the system relate and how data and information flow through it. The symbols used are not the same as for a program FLOW CHART. See the Figure for the main ones.

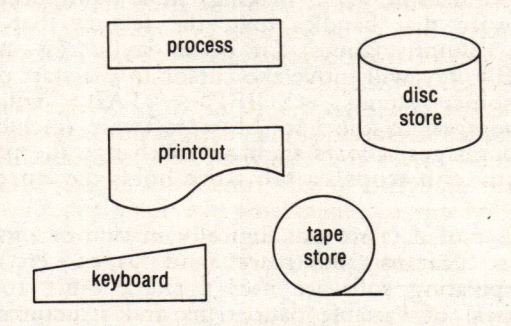

system. The main system flowchart symbols.

Systems software is the same as operating software (or operating system). A **system specification** is a detailed statement of the components of a system at the design stage: the hardware units, software required, staffing (so called liveware), even rooming, furniture and such where appropriate. See SYSTEM DESIGN above.

T

T, *symbol for* tera, a unit prefix that denotes a million million (10^{12}).

tab, *n.* (= tabulation, table making) in a word processor and other software that handles text, the feature that puts data items into columns (zones) for better layout (as in a table). The <TAB> key will move the cursor to the start of the next zone; in some systems, <SHIFT>+<TAB> will move it back to the zone to the left. Most software (including some program languages) allows the user to change the positions of the zones (the **tab stops**); a **tab store** holds the current values. See also RULER.

table, *n.* a set of data set out logically in two or more dimensions with columns and rows (and pages, etc.). An IT system's operating software uses a LABEL TABLE to hold the labels (names) of variable data items and structures, and the address that gives curent access to each. In software, the effect of a table follows the use of a spreadsheet or of an array within a program language. See also TAB. A **table plotter** is the same as a flat-bed plotter (one with the paper fixed flat).

tablet, *n.* an input unit on which one can write, draw or point; see GRAPHICS TABLET.

tag, *n.* **1.** see FLAG.
2. a label, of one or more characters, attached to a data item or data set that contains coded information about the item or set. A **tag file** is a second file that holds these tags and allows direct access to the tagged data; it is a kind of index, in other words. The contents of the tag file can be sorted separately; this **tag sort** is quicker than sorting the main file.
3. the price label on a product. A machine-readable price label offers clear benefits over others. Thus a **Kimball tag** is a type of punched card fixed to an item of clothing that carries machine-readable data as a pattern of holes. Some hotels (for instance) use key tags that involve the same approach.

tail, *n.* a flag that marks the end of a list or packet of data.

tape, *n.* a long ribbon used for data storage. See MAGNETIC TAPE, OPTICAL TAPE, PAPER TAPE, VIDEO TAPE. An open reel tape presents some handling problems; it is common, therefore, to pack the tape onto a spool in a **tape cartridge**, or two spools in a **tape cassette**. A **tape comparator** is a two-drive device that checks that the data stored on two tapes are identical. One tape may be a back-up of the other, for instance.

A **tape deck/drive** is a unit for holding a tape (or cartridge or cassette) with a system for drawing (driving) the tape past a read/write head. See DRIVE. **Tape density** refers to the concentration of data on a tape, e.g. the number of bytes per millimetre (tape is, in essence, a linear store).

Tapeless recording involves recording audio signals digitally on a computer's main and backing store (i.e. chips and/or disc). This offers far more powerful editing than working with digital or analog tape. **Tape limited** data processing occurs when the fairly slow speed of data transfers to and from tape backing store limits the overall speed of the whole process.

A **tape punch** is a device, used off- or on-line, which accepts data and converts it to patterns of holes punched in a paper tape. A **tape reader** scans the patterns and gives the corresponding data output. See PUNCHED MEDIA, a range of styles of backing storage that is very rare now.

A **tape streamer** is a fast moving magnetic tape used for backing up the contents of a hard disc (or pack). A streamer may be able to hold many tens of megabytes and to receive a backup in perhaps half an hour; streaming is, therefore, far more convenient for this purpose than using floppies. For **tape transport**, see tape drive (above). **Tape verifier** an alternative term for a tape comparator (also above).

target language, *n.* **1.** in machine translation, the human language into which the system is to translate the input.
2. an alternative term for OBJECT LANGUAGE, the machine language (usually machine code) into which a translating program translates its input. A **target program** is the same as an object program.

tariff, *n.* a system of charges made for a service. In IT, there is often a fixed (standing) charge or subscription, plus usage charges of various kinds. See, for instance, VIEWDATA.

task list, *n.* a list of the jobs a person hopes (or has) to do in the near future. Some desktop software packages include a utility to handle such lists effectively; they allow the user to enter and amend a task list, maybe with such extra data for each task as the time it may take and a prompt for an alarm.

TCM, *abbrev. for* TERMINAL TO COMPUTER MULTIPLEXER.

TDM, *abbrev. for* TIME DIVISION MULTIPLEXING.
TDMA, *abbrev. for* TIME DIVISION MULTIPLE ACCESS.
tele-, *prefix* denoting at a distance. Thus **telebooking** allows people to make bookings (e.g. for travel and theatre seats) while on line to a central computer. This must be a real-time process to avoid double bookings. Telebooking is offered by many viewdata systems, as well as being an essential tool for travel and ticket agents in many countries.

Telecommunications is the whole field of passing information and data as signals, streams, or packets, over a distance. There is no clear definition of the least distance concerned, but all methods in the field are part of 'new' information technology, i.e. they involve electricity at some stage.

A **telecommuter** is a person who works at home on information-based tasks (which very many are now), using IT for communications to offices and other people. IT offers many useful methods of communication in this context, all with advantages over mail and phone; for instance, email, teleconferring (above), and fax. People may prefer telecommuting to working in a distant office as they can work when and how they please; they also avoid the time and money costs of daily travel (commuting) and the intrusions of office life. On the other hand, telecommuting is a solitary style of working that does not suit everyone. Also, employers no longer face a united work-force, so may be tempted to keep pay rates low or avoid legal responsibilities.

Teleconferring (or more often, **teleconferencing**) systems provide a form of interactive bulletin board to users. The users log on when they wish (gain access to the host computer); they can then read the messages of others, comment on these, and add their own. Most teleconferences, like *face-to-face* (FTF) ones, have a number of topics for discussion; these appear in separate files, though it is normal to be able to copy a contribution from one to a second. Such a topic file should also be open to searching. Teleconferring is not a real-time method of communication; no system offers a method for the topic's moderator to control who should next contribute. Also, there may be problems that follow lack of eye-contact.

On the other hand, a teleconference can be of more value than an FTF one in that:

(a) each person may enter and leave at will;

(b) it is easy to scan through and select only the records that are relevant to a given user's needs;

TELEGRAPHY

 (c) the conference can last as long as people wish, even for months or years;
 (d) each person can obtain a hard copy or an editable disc copy of the records of interest;
 (e) once the hardware and software are in place, costs are low, even with 24-hour world-wide access.
 A **telecopier** is a rare name for a fax system (though commonly used in France.) The name follows the trade name of the first ones to link to the phone network (Xerox, early 1960s). **Telefax** is an absolute term for fax.

telegraphy, *n.* digital (coded) signals in the form of pulses of current in a wire which link sender and receiver. It first appeared early in the 19th century, well before telephony; it was thus a well developed system by the time the threat of the phone became real, and remains in wide use. The first telegraphs were point to point systems, i.e. a private dedicated line had to join each pair of stations. The concept is (in IT terms) almost ancient:
 (a) the first electric signal transfer (through a cotton 'wire') was in 1727 (UK);
 (b) the first system to meet success and to be based on the modern use of a low voltage battery rather than an electrostatic generator was developed almost a century later, in 1816, in the London garden of Francis Ronalds (1788–1873), who followed this a few months later with a 13 km telegraph;
 (c) the first effective long-distance telegraph was developed by William Cooke and Charles Wheatstone, UK in 1837.
 (d) the first effective long-distance telegraph was developed in the US by Samuel Morse in 1843, followed soon after by his telegraph signal coding system, which is still in use (see MORSE CODE);
 (e) the first scanned fax system (Alexander Bain, UK, 1842);
 (f) the first printing telegraph (US, 1845);
 (g) the first telegraph able to copy and transfer hand written input (F C Bakewell, UK, 1850);
 (h) the first successful transatlantic telegraph cable came into use in 1858.

Despite these developments, it was not until the 1930s that the concept of signal switching in a public network came into place. That was the birth of TELEX (= telegraph exchange). Only in the 1980s did telex, in any event a very costly affair, start to react to the threat from more modern communications methods using the world-wide phone system. The change may come too late; many people feel that telegraphy is doomed. Thus **telegrams** are no longer a major method of communication; these are telegraph messages, received and printed onto narrow sticky paper tape at a local station, and then delivered by the hand to the addressee.

telegroup, *n.* a number of people, maybe very widely apart in space and time, linked by their access to a teleconference service (see above).

telemetry, *n.* the making of measurements at a distance. It ranges from the transfer of signals from survey satellites, through the use of remote sensing to cover all the needs of a large factory, down to meters (e.g. gas, water) in homes and offices that the service company can interrogate for billing purposes. Early systems were photographic; one of the most important ones was invented by Francis Ronalds (above) in 1845 when he set up the automatic photographing of weather instruments at Kew Gardens.

tele-ordering, *n.* a modern form of mail order which allows users to order goods for delivery. It offers speed and reliability to people at home and in offices as well as to retailers.

telephone, *n.* a two-way voice communications unit; it is inexpensive but because it is linked to a world-wide network and therefore offers high-speed communication anywhere, it can be complex. A **telephone data set** is the same as a modem, i.e. a unit for linking a digital unit to a phone socket for the transfer of data through the network. For **telephone frequency**, see VOICE BAND. A **telephone handset** is the same as a telephone (above), i.e. the actual two-way voice communications unit itself. A telephone system needs to have:

  (a) a microphone to convert speech into electric signals;
  (b) a speaker for the reverse process;
  (c) a switch to access the line to the local exchange;
  (d) a method of calling the number of the other handset wanted (rotary dial or set of buttons);

Many modern handsets, however, offer a wealth of other features as microelectronics become so cheap and effective. Thus there may be:

  (a) a store for numbers the user often wants to call (from three or four to a hundred or more);
  (b) a store for the last number(s) called to make it easy to try again;
  (c) a digital display of time of day, number called, length and/or cost of current call, and (with ISDN) perhaps the

TELEPHONE

number of the line making an inward call;

(d) features such as automatic re-try (if a call doesn't get through);

(e) hands off features, such as on-hook calling and a speaker with a range of several metres rather than a few centimetres.

Handsets on extension lines in private branch exchanges may offer many more features (though most people seem not to make much use of these). As digital exchanges and ISDN spread, more and more of these will come to be on offer to handsets on exchange lines.

Portable telephones are of various types, the most important being wireless phones that can link to the main phone network. Radio phones as used on ships, for instance, and CELL phones are now under threat from CT2 systems (there being in Britain three incompatible versions by the end of the 1980s). A CT2 handset offers two-way links to the phone network when used within a few dozen metres of a special type of public access switching centre. These centres are in place in such busy places as rail stations, airports and motorway service stations.

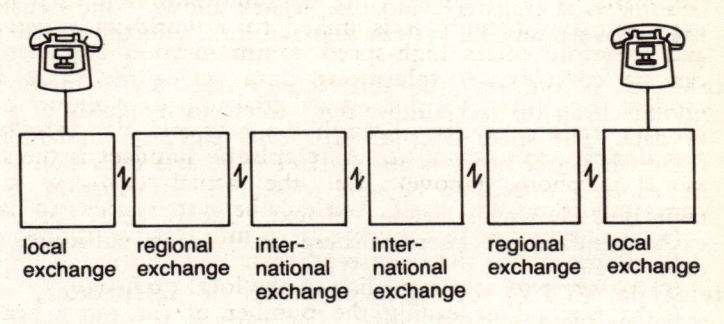

telephone. Phone networks have an hierarchy of exchanges.

The **telephone system** has often been called the world's largest network, see PSTN. By the early 1990s, not much more than a century after the first effective voice phone system (Alexander Graham Bell, 1876), the number of lines in the world approached 700 million; each has its own unique code (line number, or phone number). Insofar as each call is a point to point communication, i.e. there must be a direct link between the two handsets involved, the network must be

TELETEX

highly complex. In fact, each handset has its own line to the local **telephone exchange**, or SWITCHING CENTRE. This uses a particular method to connect a given line to any other in the local area, or to a trunk line that links it to another exchange. Most countries have a hierarchy of exchanges between local and international, with automatic switching on the basis of each line number called (see Figure).

Telephotography is yet another name for fax, also now rare, while a **teleprinter** is the common name for a teletypewriter (see below). **Teleprocessing** involves data communications as part of some data processing task, and **teleshoppping** is much the same as tele-ordering (see above), but is used specifically for retail goods such as food and clothing (rather than for items one can expect to take longer to arrive). **Telesoftware** is software (computer programs) a user can obtain or purchase through a telecommunications link, e.g. from teletext or viewdata.

teletex, *n.* a fairly modern cross between email and telex; while it offers many useful features it has come into widespread use in only a few countries in Europe. Based on international data transfer standards, teletex allows 8-bit signals to pass between any IT system that can link with the phone network.

teletext, *n.* one-way (non-interactive) VIDEOTEX; a method of giving cheap (in fact almost free) access to hundreds of pages of data. The spare lines of broadcast television signals carry these: all a user needs is an interface (e.g. in a television set or linked to a micro) to be able to see the information. Some countries, however, code teletext signals (e.g. of stock exchange data), so users wishing access must subscribe to a decoder.

teletype (TTY) or **teletypewriter** or **teleprinter,** *n.* a terminal on a telegraph line. The earliest versions were for data output only: printers that printed onto narrow paper tape the codes of an input signal (and, later, the characters the codes represented). After the telex network (below) started to spread, the machine came to offer output as well as input. By the middle of the 20th century it had a keyboard, paper tape punch, paper tape reader, and (perhaps) a typewriter style printer (but with paper on a long roll). Such a system made a useful terminal for the computer systems of the 1950s and 1960s, but now few appear in that role, and telex remains the main user. See also TELEVISION.

TELEVISION (TV)

television (TV), *n.* a technique for broadcasting moving video and sound to aerials linked to special receivers (**television sets**) in homes and elsewhere. See BAIRD for some historical notes. The principles are as follows.

(a) By a process of MODULATION, the combined video/audio signal from the source adds to a high frequency radio carrier. This passes to a transmit aerial for broadcast (but see also CABLE).

(b) As the modulated carrier passes each receive aerial, it induces a current in this. The current passes to the set; this amplifies the signal and then separates the carrier from the audio and video parts. As there are hundreds of such signals captured by the aerial, the user tunes the set to the frequency of the desired channel (carrier). The set amplifies only this signal.

(c) Amplified further as required, the audio signal passes to the speaker (or speakers if stereo).

(d) Also amplified further as required, the video signal passes to the cathode-ray tube (or other form of display). In the tube, during each fraction of a second, a beam of electrons scans the inner surface of the screen, dot by dot (see PIXEL) and line by line, to produce a FLYING SPOT. The video signal modulates the spot to build up each frame of the picture.

(e) The notes above describe how a monochrome (black and white) set receives and amplifies the signal. In a colour set, there are three electron beams, and each dot on the screen surface is in fact a triplet to output light of the three primary colours. See MASK, sense **3**.

World wide, there are three main TV standards. NTSC is the norm in North America and Japan; PAL is the most common; SECAM is the system in France, Greece, the countries of Eastern Europe and Soviet Asia, and the Middle East. These standards relate to the form of the transmitted TV signal, and therefore to the circuits in the sets. They are not compatible, but do not refer to the number of lines in a screen picture, or to the voltage and frequency of mains supply – all these are added complications. In some countries, chips are on offer to allow a TV set of a given standard to handle one or both the others. Work proceeds on a European standard (MAC), as well as on a true world-wide standard; the latter would also offer **high definition TV (HDTV)** with well over a thousand screen lines. In the early 1990s, the main contending systems were developed in Europe (not incompatible

TELEX

with MAC) and in Japan. On the other hand, a new system, also from Japan, gives near HDTV standard signals that a near normal TV set can work with; the camera works with 1125 lines, but the set displays each standard frame twice. To do this, the set needs only the store and some extra circuitry.

Current public television systems are analog (though may transfer through cable, for instance, in digital form). Fully digital television (as HDTV is) offers:

(a) much better quality pictures (with, for instance, no interference or noise);

(b) hi-fi stereo sound;

(c) several pictures on screen at once (which includes the 'picture in a picture' feature that lets the user monitor a second channel while watching the first;)

(d) interactivity;

(e) good automated and/or interactive links with recorders and with computer systems;

(f) voice control, even through the phone;

(g) storage for one or more frames;

(h) much improved TELETEXT. See also VIDEO.

telex (TX), *n.* the major type of TELEGRAPHY in public use. Widespread use only followed the introduction of telegraph switching in the 1930s which led to the development of a world-wide telex (= telegraph exchange) network, with some two million users at the system's peak in the late 1980s. Such a small number of users of a world-wide network means that capital and running costs are very high. Until the late 1980s, telex, like point to point telegraphy, used a five-bit (Baudot) code for data transfer. This is highly restrictive in the character set offered: a telex message, like a telegram, is in upper case only and can include no more than a few special symbols. Telex, in that standard form, is slow too; the system can transfer a message at a rate of only about one word a second.

The 1990s will see the spread of a more effective style of telex: faster data transfers, and using eight bits rather than five to allow far more characters. Telex machines are coming to look more and more like word processors too, and to offer features of those and of modern phones. All the same, many people doubt that telex will succeed in keeping its current market share, in view of competition from fax and email in particular.

teller, *n.* a member of a bank's counter staff, an AUTO-TELLER MACHINE (ATM) being a cash dispensing machine (often also able to give users access to other services).

tera-, (T) *unit prefix* that denotes 10^{12} (a million million), as, for instance, in teraflops, a million million floating-point operations per second (a measure of super-computer speed).

terminal, *n.* an input/output unit with little or no IN-TELLIGENCE; it gives a user access to a remote computer. In the 1950s and 1960s, a terminal was the only way a user could gain on-line access to a computer (main frame or, later, mini; there were no micros then) at not too great a cost. See TELE-TYPE for details of those machines: they consisted of little more than a poor keyboard and a poor printer. Since then, terminals have lost their punched paper tape handling units and have gained improved printers and keyboards, and screens. More significantly, they have gained more and more intelligence (local processing power and main store), and even backing store. Thus a modern terminal looks much like a stand alone micro and needs less and less access to the central computer. In turn, that central computer needs less and less power set aside for the needs of terminal users and the whole system merges into a NETWORK.

In a tree, a **terminal node** is a leaf(let), a node with no children (dependents). A **terminal to computer multiplexer (TCM)** is a MULTIPLEXER used to link a number of lines to individual terminals into a single line to the central computer. **Terminal transparency** describes the compatibility a multi-user system may offer when working with terminals that handle (e.g. code) data in different ways.

terminate and stay resident (TSR) program, *n.* see TSR.

terminator, *n.* **1.** a code that marks the end of a logical line in a computer program (e.g. the semicolon in Pascal and related program languages).
2. a program in a batching or multi-programming system that carries out the various housekeeping tasks needed at the end of each job.

termination, *n.* the end of a job or program run.

ternary, *adj.* concerned with three-state systems and data transfers, and therefore described in terms of base 3 numbers (0 1 2). Such systems are rare, and are significantly more complex than those using binary.

test, *vb.* to carry out various tasks on a hardware or software system, in order to assess how well it meets the design brief. When testing a program, **test data** is the set of data input to the program, chosen to check important special cases. The tester (possibly a systems analyst) should choose test data with great care, and then check each output against what it should be. Testing a new data processing system involves much the same approach.

text, *n.* any information in the form of words and (in most cases) sentences and paragraphs, etc. As IT makes progress, it becomes more and more common to include graphics as a component of a text (document). **Text editing** either

(a) is a better name for word processing; or

(b) uses a special program to develop an assembly or high level language program (viewed by user and software as text in the way defined above). Such a program may be a line editor, a character editor, or a screen (page) editor; this depends on what the software views the basic unit of the 'text' to be.

Like text editing (above), **text management** and **text processing** sometimes appear as names for word processing, a **text management system** being a word processor or a method for handling text files to allow document access. For **text reader/processor**, see OPTICAL CHARACTER READING (OCR). **Text retrieval** is the process of searching through files where the records are texts (e.g. references, abstracts, papers). See INDEXING.

thermal, *adj.* denoting anything concerned with heat (thermal energy). A **thermal printer** (the most common type in the case of fax machines, and also used in some other systems) needs special (**thermal sensitive**) paper. This has a coating of two separate colourless layers, one of which is a latent dye. Heat from a pin in the print head melts these at that point and the two substances mix to produce colour. Black and blue are the most common (though other colours exist); all, however, lack stability to a degree and the image tends to fade with time (especially if exposed to light). Head wear is also a problem.

In a **thermal transfer** printer, the system feeds a ribbon coated with thermoplastic ink past the plain paper. Heat from the head melts and transfers a dot of ink from one to the other. This is a very quiet and reliable printer. One form is a type of page printer where the head consists of an array of (say) 1024 pins to span the whole print width of the paper.

thermography, *n.* a process used in some forms of letterpress printing to give an embossed appearance to the characters. Printing uses a heated ink that is slow to dry; after printing, the system dusts the sheet with a plastics powder (toner). When next heated, the two combine and swell, as well as bonding to the sheet surface.

thesaurus, *n.* **1.** a collection of words (and perhaps phrases) and synonyms (which have roughly the same meaning), and perhaps antonyms (with the opposite meaning). In IT, this can be held in store and accessed by a key press from suitable software (e.g. a word processor). The purpose of a thesaurus is to help a writer choose how best to express ideas.
2. a structured set of index terms used in document INDEXING. This too may provide synonyms to help searchers. See also AUTHORITY FILE and AUTOMATED THESAURUS.

thimble printer, *n.* a fairly rare form of impact printer with the characters in the character set embossed on the surface of a head rather like a thimble. For each character printed, this twists and nods to bring the correct character to the ribbon. The system is slow and noisy, it cannot handle graphics and, for a different character set, the user must stop printing and insert a new thimble. Compare DAISYWHEEL PRINTER.

thin film, *n.* a type of magnetic storage system once fairly common for main store. See MAGNETIC FILM. **A thin window** is a small liquid crystal display (e.g. 16 or 24 characters in a line) used with some electronic typewriters to show the last few characters typed. The system gives the typist a chance to change the input before it reaches the paper. Such displays are also common on printers, copiers, fax machines and pocket computers.

third generation, *n.* an IT GENERATION in which the systems were the first to use simple integrated circuits rather than discrete transistors and diodes for switching and storage.

third party data base, *n.* a data base in a host computer to which viewdata users do not have direct access; they access their normal viewdata host, then pass through a bridge to the data they want.

thrashing, *n.* a case of usage of OVERLAYS where overlays need to come through from backing store to main store at such a rate that processing speed suffers.

three input adder, *n.* an ADDER able to accept and process three inputs at the same time; if these consist of bits from two numbers and a carry bit, this is the same as a full adder.

throughput, *n.* a jargon term for (rate of) data transfer through a processing system from input to output (with processing as required on the way).

TIE LINE

tie line, *n.* a line that carries signals only between two points, in the same way as a private line. A **tie trunk** is a trunk line between two exchanges (see TELEPHONE).

time, *n.* a crucial feature of any type of processing or transfer. There are two aspects: the time for a given action to take place, and the time period over which a process occurs. **Time assignment speech interpolation** allows voice and data to pass through a given channel; the data transfers take place during the pauses in the speech signals. A set of **time coded pages** in a videotex data base all bear the same page number. The display cycles through them at a fixed rate as they show successive blocks of information (compare CAROUSEL); the user joins the sequence at the page displayed at that moment and can leave at any time.

In MULTIPLEXING, a **time derived channel** is one with an increased signal capacity as a result of time division multiplexing (see below). This latter is not the same as **time division multiple access (TDMA)** which is a method of sharing a processor's time between the work of users on a number of terminals. In a **time division multiplexing (TDM)** system, a number of digital signals share one channel by taking turns; for instance, eight signals can pass at once, a byte from each at a time. See TDM and MULTIPLEXING. A **time out** is:

(a) when a system gives up waiting for an input or action: e.g. multi-user operating software breaks the link to a given terminal after a pre-set time (perhaps a minute) if nothing comes through. See also ABORT TIMER.

(b) the time between sending a signal along a channel and getting the acknowledgement of receipt.

Time sharing (or **time slicing**) is how the operating software of a multi-user or multi-processing system divides processor attention between the different tasks. It gives the processor a fixed time slot (e.g. one hundredth of a second) for each task in turn. As a result (in the case of multi-usage), each user can feel the system is working on those tasks alone.

TLQ, *abbrev. for* total letter quality, sales jargon for the highest quality dot printout.

token, *n.* **1.** a code that replaces a key word when a high-level program language accepts an instruction. The translator has a table of its set of key words and their tokens; this also helps it detect at once if the key word entered is not in the set (giving a syntax error message).

2. a set of bits in a certain kind of network that, when re-

TRACE

ceived by a station, allows the station to send information. As the network contains only one token, this process of **token passing** from station to station prevents clashes between signals. The kind of network that uses this approach is a **token ring**.

toll, *n.* **1.** an alternative term for TRUNK (a line that links two exchanges in a phone network).
2. a charge made by some phone networks when someone links to them from outside or from them to outside. A **toll free** call of the latter type incurs no such long-distance charge (the recipient pays).

tone, *n.* **1.** a shade of grey in a multi-tone image (see GREY SCALE and compare with HALF TONE).
2. a sound used as a signal for users of a telephone network, e.g. a dialling tone or line engaged tone. **Tone dialling** is the use of tones to signal a number to an exchange, in contrast to the sets of pulses still widely used for this purpose. The tones are produced by pressing the keys on a keypad handset. Not all exchanges can accept tone dialling, and a keypad handset can include a switch to produce pulses, if these are the only signals an exchange will accept.

top down development/programming, *n.* an approach to program development and coding which builds up more and more detail on an initial outline. The programmer breaks the starting concept into a set of stages, and repeats this process until able to code each stage as a program procedure or module. See STRUCTURE.

touch screen, *n.* an input unit that combines a display screen with a method of sensing where the user's finger is. Some types cover the screen with a transparent conducting surface (see, for example, ELECTRONIC GLASS), while others surround it with a matrix of infrared lamps and photocells. In either case, the input aspect of the display is, in effect, a grid of squares; it is the task of software to convert the signals into a coordinate and decide on action.

trace, *vb.* to follow the action of a program through in a structured way, so that the programmer can detect errors in program control (logic errors). This may be done by working through a dry run, in which the programmer takes input data sets in turn and passes manually through the program listing. On the other hand, many program languages provide some kind of trace utility to show on screen or paper which steps the run goes through. In either case, a **trace table** is useful.

TRACK

This shows how the values of variable data items change during a run.

track, *n*. **1.** a stretch along a paper tape that may carry holes when punched (see PUNCHED MEDIA). Paper-tape systems used to allow for anything from five to nine tracks. One set of hole positions in the tracks across the tape width would carry one word of data.
2. (sometimes called **band**) a stretch of a MAGNETIC MEDIUM accessed by a single magnetic read/write head. In the case of magnetic tape and stripe (as with paper tape, above), there are several tracks (often nine), each with a head to record and access data; again, the width of the tape carries one word of data (see Figure). The tracks on a magnetic disc are concentric circles on the surface (see also CYLINDER). The tracks on a magnetic drum were also circles, round the circumference. Much the same applies to OPTICAL MEDIA (tape, stripe, disc).

track(er) ball, *n*. an input device, somewhat like an upside-down mouse. A tracker ball takes up less space than a MOUSE, but many people find it harder to use. However, some keyboards have tracker balls set into the surface (as some have a joystick or paddle).

tractor feed, *adj*. denoting a method of feeding continuous paper through a printer, using sprocket holes along each edge. See also PINFEED.

traffic, *n*. the signals that pass through a channel; the more signals there are, and the more data they contain, the heavier the traffic. **Traffic control** sometimes refers to the control of input and output signals in an IT system; its concern is to achieve correct and orderly movement of data, so it covers both the hardware and the software involved.

trail, *n*. a type of trace that gives a record of the steps followed by a system as it carries out some task. An **audit trail** was originally a trail within a financial data processing system; the term now tends to refer to a log of any process that involves resources.

trailer, *n*. a set of codes at the end of a sequence of related data, e.g. a file of records. The trailer not only marks the end of the sequence, but is likely to give summary information (e.g. the number of records and check sum).

train, *n*. a sequence of pulses, perhaps all or part of a signal.

training, *n*. the process of demonstrating the workings of a system to a new user. This is a highly crucial aspect of

TRAINING

not to scale

Track	Value	T	e	s	t	i	n	g		1	,		2	,		3	!
9	parity (odd)	0	1	0	1	1	0	0	1	0	0	1	0	0	1	1	1
8	128	0	0	0	0	0	0	0	0	0	0	0	0	0	0	0	0
7	64	1	1	1	1	1	1	1	0	0	0	0	0	0	0	0	0
6	32	0	1	1	1	1	1	1	1	1	1	1	1	1	1	1	1
5	16	1	0	1	1	0	0	0	0	1	0	0	1	0	0	1	0
4	8	0	0	1	0	1	1	0	0	0	1	0	0	1	0	0	0
3	4	1	1	0	1	0	1	1	0	0	1	0	0	1	0	0	0
2	2	0	0	1	0	0	1	1	0	0	0	0	1	0	0	1	0
1	1	0	1	1	0	1	0	1	0	1	0	0	0	0	0	1	1
Character		T	e	s	t	i	n	g		1	,		2	,		3	!
Ascii code		84	101	115	116	105	110	103	32	49	44	32	50	44	32	51	33

track (sense 2.). Bits in the tracks of a magnetic tape.

343

TRANSACTION

implementing a new system (style of working in the widest sense); the staff concerned need to learn how to use the new system, and how to relate it to what they used to do. Also, training helps staff feel less threatened by new a system, and so is an aspect of user friendliness.

transaction, *n.* a single individual action or event that relates to the content of a file or data base, i.e. one that requires the up-dating of a record. In the case of a stock file, transactions would include details of sales and deliveries, changes of some aspect of a product, new products, and products no longer on offer. During each trading period a firm will build up a **transaction file**; every so often the system will sort this and merge it with the master file to produce a new master (see file GENERATION sense 1.).

Transaction processing is a crucial task for any system which allows a number of users write-access to the same files. Without care, major failures of data integrity will occur. A **transaction report** is a log of such transactions as those above, or, indeed, any log.

trans-border data flow, *n.* the transfer of information between countries. This has a variety of legal implications as well as practical ones (e.g., relating to privacy of personal data).

transceiver, *n.* any unit or terminal able to transmit and receive (output and input) data or signals. A **transceiver cable** links this to a channel.

transcribe, *vb.* to copy data from one medium to a second. A **transcriber** is a person or machine that can do this, and **transcription** is the process.

transducer, *n.* a device or unit which converts energy from one type to a second, i.e. whose input and output are in different forms. SENSORS, which always have an electrical output, are an important type of transducer.

transfer, *n.* or *vb.* passing energy, data or information from one place to a second, **transfer rate** being a measure of the speed at which this happens. **Transfer time** is the time between the start of a transfer and its finish. See also TRANSMISSION.

transistor, *n.* a semiconductor device the output of which is under the control of signals applied to one or more input contacts. A **bipolar transistor** is the most common simple type. This has three layers of semi-conductor, the central, very thin,

TRANSISTOR

layer being of opposite type ('polarity') from the other two. Figure 1 shows the two main kinds, PNP and NPN (see SEMI-CONDUCTOR), with their symbols, and the names for the three contacts.

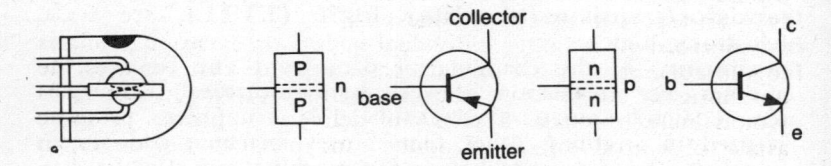

transistor. Fig. 1. Bipolar transistors.

A transistor behaves, in essence, as two PN junctions (DIODES) back to back. In normal usage, the system forward biases the base-emitter junction (giving it low resistance) and reverse biases the collector-base junction (so it has a high resistance to current). Then a signal of small amplitude at the base (input) gives a signal of large amplitude on the emitter-collector current (output): the bipolar transistor is a current amplifier. In a suitable circuit it also acts as a very fast switch (i.e., relay), and its other main use is as an oscillator: with feedback between output and input it will produce an output wave of fixed amplitude and frequency.

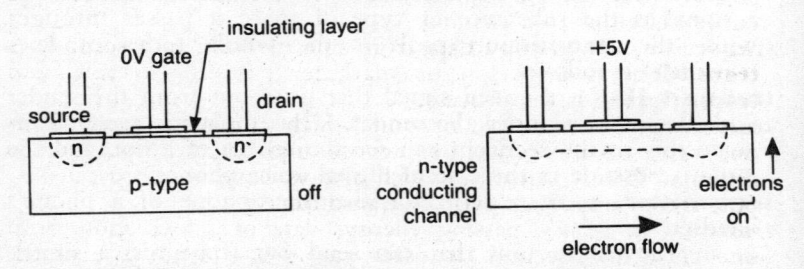

transistor. Fig. 2. Switching and insulated gate field effect transistor.

A **field-effect transistor (FET)** has a channel of semiconductor whose resistance depends on the voltage input(s) at one or more gate(s). Such transistors are, therefore, voltage-controlled. See MOS (metal-oxide semiconductor transistor), of

345

TRANSISTOR/TRANSISTOR LOGIC (TTL)

which there are two main types: NMOS and PMOS, depending on whether the channel is n-type or p-type. Whichever it is, it is a **uni-polar transistor**. See Figure 2.

transistor/transistor logic (TTL), see LOGIC (ELECTRONIC LOGIC).

transistor/transistor/transistor logic (TTTL), see LOGIC (electronic logic).

translation, *n*. the changing of data from one language to another. For translation between human (natural) languages, see COMPUTER-AIDED TRANSLATION. A computer program written in anything other than binary machine code needs translation to that code before the machine can carry it out. The amount of translation depends on the level of the source program language. Numeric (e.g. denary or hex) machine codes need little translation; programs in assembly language need rather more; high-level programs require a great deal. See also COMPILER and INTERPRETER; like an ASSEMBLER, these are translators (programs that carry out software translation).

transmission, *n*. the passing of data from one place to a second (the same as data transfer), or the signal concerned. **Transmission errors** are faults that appear in the data during transfer; various systems are able to detect and correct these to some degree. A **transmission line** is a data transfer channel, while **transmission loss** is the drop in the power of the signal during transfer (see also REGENERATOR for digital signals, and REPEATER for analog transfers). The **transmission medium** of a signal is the substance or type of space it passes through, while the **tranmission path** is the whole series of lines (channels) it follows.

transmit ID, *n*. a coded signal that goes out from the sender with details to identify the sender. Thus most fax systems include this so the recipient can see the source of a fax, and the same is possible in the case of digital voice phones.

transmitter, *n*. **1.** a term for the microphone of a phone's handset.

2. any device or unit that can send out (transmit) a signal. Various types of **transmitter cards** convert parallel data from an IT system into serial form, for transmission (and the other way for reception); see, for instance, USART.

trans-national data flow, *n*. an alternative term for trans-border data flow, the transfer of data between countries.

transparency, *n*. **1.** in a transferred signal, a feature of a bit pattern (or patterns) that makes it seem to the receiver like a control code. This similarity may cause errors at the receiving end. **Transparent data** does not appear to the receiver to contain control codes.

2. a feature of any action in an IT system that takes place without the human user being aware of it.

3. a feature of any combination of a program, and the data it needs to run, that makes it simpler for the user to work with.

transponder, *n.* a device or unit able both to receive and to transmit signals or data, where the output ('response') relates in some way to the input. It is the same in essence as a transceiver, apart from the relation between input and output. Many types of vehicle, up to and including satellites, have a transponder; this will automatically identify the vehicle on receipt of an interrogating signal. In communications satellites, a transponder receives an input signal, amplifies it, and returns it at a different frequency (and, often, with a different beam width).

Most such satellites have several transponders which allow them to handle more than one signal at a time, though a single one can also handle a number of transfers at once. By the late 1980s, some 50 communications satellites were in orbit, working with a total of almost 800 transponders; each can carry at least one colour television channel, or 1500 phone/fax calls, or data at 50 million bits per second. The difference of frequency between input and output is to prevent the strong output signal interfering with the weak input.

transport, *n.* in the case of tape backing storage, the same as DRIVE. Some people also speak of **data transport** or **document transport**, i.e. the movement of data or documents from place to place in an IT system. A network protocol may include a **transport layer**; see, for instance, OSI. The function of this is to provide the next layer with data at a set rate, and to convert a continuous stream into packets (and vice versa) as needed.

transputer, *n.* a powerful 32-bit RISC processor, with associated main store, on a single chip. The main aim of its design has been to allow its easy use within a set of such transputers to form a parallel processor. Launched in 1985 by the British company Inmos, the chip includes communications functions to aid that purpose. In itself, though, it works up to ten times faster than other 32-bit chips. New transputers are expected to provide processing speeds of 100 Mips and 20 Mflops, and data transfer rates of 100 megabits per second; they should also be easier to work with.

TRANSVERSE SCANNING

transverse scanning, *n*. an approach to the scanning of a magnetic (or other) tape by a head to allow a greater density of data storage. Used in many videotape recorders, this involves scanning at an angle across the tape; thus the head can cover a great distance in a short length of tape. See also HELICAL SCANNING.

traversal, *n*. a method of working through all the nodes and leaves (i.e. all the data items) in a tree structure. There are three styles, called IN-ORDER TRAVERSAL, pre-order, and post-order. When the traverse is of a parse tree that represents an arithmetic expression, these relate to infix, prefix (Polish) and postfix (reverse Polish) notations.

tree, *n*. a finite set of one or more nodes, with a root node, and then one or more sub-trees. In an **ordered tree** the order of the nodes in the sub-trees is significant. A tree is a hierarchical structure; you can view it logically either as a tree inverted as a directed branching graph or as a series of sets and subsets. See Figure: on the left, tree as graph, and on the right, tree as set and subsets. A **binary tree** can have no more than two descendants from each node.

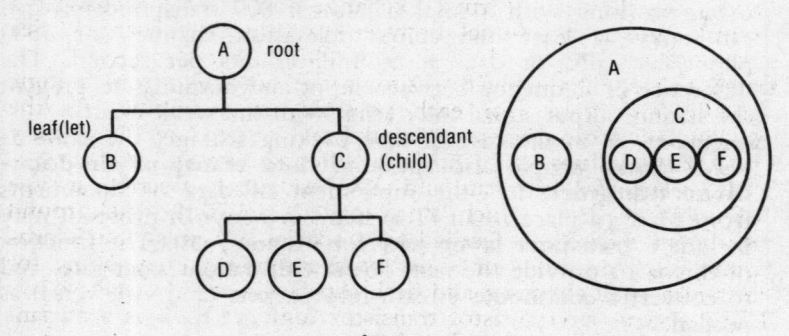

tree.

Trees appear in a number of contexts in IT theory, and not just to show hierarchical relationships and data structures. For example, **grammar trees** represent the syntax of human (natural) and the simpler program languages for the purpose of parsing and translation. A **tree search** is a method of searching a tree-like data structure for given data. See also TRAVERSAL, a method of listing all the nodes.

triad, *n*. any group of three with some significance, e.g. three bits or three characters.

tribit, *n.* a significant group of three bits (a triad of bits).

truncation, *n.* **1.** in information retrieval, cutting the suffix from a search term to leave the stem, and then searching on the basis of that. The stem of computation, compute, computed, computer, computes, computing is comput, and is likely to be a more effective search term than any of the others individually.
2. in computer arithmetic, cutting from a number the least significant bits (digits) to allow the system to store the number in the space available. This may or may not involve ROUNDING, but in any event may lead to a **truncation error**; here the loss of information caused by truncation becomes significant to the data user.

trunk, *n.* a channel that links two switching centres (exchanges) in a telecommunications network. It may be short (between centres in the same suburb), or long (such as a transatlantic cable or satellite link). A **trunk exchange** is an exchange which controls the switching of trunk calls between other exchanges (see TELEPHONE SYSTEM). A **trunk junction** is a channel between a trunk exchange and a local exchange; a **trunk line** is a channel between two trunk exchanges. See also TOLL.

truth table, *n.* a table that shows the output(s) from a logic circuit (e.g. GATE) for each possible set of inputs. As the circuit is a logic circuit, all inputs and outputs can have only two **truth values**, true and false, often shown as 1 and 0.

TSR, *abbrev. for* terminate and stay resident; it describes a type of utility program which, once loaded, sits in the background ready for action when called by a special key-press. Such programs are common for some types of micro; they offer, for instance, spell checking and desk top facilities.

TTL, *abbrev. for* transistor/transistor logic. **TTTL** is a variant with a third transistor at the output to reduce noise and improve gain. See LOGIC (ELECTRONIC LOGIC).

TTY, *abbrev. for* TELETYPE(WRITER).

tube, 1. *abbrev. for* **electron tube**, any thermionic device (in some countries, screen) such as valve or cathode-ray tube.
2. *n.*, a name in some IT hardware systems for a local (i.e., short run) high capacity data transfer channel.

Turing, Alan (1912–1954), a British mathematician who developed detailed and precise theories of computability (data processing principles). He was able to put these into practice

TURN-AROUND DOCUMENT

to some extent, by supervising the design and building of the ACE computer. An algorithm is **Turing computable** if one can design a Turing machine to work through it. A **Turing machine** (1936) is an automaton, a theoretical device with two or more possible states, and which can react to an input to produce an output. The Turing machine sits on a tape of infinite length, and starts in a given state. It can read a word from, and write a word to, the cell in the tape at its current location, and also move step by step either way along the tape. It therefore represents a programmable data processor with input and output features. A **universal Turing machine** can model the behaviour of any other Turing machine. The Turing machine concept was crucial to the design and programming of early computers, and still has value in the field of MACHINE INTELLIGENCE.

There too, the **Turing test** (1950) is of interest. A room contains two terminals, one linked to a computer and one remotely controlled by a person. If a person using the two terminals in the room cannot decide which terminal is machine controlled, we can credit the computer with intelligence. Hence the definition of machine intelligence, i.e. working in such a way that requires intelligence in a person. No machine has yet passed the Turing test in general, but many systems can do so in a limited field (e.g. playing chess).

turn-around document, *n.* a form of document output by a computer that is used as a form for people to record information; the document then returns to the computer, which reads the new data as input. The approach is common in billing for utilities (services such as phone, gas, water); the bill has a tear-off slip which contains such data as client code and amount due, in OCR characters. On receipt from the client, the amount paid is typed in, again in OCR characters, and the computer can now accept the data. The use of MICR on cheques and similar papers offers the same kind of data capture.

Many fax systems offer **turn-around polling**. This is the fax equivalent of chat mode; the polled machine then polls the poller, perhaps sending a document back on request. **Turn-around time** is:

(a) the time taken after a job goes to a computer to get the results back;

(b) the time needed to change the direction of data transfer in a half-duplex channel.

turnkey, *adj.* **1.** denoting an IT system which is so transparent (see TRANSPARENCY), that the user need have no special knowledge at all to work with it.
2. denoting an IT system delivered to the user completely ready to run as required.

turtle, *n.* a small floor robot working under the control of a computer (or its own internal microprocessor). Some turtles are on offer as toys; others are of great value in education to show the principles of control and programming. In that latter context, screen turtles (which may be no more than cursors shaped as arrows) provide for most of the learner's needs; they are cheaper and less trouble to work with too. **Turtle graphics** is a subset of many educational program languages. This approach to screen graphics involves LOGO-like commands and routines to produce designs on the display (and printout). Many turtle graphics systems can also control floor turtles fitted with pens for drawing on large sheets of paper.

twisted pair, see TWO-WIRE CIRCUIT.

two-input adder, *n.* an ADDER capable of handling only two inputs, and therefore not able to deal with carries: an alternative term for half-adder.

two-way pager, *n.* a PAGER from which the user can send at least a very simple signal (e.g. to acknowledge receipt of an inward message).

two-wire circuit or **twisted pair,** *n.* a common physical link for data transfer. Simple and cheap, this is common in local phone and computer networks; it consists of two insulated metal wires, and allows half or full duplex working. It is rare, however, to be able to induce a twisted pair to carry data at a greater rate than a few million bits per second; the distance it can carry signals is limited too.

twos (2s) complement, *n.* one greater than a number's 1s COMPLEMENT. Using numbers in 2s complement form allows a system to add values with the effect of subtraction. Forming the 2s complement of a binary number involves flipping the bits (changing 0s to 1s and 1s to 0s, to give the 1s complement) and adding 1. The result is a sign and magnitude number, with 1 in the leftmost place for a negative value and 0 there for zero and any positive number. As well as helping a computer to subtract simply, this makes it easy to convert a number between positive and negative form.

TX, *abbrev. for* TELEX.

typamatic feature, *n.* the auto-repeat feature of most modern

TYPE

keyboards; i.e. when you hold down a key, its output repeats.

type 1. or **key,** *vb*. to enter data into an IT system using a keyboard. A **type-ahead buffer** is a store that holds the codes for the key presses in such a way as to allow the operator to enter data more quickly than the system can cope with it (up to a possible limit of 16 values).

2. *n*. originally a small block of wood or metal that carried an embossed reverse image of a character for printing, or the whole set of such blocks used by a printer (body type). The term has come to mean the output of such forms of printing (letter press), and subsequently of any form. A **typeface** is a character's style (design or shape), while a **type font** or **fount** is the full set of characters in one face and of one size. Many different typefaces are available, and are distinguished by different names, such as Plantin, Times, Helvetica and so on.

typesetting, *n*. the conversion of a text into the characters of a particular typeface. It is not usually the typesetter that prints a typeset text (as a finished book, magazine et al.). This is normally the business of a printer, who most often binds the finished product also.

typo (short for **typographical error**) or **literal,** *n*. an error in printing or in keyboarding (the action of typing data into a system).

U

UART, *abbrev.* for universal asynchronous receiver/transmitter, a chip which converts both ways between serial and parallel in an interface with an asynchronous device. The most comon usage is at the join of a peripheral and a data transfer channel. Compare with USRT (which works with synchronous data), and with USART (which handles both).

UCS, *abbrev. for* any UNIVERSAL CHARACTER SET.

UHF, *abbrev. for* ultrahigh frequency, a band of RADIO waves, also often used for television broadcasts, in the frequency range 30–300 MHz.

ULA, *abbrev, for* UNCOMMITTED LOGIC ARRAY: see WAFER.

ULSI, *abbrev. for* ultra large scale INTEGRATION, a chip design that involves hundreds of thousands of elements per integrated circuit.

ultra-, *prefix* beyond or surpassing a specified range, extent or limit.

ultrafiche, *n.* a microfiche of standard size, but with such small images that a single one contains thousands rather than hundreds of pages.

ultrahigh frequency (UHF), see UHF.

ultra large scale integration (ULSI), see ULSI.

ultra-/super-fine mode, *n.* a non-standard system of fax transfer with higher resolution than normal. This is useful for documents with fine detail (e.g., drawings and text in small handwriting), but, being non-standard, works only if the system at the other end is of the same type as the sender.

ultrasonic, *adj.* denoting sound (audio) waves with frequencies above about 30 kHz (i.e., too high for normal human hearing). In industry, but not in IT, there are various uses for ultra-sonic waves of frequency above 1 MHz.

ultraviolet (UV), *adj.* denoting waves in the electromagnetic SPECTRUM on the high frequency side of visible light. The wavelength range is $10 - 10^3$ nm (1 nm = 10^{-9} m). The energy content of ultraviolet is high (and therefore poses dangers to people); but so too is the information carrying power. For this reason, a great deal of research goes on into UV carriers.

umbrella, *n.* an information provider for a viewdata system which supplies a service to other information providers.

unary, *adj.* denoting a function or operation with only one argument or operator, i.e. the same as monadic. Most common functions (e.g. SIN, SORT) are unary, but this is not so in the case of operators; examples of unary operators are the negative sign (as in −1) and the NOT operation of, for instance, NOT flag.

unbundling, *n.* the pricing of software separately from the hardware it tends to come with. Bundling involves charging a single price for a hardware item and a set of operating (and, in recent years, applications) software. Bundling has become less common as hardware prices fall but those of software rise.

uncommitted logic array (ULA), *n.* a part-made chip which is simple (and cheap) to customize; in manufacture the topmost layer is not added until the maker knows the needs of each individual client.

unconditional jump, *n.* a move outside the normal incremental flow of a program, the move being made when the program reaches that step, no matter what the circumstances. (A conditional jump, e.g. with any instruction that needs a decision, may or may not happen at that step; it depends on the circumstances.)

underflow, *n.* the effect of an arithmetic process which gives a result smaller than the smallest value a given IT system can handle. The system would therefore hold the value as zero, but, as this would not be correct, calls for an interrupt instead. Compare with OVERFLOW. Modern systems rarely meet overflow or underflow; this is because of their large word lengths compared with those of machines before the 1980s.

uninterruptable power supply (UPS), *n.* a device that sits between an IT system and its mains feed, with the aim of keeping the system running if power supply faults occur. An UPS should filter out surges and spikes, top up the power during a brown-out, and replace it during a cut. The device contains a continuously recharged battery; this should be able to keep the system running for the few minutes the user needs to back up current data.

unipolar, *adj.* denoting a type of TRANSISTOR design in which only one type of charge carrier is important. MOS devices, like the n-channel FET, are major examples.

unit buffer system, *n.* a peripheral, e.g. terminal, with no input/output buffer.

uniterm index, *n.* an approach to INDEXING which describes each document by a single index term for retrieval.

Univac, *n.* a computer from the Sperry group, the first (Univac I) coming on the market in 1951, just after the first commercial computer, the Ferranti I.

universal, *adj.* implying an international standard (but rarely so in practice). For **universal asynchronous receiver/transmitter (UART),** see UART. There are several so called **universal character sets (UCSs)** (such as ASCII), while the **universal product code (UPC)** is only one of a number of coding systems for products to which a bar code (for instance) can then be applied.

The **universal Turing machine** is an executive program for all Turing machines: given two input numbers, x and y (where x is the result of encoding Turing machine X), the output is the same as that of taking y as the input to X.

unjustified text, *n.* a block of words on screen or paper with a ragged right margin. See JUSTIFICATION.

unprotected field, *n.* an area of store, the contents of which can be changed: e.g., part of a screen display, or a field in a record of a file.

up-, *prefix.* indicating movement to a higher (or newer) level. An **updatable microfiche** is one where the contents can be changed (in most cases by some system of cross-referring), an **up-date** in any context being a newer version of something. For example, an **update file** is a newer version of a file, produced, perhaps, by an update process of merging the older version with a transaction file.

An **up(ward)-link** in a network or system with terminals is a link from a station to the centre or to a station that is closer to the centre. To **upload** data is to pass it through such a link, e.g. from a micro to a network's host computer. Compare DOWNLOAD. See also UPSTREAM.

upper case, *n.* symbols or capital letters accessed by means of a SHIFT KEY. Compare LOWER CASE.

UPC, *abbrev. for* UNIVERSAL PRODUCT CODE, a widely used (but not genuinely universal) system for giving a unique code to every product for sale to aid POS operations and stock checking at all retail outlets.

UPS, *abbrev. for* an UNINTERRUPTABLE POWER SUPPLY.

upstream, *adv.* to a higher or newer level. An upstream transfer in a cable television network is data or signal transfer towards the centre (e.g., sending a video signal from home or office to the network centre for all users to access). See also UP-LINK and UP-LOAD. A system's **up-time** is the fraction of a period during which it is working ('**up and running**') as it should (compare DOWN-TIME). A hardware or software system offers **upward compatibility** if data can transfer between it and a newer version. See COMPATIBILITY.

USART, *abbrev. for* universal synchronous/asynchronous receiver/transmitter, a chip with the same function as a UART or USRT, but able to work with both synchronous and asynchronous signals.

user, *n.* the person (or group) working with an IT system to meet individual defined needs. In a multi-user system, a **user area** is the segment of store that holds one user's programs and other data (and, often, mailbox).

User documentation is the set of instructions to help the user work with a given hardware system or program package. Alas, being often written by technical experts (such as system designers), such documentation may be far less helpful than it should be. Indeed, writing good user documentation is a crucial aspect of **user friendliness**, the technique of making a user feel at ease. See FRIENDLINESS.

A **user group** is an informal club for people who use the same hardware or software product(s). The members are able to help each other with problems, e.g. by help lines and a paper or on-line magazine; they also feel able to apply pressure to the makers of their system. A **user ID** is a code for a given user that allows access (maybe with a password too) to a multi-user system. The difference between ID (= identity code) and password is that the former comes from the system or system manager, while it is the user's job to make up (and remember) the latter. The **user interface** of a hardware or software system is where the user interacts with the system, i.e. a keyboard and screen in the former case, and a series of menus in the latter perhaps. Here, too, the concept of user friendliness is crucial.

USRT, *abbrev. for* universal synchronous receiver/transmitter, a chip in an interface with a peripheral with the task of translating either way between synchronous serial and parallel data; compare UART and USART.

utility, *n.* a program, usually small, designed to carry out a single routine task. Common **utility programs** (**utility software**) are print dumps, editors for assembly code, and error-handling routines.

V

V, 1. *symbol for* volt, the unit of electrical potential difference (PD = electrical 'pressure'), as well as for PD itself. See POTENTIAL DIFFERENCE.
2. a code for a series of international telecommunications protocols, set by the CCITT. The codes concern serial data transfer through public phone networks and, therefore, relate in the main to modems. Some of the many such protocols are **V21** (for work at 300 bits per second, bps), **V22** (1200 bps, full duplex), **V22b** (2400 baud, full duplex), **V23** (300/1200 bps), **V32** (high speed, full duplex). See also x.

VAB, *abbrev. for* VOICE answer back.

VACC, *abbrev. for* VALUE ADDED COMMON CARRIER.

vacuum device, *n.* an ELECTRON TUBE through which electrons moving in a vacuum carry current. Traditionally, electron tubes were able to provide the functions of diodes (passing current one way only) and transistors (for switching, amplification, and oscillation); apart from a few rare cases (e.g., where very heavy power throughput is involved), the only such tubes now in use are CATHODE-RAY TUBES (used for mains-powered displays). On the other hand, research starting in the late 1980s is leading to vacuum devices on the surface of chips; these would have many applications should they succeed. A vacuum triode (= transistor) of such a design is one example.

validation or **mug-trapping,** *n.* a process an IT system may use to check whether an input data item is feasible or valid. The program in question must hold the details of the range and format of each such input; in a loop, it then checks the input, and will not proceed until this meets its criteria. Thus, a program may accept a date only in the form 910713 (yymmdd), where mm must lie between 01 and 12, with dd between 01 and 31. A more sophisticated validation check on a date would allow for the fact that months differ in numbers of days. Validation can detect only invalid data; it cannot pick up incorrect but valid inputs (e.g. a date given as 190713 that should have been 910713). See also VERIFICATION, a different technique of manual input checking; this can pick up actual errors in valid data.

VALIDITY

validity, *n.* **1.** a measure of whether or not data from any source is valid, i.e. of the right format and in the right range. See VALIDATION.
2. a measure of the accuracy of a process. It is found by comparing the results of repeated runs using the same input data.

value-added, *adj.* used where a system takes a widely available service, adds extras, and then charges users for the new service. A **value-added common carrier (VACC)** is a system that carries data for others, but does not own its own channels; rather it leases or uses those of actual owners. A **value-added network (VAN)** is a service supplied within, for instance, viewdata, with extra features for an extra charge. A **value-added service** results from adding value to an existing service.

valve, *n.* a device that controls flow through itself, and therefore through the associated channel or circuit.
1. in electronics, a valve is a rectifier, a device that passes current one way only. The name came to mean any ELECTRON TUBE, for all have this property. Strictly, however, it applies only to the electron tube called a diode (a tube with two electrodes, one of which is heated to allow it to act as a source of charge). More recently the word DIODE means any rectifier, though it refers particularly to a semiconductor 'valve'.
2. IN PNEUMATICS (a technique for the transfer of control signals by pressure in a gas) and in HYDRAULICS (a similar technique using a liquid), a valve is a mechanical device that allows flow one way only. Both pneumatics and hydraulics are important methods of process and robot control.

VAN, *abbrev. for* VALUE-ADDED NETWORK.

variable, *n.* a data item where the value is likely to change during a program run, or each time the program concerned runs. Because the programmer cannot, therefore, predict what the data item's value will be, it must be coded in a special way. In fact, it receives a label which, in the operating software's label table, refers to a given storage cell.

A **variable block** is a BLOCK which may change its size in the same way. In the file of a data base, **variable (length) fields** are not fixed in size. This gives extra flexibility to the user, but makes programming harder. In programming, there are various **variable types**. Each relates to the type of data concerned, e.g. integer, real numeric, string, logic. See DATA TYPE.

VERTICAL

VCR, *abbrev. for* video cassette (tape) recorder, a machine for storing video signals (or, sometimes, other types of data) on a magnetic tape in a special box. The VCR will also be able to play back the signals or data later.

VDT, *abbrev. for* VIDEO/visual display terminal, much the same as a VDU, but not stand alone.

VDU, *abbrev. for* VIDEO/VISUAL DISPLAY UNIT. The name implies that this is the same as a screen or other display; on the other hand, however, many people use it to mean terminal (with keyboard as well as display). It is, therefore, advisable to avoid using the term.

vector, *n.* **1.** a one-dimensional array (or list); vector is in fact the equivalent mathematical term.
2. a pointer, either in the form of an address (pointing to the storage cell that holds the data in question), or as a screen address (the x/y coordinates, perhaps in terms of pixels, of a particular part). **Vector graphics** is a method of showing a graphic display on a special type of monitor. Unlike the more normal use of RASTER GRAPHICS, this stores each point in terms of its x/y coordinates, each line in terms of the co-ordinates of its ends, and so on. In other words, this a geometric, rather than a scanning, approach, is faster and has a lower storage demand.

Veitch sketch, *n.* much the same as a KARNAUGH MAP (though, in fact, the Karnaugh map is a later development).

Venn diagram, *n.* a graphic representation of the relationship between sets (in the mathematical sense). A rectangle shows the universal set (the one that holds all members); within that, circles of different sizes show actual sets, their intersection, complements, and so on. Some set-handling software is able to produce Venn diagrams as a form of graphics. John Venn (British logician, 1834–1923) devised the approach in the 19th century.

verification, *n.* the process of checking manual input that involves two separate inputs of the same data (best done using two operators). If the software notes a difference in the input values of a given data item, it requests the second operator to re-key. This process should pick up almost all input errors (often >99%); compare with VALIDATION, which detects only format and range errors (but is far cheaper). A **verifier** is a hardware and/or software system that makes verification as simple as possible.

vertical, *adj.* denoting the y direction of a graph, in most IT

VERY HIGH FREQUENCY (VHF)

cases the same as from top to bottom of a screen or printout rather than across it (this is the x, or horizontal direction). A **vertical blanking interval** is the fraction (as a period of time or number of screen lines) of a raster scan which does not form part of the displayed information. TELETEXT uses these 'blank' lines. In word processing, **vertical justification** is the same as justification, i.e. lining up the margins of text at left and/or right by control of the spacing between words and perhaps characters. The **vertical raster count** of a raster display is the number of dots in a line (the greatest number of pixels). A **vertical redundancy check** is a type of cyclic redundancy check; see, for example, GRAY CODE.

In magnetic data storage, **vertical recording** provides a much higher than normal data storage density. The approach involves holding all the bits of a word at right angles to the disk or tape surface rather than along it. Despite much research, the technique is still rare in practice: the practical problems of writing and reading are considerable. The **vertical resolution** of a scanner, display, or dot printer is the number of dots per millimetre allowed in the vertical direction. This may not be the same as the horizontal resolution (i.e. detail, see vertical raster count, above).

Where an image (e.g., that of a text in a word processor) is longer than the screen's vertical size, **vertical scrolling** allows the user to scan through from start to end. This is, in most cases, under the control of the cursor keys or a mouse. On the other hand, **vertical wrap-around** is a feature of relevant software that ensures that, if the cursor moves outside the display at top or bottom, it reappears (moving the same way) at the opposite edge.

very high frequency (VHF), see VHF.

very large scale integration (VLSI), see VLSI.

very low frequency (VLF), see VLF.

very high-level program language, *n.* a program language even more advanced than so called high-level ones. The basic definition of a high level program language is one in which a single instruction may convert to more than one machine instruction. A very high-level language, therefore, uses instructions which translate to many (e.g. hundreds of) machine instructions. Where the phrase appears, however, it tends to have a much less precise meaning that depends on the user.

vestigial side band, *adj.* denoting a form of amplitude MODULATION in which the system transfers the carrier, one full

VIDEO

SIDE BAND, and only a small part of the second. The technique is widely used for data transfer; it is as effective as double side band working but involves a smaller band width.

VHD, *abbrev. for* video high density, a technique of working with VIDEO DISC.

VHF, *abbrev. for* very high frequency, a band of radio waves (used for television as well as radio broadcasts). The frequencies lie in the range 3–30 MHz.

VHS, *abbrev. for* Video Home System, the main worldwide standard for video-cassette recording. It was devised by the Japanese Video Company (JVC), and now has several forms. However, these remain, in essence, compatible.

video, *adj.* denoting working with signals that have enough band width to carry a full moving television picture with sound. Most people take the **video bandwidth** to be several megahertz (though compression techniques exist to reduce this significantly in certain cases). A **video camera** consists of a lens system to produce an optical image of a scene, and electronics to output a corresponding video signal (in most cases an analog one). There is usually a small viewfinder display for the camera operator, and perhaps (e.g. in a studio or mobile van) a feed to a larger monitor for the producer. The main signal may pass directly to an aerial for broadcasting or for narrow band transfer elsewhere, or to a recorder (tape or disc), which may be part of the camera or close by. Many cameras have simple caption typing features. See also STILL VIDEO.

A **video cassette** is a plastic box that contains a length of video tape and fits into a **video cassette recorder (VCR)** for recording (writing) and playback (reading). A **video cassette periodical** is a serial publication (e.g. a magazine) produced and distributed by cassette.

In a **video conference** a number of people in studios in different places meet at a distance. Monitors show to each member the images of the others (and can also allow discussion of material on paper or in model form). Such a system is costly, as it requires broad-band links to carry the signals between the studios (maybe even by satellite); on the other hand, it can save a great deal of time and travel expense. Cheaper systems are being developed; these use slow-scan video phones (see below), with signal transfer through the phone network.

A **video disc** stores still or moving images at high density

VIDEO

in its surface; most use an optical approach, so are write-only (this means that you cannot re-record signals in the same place on the disc). Standard video discs are analog (while the COMPACT DISCS that use, in essence, much the same techniques are digital). All types, however, need players to read the stored data and transfer it to a display (using either a dedicated micro-processor system or a general purpose computer; see, for instance, INTERACTIVE VIDEO). Partly because of their huge storage capacity, and partly because there are several incompatible standards, video disc systems remain costly and rare, yet, since the 1960s, people have expected players to appear in every home. Indeed, the first disc was one of John Logie Baird's inventions, and the first system went on sale in the 1930s. As it is, most video disc systems appear in contexts such as libraries, schools, and training areas, and in all three remain rare. One major problem is incompatibility between the three main television standards (though it may be that this is more a political problem than a technical one: a PAL disc player on sale in Europe in 1990 can also work with NTSC discs, but must not be advertised as having this feature).

One may class the main video disc standards in a tree as in the Figure. Perhaps the most common are the reflective ('Laservision') and video high-density (VHD) types. These differ in:

(a) the storage space and total playing time (though the power of video discs is direct access to a given sequence): 72 versus 60 minutes respectively;

(b) the number of frames stored per revolution, one versus two, meaning flicker in the latter case during a freeze frame session;

(c) the ability to work with the three main world television standards (no for Laservision and yes for VHD);

(d) wear (no very significant difference).

From these comparisons, Laservision emerges as the better style, although VHD endures because a VHD disc can work in any player in the world.

A **videogram** is a rare name for a prerecorded video tape or disc, available for sale or hire. For **video high density**, see VHD in the discussion above on video discs. For Video Home System (VHS) see VHS. For **video mail**, a use of ISDN phone circuits, see VOICE MAIL.

Videomatics is a rare term for techniques that combine video and computing (e.g. the use of CD-ROM and inter-

VIDEO

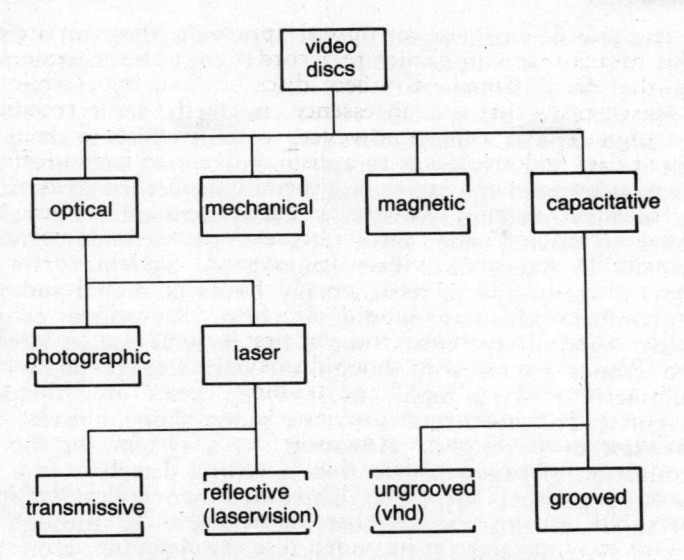

video disc. The main types of video disc.

active video). A **video phone** is a simple camera (usually fixed focus) and display (usually black and white) linked to a phone handset and key pad; this all links to the phone system. The video phone allows users to see each other (and simple documents) during a phone call, often by a slow scan that takes several seconds to transfer a single frame image. More complex systems provide for:

(a) some degree of video-conferring (above);
(b) the transfer of moving video (but this tends, at the moment, to be extremely slow; however, a full speed working system appeared in 1989: 30 colour 256×256 pixel frames a second).

For **video photography**, see STILL VIDEO. **Video publishing** involves using a DESKTOP VIDEO or other such system to produce material on video tape or disc for distribution. A **video recorder** allows a user to transfer video signals from a broadcast set or a camera to tape (e.g. see video cassette, above) or disc, for later transfer or replay. On a small scale, the most common type of disc recorder is for still photographs. The camera contains a small magnetic disc that may

VIDEOTEX

hold a few tens of images; the user can view these on a television set or monitor, produce hard copy or conventional prints/slides and then re-use the disc.

For the three main world **video standards**, see TELEVISION.

Video tape is a linear recording system which is cheap but able to offer only serial access; a VIDEO TAPE RECORDER is a machine to hold the tape, with a head for recording (writing) and re-play (reading). Most standard systems offer a couple of hours of moving video on a tape, though methods of raising that to 15 hours have been announced. Systems exist that allow a video tape to record many hours of digital audio, or to combine video with digital audio. See video cassette, above. Optical tape exists, but is not in wide use (it is costly and cannot be re-used, though the data storage density per millimetre is very high); most video tapes are, therefore, magnetic. For VIDEO TELEPHONE, see video phone, above.

videotex or (wrongly), **videotext,** *n.* a system for the dissemination of pages of data from a central data base in a host to large numbers of users. There are two styles: VIEWDATA (INTERACTIVE VIDEOTEX, where the transfer is through the phone system), and TELETEXT (BROADCAST VIDEOTEX, a one way system). The table below shows how these differ.

Teletext	*Viewdata*
broadcast	uses phone network
one way	two way
inexpensive	less inexpensive
for small data bases	no real limit on size
serial access	direct access

A teletext system using a whole television channel (e.g. in a cable network) would blur these distinctions considerably: it would allow rapid access to many thousands of frames of information.

vidicon, *n.* a tube in a common type of black-and-white video camera, hence the name for the camera as a whole.

view, see ASPECT.

viewdata, *n.* interactive VIDEOTEX: users access the central host through a micro (or dedicated terminal unit) and modem to the phone system. After logging on (and giving password etc. in the case of a subscription service), the user gains access to an individual frame of data (which may have a number of child pages) by any of the following methods:

(a) working through a sequence of menus (routing screens);

VIRTUAL

(b) giving a keyword from a restricted list of a few hundred;

(c) giving a keyword from the user's own small list, as stored in the host;

(d) quoting the page number, as acquired from a paper or on-line directory.

A given frame may:

(i) provide a block of information;

(ii) give links to other related pages;

(iii) allow the user to respond to a message from the INFORMATION PROVIDER (if it is a RESPONSE FRAME).

Also, most viewdata systems provide some kind of email and/or bulletin board feature for full two-way communications. The email service may link to other local or international email networks, as well as to fax (only outward fax is available at the moment) and telex.

Apart from the cost of the hardware and software, access costs the user:

(a) phone line charges in the normal way for on-line time;

(b) (in most cases) a subscription to the viewdata system;

(c) (in most cases) time charges to the host for access, at least during busy periods;

(d) (in some cases) payments to the host for each email, fax and telex message;

(e) (in most cases) payments to the host (and information provider) for access to at least some high value frames.

A successful viewdata system charges enough to cover its costs, but provides a sufficiently wide-ranging service to encourage a lot of subscribers. They must feel that the service saves enough in time and trouble to make subscription and usage costs worthwhile (when compared with other ways of getting the same information).

virtual, *adj.* denoting unreal, as in **virtual address**, the address of a data cell in a virtual store (see below). In packet switching, a **virtual circuit** (or **virtual link**) is a logical channel between sender and receiver; in practice, each packet may follow a different path (physical circuit). A **virtual machine** is a logical machine, the hardware that appears to be in place and working, rather than the actual set of units that comprise the machine in question. It is therefore, in effect, a simulation of an ideal machine built from real units. Much of the time, then, the operating software need not trouble with the details of specific types of action.

VISION, MACHINE

Virtual reality is the province of computer systems which are able to combine with great effect to the user's senses a mix of real world experience and computer-generated material. Current systems have a 'data glove' for the user to wear; fitted with sensors and optic fibres, this links with the computer and acts as a highly complex input unit. The virtual machine concept (see above) arose from that of the **virtual store**. This is a way to link main and backing store so they act as one, and the method (known as **virtual storage access method (VSAM)**) involves mapping each virtual address (above) to a real address, and a type of OVERLAYING. It is, therefore, a form of store management, but see THRASHING (where the practice is not as effective as the theory).

vision, machine, *n.* the simulation of human vision as input to a machine (e.g., in robotics and for surveillance). The hardware side involves the use of a video camera (in effect, an array of photocells) whereas image recognition is the task of the software. A significant aspect of current moves toward fifth-GENERATION systems, machine vision has made much progress; on the other hand, there is still a very long way to go before machines will be able to match the speed, frequency (colour) and light level range, high definition (and low cost) of the human eye and brain. A recent development is an artificial eye modelled on the eyes of flying insects: the real (scanning) or simulated motion allows this very small object to sense aspects of the scene such as the direction and distance of individual objects.

visual display unit (VDU), *n.* an output unit of an IT system that gives a visual display: but see VDU for why it is best to avoid this term.

VLF, *abbrev. for* very low frequency, a band of RADIO waves with frequencies in the range 300–3000 Hz. The main importance of these is in radio astronomy, though some types of military communication use the band.

VLSI, *abbrev. for* very large-scale INTEGRATION, building chips with many thousand elements in the surface of each. See also WAFER.

vocoder or **voder,** *n.* a 'voice encoder', a device for simple but effective SPEECH SYNTHESIS.

voice, *n.* **1.** the individual sound of a person producing speech (similarly in the case of the output of musical instruments). Some systems are **voice activated**; they remain dormant until a microphone detects a voice, and then start working. Not only does this technology include various types of recorders (e.g. for dictation and surveillance), some mobile phones and process control units also use the same approach. **Voice answer back (VAB)** is really a form of speech synthesis or playback; the system responds to user input (which may also be speech) with the speech output of the correct phrases. A **voice bank** is the store of such words and phrases. **Voice input** is the entry of data to an IT system by voice rather than some other (possibly less convenient) means. See SPEECH RECOGNITION.

voice mail or **voice messaging,** *n.* an electronic system for the transfer and storage of spoken messages. In other words, it is much like a public phone answering machine (but one that can, for instance, link with pagers to keep the addressee in touch). A private voice mail system links the phone system (ISDN provides optimum facilities) to a micro, and allows software to digitise and store inward speech phone calls. The user can then deal with these at a later time, as if working with a phone answering machine. Of more interest, however, are such features as:

(a) having the software recognise the caller and replying with a suitable digitised message;

(b) having the software recognise the caller and transferring the call to a second number;

(c) editing the stored messages.

Voice notes are a user's spoken comments on a file on screen. The comments are then stored with the file when the system saves it. Some fax machines offer a **voice request** feature. This sends a signal with the fax message asking the person at the other end to pick up the phone and talk about the contents with the sender.

2. any signal in the low audio frequency band, defined (in the case of radio) as 30–300 Hz; this is the **voice band**. In the case of phone signals, the range may be given as 300–3000 Hz, however. Thus the term **voice frequency** is not fully clear. All the same, a **voice grade** channel (e.g. phone line) is one which has a bandwidth able to carry voice signals adequately, i.e. 2 kHz or a little more. A **voice link** is such a channel. For **voice output,** see SPEECH SYNTHESIS.

3. the human technology of making speech (meaningful sound output). For **voice encoder,** see VOCODER. See SPEECH for further information on **voice recognition** and **voice synthesis**.

VOLATILE STORE

volatile store, *n.* a type of main store which needs a power supply at all times to maintain its contents. Most types of read/write storage are volatile and the contents are lost on switch-off or power failure. Many computers (especially portable ones) use an internal battery to keep refreshed the contents of at least the most important part of such a store (see SEE REFRESH).

volatility, *n.* a fraction of a file's contents (e.g. records) erased or added in a typical update session. A **volatile file** has a high turnover of records.

voltage, see POTENTIAL DIFFERENCE.

volume, *n.* **1.** a measure of the loudness of a sound signal (e.g. speaker output) and, by extension, the strength of any signal (but mainly in the audio range).
2. a large individual chunk of backing store, e.g. a floppy disk or a disk pack. The **volume label** is the name of the volume, as stored in its header; asking for the volume's contents list (by, for example, a directory call) shows the volume label in most cases.

von Neumann, Joh(an)n (1903–1957), a Hungarian mathematician who went to the US as a professor in his late 20s. Neumann's work on the US nuclear weapons programme involved him in early computing and game theory. In particular, his was the stored program concept (see also MACHINE CYCLE) that made the first electronic computers possible in the 1940s.

The **Neumann bottleneck** is the limit on data processing speed that follows using a single bus in a processor for both instructions and other data. As it is hard to tell how these differ in many cases (e.g. they both pass between main store and processor through the storage buffer register), this is not an easy bottleneck to widen. A **Neumann machine** is a serial processor with store and input/output units, the store holding and handling both program and other data in the same way (this is the stored program concept mentioned above). In other words, almost all the digital computers of the early 1990s are Neumann machines. A **Neumann sort** is a data sorting method that involves building up strings to contain the sorted items.

VSAM, *abbrev. for* virtual storage access method, an approach to handling sequential files using a virtual store. See VIRTUAL.

W

W, *symbol for* watt, the unit of power (rate of energy transfer); 1 watt = 1 joule per second.

wafer, *n.* a thin disk, cut from a long cylinder crystal (slab) of very pure semiconductor material, used in chip making. A wafer is about 1 mm thick and 100–150 mm across, and carries several hundred identical chips during manufacture. Chip-making involves adding ten or more layers of circuit elements and links; to form each one (see Figure) the wafer has as follows:

(a) an oxide layer added;
(b) a photo-resist layer added;
(c) a mask laid on top;
(d) some minutes of exposure to radiation by ultraviolet light to harden the photo-resist where exposed;
(e) the mask removed, and the unexposed photo-resist dissolved away;
(f) the now exposed oxide pattern etched away;
(g) the now exposed semiconductor pattern doped with the right impurity in an oven that contains an impurity gas, or by ion implantation.

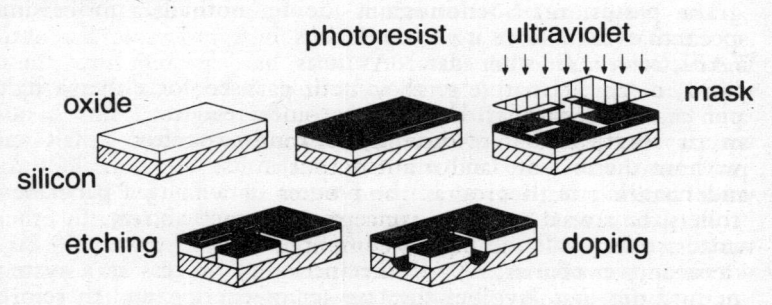

wafer. The stages of forming one layer of a wafer.

When all the layers are in place, further etching makes windows at the chip edges for the gold contact wires that will link each to the legs of the final package. Lastly, in the

WAIT(ING) TIME

process of metallization, a layer of aluminium covers the wafer.

Each chip must now pass through a testing process; if it does not work as it should, an ink spot marks it so it can later be thrown away. A diamond cutter then draws grooves between the chips so that they can be separated and packaged individually.

Wafer scale devices use all the chips on a whole wafer to form a parallel processor or store (for example). The final stage of manufacture is then (rather than breaking up the wafer) correctly linking the individual working sections into an integrated whole (i.e. using only the chips without ink spots). At the end of 1989, a British firm released the first wafer scale system, a 'solid state disk drive' based on two wafers, which gives access times as low as 200 microseconds (0.2 ms, compared to the 20 ms of hard disk). Each wafer contains 200 125 KB dynamic RAMs; with allowance for 50% DRAM failure rate, this gives the double wafer drive a storage capacity of 40 MB.

wait(ing) time, *n*. **1.** the delay between a call for data and the beginning of the actual data transfer taking place. See also LATENCY.
2. the state of a task that cannot begin until one or more events move it to the ready state. For **wait list** see QUEUE.
3. the state of a processing unit when all action is suspended. A **wait loop** in a program is a loop through which the program passes again and again, doing nothing, until some external event allows it to move on.

WAN, *abbrev. for* WIDE AREA NETWORK.

wand, *n*. an alternative term sometimes used for either a light pen or for the similar design of bar-code reader.

warm start, *n*. the re-running of a process after a halt and without the loss of data of a COLD START.

watermark magnetics, *n*. the process of writing a permanent code (like a watermark in paper) to a magnetic stripe.

watt, see W.

wave or **waveform,** *n*. a cyclic (periodic) process in a system or medium that involves the transfer of energy (and therefore, perhaps, information) from one place to another. Waves have the following main features:

(a) speed (of energy transfer through the system or medium): in the case of light, radio, and other electromagnetic waves, this can be as high as 300 000 000 m/s (3×10^8 m/s);

WEIGHTING

(b) frequency (the number of cycles in a second), the unit being the hertz, Hz;

(c) length (**wavelength;** the distance covered by a single cycle);

(d) amplitude (strength), which relates to energy content.

The basic wave equation relates the first three of these:

$$\text{speed} = \text{frequency} \times \text{wavelength}$$

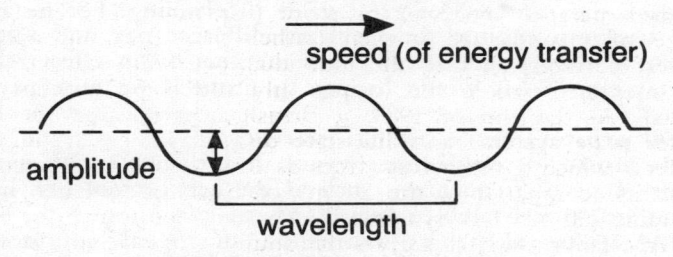

wave. The features of a wave.

Waves of electric current (often pulsed, or digital) transfer signals through the hardware of an IT system. Electromagnetic waves (e.g. radio, microwave, light) are often more efficient for long-distance transfers (but see OPTICAL PROCESSOR).

A **wave band** is a set of waves with a range of frequencies (wavelengths), within a larger spectrum. See, for example, RADIO. **Waveform digitisation** is the same process that converts an analog wave (such as that in the Figure) into a digital signal; see, for instance, PULSE CODE MODULATION. It is of great importance in many areas of IT, including speech synthesis and speech recognition.

A **wave guide** is a hollow metal tube, often of rectangular or circular section, that carries microwaves (high frequency radio waves) from place to place (up to a few hundred metres, e.g. between a signal generator and an aerial). A circular section guide can carry waves at much higher frequencies than a rectangular tube. See also HELICAL WAVE GUIDE. For WAVELENGTH, see above; **wavelength multiplexing** is much the same as most types of MULTIPLEXING.

weighting, *n.* **1.** in data processing, the factor by which to multiply a value to give the value its correct importance relative to other data.

2. in some forms of data retrieval, the factor linked to a search

WERNIKOFF, ROBERT

term to show its relative importance. When searching takes place, the software retrieves only items the combined weight of which is greater than a set value.

Wernikoff, Robert a US engineer who first developed digital fax, in the early 1960s.

what if?, *adj.* denoting the type of question widely addressed by spreadsheet users. While a major use of spreadsheets is to hold numeric data and carry out calculations (by use of formulas), they are also of great value in planning. For instance, the user can explore the result of different pay and interest rates, as they might affect profit margins by in effect asking the system 'What would happen to profit if we raise pay by 10%?'

wheel printer, see DAISYWHEEL PRINTER.

white noise, *n.* noise (interference in a channel) with a very wide range of frequencies, such as the background hiss heard from a de-tuned radio or television set.

white space skip, *n.* a method of signal compression (compaction) in which a fax system skips through a large chunk of blank paper during scanning. People use much the same method in many other kinds of data transfer.

wide area network (WAN), *n.* a NETWORK of IT systems spread over a large region, possibly the whole world (compare LOCAL and MEDIUM AREA NETWORKS). Most of the links between distant parts (stations) of the network are likely to involve telecommunications (e.g. the phone system and/or radio, cable, satellite). See also VIEWDATA.

wideband, *adj.* describes data transfers through a channel with a high enough bandwidth to carry several, perhaps even hundreds, of signals at the same time. See also BROAD BAND and MULTIPLEXING.

widow, *n.* in word processing, the last line of a paragraph or the last item of a list at the top of a page (with the rest on the preceding page). This may lead to poor communication and can look ugly, so a good program will prevent widows from appearing. Compare ORPHAN.

WIMP, *abbrev. for* a user interface that involves windows, icons, a mouse, and a screen pointer (or pull-down/pop-up menus).

Winchester, *n.* a type of small hard disk pack often used in micros. The first Winchesters were fixed in the machines; some modern ones are removable in much the same way as floppies.

window, *n.* **1.** a system used in the operating software of some micros to show on screen the identification of the file or work area in current use.
2. the screen view of part of the current file in an environment which also shows views of other files ready for access. The user can ZOOM in on one window after working in another; some systems offer screens with perhaps eight or more windows (= open files) at once. See also DESK TOP.

wired society, *n.* an alternative term for, or view of, the GLOBAL VILLAGE.

wireless, *n.* or *adj.* denoting systems which do not use wires for long-distance data transfers. The term is now rare; originally it was common to apply it to radio communication as opposed to telegraphy (which does use wires or cables). A **wireless peripheral** is one that links to the central processor by, for instance, an infra-red channel. Some keyboards and mice use this approach to free the user somewhat from constraint. (Remote control handsets for television sets are just the same.) A **wireless terminal** is a portable one that links by radio to a switching station or computer. See also CELL phone.

word, *n.* **1.** in human (natural) language, the smallest unit with meaning that can stand alone. **Word processing (WP)** is a major use of IT in all contexts; it is, however, better called **text processing,** for such a program handles the text needs of a user. A **word processor** (either a single purpose machine or a program to run on a general purpose computer) allows the user to:

(a) enter the text;

(b) edit it on any scale from character level (e.g. character insert/delete) to global level (e.g. search and replace);

(c) work on the format (layout), again locally or globally (dealing with, for instance, type styles, highlighting, justification, headers);

(d) print it out, transfer it to a second program for some other type of processing, or send it as an electronic communication (by, for instance, email, fax, teletex, or telex);

(e) save it in backing store, as an archived document and/or for further work some time in the future.

In a word processor, a **wordbreak** appears when a word splits between two lines because it cannot all fit on the first. It is best to avoid wordbreaks (and, therefore, hyphens, for these often appear in the wrong places) although people working with a justified text may use them to avoid RIVERS OF WHITE. A

word count gives the number of words in the whole or part of the document. **Word wrap** is a process whereby a word too long to fit at the end of one line moves as a whole to the next; in almost all word processors there is no need to press <RETURN> at the end of a line. People also use the term wrap to describe the same kind of effect in other types of program.
2. a set of bits treated as standard by an IT system. Most micros have a **word length** of 16 bits, though 32-bit machines are becoming popular (and, on the other hand, there are still plenty of 8-bit computers around). Main frame systems may have word lengths of 64 or even 128 bits. A system's **word time** is how long it takes to transfer a word of data from one storage cell to a second.

work, *n*. in the context of using an IT system, the user's current task and the data involved. The **work area** is the space in main store the operating software sets aside for this purpose (under the control of the program in use). A **work file** is the file (e.g. program) in current use, held in backing store.

Work(ing) space/store are the same as work area (above). A **work sheet** is the contents of a database file set out as a table, with a column for each field and a row for each record; some people use the same word for an individual spread sheet grid. A **work station** is an intelligent input/output unit at which one person interacts with a network; it is similar to a terminal, except that a work station user may carry out processing tasks for hours with no reference to the rest of the system. The machine's intelligence is as high as that of a stand-alone micro.

wow, *n*. a low-frequency variation in data transfer rate or signal frequency, as a result of a worn tape drive wheel or a warped disc.

WP, *abbrev. for* WORD PROCESSING.

WPM, *abbrev. for* words per minute, a measure of a person's rate of inputting data at a keyboard.

wrap, *n*. short for WORD WRAP, the way a word that is too long to fit the end of line moves as a whole to the next (e.g. in word processing). **Wrap round** is the process whereby, if the cursor (for example) moves off the edge of the screen, it appears at the opposite edge, moving the same way. (Programs that do not prevent the cursor moving outside the screen, and do not provide wrap round, present problems in that it is easy to lose the cursor.)

write, *vb.* to record data in a (main or backing) store, write also being a noun for the process involved. A **write after read** process is needed with stores where reading causes loss of the data items read (now rare); after reading, the system puts a copy of (writes) the data back into the store. In many kinds of storage, writing can cause loss of data already held; there is often, therefore, the need for positive action before a write can take place, known as **write enabling** (see also write protection, below). A **write head** is a unit able to transfer data fed to it into a store. See HEAD.

Write inhibiting, more often called **write protection**, involves making sure no writes can take place to a given store; this is to protect the data already in that store from loss or corruption. There are different physical methods for this in the case of cassette tapes, reel tapes (**write protect ring**: see RING), and floppy disks (**write protect notch** see DISK). Write protection using software is also available for these types of store and for hard discs. A system's **write rate** is the number of bits (or bytes or words) it can write per second.

WYSIWYG, *abbrev. for* 'what you see is what you get': in word processing and desktop publishing, a phrase that implies the screen shows exactly what will appear on paper. In fact, true WYSIWYG is rare; but plenty of systems do not even attempt to provide it.

X Y Z

X, *symbol for* transfer used, in particular, in a large number of international data transfer standards set by CCITT. Thus **X25** is a standard (protocol) for interfacing IT systems (computers, networks or terminals) to packet switching networks. It has three layers which relate to the lowest three layers of OPEN SYSTEM INTERCONECTION; these deal with the physical aspects of the interface, the link, and the packets.

X400 is the standard for message handling, for all text-based electronic mail between such diverse units as teletex, computers, telex machines, word processors, fax systems. Both private and public X400 networks exist. There are in fact dozens of X-series protocols.

xerography, *n.* an electrostatic process for the printing stage of most copiers and page printers. The first stage (making an image) involves forming the image in the form of charges on a drum. The charges attract a toner (plastic dust) which in turn transfers to the paper. A hot surface bakes the toner into the surface of the paper. The word means 'dry writing' whereas most earlier copying processes involved liquids. The Xerox company takes its name from this process.

xfer, *abbrev. for* transfer.

x-height, *n.* the measure of the size of a type face, i.e. the height of a lower case letter without ascenders or descenders (e.g. a c e m ...).

xmit, *abbrev. for* transmit.

x-on/x-off codes for transmit on/off in data transfer protocols.

XOR, *n.* the exclusive-or (or non-equivalence, NEQ) gate, with output if one or more, but not all, inputs are 1.

xy plotter, *n.* almost any type of PLOTTER, i.e. one where the pen moves over the paper between points given by their co-ordinates (x and y values). Almost all plotters are like this (other than the class of RASTER PLOTTERS) so the term is now rare. On the other hand, some people restrict the term to a FLAT BED PLOTTER.

yaw, *vb.* to turn to and fro (rock) about an axis at 90° to the direction of motion. The yawing of communications satellites affects the signal strength from moment to moment.

ZERO FILL

yoke, *n.* a bank of read/write heads linked together, as in a scanning array.

Z, *symbol for* electric impedance, the opposition of a conductor, element or system to alternating current. Resistance is the opposition to direct (steady) current. The unit is the ohm (Ω).

Z3, *n.* a programmable electromechanical calculator designed in Germany and working by 1941.

zap, *vb.* slang for erase or get rid of a file.

Zener breakdown, *n.* the sudden increase in current passed by a reverse-biassed p-n junction when the reverse voltage becomes too high (see Figure). An avalanche of current carriers appears, the process sometimes bearing the name avalanche breakdown. The **Zener diode** uses the effect for regulating a system's supply voltage (keeping it within a set range).

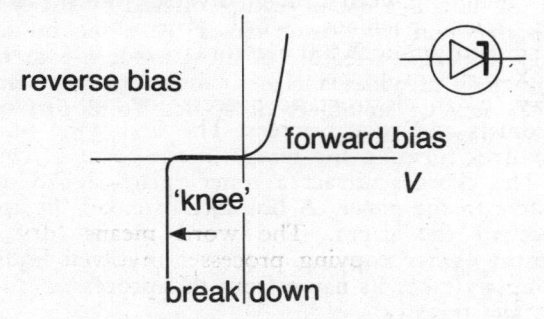

Zener. Zener breakdown and diode symbol.

zero address instruction, *n.* an instruction with no need for an address field. This is one that does not work on or with an item of data or address (e.g. STOP, CLearScreen), or one where the address field is assumed. See ADDRESSING.

zero compression/elimination/suppression, *n.* the saving of space by removing all unnecessary 0s from numeric values. Both leading and trailing zeros have no value, like the two at the start and the three at the end of the denary number 001 234.567 000, the same as 1 234.567. In IT systems with a fixed word length, leading and trailing 0s are not rare.

zero fill or **zeroize,** *vb.* to initialize a block of storage by putting 0 in each cell. On switch-on, or after running a program, the main store contains 0s and 1s unpredictably. Zeroizing makes them unreadable in the latter case (for security reasons), and avoids any danger of their corrupting later data in both cases.

zig zag, *adj.* an alternative term for FAN FOLD (printer paper).

zone, *n.* **1.** a vertical section of (column in) a screen display or printout, particularly when used to show a table of data.
2. that part of a code used for a particular type of information. For example, a file may have a single field to carry both a person's gender and age, with 'f25' for a 25-year-old female. In that case, the first byte of the field is the gender zone.

zone refining, *n.* the process used to purify a semiconductor material. A rod of the substance is pulled slowly through a heated hole, where the temperature is high enough for the impurities to migrate to the surface and pass down the rod.

zoom (in), *vb.* to increase the magnification of an image (or of part of it). This is a useful feature offered by many graphics (art) programs: you can 'come closer' to a section to edit it more finely. It is also a feature of most modern cameras: turning a zoom lens provides a closer (zoom in) or more distant (zoom out) view of an object or scene. To **zoom out** is to decrease the magnification.